RE-ENCHANTING

the

ACADEMY

EDITED BY

Angela Voss
& Simon Wilson

SCRIBE SANGUINE
QUIA SANGUIS SPIRITUS

RUBEDO PRESS
AUCKLAND · SEATTLE · 2017

132 Lone Kauri Rd	220 2nd Ave S #91
RD2 NEW LYNN 0772	SEATTLE WA 98104
New Zealand	USA

www.rubedo.press

ISBN: 978-1-943710-13-3

Cover image: 'Sophia of Canterbury' (detail)
by Judith Way, with the assistance of Derek Way.
Design and typography by Aaron Cheak.

RE-ENCHANTING THE ACADEMY

We dedicate this book to the memory of

ZOE L. WOCKNER
1980–2016

who was so looking forward to being part of
our academic community.

Acknowledgements

WE WOULD LIKE TO THANK the Faculty of Education at Canterbury Christ Church University for supporting the MA in Myth, Cosmology and the Sacred and its affiliated research programme, and honour the enthusiasm and vision of all our students. Special thanks also go to Nikki Wyrd for proofreading the text, to Judith Way and Derek Way for designing our beautiful cover image, and to Jenn Zahrt and Aaron Cheak at the Rubedo Press for their commitment to publishing our endeavours.

Contents

PART TWO

Re-enchanting the Curriculum

PART THREE

Re-enchanting the Mind

PART FOUR

Re-enchanting Nature & Body

Introduction

ANGELA VOSS & SIMON WILSON

'The modern curse is the loss of a doorway into the imaginal realm,
plus a forgetting that such a doorway and such a realm even exist'.[1]

WHAT IS ENCHANTMENT? Many of us would agree that it has something to do with imagination, and would no doubt lament with Peter Bishop that it is hard to come by in our prosaic world. To feel enchanted is to step through a hidden portal into another way of seeing, into a new reality, where the reasonable, the certain, the measurable, and the predictable give way to the awesome, the wonderful, the delightful, the paradoxical, and the uncertain—and perhaps even the longing of the soul for some other kind of life beyond the exigencies of the everyday. Indeed, it seems as though the everyday is embarrassed, wrong-footed, by such transfigurations, and conspires to keep the imaginal doorways firmly hidden from view (when not heavily barricaded by umpteen brands of fabricated fantasy).

In this book, sixteen authors encourage the modern academy to remember that portals to enchantment can be found in its hallowed halls, and indeed must be found, if education is to nourish and inspire both heart and mind, if it is to lead future generations of students out of the cave of policy-led bureaucratisation and financially-led consumerism into the creative freedom of their own souls. Our authors offer resistance to the domination of education 'by belief in the facts revealed solely by mandated standards and standardized testing'[2] through an appeal to the imagination as primary and foundational, the source of connection to self, others, and world.

---

1   Peter Bishop, 'The Shadow of Hope: Reconciliation and Imaginal Pedagogies' in *Pedagogies of the Imagination: Mythopoetic Curriculum in Educational Practice*, eds. Timothy Leonard and Peter Willis (New York: Springer, 2010), 40.

2   Leonard and Willis, 'Introduction', in *Pedagogies of the Imagination*, 1.

Enchantment catches us when we least expect it, not only through our thoughts, but through feelings, sensations, intuitions, and instincts—and as Peter Abbs reminded us nearly forty years ago, if we want to promote 'wholeness of being' as an educational ideal then our schools and academies must embrace the full spectrum of human ways of knowing, in order to bring new, integrated perspectives to our conflicted world.[3]

Has the academy, though, ever been enchanted? In his contribution to this volume, Patrick Curry reminds us that, for Max Weber (1864–1920), disenchantment was the defining characteristic of our times. Weber also believed that the process of disenchantment had been going on for thousands of years: it had simply become more pronounced, more unignorable now than ever before.[4] It is likely that every age has had its scholars and thinkers who have bemoaned this dispersal of enchantment. Simon Wilson, one of the editors of this volume, once argued—both seriously and playfully—that a Cambridge college founded well over five hundred years ago had been intended to act as a bulwark against the disenchantment which was threatening, even back then, to engulf the academy.[5] It seems probable, indeed, that there never has been a magic-drenched era when enchantment was all in all (though that does not mean that there never will be). For those with eyes to see, enchantment has probably always been thin on the ground: the problem nowadays is simply that it is thinner on the ground than ever before, and evidently getting more meagre by the year.

The reason why the world has always seemed inadequately enchanted lies in the fact that there are no structures or frameworks which can hold enchantment. It cannot be constrained, it cannot be stored, defined, or delimited. It eludes all constructions of theory, no matter how subtle or filigree. It flits at will in and out of all ideas and teachings—and indeed practices—which might want to contain it, preserve it, or hand it down through the years. It fractures our walls of words and best intentions. Indeed, it may be said that if enchant-

---

3   Peter Abbs, 'On the Value and Neglect of the Arts in Education' in *The Polemics of Imagination* (London: Skoob Books, 1996), 42.

4   See George Hansen, *The Trickster and the Paranormal* (Bloomington: Xlibris, 2001), 105.

5   Simon Wilson, 'The Imaginal College', *Fortean Times* 298 (2013): 52–53. Simon Wilson's chapter in this collection is a sequel to this.

ment were not elusively mercurial, it would not be enchantment. If its presence were steady and obvious at every moment, if it were acknowledged by all, we would be blinded and immobilised by its glamour. It would then be nothing more than compulsion. Enchantment can only work its magic if it is free of tyranny, and if we are free to ignore it, deny it, or blot it out by reasoning and logic. If scholars are willing and pay attention, however, they may perceive it and momentarily be transported as it shimmers through the cracks of discursive reasoning. It may often be seen to flash forth in the form of a vivid image which—for a second, for a lifetime—enchants us.

There is of course a history to the academy's resistance to opening the cracks. To understand the tension around imaginal and enchanted ways of knowing, one only has to look back to the European Enlightenment, where 'the Cartesian reaction to the Renaissance Exaltation of the magical powers of imaging'[6] effectively severed the lucid discourse of the rational mind from the mysterious, evocative language of dream, myth, and symbol. Whilst not in any way rejecting the immense powers of the rational mind, we can question their ever-growing insistence for autonomy. Abbs pointed to the narrowness of the rationalist and empiricist agenda back in 1979,[7] calling for a broader framework which could restore 'myth, metaphor, dream and prophecy, *and the state of mind which underlies them*' to an educational system dominated by the epistemological agendas of the scientific revolution.[8]

To reclaim this language, however precariously, therefore entails a 'going against the grain' of our contemporary scientisms, our functional instrumentalist imperatives, and even our enlightened liberal agendas of secular humanism, which will have no truck with a magical reality as, well, *true*. As Bishop points out, imagination has become subservient to our promotional culture, and reduced to 'the instrumentalization of fantasy-making'.[9] Perhaps most worrying of all, our post-modernist milieu, whilst freeing itself from the modernist world of 'monolithic monotony', seems to value a free-for-all ingenuity of empty display, 'where all values hang in quotation

6   Edward Casey, 'Toward an archetypal imagination', *Spring* (1974), 26, cited in Bishop, 'The Shadow of Hope, 37.

7   Abbs, 'On the Value and Neglect of the Arts in Education', 31–45.

8   Ibid., 35.

9   Bishop, 'The Shadow of Hope', 36.

marks and where nothing is spiritually earned'.[10] Abbs laments our culture's 'absence of interiority and profundity',[11] which denies the possibility of grounding symbolic expression in spiritual discernment, of valuing enchantment as, perhaps, a glimpse into an underlying order of reality that has always been recognised as sacred and universal. It would hardly be credited today that such glimpses may hold ethical, and even soteriological, implications beyond an anecdotal subjectivity.

It has fallen to Iain McGilchrist, in his seminal 2009 work *The Master and his Emissary*,[12] to point to what is perhaps the greatest epistemological tragedy of our times: the triumph of literalism. Metaphor and symbol enchant because they are the language of poetry, of music, art, of our great religious myths, of our emotional and somatic responses. As McGilchrist emphasises, 'metaphoric thinking is fundamental to our understanding of the world, because it is the *only* way in which understanding can reach outside the system of signs to life itself'.[13] Once upon a time in the Western world, the seven liberal arts[14] of the academy were understood as revealing a profound metaphorical ordering of reality that was empowered by the divine source of all being, an ineffable intelligence whose Providence extended through creation from the angels to the stones under our feet. Once upon a time, human reason was the servant of this universal wisdom which could only be known, or glimpsed, through contemplation, through intuition, through the revelation of nature's secrets. In the Renaissance period, McGilchrist tells us, civilisation flourished and human cultural and intellectual achievements peaked, as the mythic narrative held, inspired, nourished, and empowered human beings' creative expression and expansion of consciousness.[15] But when any grand metaphor, whether communal or personal, assumes a concretised, literal truth, a dark shadow in-

---

10   Peter Abbs, 'The Triumph and Failure of Postmodernism' in *The Polemics of Imagination* (London: Skoob Books, 1996), 21.

11   Ibid.

12   Iain McGilchrist, *The Master and his Emissary* (New Haven, CT: Yale University Press, 2009).

13   McGilchrist, *The Master*, 115.

14   Grammar, dialectic, rhetoric (the trivium), arithmetic, geometry, astronomy, music (the quadrivium).

15   McGilchrist, *The Master*, 298–329.

evitably arises which becomes projected onto all who are not seen to conform with its dogmas. The consequences are persecution, conflict, abhorrence and even demonisation. David Tacey comments, 'in drowning out the metaphorical, we have drowned out God'.[16] Or as McGilchrist puts it, the facts of the representational map have replaced the reality of the experienced territory.[17] Enchantment, immune to representation and conceptualisation, connects us directly, immediately, to the presencing of reality in its fullness.

Our prevailing myths are undoubtedly those of scientific materialism and rational empiricism, which when taken literally as ultimate truths seek to sever all ties with the images and intuitions of how the world works which arise from the wellsprings of mythopoetic imagination.[18] Perhaps more than at any time in history, we are caught between the rational mind's pursuit of *logos* and the deep intuitive apprehension of life's complex mythic dimensions—and as Angela Voss discusses in her chapter, the need to find a healthy relationship between these modes has never been so acute. For if, as McGilchrist has demonstrated, the rational mind is now pursuing complete autonomy from any grounding in 'the bigger picture' suggested by our spiritual and wisdom traditions, then the rejection of the arts and religions as guiding metaphors appears inevitable.[19] In other words, if the tremendous power of the creative imagination, as a bridge to these higher worlds, is reduced to mere fantasy (as so eloquently bemoaned by the Romantic poets), then it will seem to have nothing to do with truthfulness or knowledge. But what a high cost to human soul-life! At the centre of this plight our institutions of learning struggle to uphold any values that are non-commodifiable or non-commercially driven, despite over forty years of peda-

---

16   David Tacey, 'The Mythopoetic Approach to Belief in God: Experience, Imagination, and Faith', in *Spirituality, Mythopoesis, and Learning*, ed. P. Willis, T. Leonard, A. Morrison *&* S. Hodge (Mt. Gravatt: Post Pressed, 2009), 72.

17   McGilchrist, *The Master*, 402.

18   On the problem of reductionist approaches to spirituality, see for example Bernardo Kastrup, *More Than Allegory: On Religious Myth, Truth and Belief* (Winchester: Iff Books, 2016); Jeffrey Kripal, *Comparing Religions* (Oxford: Wiley Blackwell, 2015), 335–61; Rupert Sheldrake, *The Science Delusion*, (London: Coronet, 2012).

19   McGilchrist, *The Master*, 428–62.

gogic voices clamouring for a restoration of mythopoetic and imaginal modes of learning.[20] It is to these voices that we add our own in the ongoing work of changing the academy from within.

Transformative learning

If we are to locate this book in any educational field, it must be that of transformative learning in the transpersonal sense, that is, the movement which is concerned with individual 'soul-work' through restoring a hermeneutics of the imagination, rather than an emphasis on social change.[21] Many of the writers who would identify with this field are inspired by 20th-century developments in depth psychology, phenomenology, and philosophical hermeneutics, calling on thinkers such as C.G. Jung (1875–1961), Martin Heidegger (1889–1976), Hans-Georg Gadamer (1900–2002), Paul Ricoeur (1913–2005), and James Hillman (1926–2011). Beginning with the acknowledged pioneer James B. MacDonald in the 1970s,[22] they have developed theories and approaches for integrative pedagogies, including creative arts practice, experiential and reflexive enquiry (autoethnographic, heuristic, integral, intuitive, organic, somatic, and transpersonal), pursuing questions of wisdom and spirituality in higher education, and advocating a variety of methods for engaging both the critical mind *and* the intuitive/emotional heart (e.g., archetypal and depth psychology, spiritual hermeneutics).[23] However, as one reads more of the literature (and there is a lot of it), one begins to wonder about the impact of these innovative educators on main-

---

20   A succinct definition of mythopoetic pedagogy is given by Peter Willis and Anne Morrison as 'narrative ways of generating imaginal rather than explanatory knowing' (in 'Introduction' to *Spirituality, Mythopoesis and Learning*, ed. P. Willis, T. Leonard, A. Morrison & S. Hodge [Mt. Gravatt: Post Pressed, 2009], 2).

21   Although of course these two streams are interdependent. For an overview of transformative learning theory and development, see Edward W. Taylor, Patricia Cranton & Associates, eds., *The Handbook of Transformative Learning* (San Francisco: Jossey-Bass, 2012), 5–20.

22   For a survey of MacDonald's work, see Patricia E. Holland and Noreen B. Garman, 'Watching with Two Eyes: The Place of the Mythopoetic in Curriculum Enquiry', in *Pedagogies of the Imagination*, 12–18.

23   Key examples are listed in the Select Bibliography on page 25.

stream educational discourse. Bishop speaks of an 'extraordinary dullness, if not direct hostility, of much contemporary social science towards mythopoetics', suggesting that it will always need to operate 'from the margins'.[24] It is certainly a struggle to make explicit the implicit meanings glimpsed in moments of enchantment, ecstasy, love or inspiration, a fact which McGilchrist explains in terms of the often conflicting functions of the two brain hemispheres.[25] All the more reason, then, not to shy away from their discourse of 'affect' whose authenticity silently underpins so much cognitive busy-ness.

So where are the teachers as 'myth-makers'[26]—teachers trained in MacDonald's imaginal knowing as pedagogy, Jerome Bruner's 'narrative knowing',[27] Hillman's 'enchantment of imaginal knowing',[28] Rosemarie Anderson's 'intuitive inquiry',[29] John Dirkx's 'soul-work',[30] or Christopher Bache's 'living classroom'?[31] Where is the desire, articulated by religious studies professor Jeffrey Kripal, to push past the discourses of 'faith' and 'reason' which have so dominated academic models, to the 'third classroom' of reflexivity and imaginal consciousness?[32] Where is a sense of the sacred, and where the hermeneutic to engage, reflect and interpret it in order to return it once again to the really big questions that we, as postmoderns, must put to ourselves, questions that may 'help make students

---

24   Bishop, 'The Shadow of Hope', 35.

25   McGilchrist, *The Master*, 172–96.

26   Leonard and Willis, 'Introduction', 1.

27   See Holland and Garman, 'Watching with Two Eyes', 21.

28   See e.g., James Hillman, *The Thought of the Heart* (Dallas, TX: Spring, 1981); Peter Willis, 'De Profundis: Spirituality, Mythopoesis, and Learning for Hard Times', in *Spirituality, Mythopoesis, and Learning*, 23.

29   See e.g., William Braud and Rosemarie Anderson, *Transpersonal Research Methods for the Social Sciences* (London, New Delhi: Sage Publications, 1998), 69–94.

30   See e.g. John M. Dirkx, 'Nurturing Soul in Adult Learning', in *Transformative Learning in Action: Insights from Practice (New Directions for Adult and Continuing Education, no. 74)*, ed. P. Cranton (San Francisco: Jossey-Bass, 1997), 79–88.

31   Christopher Bache, *The Living Classroom, Teaching, and Collective Consciousness* (Albany: SUNY Press, 2008).

32   See Jeffrey J. Kripal, *The Serpent's Gift* (Chicago: Chicago University Press, 2007); and Kripal, *Comparing Religions*.

capable of truth'?[33] For it is not enough to indulge in enchanted spaces (the New Age counter-culture offers unlimited opportunities for that). The academy can offer a great gift—the training of the critical powers of mind to discern and reflect on what the imagination may reveal, in order to bring interpretation, clarity, and wisdom to bear on enchantment and all that it means for individual and collective spiritual health. As Holland and Garman put it (following Ricoeur), *both* the restoration of meaning and the reduction of illusion are required 'for a complete range of vision and adequate depth perception'.[34] The split must be healed, the dialogue must be had, the flow unblocked between our two worlds—to reach a new synthesis, a greater consciousness, an entering into mythic truth *and* a standing back, the willingness to be open to mystery, and the willingness to submit to the task of reflexive appraisal and theorising on that mystery: the human as 'two and one'.[35] One without the other, or one in wrong relationship with the other, just won't work, if we want to educate a new generation to be both intellectually robust and morally empowered.

Our contributors

In the MA in Myth, Cosmology and the Sacred at Canterbury Christ Church University, we draw not only on a rich field of transformative pedagogy, but also on an even richer and deeper field of esoteric philosophy and wisdom traditions to create a bridge between spiritual practice and critical engagement. In this sense, we identify with what Richard Tarnas has called a 'heroic community',[36] an

---

33   Leonard and Willis, 'Introduction', 6.

34   Holland and Garman, 'Watching with Two Eyes', 16.

35   See Jeffrey J. Kripal, *Authors of the Impossible; The Paranormal and the Sacred* (Chicago: Chicago University Press, 2010), 270.

36   Richard Tarnas, 'The Role of "Heroic" Communities in the Postmodern Era', *Founders Symposium, 2013,* Paper 30. (http://digitalcommons.ciis. edu/founderssymposium/30/). Other academic examples (non-academic examples are too numerous to cite) include The Alef Trust (UK), The California Institute of Integral Studies, The Esalen Institute (California), The Laszlo Institute (Lucca, Italy), The Pacifica Institute (California), The Ubiquity University (California), Schumacher College (Devon, UK), The Prince's School of Traditional Arts (London), The Temenos Academy

educational endeavour which is consciously orientated towards values which challenge those of mainstream society. The heroic stance defines a moral vision which fosters the individual's courage to speak out for change, and in this sense, is in service to what Joanna Macy and Molly Brown have called the 'Great Turning'. The Great Turning involves a necessary 'shift in perception of reality, both cognitively and spiritually' and requires creation of institutional forms rooted in deeply held values, which are 'both very new and very ancient, linking back to rivers of ancestral wisdom'.[37]

To reach out to academic colleagues who are also 'heroically turning' in their classrooms and publications, we held an international conference in September 2015, in Canterbury, UK, on 'Reenchanting the Academy'. The contributions to this volume arise out of this project, and represent a variety of ways in which that elusive door to enchantment is being kept open by lecturers, researchers, and postgraduate students. They will hopefully convince you by the power of their reason and logic, *and* also enchant you through their images (which they have to do if this collection is to have any meaning). Towards the end of his chapter, for instance, Patrick Curry writes of wonder as 'the inner lining and depth of things, [...] at the very heart of our ordinary, normal, carnal lives'. The heart, our ordinary, normal, carnal heart, we understand, may also be the organ of enchantment. When we see and touch and feel with our heart, that enchantment may fill us, body, mind, and spirit. If learning is to be enchanted, then, it must address the heart. Otherwise, as our contributor Linden West writes, we will remain 'frozen in the gaze of destructiveness', hard as ice and cold as marble, like mad statues.[38]

(London), Trans4M (international), and Waldorf communities (international). There are also many individual researchers and teachers engaged with transformational approaches.

37   Joanna Macy and Molly Brown, *Coming Back to life: Practices to Reconnect our Lives, our World* (Gabriola Island, BC: New Society Publishers, 1998). See also Kathleen Taylor and Dean Elias, 'Transformative Learning, a Developmental Perspective', in *The Handbook of Transformative Learning*, 165.

38   The choice of the phrase 'mad statues' was influenced by a recurring image from the works of Nicholas Mosley. See, for example, *Hopeful Monsters*, where a character, talking of a trip to Nazi Germany, says '[...] everyone there seemed so confident, all-of-a-piece; striding forwards like mad archaic statues'. Nicholas Mosley, *Hopeful Monsters* (London: Mandarin

Scholars will then surrender to their 'mollusc tendencies' in 'academies which themselves are become carapaces' (Simon Wilson).

Anita Klujber reminds us of the musical nature of enchantment when she describes how she has 'orchestrated' her chapter 'to approximate the concept of musical thought'. The heart too appears as a leitmotif in her piece: her essay is a song of the heart, which is perhaps what we hear when we think with the heart. Laura Formenti and Silvia Luraschi, meanwhile, sing the breath of the heart, and invite us to breathe in and out with them. The learning they envisage is a taste and an embodying of *pneuma*, the breath of life and of enchantment. Angela Voss, drawing on Plato and Ibn 'Arabi, describes, too, a kind of revelation through 'tasting', ingesting what is known and absorbing it in the whole being.[39] Many scholars do not really want to taste their work, and while that is their right, Angela mischievously expresses a desire to 'shove' them out of their taste-free domain into a world less bland.

Already in the world beyond the bland, Chara Armon and Joan Armon's students learn how to 'rewild' their hearts. The life they take into the depths of their being is that of the animals, the plants, and the soil itself, until their hearts grow with the forces of nature and burst free of utilitarian or consumerist bonds. Becca Tarnas, discussing the works of Tolkien, draws on the same archetypal set of images when she offers to 'the disenchanted heart' of modernity the possibility of being nourished by seeing that 'the roots of Middle-earth extend deeply into the rich soils of our own world'. Again we sense the kinship of soil and soul, humus and humans.

Lisa McLoughlin's chapter is similarly 'haunted by the underlying tangle of roots'. This tangle does not ensnare. Rather, in its labyrinthine and ever-growing complexity, it guides our steps through 'the lonely enchanted holloways throughout and outside the academy'. Equally, it leads us through 'the blood vessels in [our] body' (in the words of Paul Stevens), to the academy of the heart, which is

---

Paperbacks, 1991), 248.

39   Mediaeval monastic reading, too, was a slow and laborious tasting, chewing, and ingesting of what is read and learnt. Ivan Illich argues that this tasty road to wisdom ended with the advent of silent reading and new technologies of the book in the late Middle Ages: see Ivan Illich, *In the Vineyard of the Text: A Commentary to Hugh's 'Didascalicon'* (Chicago: University of Chicago Press, 1993).

not confined to one place but which is everywhere. Robert Bowie, too, invites us to walk into a transfigured world which is also the transfigured heart, by stepping through the pages of the Bible into the Gospels, and thus throwing down any hermeneutic fences which may stand between us and the stories they tell. This is an experience which enables individuals to taste and see with their hearts, thus filling them with enchanted knowing.

Julia Moore's version of this experience is perhaps more playful, perhaps even a little spooky. She does not want us to follow in her footsteps; rather we are asked to sit. Specifically, we are asked to sit in a dark room where the table turns, and loud raps, bangs, and even laughter can be heard. She reminds us that the astructural workings of enchantment can seem uncanny, eerie, and not a little disreputable: her academy is haunted as much as it is enchanted; its gloomy corridors are paced by ghosts, perhaps even by the walking dead of Sonia Overall's piece. Embracing paradox (which, being arational and alogical, can lead to enchantment), Sonia Overall recommends the zombified walking of Phil Smith as an antidote to the disenchanting somnambulism of everyday routine. For our hearts truly to be alive to the world in the fullest sense of the word, it seems we must unleash the liminal walk of the living-dead.

Laura Shannon invites us neither to walk nor to sit, but to join her winged women as they dance and fly, fly and dance, all at the same time. And as their flying/dancing weaves its way through our consciousness, it 'reweave[s] intellect and intuition' and we fly 'over the garden wall'. Once there, in the enchanted realm beyond, we may 'take the thread and keep on weaving' (Judith Way), endlessly and intricately.

Or perhaps our hearts will see and feel enchantment fly in through the bathroom window (as in Eduard Heyning's playful appropriation of Paul McCartney's song), breaking proper bounds, smashing the fragile limits of discursive reason into a 'fractal kaleidoscope' (Paul Stevens) of enchanted and endlessly refractive images, such as those found within these pages.

∾

If what we have said about enchantment is true, it is inevitably the case that our book's structure, so hard-won, is arbitrary and inherently disenchanting. Anyone, however, who thinks they can solve this problem by devising a more enchanted sequence for these chapters is invited to email their suggestions to us (at *angela.voss@ canterbury.ac.uk* or *simon.wilson@canterbury.ac.uk*).

CANTERBURY, JANUARY 2017.

SELECT BIBLIOGRAPHY

ABBS, Peter, *The Polemics of Imagination*. London: Skoob Books, 1996.

ANDERSON, Rosemarie, and William Braud, eds., *Transforming Self and Others through Research*. Albany, NY: State University of New York Press, 2011.

ANGELO, Marie, 'Imaginal Inquiry: Meetings with the Imaginal Intelligence', in A. Voss and W. Rowlandson, eds., *Daimonic Imagination: Uncanny Intelligence*, Newcastle: Cambridge Scholars Publishing, 2013, 357–73.

BRAUD, William, and Rosemarie ANDERSON, eds., *Transpersonal Research Methods for the Social Sciences*. London and New Delhi: Sage Publications, 1998.

HENDERSON, James G., and Kathleen R. KESSON, eds., *Curriculum Wisdom; Educational Decisions in Democratic Societies*. Pearson Education: New Jersey, 2004.

LEONARD, T., and P. WILLIS, eds., *Pedagogies of the Imagination; Mythopoetic Curriculum in Educational Practice*. New York: Springer, 2010.

MCGILCHRIST, I. *The Master and his Emissary*. New Haven, CT: Yale University Press, 2009.

ROMANYSHYN, Robert D., *The Wounded Researcher: Research with Soul in Mind*. New Orleans: Spring Journal, 2005.

TAYLOR, Edward W., Patricia CRANTON & Associates, eds., *The Handbook of Transformative Learning: Theory, Research and Practice*. New York: Jossey-Bass, 2012.

TISDELL, Elizabeth J., *Exploring Spirituality and Culture in Adult and Higher Education*. San Francisco: Jossey- Bass, 2003.

VOSS, Angela, 'A Methodology of the Imagination', *Eye of the Heart Journal*, vol. 4, 2009, 37–52.

WILLIS, P., T. Leonard, A. MORRISON, and S. HODGE, eds., *Spirituality, Mythopoesis and Learning*. Mt. Gravatt: Post Pressed, 2009.

About the Contributors

CHARA ARMON PHD is an Assistant Professor in the Lawrence Gallen Teaching Faculty at Villanova University, where her teaching focuses on environmental humanities, ecology and spirituality, and sustainable and justice-oriented agriculture. Her recent publications explore pedagogy within the environmental humanities.

JOAN ARMON PHD is Associate Professor in the Department of Education at Regis University in Denver, Colorado. Her teaching, research, and publications focus on justice-oriented and garden- or farm-based sustainability education in teacher preparation and integrative core courses.

ROBERT A. BOWIE PHD is Director of the National Institute of Christian Education Research at Canterbury Christ Church University. His interests centre on values and human rights education, religious education, and Christian education, and his most recent book is *Dignity and Human Rights Education* (2016) with Peter Lang and *Oxford A Level Religious Studies: Christianity, Philosophy and Ethics* (Books 1 and 2) (2016 and 2017) with OUP.

PATRICK CURRY PHD is a scholar and writer living in London. Formerly a Lecturer at the universities of Bath Spa and Kent, he is the author of books on the history of astrology, the work of J.R.R. Tolkien, and environmental philosophy. He is currently completing a book on enchantment.

LAURA FORMENTI PHD is Professor and Coordinator of the Doctorate in Education at Milano Bicocca University. Her interests are focused on family relations, adult education and learning, training of professionals in education, health, and social care, in a systemic, constructivist, and complexity framework. Among her publications in English are *Embodied Narratives* (2014, co-editor) and *Stories that Make a Difference* (2016, co-editor).

EDUARD HEYNING is a PHD student of Myth, Cosmology, and the Sacred at Canterbury Christ Church University. His thesis, *Star Music*, addresses the creation of music inspired by the Pythagorean-Platonic cosmology. Eduard has a background in classical music and medieval studies in the Netherlands.

ANITA R. KLUJBER PHD is an independent scholar, affiliated with the University of Essex, where she is visiting fellow at the Department of Literature, Film, and Theatre Studies. She is also a member of the collaborative research group 'From Periphery —To Centre' at the University of Pécs, Hungary, working on a project in contemporary World Literature. Her main research interest is the exploration of the imagination in an interdisciplinary context, mainly within the fields of comparative literature, mythology, education, and psychology. Her professional aspiration is to promote the nurturing of the imagination through applied literature and transformative pedagogy.

SILVIA LURASCHI is a Pedagogist, a PHD student in Educational and Communicational Sciences at the University of Milan Bicocca, and a qualified practitioner of the Feldenkrais Method. She is interested in studying embodied and aesthetic transformation in contemporary social contexts for an ecological, holistic, critical, and reflective approach to education and learning.

LISA MCLOUGHLIN is co-president and field programme coordinator of the non-profit Nolumbeka Project. She holds a PHD in Science and Technology Studies; a M.ED in Math, Science, and Instructional Technology; and a BS in Civil Engineering. Her current research focuses on the intersections of archæology, engineering, and religion in ceremonial stone landscapes.

JULIA MOORE is a PHD researcher at Canterbury Christ Church University. Her research investigates the role of intuitive methods inspired by mediumship development and surrealist games in academic practices of reading and writing. She is also an artist with a practice encompassing film and video, collaboration, and automatic techniques. Recent works include Experimental Séance parts I and II (2014/2015).

SONIA OVERALL SFHEA is a Senior Lecturer in Creative and Professional Writing at Canterbury Christ Church University. Her research interests include psychogeography, intertextuality, and experimental forms of creative writing. Her publications include *The Realm of Shells* (2006), a novel, and *The Art of Walking* (2015), a chapbook of poems.

LAURA SHANNON has researched and taught traditional Balkan dance since 1985, with a particular focus on women's dances and rites of passage. Trained in Intercultural Studies and Dance Movement Therapy, Laura is on the faculty of the Sacred Dance Department at the Findhorn Foundation, Scotland, and is currently pursuing postgraduate studies in Myth, Cosmology, and the Sacred at Canterbury Christ Church University.

After twenty years as an academic researcher and lecturer in psychology, PAUL STEVENS is now a hypnotherapist and consultant at *NaturalResourcesWellbeing.com*. He is interested in ecological models of the self as part of a wider exploration of systemic perspectives on humanity's place within the natural world.

BECCA S. TARNAS is a doctoral candidate in the Philosophy and Religion department at the California Institute of Integral Studies. Her dissertation research is focused on the theoretical implications of the synchronicity between the Red Books of C.G. Jung and J.R.R. Tolkien. Becca received her MA from CIIS, and her BA from Mount Holyoke College. Her research interests include ecology, imagination, philosophy, and depth psychology, and she is also co-editor of *Archai: The Journal of Archetypal Cosmology*.

LINDEN WEST PHD, FRSA is Professor of Education at Canterbury Christ Church University. He employs psychosocial perspectives and auto/biographical narrative research in his work on lifelong learning and adult education. His books include *Distress in the City: Racism, Fundamentalism, and a Democratic Education*, Trentham; *Using Biographical Methods in Social Research* (with Barbara Merrill), Sage; and *Beyond Fragments: Adults, Motivation, and Higher Education*, Taylor and Francis. Linden jointly coordinates a European research network and is a psychoanalytical psychotherapist.

ANGELA VOSS PHD is a senior lecturer in the School of Childhood and Education Sciences, Canterbury Christ Church University, and programme director for the MA in Myth, Cosmology and the Sacred. Her teaching and research centre on the role of the symbolic imagination in western philosophical, spiritual, and cultural traditions, and she has written extensively on the astrological music therapy of the Renaissance philosopher Marsilio Ficino (*Marsilio Ficino*, 2006). She is a 'walker between the worlds' of esoteric practice and transformative learning.

JUDITH WAY is an artist, poet and writer, and teacher. She teaches art, yoga, and sacred dance, and lectures on the sacred dimensions of creativity. Having recently completed the MA in Myth, Cosmology and the Sacred in Canterbury, she is currently engaged in an artistic project, Sophia of Canterbury, which aims to bring the image of Sophia into a visible form for contemporary veneration and acknowledgement of her place within esoteric Christianity and modern symbolic language.

SIMON WILSON PHD is a senior lecturer in the School of Childhood and Education Sciences at Canterbury Christ Church University, where he teaches on the Myth, Cosmology, and the Sacred MA and supervises PHD students. He is also a member of the Institute for Orthodox Christian Studies in Cambridge. Simon has published widely on subjects such as the Grail, René Guénon, and the writings of Charles Fort. His current research interests include icons, the mystical theology of the Eastern Church, and fortean phenomena.

PART ONE

*Re-enchanting the
Institution*

The Enchantment of Learning and 'the Fate of Our Times'[1]

PATRICK CURRY

I AM GOING TO PROCEED by supplying some examples of the enchantment of learning before getting to the bad news: the modern academy. I will conclude with a look at what we might do about it. First, let me define my terms a bit. The question of what 'enchantment' is could be unpacked at length, but you will not go far wrong if you remember that it is essentially a state of wonder, as opposed to will or power, or any of its variations like the will-to-power and power-knowledge. 'Learning' includes education, although it exceeds it, and education includes the academy, meaning universities, so what I have to say ideally takes in all of them.

The 'fate' part of my title refers to Max Weber's pronouncement in 1918, based on a keen mind and a lifetime of consummate scholarship, that 'The fate of our times is characterised by rationalisation and intellectualisation and, above all, by the "disenchantment of the world"'. That disenchantment results not from thinking or reasoning as such but rather from 'the belief [...] that one can, in principle, master all things by calculation'. The programme to do so has deep religious, philosophical, and cultural roots in Western culture. It proceeds mainly by splitting what Weber called the 'unity of the primitive image of the world, in which everything [is] concrete magic', into two exhaustively polarised and hierarchically valued categories: spiritual *vs.* material, mental *vs.* physical, and, above all,

1   I would like to thank Leslie van Gelder, Susan Peters, Wendy Wheeler, and Michael Winship for their comments on earlier drafts. I am also grateful to Liz Greene, Suzanna Saumarez, and Tom Shippey for helpful discussions.

Being *vs.* mere appearance.[2] Mapping directly onto that distinction is another: true *vs.* false.

'Concrete magic' was thus Weber's definition of enchantment: an experience of someone or something that is at once sensuous, particular, and contingent; *and* deeply, ineffably mysterious. When and where this happens, everything is important, even necessary, and nothing is inferior, inessential, or merely phenomenal. Put at its simplest, therefore, enchantment is the realisation—in varying degrees of intensity, the becoming real—of wonder.[3]

WHAT IS THE ENCHANTMENT OF LEARNING?

Now the wonder of learning, the delight of discovering what (it turns out) you wanted to know, the joy of a new world to inhabit, seen through other than your own habitual eyes—these things are so undervalued in our current educational institutions that we need to take a moment to remind ourselves of what we are talking about. Here are three examples. Niccolò Machiavelli has been exiled from Florence to his family farm, and in a letter of 10th December 1513, to his friend Francesco Vettori, he writes:

> On the coming of evening, I return to my house and enter my study, and at the door I take off the day's clothing, covered with mud and dust, and put on garments regal and courtly; and reclothed appropriately, I enter the ancient courts of men of antiquity where, affectionately received, I partake of that food which only is mine and for which I was born, where I am not too timid to speak with them and ask them the reasons for their actions; and they in their courtesy answer me; and for four hours of time I feel no weariness, I forget every

---

2   H.H. Gerth and C. Wright Mills, eds., *From Max Weber: Essays in Sociology* (London: Routledge, 1991), 155, 139, 282.

3   J.R.R. Tolkien defines enchantment as 'the realisation, independent of the conceiving mind, of imagined wonder'; Verlyn Flieger and Douglas A. Anderson, eds., *Tolkien on Fairy-stories* (London: HarperCollins, 2008), 35.

trouble, I do not fear poverty, death does not dismay me; I give myself over entirely to them.[4]

This passage is usually assumed by modern scholars to be a mere humanist trope, a literary flourish. It is both more respectful and more economical, however, to assume that Machiavelli meant exactly what he said, and that what he describes is just what happened. Or are we too jaded to believe it? Too bad for us, if so!

Another example: in 1934, after a time of sleeping rough in his long walk across Europe, the great travel writer Patrick Leigh Fermor found himself a guest of the British Consul in Sofia. He luxuriated in the hot baths, clean linen, and fine food, but '[b]est of all,' he said, 'the *Encyclopædia Britannica*; I leapt at it like a panther'.[5]

More recently still, another writer, Eva Hoffman, recalls emerging from her fortnightly trip to the local library in her Warsaw neighbourhood, the interior of which was 'a space of mystery and magic, on whose threshold I stand a humble acolyte': 'I come out, usually into the dim evening streets, enchanted with what awaits me, and as soon as I come home, I pounce on one of the volumes'.[6] (Note the pantherine resonance with Leigh Fermor; the soul is hungry for living knowledge, and only that can satisfy it.)

This sort of relationship with learning—not only enchanted, but passionately so—is the true benchmark for understanding, appreciating, and encouraging its wonder, so let me try to tease out some of the dynamics at work. One is the seriousness of play: improvised but not random, intentional but not goal-directed, and relational, involving other beings, of whatever kind, whether present physically or imaginally. When it takes place free from any attempt to direct or manipulate or use it, play is fundamental to the way we learn how to be ourselves: as well as how others tick, how to create and innovate and, perhaps most importantly, how to learn at all. The enchantment resulting from play leads you deeper into whatever you're doing,

---

4   This passage can be found, in only very slightly differing translations, in any of the many biographies of Machiavelli, e.g., Michael White, *Machiavelli: A Man Misunderstood* (London: Abacus, 2004), 183–84.

5   Patrick Leigh Fermor, *The Broken Road: From the Iron Gates to Mount Athos*, ed. Colin Thubron and Artemis Cooper (London: John Murray, 2013), 8.

6   Eva Hoffman, *Lost in Translation* (London: Vintage Books, 1998), 26.

which in turn generates a deeper enchantment.

Another aspect of the enchantment of learning is the intrinsic value of what is being learned. As John Henry Newman insisted long ago in *The Idea of a University*, 'any kind of knowledge, if it be really such, is its own reward'. It is valuable not for its instrumental or exchange-value, in order to attain some other goal, no matter what, but, he wrote, 'for what its very presence does for us'.[7] And the experience of that presence is one of wonder.

In an essay of the same title, Simon Leys has restated Newman's thesis, writing that, '*a university is a place where scholars seek truth, pursue and transmit knowledge for knowledge's sake—irrespective of the consequences, implications and utility of the endeavour*'. No matter how anachronistic or impractical it may seem, it is necessary, now more than ever, to insist on this humanist ideal, even if only so we can realise how far we have fallen. As Leys says, 'When a university yields to the utilitarian temptation, it betrays its vocation and sells its soul', without which it cannot fulfil its very *raison d'être*.[8]

A third dynamic is metaphor. Metaphor is the life-blood of learning, and of the humanities in particular, because there can be no empathic, imaginative, or narrative understanding without understanding-*as*; that is, without the tensive truth of being, at one and the same time, who you are as the reader, listener, viewer or whatever, and simultaneously (in defiance of Aristotle's logical laws) as the other person, or indeed thing, you are hearing, watching, or reading, or about whom you are reading.

Science has different goals: explanation, prediction, mastery.[9] Accordingly, it may start in wonder but can only progress, in its own terms, by trying to 'resolve' or otherwise eliminate explicit metaphor, ambiguity, and paradox. To quote the Nobel Prize-winning scientist Sir Peter Medawar (in a passage I find quite chilling): 'As science advances, particular facts are comprehended within, and therefore in a sense annihilated by, general statements of steadily

---

7   John Henry Newman, *The Idea of a University* (Notre Dame: University of Notre Dame Press, 1982 [1853]), 77, 78.

8   Simon Leys, *The Hall of Uselessness: Collected Essays* (New York: NYRB, 2013): 463, 464. Emphasis in original.

9   See the work of Mary Midgley, Paul Feyerabend, and many others, including my own 'Defending the Humanities in a Time of Ecocide' (http://www.patrickcurry.co.uk/papers/Rio%20paper%20-%20Feb%202015.pdf).

increasing explanatory power and compass [...] In all science we are being progressively relieved of the *burden* of singular instances, the *tyranny* of the particular.'[10]

What is valued here is increasingly generic abstraction, whose ultimate model is mathematics. Contrast this worldview with that of Freya Stark, the great travel writer and essayist, who affirms that 'truth is *never* average. Since there is not one single thing in the world exactly like another, the very essence of truth is that it leaps across averages to the particular [...]'[11] Certainly this kind of truth is essential to enchantment, whose 'magic' is always to be found in, and as, the 'concrete'. But I see it as essential to life itself.

This is where metaphor comes in. As its great theorist Paul Ricoeur put it, metaphor discovers as it creates, and makes as it finds.[12] And it does so together with an other, whoever that may be. This is not truth as accurate representation, nor as deductive syllogism, but as relationship and its effects. Hence Weber's definition of truth, respecting its wildness and autonomy: 'only that which *wants* to be true for all those who *want* the truth'.[13] The contrast with the starveling captive of modern power-knowledge could hardly be clearer.

This mode is not about knowing and manipulating an item. It is participatory, both affecting the other party or parties and being affected by them. It follows that the actual individuals involved are of paramount importance. It is above all from and in relationship with a particular ('concrete') teacher that one learns, and one does in a way that includes but transcends any methods or propositional content. This relationality extends to communities of teaching and learning—some of whose members (as in the experience of Machi-

---

10   Quoted in Paul Feyerabend, *Conquest of Abundance: A Tale of Abstraction versus the Richness of Being* (Chicago: University of Chicago Press, 1999), 250, 251 (my emphases). Feyerabend's discussion here is typically lucid and humane.

11   Freya Stark, *Perseus in the Wind: A Life of Travel* (Tauris Parke, 2013 [1948]), 81. Emphasis in original.

12   See Paul Ricoeur, *The Rule of Metaphor,* trans. Robert Czerny (London: Routledge, 2003).

13   Weber quoted in Lawrence A. Schaff, *Fleeing the Iron Cage: Culture, Politics, and Modernity in the Thought of Max Weber* (Berkeley: University of California Press, 1989), 118. Emphases in original.

avelli) may not be present in the narrowly physical sense—and their various traditions. And it leaves thinking as only a process that does not already know, although it may sense, its conclusion in advance.

I was lucky enough to have this kind of experience in Gregory Bateson's classes at the University of California (Santa Cruz) in the mid-1970s. It comprised learning new things about both the world and myself, and with each one, a significantly new world and self came into being. But not only that; the excitement was both subtler and more sweeping. To borrow Bateson's own terms, I was learning how to learn. And that only happened in his presence, in a way that cannot be reduced to concepts alone. Yet I was also aware of the presence, not literally but unmistakably nonetheless, of those from whom he had learned, and learned how to think: Blake, Lamark, his father the scientist William Bateson and, not least, the author of *The Book of Job*.

THE MODERNIST DISENCHANTMENT OF LEARNING

Learning of this kind is under assault everywhere in the modern world, but for reasons of time and context I shall concentrate on universities, and compress even that. Also, I am addressing, in necessarily general terms, only the Anglo-American situation, and especially the British, where the situation is probably worst.[14] At the same time, the trend is global. So what place is there now in our educational systems, including the academy, for the enchantment of learning? The answer is grim, but there are two good reasons for running this gauntlet: it is important to know what we are up

---

14   See, among others, Stefan Collini, 'Sold Out', *London Review of Books* [henceforth *LRB*] (24.10.13): 3–12; *What Are Universities For?* (London: Penguin, 2012); and 'Impact on the Humanities', *Times Literary Supplement* [henceforth *TLS*] (13.11.09): 18–19; Anthony T. Grafton, 'Britain: The Disgrace of the Universities', *New York Review of Books* (8.4.10); Mark Slouka, 'Dehumanized: When Math and Science Rule the School', *Harper's Magazine* (Sept. 2009): 32–40; Nicholson Baker, 'Wrong Answer: The Case Against Algebra 11', *Harper's Magazine* (Sept. 2013): 31–38; Caleb Crain, 'Counter Culture: Fighting for Literature in an Age of Algorithms', *Harper's Magazine* (July 2015); 78–83, Stefan Collini, 'Who are the Spongers now?', *LRB* (21.1.16): 33–37; and, most recently, Marilynne Robinson, 'Save Our Public Universities', *Harper's Magazine* (March 2016): 29–37.

against, and in order to understand enchantment it helps to be clear about what it is not.

The principles of modern education follow from the central project of modernity: the rational mastery of nature, both human nature and non-human, in the name of efficiency, convenience, and security.[15] This programme is pursued as impersonally as possible, through a battery of instruments of power and universally applied techniques, and its work consists of what Weber called 'rationalisation': abstracting, objectifying, explaining, domesticating, controlling, managing, commodifying, exploiting, and if necessary destroying (as in the immortal words of the American major in Vietnam—which any officer of the Inquisition would have immediately grasped—'It became necessary to destroy the village in order to save it').[16]

The chief instrument of modernity is what the historian of technology Lewis Mumford called the Megamachine, and it has, I suggest, three engines: capital, the state, and technoscience.[17] Since the chief of these is capital, they work together to enforce the market fundamentalism known as neoliberal economics, with its relentless focus on money and the 'bottom line', and therefore privatisation, deregulation, and 'austerity' for the poor. In the overdeveloped world, this imperative is obeyed by all political administrations, whether 'conservative' or 'liberal', and defended, ever more desperately, even as it staggers from crisis to crisis.

The dominant ideology which has justified this programme over the last few decades comprises another trinity: cognitive psychology, which defines human singularity (and therefore human privilege) as thinking, and thinking in turn as superior to all other possible candidates like emotion, imagination, intuition and so on; biology, especially neurophysiology and genetics, thus marginalising what is environmental, or rather, ecological; and neo-Darwinism, exalting a crude concept of 'adaptation' over all other considerations. The effect is a weird synthesis of hyper-abstraction and hyper-materialism, both in service of an ultra-determinism that elites think they

---

15   'The rational mastery of nature' is borrowed from Val Plumwood, *Environmental Culture: The Ecological Crisis of Reason* (London: Routledge, 2002).

16   This took place after the destruction of the Vietnamese village Ben Trê, 7th February 1968.

17   On technoscience in particular, see Curry, 'Defending the Humanities'.

will nonetheless be able to manipulate in their favour.[18]

What are the consequences for higher education—until recently under the rule, in the UK, of the Department of Business, Innovation and Skills, and now, equally tellingly, the Ministry of Universities, Sciences and Cities? Perhaps the most obvious is the dominance of managers and administrators over academics, under the rule of VCs indistinguishable from CEOs (average annual salary: £250,000). This ascendency is partly engineered by promoting academics with apparatchik potential over the head of those who are merely good at teaching and scholarship.

Now in order to obtain funding in these circumstances, the humanities in particular—literature, philosophy, religious studies, history, and studies of the arts—have frequently been obliged, and still are, to pretend they are like sciences (themselves modelled on technoscience, with a supposedly singular scientific method).[19] The resulting flight from relationality, participation, and subjectivity (which is now treated as a synonym for mere arbitrary preference) encourages a fetishisation of methodology that slips easily into methodolatry, the worship of method. The emphasis on standardisation, quantification, and 'objectivity' (which is enacted as depersonalisation) then redefines the field in such a way as to make them appear appropriate. Thus, applicants for funding to the Arts and Humanities Research Council, no less, are required, without a blush, to demonstrate the 'social and economic impact' of their work on Herodotus, or Chaucer, or Leibnitz... Good luck!

---

18   See Hilary Rose and Steven Rose, *Genes, Cells and Brains: The Promethean promises of the New Biology* (London: Verso, 2013); and the essays in Hilary Rose and Steven Rose, eds., *Alas, Poor Darwin: Arguments Against Evolutionary Psychology* (London: Jonathan Cape, 2000); Paolo Legrenzi and Carlo Umilta, *Neuromania: On the Limits of Brain Science*, trans. Frances Anderson (New York: Oxford University Press, 2011); Raymond Tallis, *Aping Mankind: Neuromania, Darwinitis and the Misrepresentation of Humanity* (London: Routledge, 2014).

19   On scientism and the humanities, see Ray Monk, 'Wittgenstein and the Two Cultures', *Prospect* (July 1999): 66–67; Marilynne Robinson, *Absence of Mind: The Dispelling of Inwardness from the Modern Myth of the Self* (New Haven: Yale University Press, 2010); and Barbara Herrnstein-Smith, 'Scientizing the Humanities: Shifts, Collisions, Negotiations', *Common Knowledge* 22.3 (2016): 353–72. The classic critique of a singular scientific method is Paul Feyerabend's *Against Method* (London: New Left Books, 1975).

One curious and damaging effect is that what becomes valued is not the subject itself, whatever it may be, but how to study it. To pick another personal example, my first degree, in psychology, ended up teaching us students not so much about the human mind, which we had naïvely been expecting, as about the study of it, reduced in turn to methodology. Not surprisingly, since our professors believed that if you get that right, the truth will necessarily follow, no matter who applies it. Ironically, this is magical thinking. The judgement of the person using the method *does* matter, in a way that cannot be formalised; rules, even algorithms, do not apply themselves. And one size does *not* fit all. Yet whatever does not fit the metric—whatever is real but incalculable, irreducibly qualitative, ultimately valuable rather than justifiably useful—all this gets cut or stretched until it does fit. The result is yet another disenchanted department of Procrustean Studies.

One of Saul Bellow's characters, the rebel Dean of a Midwestern university, puts it this way: 'he had taken it upon himself to pass Chicago through his own soul ... there was no other way for reality to happen. Reality didn't exist "out there." It began to be real only when the soul found its underlying truth. In generalities there was no coherence—none.'[20] That 'underlying truth' is upstream of the disenchanting division into a knowing subject ('mind') and a known object ('world'), which creates what Bellow calls 'the generality-mind'.[21] This is why the concrete magic of enchantment is often unwelcome; it is truly transgressive, because it fuses what modernity tries to keep chastely apart.

There have been many warnings. A plangent one was sounded by the philosopher and musicologist Vladimir Jankélévitch:

> In an era when pastiches of 'scientific investigation' have become quasi-universal, musicians owe it to themselves to become 'researchers' just like everyone else. But what are they looking for, in the end? A previously unknown chord? A new musico-atomic particle? It is a safe bet

---

20   Saul Bellow, *The Dean's December* (London: Secker and Warburg, 1982), 266.

21   Upstream: see the discussion in Henri Bortoft's excellent *Taking Appearance Seriously: The Dynamic Way of Seeing in Goethe and European Thought* (Edinburgh: Floris Books, 2012).

that a decline in inspiration translates into this thirst for innovation. Scriabin was a genuine 'researcher' because he was inspired as well. And vice versa, those with nothing to say attach exaggerated importance to novelties of vocabulary.[22]

This was in 1961. Now I'm not saying there weren't real insights involved, but by then structuralism was already well-established in the humanities, especially linguistics and anthropology, and all its hallmarks—objectivism, an uncritical veneration of method, and an aspiration to universal truth—were disenchanting. And these, along with an unmistakably exaggerated sense of the importance of novel vocabularies, also characterise the various hermeneutics of suspicion that have excited and dominated the humanities since then: Derridian post-structuralism, Foucauldian archaeology and genealogy, Lacanian psychoanalysis, Homi Bhabha's post-colonialism, Deleuzian metaphysics, and most recently the shotgun wedding, conducted by Slavoj Žižek, of Hegel and Lacan.

The gross reductionism of cognitive psychology, neurophysiology, and ultra-Darwinism is plain enough, but perhaps the time has now come to recognise these schools too as squabbling sibling offspring, born of humane studies, but sired by scientism. And too often, the outcome resembles the old medical joke: the operation was a success, although the patient died. In departments of English, for example, the patient was mostly literature itself—especially its heart: story—and consequently, reading as an enchanting experience. Readers were left to find their own way to what Ricoeur called a second *naïveté*, and recover a sense of wonder as best they could.[23]

These schools' esoteric, self-referential, and stylistically-challenged vocabularies are bad enough, but those of our new masters are still worse. You are probably sadly familiar with the spectral

---

22   Vladimir Jankélévitch, *Music and the Ineffable*, trans. Carolyn Abbate (Princeton: Princeton University Press, 2003), 108. See also, for example, Ivan Illich, *Deschooling Society* (London: Marion Boyars, 1971); and Lionel Trilling, *Mind in the Modern World* (New York: The Viking Press, 1972).

23   'Hermeneutics of suspicion' was famously coined by Ricoeur; also 'second naïveté', in Paul Ricoeur, *The Symbolism of Evil*, trans. Emerson Buchanan (Boston: Beacon Press, 1967), 351–52.

metaphors, dead on arrival, of targets, outcomes, benchmarks, outputs, resources, impacts and other items of neo-liberalese, so I will mention only one recent example. The Warburg Institute in London, founded by scholars fleeing the Nazis, is renowned for the study of European history and culture, and its glory is an open-shelved and thematically-arranged library, which gives full scope to the possibilities of scholarly serendipity. In the course of the University of London's attempt to modernise (for which read: destroy) the Warburg Institute, the pro-vice-chancellor described its library as a 'space hungry' policy that resists 'adopting sector best practice to apportion costs more transparently'.[24] What this means in plain English is that since the resulting benefits to scholarship cannot be quantified, they can be ignored; and since a website is cheaper to maintain than a library of what we must now call actual books, they should be mostly converted into binary pixels and then sacrificed.[25]

What I am describing is really new only in its scope. Already in 1969, the Canadian philosopher George Grant, in an essay on the university, decried 'this growing victory of power over wonder', in which 'technical reason has become so universal that it has closed down on openness and awe, questioning and listening'.[26] But these disenchanters, described by Weber even earlier as a 'nullity', '[s]pecialists without spirit', aren't listening.[27] And they are no longer at the gates of the academy, but in charge.

The effects are about as discouraging to enchantment as can be imagined: working academics are forced to engage in permanent 'grant capture', complete meaningless and demeaning forms, and continually adjust to change for its own sake, while students are discouraged from any apprehension of what they are studying, and why, outside the brutally instrumentalist box of career, status, and money. By the same token, they are encouraged to think of themselves not as students, here first and foremost to learn, but as customers, whose priority is a practical return on their 'investment'. But

---

24   Pro-vice-chancellor quoted in a letter by David Norbrook in the LRB (8.1.15).

25   See also 'Charles Hope writes about the battle over the Warburg Institute', LRB (4.12.14): 32–34; Adam Gopnik, 'In the Memory Ward', *The New Yorker* (16.3.15): 34–41.

26   George Grant, *Technology and Empire* (Toronto: Anansi, 1969), 116, 24.

27   Gerth and Mills, *From Max Weber*, 182.

for both parties, enchantment still requires (and encourages) scholarship in which the person is not just bent on mastering a passive subject but is in an ongoing relationship with it, ideally one in which a chief concern is that *it* may flourish.

The natural habitat of such scholarship in the academy has long been the humanities. There was never a time when they were wholly unhampered, of course, but now their very ground is under attack, in at least two ways. One I have mentioned; partly driven by capital and partly collaborating with it, scientism infiltrates and informs models of inquiry in unhelpful ways. Two, humanities courses are increasingly designated 'non-strategic' and cut in favour of STEM studies: science, technology, engineering, and maths. (Actually, it turns out maths and even science enrolments are declining. Only technology and its subset engineering are booming.)[28] Meanwhile, the financial services industry, which actively promotes parasitic self-interest, creams off if not the best, then many of the brightest— at least 40 per cent of Ivy League graduates, for example, in the early years of this century.[29]

Studies have repeatedly shown that reading on a screen rather than paper depresses both comprehension and retention, and that students who take notes with a pen rather than a laptop end up with a better grasp of the subject which they remember for longer.[30] Then there is the move to MOOCS (Massive Open Online Courses), a medium which seriously weakens the presence and personality of the particular teacher along with meaningful interaction. But replacing face-to-face learning is not driven by the desire to provide a better education, rather by its cheapness and convenience for educational institutions. The outreach is played up, but not the sacrifice in quality.

---

28   See William Deresiewicz, 'The Neoliberal Arts: How College Sold its Soul to the Market', *Harper's Magazine* (Sept. 2015): 25–32, which was published after I had written this paper. (I draw comfort from the fact that despite being much better-informed than I am, Deresiewicz says many of the same things.)

29   Joyce Appleby, *The Relentless Revolution: A History of Capitalism* (New York: W.W. Norton & Co., 2010), 406.

30   See research reported in *The Guardian Weekly* (19.12.14) and elsewhere. Relatedly, children are thirty-four times more likely to read storybooks daily than stories on a tablet, and four times more likely to read them for more than 30 minutes; *The Guardian Weekly* (2.2.15).

Courses cut, arbitrary demands, short-term contracts, pitiful pay, humiliating conditions, lack of trust and bullying, patronising, infantilising treatment by overseers: all these have resulted in unprecedented stress on teaching staff, especially in the humanities. At the same time, however, it must be said that academic resistance to the disenchantment of the academy has fallen short of admirable. Often it has consisted of what Marina Warner describes as 'an ecstasy of obedience'.[31]

One reason is a mindset that already militates against enchantment, even without any help from modernisation. As C.S. Lewis discovered in Cambridge; 'those who might be expected *ex officio* to have a profound and permanent appreciation of literature may in reality have nothing of the sort. They are mere professionals.'[32] Of course, a desire to advance one's career is perfectly legitimate. But when it becomes the overriding concern—which is what the modern academy encourages and exploits—the effects for the enchantment of learning are dire. One is to make the institution as such, which provides that career, one's first priority, over and above the learning it supposedly exists to serve. The resulting conspiracy of individual careers undermines true solidarity, along with one of the academy's *raisons d'être*: bringing together disinterested minds.

By the same token, excellence (which by definition stands out) is discouraged in favour of the average, individual judgement and conscience are disparaged as eccentric or dangerously maverick, and unlicensed insight is sacrificed for collective security. Mere professionalism or careerism, with no other values to defend, also offers conveniently little resistance to a managerial and technical takeover of what it actually means to be 'professional'. That mode in turns takes the human constant that (in Leys's words) 'inspired talent is an intolerable insult to mediocrity' and turns it into a principle.[33]

Partly as a result of these pressures, then, but to an extent they do not justify, academic practitioners of the humanities have been willing to abandon what people, including students, most want and need, wherein lies their enchantment: story, narrative, and meta-

---

31   Marina Warner, 'Why I quit', *LRB* 36:17 (11.11.2014): 43. Also see her 'Learning my lesson', *LRB* 37:6 (19.3.2015): 8–14.

32   C.S. Lewis, *An Experiment in Criticism* (Cambridge: Cambridge University Press, 2012 [1961]), 6.

33   Leys, *Hall*, 42.

phor. If you replace understanding with explanation and interpretation with analysis (when the latter two are presented as substitutes for the former two, not versions of), and add the understandable disincentive of an uncertain future career, is it any surprise that enrolments are plummeting?

WHAT CAN WE DO?

To quote someone speaking from long and bitter experience, 'There is naught you can do other than to resist, with hope or without it'.[34] That seems to me to be fundamental, within universities or outside them.

We should not give up on the academy without a fight, of course, but it is not the only possible site of resistance. The Nobel Prize-winning novelist J.M. Coetzee once discussed what happened to universities beginning in the 1980s and 1990s, 'as under threat of having their funding cut they allowed themselves to be turned into business enterprises, in which professors...were transformed into harried employees required to fulfil quotas under the scrutiny of professional managers'.

He reminds us that in some Eastern European countries under Communist rule, dissidents conducted night classes in their homes, teaching banned subjects and authors, adding that:

> If the spirit of the university is to survive, something along those lines may have to come into being in countries where tertiary education has been wholly subordinated to business principles. In other words, the real university may have to move into people's homes and
>
> grant degrees for which the sole backing will be the names of the scholars who sign the certificates.[35]

---

34   Elrond: See J.R.R. Tolkien, *The Lord of the Rings*, vol. 1 (London: George Allen and Unwin, 1953), 255. On enchantment as a primary value in Tolkien's work, and both its popular and critical reception, see my *Deep Roots in a Time of Frost: Essays on Tolkien* (Zurich: Walking Tree Books, 2014).

35   J.M. Coetzee, *Diary of a Bad Year* (London: Harvill Secker, 2007), 35–36.

We should also avail ourselves of the elders who have seen through the disenchanted modernist paradigm, and spoken truth to its power: people like some of those I have quoted, plus Edith Cobb, Ivan Illich, Neil Postman, Wendell Berry, and many others. There is a powerful counter-cultural tradition, with many tributaries, upon which to draw.

Relatedly, let's take every opportunity to value and protect teachers—and especially those who are themselves enchanted by the intrinsic worth of what they are teaching—as individuals, above and beyond any methodology, system, or programme. To the extent they are diminished, so are the relationships that are integral to wonder in learning.

To this perhaps not very original advice, I would like to add something else that I feel is both important and too-little-known. It concerns re-enchantment. There is a paradox at the heart of any such desire or attempt, because enchantment is wild. It cannot be rationally administered. We might even say that it *is* what cannot be administered, managed, or controlled—all modes of disenchantment. In learning, the paradox was perfectly summed by Ivan Illich: 'what people most need to learn, they cannot be *taught* [...]'[36]

It follows that a method or programme of positive re-enchantment is doomed to failure or worse ('worse' is when enchantment, having died in captivity, is surreptitiously replaced by something else under the same name). Especially to be avoided is any attempt to justify it in empirical or utilitarian terms, which cedes the very ground of the debate to the modernists. ('Learning can be shown to improve if wonder is included.' 'Oh really? Ok, we'll help you organise that.' Next up: enchantment targets, impact assessment, rating your enchantment experience on a scale of one to ten...)

This point, which is basic, seems to be difficult to accept, especially for progressive people, because it apparently leaves them helpless to protect or promote a sense of wonder in learning. But that is a misunderstanding. Things that matter do follow. One is that doing itself—that old itch to just *fix* things—is less important than *un*doing. Both individually and collectively, the way to encourage enchantment in learning is become aware of, and let go of, the habitual attitudes, practices, and rules that suppress it.[37] Leave room

---

36 Ivan Illich, *Tools for Conviviality* (London: Fontana, 1975), 81.

37 The therapeutic practice known as the Alexander Principle proceeds on just such a basis.

for it, resisting the temptation to try to meddle and control the outcome, and create the conditions it favours, where profit of any kind,
use-value, and efficiency are not allowed to dominate.[38] This is not
the same as making it happen. The point is to *let* it happen, and
the difference is crucial. Wonder, like love, is not a method, and it
cannot be applied, tested, or systematically improved. All we can
do is create the conditions it favours—usually through appropriate
ritual for that purpose—and invite it to be present. As Robert Frost
famously said, the movement in poetry is from delight to wisdom.
Delight is where we must start.

We need to remember that meeting, relating, and discovering,
and the enchantment that accompanies them, are our birthright as
embodied and ecological beings, so they are always potentially present. And we need to avoid the illusion that we know exactly what to
do. The best course is therefore to place (as the poet Seamus Heaney
said) our 'love and trust in the good of the indigenous'.[39]

Finally, I would like to leave you with this thought. As yet another poet, Wallace Stevens, puts it, 'Realism is a corruption of reality'.[40]
This is closely related to Tolkien's point that enchantment, although
irrelevant (at best) to the programme of rational mastery, 'is as necessary for the health and complete functioning of the Human as is
sunlight for physical life [...]'[41]

Now it is true that modernist education denies and suppresses
certain extraordinary experiences because they cannot be accom-
modated within the rationalist-realist worldview. But as Weber
pointed out, disenchantment characteristically proceeds by dividing
concrete magic 'into rational cognition and mastery of nature, on

---

38   See Anna L. Peterson's excellent *Everyday Ethics and Social Change: The
      Education of Desire* (New York: Columbia University Press, 2009). And cf.
      another poet: 'In the end, we can only prepare a space, a field, for inspira-
      tion to occur. This, of course, is contrary to the way we're taught to believe
      we should accomplish anything: by deciding to do it, then figuring out
      how, then making it happen.' (C.K. Williams, *In Time. Poets, Poems, and
      the Rest* [Chicago: University of Chicago Press, 2012], 88).

39   Heaney quoted in *Poetry Ireland Review* (2013): 27.

40   Wallace Stevens, *Collected Poetry and Prose* (New York: The Library of
      America, 1997), 906.

41   J.R.R. Tolkien, *Smith of Wootton Major*, extended edition, ed. Verlyn
      Flieger (London: HarperCollins, 2005), 101.

the one hand, and into "mystic" experiences, on the other'.[42] One side disenchants by forcing experience to be only concrete, the other by forcing it to be only 'magic'. One reduces down, the other up, but neither questions the distinction they both assume, nor their shared imperial ambition. That is why Gregory Bateson said that 'These two species of superstition [...] the supernatural and the mechanical, feed each other'.[43]

This truth is a clear warning not to accept the spiritual as a separate domain from the material, whatever is left over after the rest of the world has been rationalised and mechanised. So although I fully support the effort to rescue the paranormal (for want of a better term) from the enormous condescension of modernity, let's be wary of treating it as a wholly other domain.[44] We need to remember that what is stigmatised by modernism as spooky, superstitious and illusory is also a dimension of being *human* and of being *alive*. As Val Plumwood says, 'it is the space of everyday wonder and quotidian enchantment that is in need of reclamation and recovery'.[45]

Wonder itself is extraordinary, of course. But what it signals and shows us is the inner lining and depth of things, not as altogether somewhere else, another realm, but at the very heart of our ordinary, normal, carnal lives.[46] And its mystery cannot be explained, as if we could stand outside it. It can, however, be lived, and celebrated, and maybe even understood.

---

42   Gerth and Mills, *From Max Weber*, 282.

43   Gregory Bateson and Mary Catherine Bateson, *Angels Fear: An Investigation into the Nature and Meaning of the Sacred* (London: Rider, 1987), 51.

44   'The enormous condescension of modernity' is adapted from E.P. Thompson's resonant phrase in *The Making of the English Working Class*, in which the last word is 'posterity'.

45   Val Plumwood, 'Journey to the Heart of Stone', in *Culture, Creativity and Environment: New Environmentalist Criticism*, ed. Fiona Becket and Terry Gifford (Amsterdam: Rodopi, 2007), 17.

46   'Its lining and its depth': Maurice Merleau-Ponty, *The Visible and the Invisible*, ed. Claude Lefort, trans. Alphonso Lingis (Evanston: Northwestern University Press, 1968), 144.

Select bibliography

Bateson, Gregory and Mary Catherine Bateson. *Angels Fear: An Investigation into the Nature and Meaning of the Sacred.* London: Rider, 1987.

Bellow, Saul. *The Dean's December.* London: Secker and Warburg, 1982.

Collini, Stefan. *What Are Universities For?* London: Penguin, 2012.

_____, Stefan. 'Who are the Spongers Now?', *LRB* (21.1.16): 33–37.

Curry, Patrick. *Deep Roots in a Time of Frost: Essays on Tolkien.* Zurich: Walking Tree Books, 2014.

Fermor, Patrick Leigh. *The Broken Road: From the Iron Gates to Mount Athos.* Edited by Colin Thubron and Artemis Cooper. London: John Murray, 2013.

Feyerabend, Paul. *Conquest of Abundance: A Tale of Abstraction versus the Richness of Being.* Chicago: University of Chicago Press, 1999.

Flieger, Verlyn, and Douglas A. Anderson, eds. *Tolkien on Fairy-stories.* London: HarperCollins, 2008.

Hoffman, Eva. *Lost in Translation.* London: Vintage Books, 1998.

Jankélévitch, Vladimir. *Music and the Ineffable.* Translated by Carolyn Abbate. Princeton: Princeton University Press, 2003.

Leys, Simon. *The Hall of Uselessness: Collected Essays.* New York: NYRB, 2013.

Newman, John Henry. *The Idea of a University.* Notre Dame: University of Notre Dame Press, 1982.

Plumwood, Val. *Environmental Culture: The Ecological Crisis of Reason.* London: Routledge, 2002.

Ricoeur, Paul. *The Rule of Metaphor.* Translated by Robert Czerny. London: Routledge, 2003.

Schaff, Lawrence A. *Fleeing the Iron Cage: Culture, Politics, and Modernity in the Thought of Max Weber.* Berkeley: University of California Press, 1989.

Stevens, Wallace. *Collected Poetry and Prose.* New York: The Library of America, 1997.

Tolkien, J.R.R. *Smith of Wootton Major.* Edited by Verlyn Flieger. London: HarperCollins, 2005.

WARNER, Marina. 'Why I Quit'. *LRB* 36:17 (11.11.2014): 42–43.

———. 'Learning my Lesson'. *LRB* 37:6 (19.3.2015): 8–14.

WHITE, Michael. *Machiavelli: A Man Misunderstood*. London: Abacus, 2004.

'Clutching the Wheel of St Catherine'

Or, A Visit to a Re-enchanted College

SIMON WILSON

ENCHANTMENT IS THE OPPOSITE OF DEADNESS. It is a living thing, perhaps a manifestation of life itself. It has close synonyms, such as imagination, inspiration, transfiguration, enspiritment, ensoulment, Eden, Paradise, love. But, as the irruption of life into the world, it cannot be defined, only experienced. And in order to be experienced it has first to be acknowledged.

In an academia obsessed with quantifiable outcomes and outputs, with metering and monitoring, this powerful life force evidently remains unacknowledged, unperceived. If we ascribe this failure to specific ideologies—neo-liberalism, managerialism, scientism, and what have you—we fail to see the spiritual wood for the material trees: that disenchantment is a symptom of a universal spiritual malaise, what the French thinker René Guénon called the Reign of Quantity.

René Guénon was the founder of what has been called the Traditionalist or Perennialist school of thought.[1] His whole life bears witness to his search for an authentic spiritual tradition to which he could attach himself. Born in 1886, he studied mathematics in Paris, but soon abandoned his course to immerse himself in a whole swathe of esoteric societies and movements. In 1912 he married a devout Catholic, and began to remove himself somewhat from the

---

1   See for instance Harry Oldmeadow, *Frithjof Schuon and the Perennial Philosophy* (Bloomington: World Wisdom, 2010), 23. Guénon however did not apply either of those labels to himself, and indeed reserved the term 'Traditionalist' for those who had no real understanding of true tradition: see René Guénon, *The Reign of Quantity and the Signs of the Times*, trans. Lord Northbourne (Hillsdale: Sophia Perennis, 2004), 208–14.

occult *milieu*. His wife's unexpected death in 1928 seems to have affected him deeply, and two years later he took up residence in Cairo, where he spent the rest of his life as a Muslim and a member of a Sufi order. He died in 1951.

Guénon was the author of numerous books and articles, which have had an enormous intellectual influence.[2] His magnum opus is perhaps *The Reign of Quantity and the Signs of the Times* (1945), in which he assumes the mantle of a prophet, and meticulously takes apart the foundations of modernity, describing a world in which 'everything is counted, recorded, and regulated'.[3] His theme, in his own words, is 'the pure multiplicity toward which the present world is straining with all its might'.[4] People, although they may be unaware of it, are plunging headlong into an exclusively quantitative existence, into 'quantity itself, deprived of all quality', a state in which only numerical distinctions are perceived or allowed.[5]

This is, he argues, essentially a spiritual predicament, resulting from modernity's drift from what he calls the Centre. His writings turn again and again to the idea of the Centre, and he defined it as follows:

> The Centre is before all else the origin, the point of departure of all things; it is the principial[6] point, without form, without dimensions, therefore indivisible, and consequently the only image that can be given to primordial Unity. From it, by its radiation, all things are produced [...] The central point is the Principle, it is

---

2   Many thinkers have been directly influenced by Guénon, including Ananda Kentish Coomaraswamy, Frithjof Schuon, Seyyed Hossein Nasr, Mircea Eliade, Lord Northbourne, and Philip Sherrard. See Mark Sedgwick, *Against the Modern World: Traditionalism and the Secret Intellectual History of the Twentieth Century* (Oxford: Oxford University Press, 2004), passim.

3   Guénon, *Reign of Quantity*, 144.

4   Ibid., 8.

5   Ibid., 9, 49.

6   'Guénon used the neologism *principiel* as an adjective derived from *Principe*, the primary Source and Origin of everything.' Graham Rooth, *Prophet for a Dark Age: A Companion to the Works of René Guénon* (Brighton: Sussex Academic Press, 2008), xxviii. 'Principial' is the equivalent English neologism adopted by most translators of Guénon.

pure Being, and the space which it fills by its radiation and which exists only by that same radiation (the *Fiat Lux* of Genesis) [...] is the World in the widest sense of the word, the totality of all beings and all states of existence constituting universal manifestation.[7]

The Centre is life itself. It is being, pure essence, and contains all that exists and can exist. Offering fullness of life for those who can perceive it, it is the eternal moment of enchantment, and is utterly shot through with—and shines always with—the presence of the divine. It is not however limited to any particular place: suffusing the whole of the cosmos, it is truly ever-present to those with eyes to see, 'penetrat[ing], sustain[ing], and illuminat[ing] all things'.[8] Thus we all of us carry around in us our own interior Centre, in the form of our heart. Illumination and enchantment takes place in our heart, from which it radiates through our whole being.[9]

Although Guénon's descriptions of the Centre tend to be somewhat abstract, they come to life in many of the symbols he finds for it, such as the heart itself, Eden, the Land of the Living, and, perhaps pre-eminently, the Grail.[10]

Humanity however has drifted away from the life-giving Centre to the circumference, and the result is a robotic and monotonous

---

7   René Guénon, *Symbols of Sacred Science*, trans. Henry D. Fohr (Hillsdale: Sophia Perennis, 2004), 57–58. Guénon's conception of the Centre evidently had a huge influence on the great scholar of religion Mircea Eliade, whose own writings on the Centre often read like close paraphrases of Guénon's. See, for example, Mircea Eliade, *The Sacred and the Profane: The Nature of Religion*, trans. Willard R. Trask (Orlando: Harcourt Inc., 1987), 36–47, 64–65; and Mircea Eliade, *Cosmos and History: The Myth of the Eternal Return*, trans. Willard R. Trask (New York: Harper & Row, 1959), 12–21. Eliade, however, seems never publicly to have acknowledged the huge debt that he owed to Guénon: see Sedgwick, *Against the Modern World*, 111–12.

8   Guénon, *Symbols*, 441.

9   Ibid., 406.

10   See, for example, ibid., 12–37, 79–95; and René Guénon, *The King of the World*, trans. Henry D. Fohr (Hillsdale: Sophia Perennis, 2004), 27–32, 49–66. For a discussion of the role of the Grail in Guénon's thinking, see Simon Wilson, 'René Guénon and the Heart of the Grail', *Temenos Academy Review* 18 (2015): 146–67.

parody of life.[11] More and more we are 'reduced to nothing more than simple numerical "units".[12] Robbed of our proper qualities, we are turned, Guénon writes, 'into something as nearly as possible like mere machines'.[13] Cyborg beings at best, our perceptions of the world have become narrowed: the faculties which had once enabled us to experience super-sensible realities in the world have atrophied, and the material world responds by actually—literally—forming a hard shell around those who inhabit it so that it seems to be all that *can* be known. Guénon believes that the work of most modern scholars, no matter how eminent they may be, reinforces these effects:

> It can be said with truth that certain aspects of reality conceal themselves from anyone who looks upon them from a profane and materialistic point of view, and they become inaccessible to his observation [...] That is why there are some things that can never be grasped by men of learning who are materialists or positivists, and this naturally further confirms their belief in the validity of their conceptions by seeming to afford a sort of negative proof of them, whereas it is really neither more nor less than a direct effect of the conceptions themselves.[14]

Scholars' mollusc tendencies have if anything worsened since Guénon was writing, as pressures to be business-oriented fundraisers have been brought to bear on them, and they are now each encased in their individual entrepreneurial shells in academies which themselves are become carapaces.[15] Enchantment has no chance: unperceived, unacknowledged, it is blocked out. That was certainly my own experience as an undergraduate reading English at St Catha-

---

11   See for example Guénon, *Reign*, 162–63.

12   Ibid., 51.

13   Ibid., 51.

14   Ibid., 117. For Guénon's discussions of the process, which he calls 'solidification', see for example ibid., 101, 106, 113–19, 134.

15   The notorious atomisation of knowledge is the result: universities are now multiversities. On Guénon and modern universities, see also David R. Lea, 'The Managerial University and the Decline of Modern Thought', *Educational Philosophy and Theory: Incorporating ACCESS* 43 (2011): 816–37.

rine's College, Cambridge, in the 1980s. Romantically I had hoped to feed my soul, but had largely found uncomprehending materialism and empiricism instead.[16] Later, however, I became drawn to the story of the college's patron saint, and in the light of that legend looked again at the early years of the college: the result was an article on a St Catharine's of the imagination, in which I attempted—or perhaps just claimed—to uncover the tradition of enchantment at its heart.[17]

Founded in 1473, the College was dedicated to St Catherine of Alexandria, the patron saint of theologians, philosophers, and scholars. According to her legend, she had rebuked the Emperor Maxentius in the early 4th century for cruelly persecuting Christians and worshipping idols. Maxentius responded by calling in the empire's wisest men to confound her: victory however was hers as she was able to refute their best arguments with ease. The emperor then ordered that Catherine be executed on the wheel: the instrument of martyrdom however shattered at her touch and Maxentius resorted to having her decapitated.

The arms of the College represent the saint's wheel, displaying a golden Catherine Wheel against a red background.[18] These arms symbolise the nature of Catherine's wisdom. The hub of the wheel is the very Centre itself, the spokes signify its radiation as it illumines and enchants the world into being.[19] As the wheel set up by Maxentius turned, Catherine was not flung to the circumference to be torn to pieces—fragmented, atomised—by the hard facts of the material world: rather, she was drawn back to the Centre. So it was the killing reign of quantity which was shattered, and not the saint, who in-

---

16   Seventeen years or so earlier Patrick Harpur had had a similar experience, despite the presence of T.R. Henn: he refers to 'the disenchantment with my teachers and colleagues whom, when I arrived [at St Catharine's], I was sure would be infinitely cleverer and wiser than I, and from whom I hoped to learn so much.' Patrick Harpur, email message to author, 26th June, 2015.

17   Simon Wilson, 'The Imaginal College', *Fortean Times* 298 (2013): 52–53.

18   Or, in the language of heraldry, 'Gules a Catherine wheel Or'. See W.H.S. Jones, *A History of St Catharine's College Once Catharine Hall Cambridge* (Cambridge: Cambridge University Press, 1936), 47.

19   As Guénon points out, an alternative term for 'hub' is 'nave,' which has the same etymological root as 'navel'. See Guénon, *King*, 56. The hub of a wheel is thus symbolically an *umbilicus* or *omphalos*: it is the nave (l) or centre of the world, and a manifestation of the very Centre itself.

stead shone triumphantly from the Centre with life and truth.

In its early years (so I argued in my aforementioned article) the College named after St Catherine became itself a manifestation of the ever-present Centre, from which enchantment emanated. I have since discovered that, in a modest way, it still fulfilled this role in the last century (though sadly before my time). That is perhaps an eccentric claim, and in making it I hope that I am not confusing enchantment with delusion. It would not be the first time that the college's arms have led the mind a merry dance. In the 17th century, Thomas Bancroft (c. 1596–1658) wrote the following lines to his friend James Shirley (1596–1666), a successful poet and dramatist of the time:

> Iames, thou and I did spend some precious yeares
> At Katherine-Hall; since when, we sometimes feele
> In our poetick braines, (as plaine appears)
> A whirling trick, then caught from Katherine's wheele.[20]
> [sic throughout]

That whirling trick can leave one dizzy and confused. Which is why we need to gaze at the centre of the wheel of St Catharine's. If we are able to do that we may discover the distinguished Anglo-Irish Yeats scholar Thomas Rice Henn (1901–1974).[21] A fellow of St Catharine's from 1926 until 1969, T.R. Henn dominated the teaching of English Literature at the college for over forty years, transfixing undergraduates and colleagues alike with his personality and with his voice. Kathleen Raine, who became a friend of Henn's when she was a research fellow at Girton from 1955 to 1961, recalled him reading Yeats aloud 'in what an Irishman in Sligo called "his great cathedral voice that comes from the heart".[22] Patrick Harpur writes that

---

20   Francis Warner, 'St Catharine's Poets in the Master's Lodge', *St Catharine's College Society Magazine* (1998): 15. The college was usually referred to as 'Katherine Hall' until 1860, when 'St Catharine's College' became its official title: see Jones, *History of St Catharine's*, 46, n. 2.

21   Director of the Yeats International Summer School in Sligo from 1962 to 1968, Henn had met the great Irish poet in person: see T.R. Henn, *The Lonely Tower: Studies in the Poetry of W.B. Yeats* (London: Methuen, 1950), xiii.

22   Kathleen Raine, *Autobiographies* (London: Skoob Books Publishing,

he and his fellow students 'spent hours regaling each other in faux Tom [Henn] accents [...] with the latest bon mots and throwaway lines we'd got from our separate encounters with him'.[23] Much more than a mere 'character', however, Henn was a charismatic teacher who knew that literature, when properly studied, was not a luxury or mere fantasy: it had the power to revitalise mechanised and moribund hearts and souls by reconnecting them to archetypal symbols with their origins in the profundities of the individual psyche, in the transpersonal ancestral mind of humanity, and ultimately in the *anima mundi*, 'that strange company of spirits' as he called it.[24] Studying literature with Henn could thus cure what he called 'that starvation, that atrophy of the traditional life of the spirit, which many moralists have diagnosed as a malaise of the culture'.[25]

His teaching, then, represented an attempt to open his students to this life-giving experience of literature, and so to cleanse them of the deadening materialism of the world. I.A. Richards, writing in *The Times* on the occasion of Henn's death, bore witness to the fact that this attempt frequently succeeded: Henn would be remembered, he wrote 'especially by his pupils for his insight into the learning of the imagination (a tradition not often taught in schools) which opens up the visionary world beyond the confines of material things until "soul clap its hands and sing"'.[26] His supervisions[27] were in effect a kind of initiation, in which the students would, through

---

1991), 328.

23   Patrick Harpur, email message to author, 25th June, 2015.

24   Henn, *Lonely Tower*, xiv.

25   T.R. Henn, *The Bible as Literature* (London: Lutterworth Press, 1970), 20. If a culture without spiritual content was a dead thing for Henn, the same was equally true for the study of culture: as he wrote in his autobiography, 'I do not think it is possible to make the teaching of literature a living thing without attention to the transcendental values'. See T.R Henn, *Five Arches: A Sketch for an Autobiography* and *'Philoctetes' and Other Poems* (Gerrards Cross: Colin Smythe, 1980), 201.

26   Quoted in Edward Malins, 'Dr. T.R. Henn: An Appreciation', *The Canadian Journal of Irish Studies*, 1.1 (1975): 8. The reference is to 'Sailing to Byzantium' by Yeats. I.A. Richards (1893–1979) was a hugely influential scholar, one of the founders (perhaps *the* founder) of the academic subject of English Literature.

27   'Supervision' is the term used at Cambridge for a one-to-one tutorial, or a tutorial for a small group of students.

their encounter with symbols and imagery, gradually come to incarnate the vital impulse carried by great writing and channelled, as
it were, through Henn. His pupils were being transported into the
illumined and enchanted Centre, where being alive took precedence
over slavishly sticking to the syllabus or even to the ostensible aim of
the supervision. 'He paid scant attention to our essays,' remembers
Patrick Harpur, 'but held forth on random topics. His aim seemed
to be to wake us up'.[28]

Being properly awake and properly alive—living connected to
the Centre as it were—could mean actually encountering the archetypes and living the myths. Sitting on a train to Manchester, Henn
heard the spine-chilling cry of the banshee: later he discovered that
his elder brother had at that moment died in Ireland.[29] Being alive
also meant being free to startle and even shock: that was sometimes
necessary to crack open the carapace and revive the moribund mollusc within. Patrick Harpur recalls that, during a supervision, Henn
suddenly turned to a particularly uptight—and indubitably virgin-
al—student and said "'Have you noticed, Mr Hill, that when you
make love to your girlfriend [...] that her armpits smell like the musk
rat's earlobes?'"[30] While Harpur's story may be meant to convey a
flavour of the man rather than to be taken as an absolutely literal
report, other students who knew Henn have told similar tales. The
theatre director and founder of the Royal Shakespeare Company,
Sir Peter Hall, who studied English at St Catharine's from 1950 until
1953, writes that while discussing imagery in a Yeats poem, Henn
suddenly demanded of his supervisees, "'Have you ever made love
—to a girl—in a cave?'"[31]

Henn could also be disconcerting or startling rather than shocking. Once, shortly after he had graduated, Patrick Harpur returned
to college to see his old supervisor. Henn stared deeply into his eyes
and then asked him if he could see his [Henn's] aura, adding, "'I
think you can probably see these things. I'm told it's a kind of light
brown. The academic colour'".[32] This comment was probably all the

---

28   Patrick Harpur, email message to author, 25th June 2015.

29   Patrick Harpur, *Daimonic Reality: A Field Guide to the Otherworld* (Lon-
      don: Arkana, 1995), 113–14.

30   Patrick Harpur, email message to author, 25th June 2015.

31   Ibid.

32   Ibid.

more perplexing as it is hard to imagine that Henn's aura was actually so drab a hue as light brown.

I'd like to briefly explore Henn's influence in the work of two students who bookend his supervising career: Malcolm Lowry and Patrick Harpur. In different ways they have both carried forth Henn's initiatic impulse into the world.

Malcolm Lowry read English at St Catharine's from 1929 to 1932.[33] Although he and Henn evidently didn't get on,[34] Lowry's works are heavy with the archetypes and symbols which were so crucial for his supervisor. That is especially true of his College's central symbol, the Catherine Wheel.

Lowry makes repeated references in his works to a re-imagined college. Sometimes the reference could be explicit, as in the short story 'Through the Panama', for instance, where the protagonist dreams of Death leading him to 'St Catherine's [sic] College, Cambridge, *and the very room*'.[35] At other times Lowry thinly disguises his college, as is the case in the unfinished novel *October Ferry to Gabriola*, in which the main character has studied at 'the college of Ixion, at the University of Ely'.[36] But it is the Catherine Wheel which

---

33 Lowry was certainly the greatest novelist Henn had taught, yet when Henn, shortly before his death, listed the eminent authors he had supervised at St Catharine's, he omitted Lowry altogether. See T.R. Henn, 'The College 1919–70', in *St Catharine's College Cambridge 1473–1973: A Volume of Essays to Commemorate the Quincentenary of the Foundation of the College*, ed. E.E. Rich (Cambridge: St Catharine's College, 1973), 283. Lowry's biographer puts the omission down to fundamental differences in temperament between the two men: see Gordon Bowker, *Pursued by Furies: A Life of Malcolm Lowry* (London: Flamingo, 1994), 94–95. Patrick Harpur, however, suggests that Henn had little knowledge of the novel and had simply not read Lowry's works: see Patrick Harpur, email message to author, 26th June 2015.

34 Bowker, *Pursued by Furies*, 94–95.

35 Malcolm Lowry, *Hear Us O Lord From Heaven Thy Dwelling Place* and *Lunar Caustic* (Harmondsworth: Penguin Books, 1979), 37. The reference is to the room which Lowry briefly shared with a fellow student, and in which the student subsequently killed himself. The incident fed Lowry's sense of personal guilt. See Bowker, *Pursued by Furies*, 96–99.

36 Malcolm Lowry, *October Ferry to Gabriola* (Harmondsworth: Penguin, 1979), 61. If Lowry associates his old college with death in 'Through the Panama', in *October Ferry to Gabriola* he links it with endless pain and

frequently appears as a truly pivotal symbol in Lowry's works, in a variety of guises. At times it threatens to fling protagonists off into dizzy disintegration and death, at others it offers a moment of stability and peace in a chaotic world.

Lowry's masterpiece is *Under the Volcano*, and it is there that the wheel, under its various aspects, also plays its most prominent role. The novel tells of the last day in the life of Geoffrey Firmin, but is just as much about the tragic wreck of mankind in the 20th century.

In a 1946 letter to his publisher, Lowry himself described the book as '*trochal*', i.e., having the form of a wheel.[37] This formal principle is symbolised in *Under the Volcano* by a fairground Ferris wheel, which makes its most famous appearance at the end of the first chapter: 'Over the town, in the dark tempestuous night, backwards revolved the luminous wheel'.[38] In his letter, Lowry called the big wheel, 'Buddha's wheel of the law [...], it is eternity, it is the instrument of eternal recurrence, the eternal return'.[39]

The revolving wheel is also a metaphor for drunkenness. Firmin is an alcoholic, and his world—his 'drunken madly revolving world'— spins around him like a crazy Catherine Wheel.[40] Even worse is the uncontrollable spinning of his thoughts, 'a whirling cerebral chaos' in which reality disintegrates.[41] Firmin's condition symbolises, as Lowry put it, 'the universal drunkenness of mankind during the [Second World] war, or during the period immediately preceding it'.[42] Thomas Bancroft's 'whirling trick, [...] caught from Katherine's wheele', to which I referred earlier, has, in the 20th century, turned insane, demonic even, and infected the entire globe.

---

punishment. Ixion, in Greek mythology, had been helplessly bound to a rolling wheel for all eternity, a punishment for his sins. Lowry thereby transforms the liberating wheel of St Catharine's into a symbol of the harsh and pitiless laws of the gods of this world, a wheel whose turning brings not life but eternal and inescapable suffering. Ely, the location of the fictional college, is a venerable cathedral city a few miles from Cambridge.

37   Malcolm Lowry, *Under the Volcano* (Harmondsworth: Penguin, 1985), 44.

38   Ibid., 87.

39   Ibid., 23.

40   Ibid., 238.

41   Ibid., 349.

42   Ibid., 17–18.

At the end of the novel Firmin is murdered. His consciousness, and the world, and all civilisation, disintegrate together:

> the world itself was bursting, bursting into black spouts of villages catapulted into space, with himself falling through it all, through the inconceivable pandemonium of a million tanks, through the blazing of ten million burning bodies, falling, into a forest, falling—[43]

The book has spun like a wheel, and flung existence into a nightmare of demonic, mechanised, and quantified death ('a million tanks', 'ten million burning bodies'). But the Catherine Wheel at the novel's centre offers brief and fragile respite from these centrifugal forces. In the sixth chapter of *Volcano*—'the heart of the book' as Lowry described it—Firmin's half-brother Hugh recalls his time at Cambridge, and wonders what he had done there. Did he 'climb the gateway [...] to visit Bill Plantagenet in Sherlock Court, and, clutching the wheel of St Catherine, feel, for a moment asleep, like Melville, the world hurling from all havens astern?'[44] Surrounded in the novel by wheels of all kinds, Hugh sees himself as a student tipsily climbing over the main gates into St Catharine's, to see a friend living on the college's Sherlock Court. Prominently displayed on these gates is the Catherine Wheel, which, in this moment of great vulnerability, he grabs hold of, and it steadies himself in the whirling world, like a ship's helm on a stormy sea (Catherine is after all the patron saint of mariners). Perhaps it cannot save Hugh completely, but the stability and orientation it offers provides a kind of support: better than nothing in the disintegrating universe of this novel. Even if Hugh drunkenly falls asleep, that does not mean that the hint, the hope is not there.

---

43   Ibid., 415–16.

44   Ibid., 28, 219–20. The reference is to a passage in *Moby-Dick* in which Ishmael falls asleep at the tiller, to wake up disoriented, facing the wrong way round, the ship apparently 'rushing from all havens astern'. Herman Melville, *Moby-Dick*, ed. Harrison Hayford and Hershel Parker (New York: W.W. Norton & Company, 1967), 354. Melville's point is the necessity of true orientation, of not being lulled by the sleep of delusion. Hugh, however, is offered a momentarily safe haven: not the tiller of a ship but the Catherine wheel.

Decades later, in the academic year up to his retirement in 1969, Henn supervised Patrick Harpur. Harpur's works are full of the archetypal imagery his old supervisor regarded as essential for spiritual health.[45]

Considerably less tentatively than Lowry, Harpur carries a broad spiritual resistance to the pulverising centrifugal forces of the modern world, and so communicates the enchantment woven by Henn. He writes of cathartic moments when the imaginal world, which is really always there behind the surface, stands revealed:

> The whole world is trembling on the edge of revealing its own immanent soul. We see it in moments when our perception is raised by imagination to vision [...] We see it when, as Blake says, the doors of perception are cleansed and everything appears as it is, infinite.[46]

This experience is the result not of a particular pedagogy, methodology, or philosophy but of a completely traditional 'way of seeing'.[47] Harpur, like his old supervisor, wants to rattle at our carapaces and awaken us to that vision, to revitalise us. All who are thus enchanted are, as he puts it, links in an 'Aurea Catena', 'a Golden Chain of initiates',[48] which has always existed and will always exist, not on the level of exoteric history but on the level of the spirit.

Reading his books we too may experience enchantment, feel the proximity of the Centre, and be saved from the pulverising Reign of Quantity described by René Guénon. Tom Henn's college at last spreads beyond Cambridge, its Golden Chain of initiates like a shining Catherine Wheel. This life-giving wheel illuminates Canterbury

---

45   Harpur, *Daimonic Reality*, 113–14. Harpur has—not entirely seriously—indicated that he is Henn's intellectual heir: he tells the story of how he came into possession in a roundabout way of Henn's old Barbour, 'a fantastic old brown waterproof from the 1930s, which I wear to this day, literally taking on, perhaps, his mantle!' Patrick Harpur, email message to author, 25th June 2015. Thus Henn has not only been able to protect Harpur's spiritual health but his physical health, too.

46   Harpur, *Daimonic Reality*, 123.

47   Patrick Harpur, *The Philosophers' Secret Fire: A History of the Imagination* (London: Penguin Books, 2002), 2.

48   Harpur, *Daimonic Reality*, 297; Harpur, *Secret Fire*, 287.

Christ Church University, where I now teach, and you, the reader of this chapter, are at its hub.

SELECT BIBLIOGRAPHY

BOWKER, Gordon. *Pursued by Furies: A Life of Malcolm Lowry.* London: Flamingo, 1994.

GUÉNON, René. *The King of the World.* Translated by Henry D. Fohr. Hillsdale: Sophia Perennis, 2004.

_____. *The Reign of Quantity and the Signs of the Times.* Translated by Lord Northbourne. Hillsdale: Sophia Perennis, 2004.

_____. *Symbols of Sacred Science.* Translated by Henry D. Fohr. Hillsdale: Sophia Perennis, 2004.

HARPUR, Patrick. *Daimonic Reality: A Field Guide to the Otherworld.* London: Arkana, 1995.

_____. *The Philosophers' Secret Fire: A History of the Imagination.* London: Penguin Books, 2002.

HENN, T.R. *The Bible as Literature.* London: Lutterworth Press, 1970.

_____. *Five Arches: A Sketch for an Autobiography* and *'Philoctetes' and Other poems.* Gerrards Cross: Colin Smythe, 1980

_____. *The Lonely Tower: Studies in the Poetry of W.B. Yeats.* London: Methuen, 1950.

LOWRY, Malcolm. *Hear Us O Lord From Heaven Thy Dwelling Place* and *Lunar Caustic.* Harmondsworth: Penguin Books, 1979.

_____. *October Ferry to Gabriola.* Harmondsworth: Penguin, 1979.

_____. *Under the Volcano.* Harmondsworth: Penguin, 1985.

MALINS, Edward. 'Dr. T.R. Henn: An Appreciation'. *The Canadian Journal of Irish Studies* 1.1 (1975): 5–8.

OLDMEADOW, Harry. *Frithjof Schuon and the Perennial Philosophy.* Bloomington: World Wisdom, 2010.

RAINE, Kathleen. *Autobiographies.* London: Skoob Books Publishing, 1991.

ROOTH, Graham. *Prophet for a Dark Age: A Companion to the Works of René Guénon.* Brighton: Sussex Academic Press, 2008

SEDGWICK, Mark. *Against the Modern World: Traditionalism and the Secret Intellectual History of the Twentieth Century.* Oxford: Oxford University Press, 2004.

WARNER, Francis. 'St Catharine's Poets in the Master's Lodge'. *St Catharine's College Society Magazine* (1998): 15.

WILSON, Simon. 'The Imaginal College'. *Fortean Times* 298 (2013): 52–53.

_____. 'René Guénon and the Heart of the Grail'. *Temenos Academy Review* 18 (2015): 146–67.

Re-enchanting the Academy

Popular Education and the Search for Soul in the Modern University

LINDEN WEST

INTRODUCTION

Contemporary universities, at least on their websites, can seem pre-occupied rather with the allure of world-class research status or with their positioning in diverse league tables of student satisfaction, than with bigger questions as to their purpose and values in an increasingly conflict-ridden world. Universities may be located in troubled and troubling marginalised communities, where there are tensions between different cultural groups, and a rise of racism, xenophobia, as well as of mental illness, educational failure, and alienation from conventional politics. But the big questions that may be provoked by this, in part cultural, social, educational and political, may be marginal in many parts of the business university.[1] I will focus on the responsibilities, if any, of universities in the face of the crisis of faith in multiculturalism and the rise of racism and xenophobia. How should universities respond to profound challenges such as social injustice, growing inequalities, insecure labour markets and the troubling rise in mental ill-health? These problems may demand new, critical and interdisciplinary interrogation, but academic disciplines can be dominated by narrow perspectives remote from 'real' world concerns. They can be trapped in acritical assumptions about neo-liberalism, for instance, to the dissatisfaction of many students in various universities.[2]

Moreover, research agendas can be fixated on the pursuit of the most income, perhaps involving research of a quick fix, 'don't ask

---

1   See Ronald Barnett, *Being a University* (London: Routledge, 2011).

2   See Post-Crash Economics Society, *Economics, Education, and Unlearning* (Manchester: University Post-Crash Economics Society, 2014).

too many questions' kind. This may apply in educational research: it can be difficult to get funding for forms of research that take time, are in-depth as well as traversing disciplinary boundaries, and are relatively expensive. Studying the present crisis of mental illness, for instance, may not simply be a personal or psychological matter but can be interconnected with the health of families and whole communities and the resources available to them. Such issues become acute when thinking of the university's social responsibilities in marginalised post-industrial communities.[3] I have been interrogating the rise of racism and fundamentalism, for instance, as well as a crisis of mental health and education, in a post-industrial city in the English Midlands called Stoke-on-Trent; the place where I was born.

There are echoes in the research of the values and methodologies of the Chicago School of Sociology, with its psychosocial interdisciplinarity, and its conviction that the city was a legitimate source for normative enquiry. In-depth ethnography and biography provided the university with powerful intellectual resources, social purpose, and a civic rationale.[4] I have been trying to do something similar, if on a much smaller scale. To reach out to the people who may be struggling the most, like the racist or someone attracted to violent Islamism, and to gather their stories and to try to think about them in new ways. The trouble is that a university's gaze is often elsewhere, neurotically obsessed with what governments or powerful others think they should be doing. Carl Gustav Jung applied the quasi-metaphysical term 'soul' to the well-being of people and whole cultures in the shadow of the First World War.[5] Belief in confident modernity, in the idea of progress, or in God, lay twisted and broken in the mud of Flanders, and he was exercised by the struggle for something new and better. Perhaps there is also a crisis in the soul of the modern university and we need to ask awkward questions.

Jung saw that crisis as an opportunity to learn and think afresh, to consider what had gone wrong, and to find new meta-understandings of what it means to be human, and of the prerequisites for

---

3   See Linden West, *Distress in the City: Racism, Fundamentalism and a Democratic Education* (London: Trentham/UCI Books, 2016).

4   Barbara Merrill and Linden West, *Using Biographical Methods in Social Research* (London: Sage, 2009).

5   C.G. Jung, *Modern Man in Search of a Soul* (New York: Harvest, 1933).

well-being, in a world of lost faith and disenchantment. We too seem frozen in the gaze of destructiveness, of growing terrorism, barbarity, and xenophobia in many parts of the world; and in awareness of the continuing capacity of people to do terrible things to each other. The emotional and physical suffering of countless refugees and innocents fleeing from or trapped in war zones and oppressive regimes is overwhelming. We also face the disturbing ecological crisis of the sustainability of our planet, co-existing with an insatiable appetite to consume more and to care less. For Jung, troubling times required serious thinking about a culture's soul, and the nature of our humanity, and why we act in destructive, self-serving, and thoughtless ways. Perhaps we really should ask fundamental questions about the state we are in, and of the university's responsibilities to encourage serious and critical thinking across various populations.

Arguably such questions are often avoided. We (and this includes academics) may prefer to bury our heads in the sand, and get on with what we are doing, because to do and think otherwise is too daunting a task. The university itself may seem deeply incorporated in the neo-liberal project. Governments have mobilised a discourse of economic crisis to stress the university as a servant, predominantly, of the economy and, in effect, of the established order. Servanthood is to be achieved, in part, by producing forms of knowledge that are more easily consumed and translated into new goods, services, and patents; and by providing courses that students pay for, and exchange for employment.[6] The difficult business of thinking about what troubles and disenchants us could be the casualty. The desire within liberal education, or *Bildung*, was to create autonomous, thinking citizens, free from the heteronomy of the Church. But the critical theorist Theodor Adorno thought that *Halbbildung*, or half-education, had replaced the heteronomy of formal religion.[7] This involves compliance with current cultural, social, and economic assumptions, including, for present purposes, the heteronomy of neo-liberalism.

---

6   See Keri Facer, 'Claiming the Crisis: Education Research, Activism and Opportunities for Renewal: Notes Towards a Civic, Critical, and Popular University' (paper presented at the European Conference on Educational Research, the University of Cadiz, 21st September 2012).

7   Cited in Anastasios Gaitanidis, 'Anxiety, Psychoanalysis, and Reinvigorating Education', in *Psychoanalysis and Education: Minding a Gap*, ed. Alan Bainbridge and Linden West (London: Karna, 2012), 41.

Students, from such a perspective, are provided with sets of pre-sumptions that filter their actual experience as classed, gendered, raced, psychosocial as well as historical beings, and integration, con-formity, and a thoughtless, even selfish adaptation to what presently exists becomes the norm.[8] The struggle to think difficult thoughts is replaced by a mantra of objective and non-conflictive knowledge and the relatively unquestioning adaptation to the status quo. This was what the economics students at Manchester University and in several other universities were in effect complaining about in 2012, which led to the creation of the Post-Crash Economics Society. The accusation was that the study of economics was confused with a single methodological framework—the neo-classical—that could easily degenerate into dogma. In the light of the 2008 financial cri-sis, such foundations seemed increasingly questionable. Unfettered competition, in the financial sector and elsewhere, was shown to be socially destructive. Greed, if taken to excess, was found to be plain bad. The Invisible Hand, if taken to extremes, appeared malevolent, contributing to a severe loss of global income and output. Pursuing self-interest, by firms and individuals, had made society poorer.

Even worse, students were penalised for considering variety and rewarded for reproducing existing thought by rote. Their teachers were telling them 'truths' that were unravelling before their eyes, but the message rolled endlessly on to their increasing disenchant-ment.[9] The complexity of people's actual problems in the face of the financial crash, and the illusions of a marketised world, cried out for new, critical attention.

For me, as a historian and auto/biographical narrative researcher, engaging with the past and present of a particular city offered both consolation and new ideas. There have been times and places where really serious knowledge was generated, alongside a concern for all the people rather than a few. We can learn, at least, that it was not always like the present, and need not be so in the future. But the struggle towards greater consciousness of the disturbing state we are in requires sustained effort and struggle, although there is already resistance in parts of the academy to the neo-liberal zeitgeist. There are deep anxieties around how knowledge itself gets commodified, packaged, in effect, for extrinsic, individualistic, and even illusory

---

8   See Gaitanidis, 'Anxiety', passim.

9   See Post-Crash Economics Society, *Economics*.

ends. There is antipathy towards the notion that a student 'buys' a particular degree, in a specific institution, as a product to be enjoyed rather than a difficult space in which to build insight and knowledge in the company of others. Freud thought education to be an impossible business, and that the work of self-exploration, including what destroys the possibilities of a good enough relation with the other, or sensitivity to fragile ecologies, is demanding work.[10] But the spiritual quality of education, the making of souls, derives from understanding, experientially, how much serious thinking we must do. The language of student satisfaction mocks the endeavour.

The historic idea of the university's civic responsibility and of the role of popular education within this, has been lost. Disenchantment, I suggest, is a consequence, within and outside university walls, as chronicled in my recent book. The city constitutes a case study of many interconnected discontents, which includes questions about the role of local universities.[11] Education, especially university education, can be remote from most people, in a context of growing social and economic inequality, mental illness, and a fractured economy. Moreover, representative democracy is hollowed out, smaller numbers of people bother to vote, and the mechanisms of traditional political party organisation have atrophied.[12] The racists and fundamentalists exploit these vacuums. Alternative public spaces where diverse peoples can meet and troubles can be translated into a language of public deliberation and action have withered too. A cultural solipsism is the norm. The people of Muslim communities are fearful of going anywhere near the predominantly white working class estates, for fear of abuse; white working class people easily stereotype the Muslim other as alien and threatening. Many ordinary people consider the two universities in the city—Staffordshire and Keele—largely irrelevant in these troubling dynamics.

AN OLDER WORLD

I began my academic career as a historian of popular or workers' education.[13] I recently revisited some of this work and older ideas

---

10   See Deborah Britzman, *After-Education* (New York: SUNY Press, 2003).

11   See West, *Distress in the City*.

12   Ibid.

13   See Linden West, 'The Tawney Legend Re-examined', *Studies in Adult*

of serious, questioning university education with a social purpose, as part of thinking about the troubles of the contemporary city and universities. How then might struggles to spread forms of higher education beyond the walls speak to our present disenchantment? I am thinking especially of the work and values of Christian Socialists like Richard Henry Tawney and A.D. (Sandy) Lindsay, as well as humanist Marxists such as Raymond Williams. Each of them saw in forms of popular education—created in an alliance between progressive elements in universities and workers' organisations—glimpses, in microcosm, of the good, fraternal, more egalitarian as well as educated society. Knowledge, in this tradition, represented a personal as well as collective struggle for enlightenment in which difficult, awkward, troubling questions were encouraged rather than avoided. Worker-students themselves frequently sought answers outside conventional and sometimes oppressive systems of thought that seemed to deny the realities of their experience.

Tawney and the others perceived the university's prime purpose to be one of cultivating a more humane, thoughtful, inclusive, questioning, democratised, learning society. This, Tawney thought, would release the better angels of human nature. As a sergeant in the First World War he had led his men out into the Battle of the Somme. He believed that human society and life could never reach a state of repose and that life and learning was a perpetual, never resolved crisis. People and societies, he said, walk between precipices, and do not know the rottenness in them till they crack.[14] Education had to do with a collective as well as individual commitment to make things better, for everyone. The New Jerusalem, in any absolute or even metaphoric sense, was always contingent, but an ideal worthy of struggle, grounded in values of social justice.

Of course, that older, non-conformist culture of working class autodidacticism and self-help institutions has largely disappeared, as have the industrial economies which gave them birth in places like Stoke. Notwithstanding, there are shafts of light in historical analysis, about why and how students were motivated to ask demanding questions and to care for others. A reappraisal of the work

---

    Education 4.2 (1972): 105–19.

14   Norman Dennis and A.H. Halsey, *English Ethical Socialism; from Thomas More to R.H. Tawney* (Oxford: Clarendon Press, 1988): 169.

then, and its relevance to now, has been underway for some time.[15] Maybe history offers what Raymond Williams called 'resources of hope'; possibilities, however difficult, to renew a commitment to serious questioning of dominant truths, alongside concern for those who may be struggling the most.[16]

RICHARD HENRY TAWNEY: CULTIVATING FRATERNITY AND THE HUMAN SPIRIT

Tawney was born in November 1880, in Calcutta, India, the child of upper middle class, highly educated parents. He was privately educated and became a committed Anglican who was well furbished with social and cultural capital.[17] He was to play an inspirational role in thinking about the nature and purposes of university education and the responsibilities of universities to the communities in which they were located. In a recent re-evaluation of Tawney's contribution to educational and social thought, the historian Lawrence Goldman suggests that Tawney's earlier spiritual emphasis on the role of fraternal association in individual and collective development has been lost in a preoccupation with his later, Fabian-like, top-down instrumentalism.[18] The earlier Tawney had a stronger understanding of the prerequisites for serious questioning and for social change, through working with men and women who belonged to collective organisations like non-conformist churches, trade unions, cooperative and mutual societies, and bodies like the Workers Educational Association (WEA).

---

15   See Jonathan Rose, *The Intellectual Life of the British Working Classes*, 2nd ed. (New York: Yale University Press, 2010; Lawrence Goldman, *The Life of R.H. Tawney: Socialism and History* (London: Bloomsbury Academy, 2013); John Holford, 'Adult and Higher Education in the Early Work of T.H. Tawney' (paper presented at the Standing Conference of University Teachers and Researchers in the Education of Adults held at the University of Leeds, 7th–9th July 2015).

16   See Raymond Williams, *Resources of Hope: Culture, Democracy, Socialism* (London: Verso, 1989).

17   See Holford, 'Adult and Higher Education'.

18   See Goldman, *Life of R.H. Tawney*.

Tawney thought that experiences of fraternity in workers' education encouraged students to take risks and engage in serious thinking, through new and better qualities of human relationship. Cultures of lived equality, mutual respect, dialogue, and liberty of thought were essential to these dynamics, which Anthony Giddens calls the democracy of the emotions.[19] Such a democracy is characterised by trust in others, as well as the capacity for dialogue and serious listening, which enables students to feel both recognised as well as part of a bigger progressive project. The qualities of the cultures in which people were embedded mattered, in these terms, as much as economic relationships. Capitalist or some Marxist interpretations of the human condition emphasised the primary importance of material and work relationships, rather than culture *per se*. Economics was fundamental, rather than mutual societies. It was a person's experience of relationships in work, and of material rewards, that shaped, even determined human consciousness. Tawney considered this to be a flawed, reductionist understanding, as did the Oxford Idealists who inspired him. The apotheosis of the human spirit was to be found in the fraternal, egalitarian relationships cultivated in workers' education, which developed the appetite to think radically. It represented, in microcosm, the good society and gave energy to the struggle to change society for the better. In other words, the spiritual quality of people's lives shaped their consciousness of work and its disenchantments, and generated resources of hope. Tawney thought everyone equal in the eyes of God, and human differences were trivial when viewed through the lens of the divine.

Tawney's ideas on university education were grounded in a mix of Enlightenment and Oxford Idealism as well as religious belief. The tradition and social movement he helped build played a key role in critiquing capitalist economics, and imagining and creating the welfare state after the Second World War.[20] His first ever university adult education 'tutorial class', as they were known, was held in Longton in 1908, one of the Pottery towns which later became the city of Stoke-on-Trent. They were tutorial classes, not lectures, in which Tawney encouraged the thirty or so worker-students to engage with primary source material rather than secondary interpretation; and to interrogate ideas and evidence in the light of person-

---

19   See Anthony Giddens, *Runaway World* (London: Profile Books, 1999).

20   See Rose, *Intellectual Life.*

al experience, as miners, potters, steel workers, elementary school teachers, men as well as women. The curriculum was negotiated and largely free from outside influence; there were no external examinations to distort or disrupt the questioning or what people wanted to study and how they might go about it. The classes were intellectually demanding, and students were expected to produce fortnightly essays, although this could be too much for particular students. At their best they were communities of imaginative, caring, committed, and thoughtful learners in which all could be teachers and students. Jonathan Rose especially has drawn on diverse life testimonies and biographies to illuminate the powerful cultural as well as personal significance of this work.[21]

According to Tawney, the movement was founded on three core principles. First, the opposition to revolutionary violence: 'one may not do evil that good should come', in Cobbett's dictum of a century before.[22] Second, no institution, however perfect in conception, could be made to work effectively by individuals whose morality was inadequate. Third, where a sound morality was lacking, this could be forged in a community of scholars seeking truth and the common good.[23] There were Aristotelian ideals at work, alongside Oxford idealism;[24] an ideal of the fully developed person living in communities, building and sustaining virtue—communities cultivating not self- but other-regardedness, and collectively directing themselves to higher aims than the purely egotistic, materialistic, or narcissistic.[25] The idealists at Oxford who influenced Tawney were opposed to individualism, utilitarianism and social atomism. They drew on German philosophers, especially Kant and Hegel, and the notion that individuals could only be understood and realise their potential in the collective. Men and women were part of social and political communities from which they could not be divorced for analytic or practical purposes. They were linked together by values and institutions rather than simply webs of economic relationships. There are curious contemporary echoes of this in discussions about

---

21   Ibid.

22   See Dennis and Halsey, *English Ethical Socialism*.

23   Ibid.

24   See Lawrence Goldman, *Dons and Workers: Oxford and Adult Education Since 1850* (Oxford: Clarendon Press, 1995).

25   See Dennis and Halsey, *English Ethical Socialism*.

the priority of the other and the tradition of thinking that looks to our relations with objects outside us—other people, art or God—to draw us beyond our own borders, towards kinship with others and the world.[26] This has to do with the human spirit and its capacity for enchantment.

More recently, I have applied the insights of critical theory and psychoanalysis to the reassessment of the tutorial class movement, by engaging with the narratives of some of the autodidacts themselves.[27] We may observe in their testimonies the commitment to serious learning and social purpose but also processes of self-recognition at work, in the language of critical theorist Axel Honneth. These have to do with the importance of feeling understood by significant others; which operates at a primitive or early emotional and unconscious level; feeling loved, in short, in a non-narcissistic sense, which provides a building block for selfhood. Self-confidence, as Honneth frames it (or what I term more open, spontaneous experiences of self, drawing on the ideas of psychoanalyst Donald Winnicott),[28] is created when people feel themselves to be accepted and acceptable, and that they have things to say which are valued by people they admire and respect.

Honneth takes us into thinking at a group and collective as well as more intimate, inter-subjective level. He applies the term 'self-respect' to describe what happens when people feel part of a purposeful, valued group, with rights and responsibilities, and that they have a right to be listened to and fully participate, which encourages responsibilities towards others.[29] Self-esteem, Honneth's third category, can then be nurtured when people become aware of their importance to the group and of their value to others. Crucially we can then better recognise and appreciate others, and otherness, of different ways of thinking, which helps create new forms of social solidarity. It is important to emphasise this as an intellectual, imaginative as

---

26   See Mark Freeman, *The Priority of the Other* (Oxford: University Press, 2014).

27   See West, *Distress in the City.*

28   See Donald Winnicott, *Playing and Reality* (London: Routledge, 1971).

29   See Axel Honneth, *Disrespect: The Normative Foundations of Critical Theory* (Cambridge: Polity Press, 2007); and Axel Honneth, *Pathologies of Reason: On the Legacy of Critical Theory* (New York: Columbia University Press, 2009).

well as profoundly relational process. We may also find self-recognition in a character in literature with whom we identify, as well as a new idea that may speak to our experience. There are psychological dynamics of projective identification in play, as we project parts of ourselves into the other's experience, someone we admire, say, for their resilience, and then introject changing qualities of self, and self-understanding, in the language of psychoanalytic object relations theory.[30]

Of course, something quite different can happen in groups, as they close themselves down to difference and the other, not like us; or is inferior or corrupt, as, at an extreme, happens in the racist gang or Islamist group.[31] But a good, diverse group (and here Honneth draws on the ideas of educator John Dewey),[32] will remain open to diversity and thrive precisely because of this. Experience is never finite, or another point of view denied, in the name of some absolute truth, because there is always a different perspective, another set of experiences to engage with. Education becomes a perpetual struggle to understand and build forms of knowledge, which embrace the cosmopolitanism inherent in encounters with the other. Bigotry and prejudice are correspondingly challenged, as chronicled in various student accounts.[33] Such understanding of educational process and of the intersubjective, highly contingent, developmental, vulnerable but also potentially resilient as well as generous self, is far removed from the autonomous, acquisitive, egotistical, materialistic subject that dominates the contemporary academic mind.

Unfashionable

Notwithstanding, Tawneyite ways of thinking about the human subject, education, universities, and the nature of social change became unfashionable after the Second World War. He himself had doubts

---

30   See West 1996, *Beyond Fragments*; and West, *Distress in the City*.

31   See West, *Distress in the City*.

32   See John Dewey, 'The Ethics of Democracy', in *The Early Years of John Dewey*, ed. J.A. Boydston (Carbondale: Southern Illinois Press, 1969), 227–49.

33   See Nancy Dobrin, *Happiness* (Kings Langley: Sacombe Press, 1980); and Rose, *Intellectual Life*.

about the tutorial classes, not least the intellectual and emotional effort required from worker students. Tawney was far from a naïve idealist and there were 'limits to his moralising', as Lawrence Goldman notes.[34] He was aware that the same spirit of non-conformity that drove some worker students could narrow viewpoints and bring a tendency to over-proselytise that made it difficult to take on board different perspectives. He was also aware that material conditions mattered. Writing to Cartwright, one of his first students, in response to a first essay (Cartwright was later to play a key role in university adult education, and become Tawney's lifelong friend), he stated:

> our problem at the present day is to put economic activity in proper relation to the other elements of human life. But if we forget the economic motive altogether and overlook the material conditions on which the production of wealth depends, we become mere sentimentalists and dreamers.[35]

This takes us to the nub of an historic and contemporary question: what weight should we give to motives other than economic or materialistic? Motives like the need to understand, to feel loved and lovable, and to find meaning, purpose and recognition in a life? This is where our contemporary societies, including universities, have lost their way in the privileging of *Homo economicus*.

Tawney's views on the role of religious belief and conviction in economic development were also disparaged by economic historians, who considered their place to be tangential in economic or cultural change processes.[36] As early as 1925, Trotsky dismissed any notion of social progress based on a Tawneyite Protestant piety and uncritical mystification of the working class. Much later, in the 1960s, the rise of critical sociology led to a renewed dismissiveness of Tawney and his work as 'bourgeois reformism'. His writings were said to be overly descriptive, lacking a rigorous theoretical base, while his view of character and choice was naïve and idealistic. Tawney's notion of socialism and workers' education became derided as

---

34   Goldman, *Dons and Workers*, 160.

35   Ibid., 160.

36   See Dennis and Halsey, *English Ethical Socialism*.

high-minded cliché, even by some who admired him like sociologist Richard Titmus.[37]

The tutorial classes themselves became unfashionable as universities gradually opened their doors to more working class students, and older routes to higher education seemed redundant. By the 1970s, the tutorial class movement appeared exhausted and passé.[38] By then, in Stoke and North Staffordshire, over 80 per cent of working class people claimed never to have heard of the WEA.[39] For some on the left, the critique was part of a broader disdain for a paternalistic welfare state and the deference towards universities and high culture they thought embodied in Tawney-type university adult education. In contrast, that is, to the overtly Marxist National Council of Labour Colleges (NCLC). Educators like Tawney and the tutorial class movement were even said to have castrated a potential proletarian autodidactic radicalism.[40] In one influential view the tutorial classes, and some of the WEA, offered 'about the best police expenditure [...] that could be indulged in [...]'.[41] They constituted in effect a form of social control.

That was never quite my view but at the start of my academic career, in the 1970s, I too embraced the paternalistic critique, accusing figures like Tawney and some of his students of a simplistic faith in the social democratic project and university education. My own research acknowledged, if begrudgingly, aspects of Tawney's achievements and those of tutorial class students, but I was still dismissive of what was achieved and its relevance to renewing workers' education in the 1970s.[42] I was young, ambitious and easily seduced by academic fashion. I was envious too of those who seemed better able to play grand theoretical Marxist games, and who were dismissive

---

37   Ibid.

38   See West, 'The Tawney Legend'; and Goldman, *Dons and Workers.*

39   See Roy Shaw, 'Adult Education and the Working Class', *Studies in Adult Education.* 2.3 (1970): 132–46.

40   See Stuart Macintyre, *A Proletarian Science: Marxism in Britain, 1917–1933* (London: Lawrence and Wishart, 1986).

41   Roger Fieldhouse, 'The Workers Educational Association', in *A History of Modern British Adult Education*, ed. Roger Fieldhouse and Associates (Leicester: National Association of Adult Continuing Education 1996), 176.

42   See West, 'The Tawney Legend'.

of purely descriptive studies or of Idealism, especially the role of the spirit and character in human betterment. I felt out of my depth, and needed time to learn to swim. But that world, and Tawney's experiment in democratic education, seem different now, viewed through the lens of subsequent history and the rise of neo-liberal orthodoxy.

Interestingly, in my earlier account of the tutorial classes, published in 1972, I noted how they offered space for new kinds of thinking among different and diverse working-class people. And, that they stimulated new forms of educational and democratic activism in the mining communities across North Staffordshire:

> The Longton Tutorial Class [as one student recalled], attracted the political and union activist. Many of them were already leaders in various working class organisations. One indication of political activity can be seen in the impact on class work of national and local elections [...] and the elections for the newly formed Country Borough of Stoke-on-Trent [...] the logic of their [the students'] attitude to education as an emancipating force [was that] by 1913–14 of the eighteen tutorial classes organised by Oxford, four were in the Potteries [...] As well as spreading the tutorial classes proper there were demands for the spreading of educational provision among the miners of North Staffordshire. The North Staffs Miners' Higher Education movement was an expression of this demand. Cartwright outlines the inspiration behind the movement as being 'to bring higher education of a humanistic type to those who had hitherto lain outside its range'.[43]

Tutorial class students themselves took classes to remote areas. One course in the bleak moorland of North Staffordshire devoted to the French Revolution attracted twenty-nine students, and forty-one essays were written. But in a slightly condescending conclusion, I stated that 'Tawney's ideas were a product of an age very different from the Britain of 1972'. 'It is time', I wrote, 'people ceased to cling so uncritically to what he stood for and the movement he helped

---

43   Ibid., 115–16.

shape'.[44] Some of the condescension, I now believe, was the stuff of 1960s' hubris, of how we easily forgot or disparaged our parents' achievements in the grandiose fantasy that the future was incomparably ours. We also could behave like a good, radical bourgeois 'frankly contemptuous of a culturally conservative working class'.[45] Student cultures of drugs, vandalism, laziness and general disdain also led to the exploitation of precisely the sorts of people who were to be the subjects of our putative revolution: the porters, cleaning ladies, and kitchen staff who tidied up our mess.

Working-class people, as Rose notes, had long observed such behaviour among the exclusive castes of bohemians: 1960s students, despite or perhaps because of their ideological socialism, could look forward to employment in the creative industries, and a little later in finance. Listening to them, one university porter observed, 'was like being in a mental hospital where everyone was pretending to be someone else',[46] including acting as revolutionaries. There is now a wider questioning of what the 1960s 'did for us', in the light of the neo-liberal fundamentalism that followed.[47] Lynne Segal has countered some of the revisionism by arguing that it was the rise of neo-liberalism *per se* rather than the behaviour of student radicals that was to blame for what subsequently transpired.[48] But this is a matter of debate, not least because, as Rose observes, cultural politics from the 1980s onwards were saturated by an obsessive individualistic spirit, which was to energise the emergent neo-liberalism.[49]

RAYMOND WILLIAMS

Williams was of the same broad tradition as Tawney, although of a later generation; there were differences between them in their

---

44   Ibid., 117.

45   Rose, *Intellectual Life*, 462.

46   Ibid., 463.

47   See Francis Beckett, *What Did the Baby Boomers Ever Do For Us: Why the Children of the Sixties Lived the Dream and Failed the Future* (London: Biteback, 2010).

48   See Lynne Segal, *Out of Time: The Pleasures and Perils of Ageing* (London: Verso, 2013).

49   Rose, *Intellectual Life*.

political philosophies, alongside pedagogic similarities and shared convictions that appear more obvious now. Both understood that the WEA's historic mission was far from over by the 1950s, or since: if 'exceptional minds' from diverse backgrounds go to university more easily, wrote Williams in a letter to WEA tutors, the question remained of 'what about everyone else?' Were they simply to be treated as rejects, suitable only for narrow vocational training? The WEA stood for something that even educational reformers tended to forget, obsessed as they could be with schooling: 'It stands for an educated democracy, not for a newly mobile and more varied élite.'[50] And even if Williams might have been overly dismissive of vocational education, questions remain about the education of all the people as citizens, with rights and responsibilities.

Like Tawney, Williams was deeply critical of people who presumed to deliver the answers to ordinary people or provide ideological texts to shape their minds and actions, without requiring active engagement from those concerned. Such teaching was the antithesis of a democratic university education, as Tawney and Williams understood it: it was demeaning, infantilising, and anti-educational to proffer conclusions—people needed to reach them on their own, in fellowship, over time.

In his writing on 'culture as ordinary',[51] Williams observed how the advertising men and women held the same essential view of the masses as the authoritarian left (maybe some in universities too). Expensively educated people were 'now in the service of the most brazen money-grabbing exploitation of the inexperience of ordinary people'.[52] 'The old cheapjack is still there in the market [...] he thinks of his victims as a slow ignorant crowd. The new cheapjack is in offices with contemporary *décor*, using scraps of linguistics, psychology, and sociology to influence what he thinks of as the mass mind'.[53] But Williams' scorn was not confined to the marketing men and women. He was angry with those of his friends who talked of the ignorant masses: 'one kind of Communist has always talked like this, and has got his answer [...] at Budapest', in the Hungarian uprising of 1956. This, in retrospect, was the opening scene in the

---

50   Cited in Goldman, *Dons and Workers*, 252.

51   Raymond Williams, *Resources of Hope*, 3–18.

52   Ibid., 6.

53   Ibid., 7.

eventual demise of 'communism'. Williams wrote that the Marxist interpretation of culture is not acceptable while it insists that people should think in prescribed ways: 'It is stupid and arrogant to suppose that any of these meanings (within cultures) can in any way be prescribed: they are made by living people, made and remade, in ways that we cannot know in advance'.[54]

The Marxist interpretation of culture, he argued, was unacceptable if it retained a directive element. This is the insistence that if you desire socialism, you must learn to think and write in prescribed ways.[55] Thus Williams' idea of learning democracy is an open and negotiated process, an effort to build a culture of shared meanings, under the influence of everyone, in fraternal relationship. Such a message, alongside Tawney's, is deeply relevant to our present crisis of multiculturalism, of xenophobic disrespect of the other and the metropolitan elite sneering at ordinary people. Ironically, it might also be spiritual, in the respect shown for ordinary people and what they could offer. There is also in Williams' writing an explicit acknowledgment of the unpredictability of the human condition and how the future is not pre-determined, in some grand leftist Hegelian dialectic. Human beings are far more than economic creatures: they make and are made by culture. The point of education was to liberate the creative cultural potential within everyone.

If Williams had none of Tawney's Christian piety, his faith in ordinary people is in stark contrast to the marketing 'men' and leftish authoritarians as well as neo-liberal ideologues. People, here too, are objectified, reduced to fulfilling economic roles in selfish and unthinking consumption. Economic growth is driven by a desire for status, display, for triumph, power and performance, and too much thinking gets in the way.[56] Philip Mirowski, drawing on Hayek's free market ideas, argues that neo-liberalism is profoundly anti-educational in its attitudes to the masses who must be perpetually encouraged to consume.[57] Moreover, a liberal, humane education is perceived to be the province of an elite, the educable, who are always

54   Ibid., 8.

55   Ibid.

56   See Paul Verhaeghe, *What About Me? The Struggle for Identity in a Market-based Society* (London: Scribe, 2014).

57   See Philip Mirowski, *Never Let a Serious Crisis Go to Waste* (London: Verso, 2013).

the minority. More means worse for universities and too much education is antithetical to the efficient functioning of markets and the desire, discontent, and the illusions on which their efficacy depends.

If Williams criticised Tawney for making too much of the cult of impartiality in university adult education, particularly in his refusal to take a stand, any stand (even against the zealot), other than offering a different point of view, both shared a pedagogy of hope and belief in the necessity of public/educational space where all partialities of opinion could enter and people might learn across difference, in fraternal ways.[58] This was the central conviction of Williams' 'the long revolution', the title of one of his most important books: learning democracy, of the kind that ensued in the tutorial classes, took time, was never complete, and always difficult. In Stoke today, the WEA struggles in the face of inadequate, short-term funding to bring white working class and Muslim people together in health groups, to build mutual respect and a sustainable learning environment. But the work is hard and achievements fragile.[59] Williams, in his later writing, predicted how difficult things would become. He talked of a long counter-revolution, in the new rampant individualism and seductive consumerism, combined with growing inequality and poverty.[60]

Derek Tatton, one-time student of Williams, was schooled in the university adult education tradition. He was one of the biographical subjects in my study of Stoke.[61] Tatton, in his own writing, has been preoccupied with how—in the face of contemporary neo-liberal trends—we can revitalise the 'very concept of human reason and value'.[62] Tatton writes of the pessimism generated by conflicts in Syria, Iraq, Egypt, Gaza, and Palestine, and the widening gap between rich and poor, as well as a deep ecological crisis of sustainability. To which we could add the rise of diverse fundamentalisms, and fascistic violence in Paris, Nice, Rouen, Pakistan, Madrid, Germany, Italy, Nigeria, and other parts of Africa; and in small pockets in Stoke and

---

58   See Goldman, *Dons and Workers*.

59   See West, *Distress in the City*.

60   See Raymond Williams, *The Long Revolution* (Cardigan: Parthian Books, 2011).

61   See West, *Distress in the City*.

62   Derek Tatton, 'Resources for a Journey of Hope' (unpublished paper, 2011).

other post-industrial cities. Derek quotes Chomsky in observing
how the optimism of the 1950s and 1960s was displaced by pessimism about the prospects of human betterment.[63] The 1970s evoked
growing feelings of hopelessness and despair among progressive
forces. Chomsky thought the reversal of centuries-long movement
towards industrialisation was important, with the economic shift
from productive enterprise to financial manipulation.[64] Williams
himself in his book *Towards 2000*, published in the 1980s, was troubled by an emerging self-consciousness among elites—political,
cultural, military, and in the media—who constantly calculate their
relative advantage over others in a war of appearances and display.
This is Williams' *Plan X*: we could call it neo-liberal narcissism and
the marginalisation of profounder forms of inclusive education for
the collective good.[65]

Pessimism and even cynicism towards representative democracy
go hand in hand with these tendencies, Tatton and Williams note.
Decreasing numbers of people exercise their right to vote and Tatton quotes Williams, from *The Long Revolution*:

> A tightly organised party system and parliament seems
> to have converted the national franchise into the elec-
> tion of a court. As individuals we cast one vote at inter-
> vals of several years on a range of policies and particu-
> lar decisions towards which it is virtually impossible to
> have one single attitude [...] [F]rom this [...] a court of
> ministers emerges [...] and then it is very difficult for
> any of us to feel even the smallest direct share in the
> government of our affairs.[66]

Tatton also mentions Williams' concern over militaristic metaphors and the fetish of violent 'solutions' among some so-called
progressive forces. When power is monopolised by unresponsive
elites, divisions can constantly open among those who seek to op-

---

63   Ibid.

64   See Noam Chomsky, *Hopes and Prospects* (Chicago: Haymarket Books,
     2010).

65   See Raymond Williams, *Towards 2000* (London: Chatto and Windus,
     1983).

66   Tatton, 'Resources'.

pose them: some may find violence attractive. Williams is quoted, in the introduction to a new edition of *The Long Revolution*, published in 2011, as saying that he was deeply uneasy with a language of short or violent responses to injustice. Metaphors of assaulting citadels, he observed, are the wrong kind of metaphor. Any struggle needed to be slow, democratic, non-violent, and fundamentally educational, in the broadest terms.[67] Interestingly, as organised working class traditions waned, he saw potential in new forms of communication technologies, and their capacity not only for encouraging political activity but also for experimenting with forms of self-government. The long revolution might partly be digital: in the interplay of diverse communities, local and global; and in a determination to occupy or reclaim parks, halls, schools, universities, churches, synagogues, and mosques for building horizontal forms of dialogue, learning, and decision-making. Of course, a major question emerges: how might it be possible in the present to create new and diverse experiments in democratic education, sustained and sustaining, inclusive, energetic, working across difference, to reinvigorate civil society as well as cultural and political life? And what role for universities, or groups within them, in such a project?

A.D. (Sandy) Lindsay

That older, successful experiment in university adult education was founded on the ideal of the active participation by informed citizens in the polis and inclusive policymaking, rather than things being done to people from on high. The University of Keele, close by to Stoke, grew out of this tradition. The first Principal of the then University College of North Staffordshire, A.D. 'Sandy' Lindsay, had been deeply involved in workers' education in Stoke and its environs. From 1947 he served on the Commission into German Universities, investigating their shortcomings in the light of the War and Nazism. The Commission explored the contribution universities and colleges could make to the development of a democratic society and education.[68] As Master of Balliol College in Oxford before the

---

67   Cited in Tatton, 'Resources'.

68   David Phillips, 'Lindsay and the German Universities: An Oxford Contribution to the Post-war Reform Debate', *Oxford Review of Education* 6.1

War, Lindsay encountered many German Jews fleeing persecution and had wondered why universities there had done relatively little to resist the rise of a virulent fundamentalism.

The minutes of the Commission note how Lindsay attempted to define the problem as to do with an absence of university adult education in many communities. The problem, he thought, stemmed partly from elitism and the disconnection of universities from ordinary Germans. He wanted to open the academy to a wide range of people from all backgrounds and to build stronger relationships with local communities. He encouraged people to think beyond the fragments of the polis and the academy, towards a dynamic notion of democratic education in which universities were centrally involved. The function of the university, he asserted, was not simply to produce a society of specialists, in research or teaching, but also 'to awaken social understanding'.[69] For this reason, universities should take over responsibilities for adult education. 'A country can only be democratic if all its men and women can be active citizens.'[70] Lindsay worried at how academics easily become divorced from ordinary life and the needs of society, most of all, as Williams and Tawney also saw it, from the citizens left behind by education selection processes.

Lindsay was influenced by the WEA but also by the Scottish concept of the university, with its long democratic tradition as well as Christian socialism. He thought universities should cultivate in their students a developed sense of moral and political responsibility. Such sentiments, like Tawney's, may seem out of place in a modern secular, sceptical environment. And they may even have struggled to find space at Keele, in earlier times, as one involved commentator has suggested.[71] Lindsay wrestled with various influences in the founding of Keele, and Hall detects ambivalence in some of his attitudes towards Stoke. The man who in 1925 had called for 'a real people's university', and in 1947 was struggling to achieve it, was by 1948 tending more towards opposition to specialism and the relative importance of a residential institution than the more inclusive university. The very title of the University of Keele expressed distance

---

(1980): 91–106.

69 Ibid., 96.

70 Ibid., 97.

71 See A. Hall, 'Mountford's Keele and Ours: A Review of Mountford, J., *Keele: An Historical Critique*, RKP' (unpublished paper, 1972).

from the city of Stoke.

Furthermore, Lindsay's rhetoric, like Tawney's, does seem of another age, and universities are products of the times in which they are located. Notwithstanding, David Watson and others make the case that universities are important resources to address the very real economic and social needs of local communities, and in new ways. He concludes that the UK has got things badly wrong in its state-sponsored, brittle, nationalistic, politically colonised view of the education of citizens. It moves too easily from rights to duties, and a presumption that obedience and patriotism are inviolable.[72] It also neglects the experiences of groups across the population, and ignores the impact of exclusionary and plain nasty 'British values' like Islamophobia on the streets. The university, Watson concludes, has neglected its civic responsibilities and local communities in ways that echo disturbing periods in other countries.

Ronald Barnett similarly challenges the absence in many universities of a clear commitment to the well-being of communities and the need to encompass, in what he calls 'the ecological university', a concern for sustainability and well-being from the global to the local, from social relationships to the planet, from work to human psychological well-being.[73] The ecological university should encourage serious thinking about the interplay of global and local, within an ethic of care. If this seems vague, Barnett stresses that his writing is deliberately utopian so as to challenge the assumptions of the conventional business university. Moreover, in the rediscovery of a living connection between the local and global, between one group of marginalised people and another, and between personal and collective well-being, universities can discover a renewed sense of civic responsibility. Students and teachers might also find renewed enchantment in what they are asked to do and think about, beyond their own narcissistic concerns.

Conclusion

The idea of the university's role and values, and of the nature of our

---

72   David Watson, *The Question of Conscience: Higher Education and Personal Responsibility* (London: Institute of Education Press, 2014), 54.

73   Barnett, *Being a University*, 141–51.

humanity in disturbing times, lies at the heart of this chapter. The notion of the university is deeply contested, and it may be, for some, that the heterogeneity of institutions in mass systems of higher education, with diverse missions, makes the question redundant. Some universities will be bothered by this; others will get on with different priorities. Conversely, as academics and students, we can struggle to build new social purpose in a troubled, fragmented and fragile world.[74] Alternatively, we may content ourselves with thinking of people as consumers: as inherently selfish, egoistic, and acquisitive; or, we can imagine people, including ourselves, as potentially questioning, moral, agentic beings, when we feel cared for and recognised by significant others. But such capacity depends on mobilising resources and involving universities to create more and better qualities of public space, within and outside formal settings, where dialogue across difference becomes possible. The public realm has been a casualty of what David Marquand calls the revenge of the private against the public, and the disparagement of collective action and democratic process.[75] I argue that we neglect the public realm at our peril, and earlier experiments in democratic education can teach us about what should be done.

The significance of the older, fraternal, working class, self-help, autodidactic tradition is largely forgotten, in the mainstream, and even among progressives. But it deserves to be rescued from the enormous condescension of posterity; in fact, the loss of strong working class self-help cultures has been calamitous for our whole social fabric.[76] A centralist, Fabian instrumentalism and bohemian contempt have dominated British progressive thought, while the neo-liberal is implicitly contemptuous of the masses. Fabianism thought it possible to calculate needs and demands centrally: if you had a big enough computer, you could plan rationally for the future. This perspective viewed workers' education as peripheral, and worker representation in enterprises or local institutions built by people themselves as marginal. Under New Labour, Maurice Glasman argues, it was the centralised state that was going to make 'the

---

74 See Barnett, *Being a University*.

75 See David Marquand, *Decline of the Public: The Hollowing-Out of Citizenship* (London: Routledge, 2004).

76 See West, *Distress in the City*.

fat thin, teenagers chaste, [and] bad people into good parents'.[77] However, mediating organisations such as the WEA and new initiatives like the family 'support' programme Sure Start, (documented in my earlier work)[78] have been ignored, at least with regard to their democratising, educational potential. We really need to create new spaces in which people can learn to talk to and appreciate one another, in cultures of equality, respect, trust, openness and dialogue, rather than shout, and reduce each other to stereotypes. To create such educational space in the university and in local communities, could be a re-enchanting, soul-full process.

Universities, or more likely groups within them, might cultivate more and better relationships with local as well as global communities: in alliance with diverse agencies like Citizens UK, Philosophy in Pubs, the churches, adult education organisations, Children's Centres, mental health campaigners, etc. Maybe they could re-establish university settlements in marginalised places. Academics and students would find greater meaning by giving to others. Anastasios Gaitanidis questions the consumerist model of education that promises satisfaction.[79] Like the tutorial class students of old, education has in fact to embrace and encourage dissatisfaction and anxiety. And in the process, to nurture a shared questioning of a deeply unequal, overly individualistic, pathological, structurally narcissistic and ultimately destructive status quo. Tawney, Williams, and Lindsay would have understood this, if using different language and frames of reference. But the necessity of building more inclusive, democratic university education is becoming clear once more (as is the cost of neo-liberalism): to create greater dialogue across difference and processes of mutual recognition in serious learning, so as to strengthen social solidarities, however long and hard the process might be.

---

77   Maurice Glasman, '1945 and all that' (keynote paper presented at the Thirteenth Biennial Conference of the Australian Society for the Study of Labour History, Sydney, 11th–13th July 2013), 4.

78   See Merrill and West, *Using Biographical Methods*.

79   See Gaitanidis, 'Anxiety'.

SELECT BIBLIOGRAPHY

DENNIS, Norman, and A.H. HALSEY. *English Ethical Socialism; from Thomas More to R.H. Tawney*. Clarendon Press: Oxford, 1988.

DEWEY, John. 'The ethics of democracy'. In *The Early Years of John Dewey*, edited by J.A. Boydston. Carbondale: Southern Illinois University Press, 1969: 227–49.

GAITANIDIS, Anastasios. 'Anxiety, psychoanalysis and reinvigorating education'. In *Psychoanalysis and Education: Minding a Gap*, edited by Alan Bainbridge and Linden West, 37–50. London: Karna, 2012.

GOLDMAN, Lawrence. *Dons and Workers: Oxford and Adult Education since 1850*. Oxford: Clarendon Press, 1995.

_____. *The Life of R.H. Tawney: Socialism and History*. London: Bloomsbury Academic, 2013.

HONNETH, Axel. *Disrespect: The Normative Foundations of Critical Theory*. Cambridge: Polity Press, 2007.

_____. *Pathologies of Reason: On the Legacy of Critical Theory*. New York: Columbia University Press, 2009.

JUNG, C.G. *Modern Man in Search of a Soul*. New York: Harvest, 1933.

MERRILL, Barbara, and Linden WEST. *Using Biographical Methods in Social Research*. London: Sage, 2009.

POST-CRASH ECONOMICS SOCIETY. *Economics, Education, and Unlearning*. Manchester: University Post-Crash Economic Society, 2014.

ROSE, Jonathan. *The Intellectual Life of the British Working Classes*. 2nd ed. New York: Yale University Press, 2010.

TATTON, Derek. 'Resources for a journey of hope'. Unpublished paper, 2011.

WEST, Linden. *Distress in the City: Racism, Fundamentalism, and a Democratic Education*. London: Trentham/UCL Books, 2016.

_____. 'The Tawney Legend Re-examined', *Studies in Adult Education*, 4.2 (1972): 105–19.

WILLIAMS, Raymond. *The Long Revolution*. Cardigan: Parthian Books, 2011.

_____. *Resources of Hope: Culture, democracy, socialism*. London: Verso, 1989.

_____. *Towards 2000*. London: Chatto and Windus, 1983.

'Not to explain the world, but to sing it'

Panpsychism and the Academy

EDUARD C. HEYNING

IT WAS 1969 when a female fan broke into Beatle Paul McCartney's house in his absence through the bathroom window, and opened the front door to let the others in. Paul turned the experience into the song 'She Came In Through The Bathroom Window'. Beatle fans would do anything to get close to their idol, and Beatlemania unlocked hysterical energies on a scale completely beyond any expectations or explanations, taking over the music industry and popular culture. What on earth caused this enchantment? Did The Beatles have a special message? Their songs were about love, playfulness, liberating the imagination, not about belief or ideology. In the 1960s, anything new was worth trying as a liberation from the past. Within a decade this urge to freedom sparked off a movement called New Age, but what exactly was new? Wouter Hanegraaff has painstakingly analysed New Age publications and concluded that 'most of the beliefs which characterise the New Age were already present by the end of the 19th century, even to such an extent that one may legitimately wonder whether the New Age brings anything new at all'.[1] The girl who so longed to meet her beloved idol was standing in a long tradition, with roots that can be traced back to classical antiquity. Longing to free the body and the mind from outdated restrictions to realise wholeness was nothing new. However, to get really close to the magic, she had to come in through the bathroom window, instead of walking up the steps of a temple.

In the academic world, something similar has happened. The motto of Western science has always been 'mind over matter': true knowledge can only be obtained by the intellect, because the senses

---

1   Wouter J. Hanegraaff, *New Age Religion and Western Culture: Esotericism in the Mirror of Secular Thought* (Albany, NY: SUNY Press, 1998), 482–483.

are unreliable. From Isaac Newton on, this was narrowed down to proof by the laws of physics. It led to an atmosphere of contempt within the academic world of the subjective, the emotional, and the intuitive. Challenges to this position came from the 1960s onwards as more people—and more girls—with different mindsets entered the academy. Increasingly, truth was sought beyond reason: in imagination, creativity, the spiritual, and the esoteric—it was all there in the lyrics of The Beatles, including visions inspired by drugs.

The British writer Aldous Huxley (1894–1963), looking at a flower arrangement under the influence of the hallucinogenic drug mescaline, wrote in 1954:

> I was seeing what Adam had seen on the morning of creation—the miracle, moment by moment, of naked existence [...] The Being of Platonic philosophy—except that Plato seems to have made the enormous, the grotesque mistake of separating Being from becoming, and identifying it with the mathematical abstraction of the Idea. He could never, poor fellow, have seen a bunch of flowers shining with their own inner light and all but quivering under the pressure of the significance with which they were charged; could never have perceived that what rose and iris and carnation so intensely signified was nothing more, and nothing less, than what they were—a transience that was yet eternal life, a perpetual perishing that was at the same time pure Being, a bundle of minute, unique particulars in which, by some unspeakable and yet self-evident paradox, was to be seen the divine source of all existence.[2]

It seems Huxley makes a fool of Plato. Indeed, in the *Timaeus* 28–30, Plato proposed a separation of 'being' from 'becoming', for an understanding of the universe. Plato, however, did not confine mind to human mathematical imagination, but saw the entire universe permeated with it through the presence of the *anima mundi*, the world soul, which displays eternal beauty in nature. Plato also introduced a mysterious 'receptacle', prior to time and creation, in-

---

2   Aldous L. Huxley, *The Doors of Perception* (Harmondsworth: Penguin Books, 1971), 17.

accessible to rational thought (*Timaeus* 48B). As Gregory Shaw has shown, this mystical vision has over the ages been stripped of its metaphysical beauty, first by Aristotle and subsequently by scholars and scientists, reducing it to a dualist theory of divine reason versus dead matter.[3] Huxley, in effect, is siding with Plato against the desacralisation of the material world by the scientific worldview.

In the 1960s the attitude that Huxley was expressing became fashionable among students, questioning the exclusive authority of physicalism. From the Sorbonne to the Kent State shootings, protests would rock the academic world. But the academy showed enough resilience to adapt itself to the new ideas by allowing the development of new forms of scientific practice during the remainder of the 20th century—but only within the old paradigm. The new forms embraced a more intuitive, reflexive or creative approach to studying in general, and a more soulful or metaphorical approach to reality. Sometimes this involved a return of an ancient wisdom in a new guise; an example of such a newcomer with an ancient past, and the subject of this chapter, is the philosophical theory of *panpsychism*.

Panpsychism as a term was first introduced by the Italian Platonic-Hermetic philosopher Francesco Patrizi (1529–1597). Patrizi, following Marsilio Ficino (1433–1499), theorised a system of emanations based on the works of Plato, Proclus, the *Corpus Hermeticum*, and the Chaldean Oracles. As Lee Irwin writes, he argued for a principle he called *pampsychia* [sic], 'all-soulness', as the medium through which all of nature is vivified and uniquely animated. Patrizi taught that the whole cosmos is filled with soul, including the inorganic and elemental realms and the earth itself, as well as all plants, animals, and humans.[4] Patrizi described the *anima mundi* not as a unified collection of souls, but as distinctive forms of 'soulfulness' inherent to each and every order of creation.[5] He believed this idea belonged to the *prisca theologia*, which preceded, in the Re-

3   Gregory Shaw, 'The Chôra of the Timaeus and Iamblichean Theurgy', *Horizons* 3.2 (2012): 103–29.

4   Lee Irwin, 'A World Full of Gods: Panpsychism and the Paradigms of Esotericism', in *Esotericism, Religion, and Nature*, ed. Arthur Versluis, Claire Fanger, Lee Irwin and Melinda Phillips, ASE series 2 (Lansing, MI: Michigan State University Press, 2010), 31.

5   Irwin, 'A World Full of Gods', 28.

naissance view, Plato and Aristotle.[6] Indeed, panpsychist ideas can be found in practically all Greek and Roman philosophers, though there are many varieties.

Pan is Greek for 'everything' (with a naughty hint of the hooved god of Arcadia). In short, panpsychism stands for 'something mind-like everywhere and always'. But what contemporary panpsychism exactly means is far from clear. It is a theory, but it is also a feeling or experience. That makes it interesting. Panpsychism goes beyond Cartesian dualism of mind and matter as ontologically separate categories. It challenges the monism of materialism (everything is fundamentally matter) and idealism (everything is fundamentally mind). For the materialist, consciousness is a function of the brain. Everything can be explained in terms of physics, if not now then surely in the future. For the idealist, consciousness is the ground of all being. We cannot know anything without consciousness. Pan-psychism however ascribes to neutral monism, which sees mind and matter as two equivalent aspects of a single reality, to which both can be reduced. The clearest definition I have found so far is by Emma Restall Orr, who defines panpsychism as 'a monist meta-physical stance, based upon the idea that mind and matter are not distinct and separate substances but an integrated reality, rooted in nature' and 'based upon ubiquitous and integrated mindedness'.[7] Does panpsychism mean that plants, trees, rocks, stars, and the earth can contain something mind-like? For the ancient Greeks, yes; for Renaissance man, yes; for a handful of people today, yes. Any academics? Very few.

Freya Mathews (b. 1949) is a panpsychist philosopher, author, poet, and adjunct professor of environmental philosophy at Latrobe University in Melbourne. She also manages a private biodiversity re-serve. In 2003 she published *For Love of Matter*, a passionate appeal to change our attitude to nature from exploitation of dead matter

---

6   On the *prisca theologia*, see Christopher S. Celenza, 'Marsilio Ficino', in *The Stanford Encyclopedia of Philosophy*, ed. Edward N. Zalta (Redwood City: Stanford University Press, 2015).

7   Emma Restall Orr, *The Wakeful World: Animism, Mind and the Self in Nature* (Alresford: Moon Books, 2012), 104–06. There are however many different definitions of panpsychism; for the sake of clarity I ignore the diversity in this article. For an overview, see David Skrbina, *Panpsychism in the West* (Cambridge, MA: MIT Press, 2005).

into an erotic encounter with an enchanted world, using poetry and music. Mathews argues that a holistic or cosmological version of panpsychism functions not merely as a rival theory but as a rival paradigm to materialism.[8] In this she is joined by the biologist Rupert Sheldrake in his article 'Setting Science Free From Materialism'.[9] Is panpsychism a paradigm for the new millennium, entering the academy by the bathroom window? Mathews argues that the promise of panpsychism is to awaken 'the metaphysical yearning, the desire for world', that is 'innate to subjectivity per se and hence the core to our being', and so 'to re-enter the terrain of enchantment'.[10] 'To abide in an enchanted state', says Mathews, is 'to live in communicative exchange, erotic engagement, with one's own immediate environment'.[11] 'How can we sing back to life a world that has been so brutally silenced?' she asks.[12] I think she is making a promising case for a new paradigm. Below I will come back to her ideas; but first I will sketch a general background to her theory of panpsychism.

MIND AT LARGE

A prerequisite for understanding panpsychism is the acceptance that human consciousness is, in principle, not different from animal consciousness. In 2012 a prominent international group of cognitive neuroscientists, gathered at Cambridge, unequivocally stated that

> non-human animals have the neuroanatomical, neurochemical, and neurophysiological substrates of conscious states along with the capacity to exhibit intentional behaviours. Consequently, the weight of evidence indicates that humans are not unique in possessing the neurological substrates that generate consciousness.

---

8   Freya Mathews, *For Love of Matter: A Contemporary Panpsychism* (Albany, NY: SUNY Press, 2003).

9   Rupert Sheldrake, 'Setting Science free from Materialism', *Explore: The Journal of Science and Healing* 9.4 (2013): 211–18.

10   Mathews, *For Love of Matter*, 22.

11   Ibid., 18.

12   Ibid., 8.

> Non-human animals, including all mammals and birds, and many other creatures, including octopuses, also possess these neurological substrates.[13]

In this sense, we *are* animals. We have left behind the Cartesian theory that humans are superior to animals because they can control their natural desires. Since Sigmund Freud we have developed a different valuation of the suppression of instincts, and the resulting neurosis. We also know that brain size does not explain intelligence. However, there is another problem; the Cambridge statement sees consciousness as emerging from neurons. This theory of emergentism teaches that consciousness is a new, unexpected and different outcome of the material world, which is in opposition to panpsychism. How panpsychism connects consciousness with *all* matter begs the question of what defines consciousness.

I should mention that I am not discussing the theory of pantheism, God and the world being one.[14] This supposes God to be immanent, not transcendent. The majority of the major religions have been teaching God's transcendence and thus many pantheists found themselves in trouble, such as Baruch Spinoza (1632–1677), who was excluded from both the Jewish and the Christian faiths. Panpsychism however substitutes *psyche* (soul) for *theos* (God), allowing for religious syncretism. Ultimate reality is not named; god or gods are only part of it. *Psyche* is an ancient Greek concept, but the Greeks did not have a word for consciousness, and it can be confusing to substitute 'consciousness' or 'mind' for 'soul' as pervading all matter. To make things even more complicated, contemporary concepts must be flexible enough to accommodate *altered states* of consciousness, which is the domain of a range of sciences, including transpersonal psychology.

In 1872, the Canadian psychiatrist Maurice Bucke (1837–1902) had a religious experience in London which he described as 'cosmic consciousness'. Bucke relates this in the third person:

> He found himself wrapped around as it were by a flame-coloured cloud. For an instant he thought of fire, some sudden conflagration in the great city; the

---

13   Philip Low, *The Cambridge Declaration on Consciousness* (2012).

14   Timothy L.S. Sprigge, 'Pantheism', *The Monist* 80.2 (1997): 191–217.

next, he knew that the light was within himself. Directly afterwards came upon him a sense of exultation, of
immense joyousness accompanied or immediately followed by an intellectual illumination quite impossible
to describe.[15]

The experience meant to Bucke that the 'Cosmos is not dead matter but a living Presence, that the soul of man is immortal, that the
universe is so built and ordered that without any peradventure all
things work together for the good of each and all, that the foundation principle of the world is what we call love'.[16] Subsequently
Bucke developed a sweeping theory of the nature of consciousness
across all races and religions, and its historical evolution to a new
global level based on cosmic consciousness, which he projects into
the future. We can take Bucke's statement that the cosmos is 'a living
Presence' as a proclamation of panpsychism.

Bucke influenced William James (1842–1910), who has often been
called the 'Father of American psychology'. James was very influential as philosopher, positing the role of the brain as not productive of consciousness but permissive or transmissive; James spoke
variously of the brain as straining, sifting, canalising, limiting, and
individualising a larger mental reality existing behind the scenes.[17]
This view of consciousness and the brain came to be known as the
'filter model'.[18] James was deeply convinced that the filter model is
compatible with the possibility of post-mortem survival of individual consciousness, seeing cosmic consciousness as collective, like a
reservoir.[19] Aldous Huxley calls this idea 'Mind at Large', and quotes
the English philosopher C.D. Broad (1887–1971):

Each person is at each moment capable of remembering

---

15   Maurice Bucke, *Cosmic Consciousness. A Study in the Evolution of the Hu-
      man Mind* (Mineola: Dover Publications, 2009), 10.

16   Ibid.

17   Edward F. Kelly, Emily W. Kelly, and Adam Crabtree, eds., *Irreducible
      Mind: Toward a Psychology for the 21st Century* (Lanham: Rowman & Lit-
      tlefield, 2007), 28.

18   Ibid., 29 n.23. Kelly argues that the 'filter model' can be found in Kant and
      perhaps in Plato.

19   Ibid., 591–92.

all that has ever happened to him and of perceiving everything that is happening everywhere in the universe. The function of the brain and the nervous system is to protect us from being overwhelmed and confused by this mass of largely useless and irrelevant knowledge, by shutting out most of what we should otherwise perceive or remember at any moment, and leaving only that very small and special selection which is likely to be practically useful. An extension or modification of this type of theory seems to offer better hopes of a coherent synthesis of normal and paranormal cognition than is offered by attempts to tinker with the orthodox notion of events in the brain and nervous system generating sense-data.[20]

Today, this is still an ongoing debate. For instance, Rupert Sheldrake recently stated that 'if our minds are not just the activity of our brains, there is no need for them to be confined to the insides of our heads [...] Our minds are extended in every act of perception, reaching even as far as the stars'.[21]

Natural mind

The theory that individual human and non-human entities—such as animals, plants, geographic features such as mountains or rivers, or other entities of the natural environment, including thunder, wind, and shadows—possess a soul or spirit is called *animism*.[22] In ancient Greece, the animist view of an enchanted world preceded the belief in personal gods, as in Homer, and consisted of spirits of vaguer individuality and narrower functions, expressed by such terms as the Greek *daimon* and Latin *numen*, that are quasi-material and can act.[23] Animism existed alongside the traditional cult worship of the pantheon, especially in the Roman world, where much of its my-

---

20   Huxley, *The Doors of Perception*, 21.

21   Sheldrake, 'Setting Science Free From Materialism', 217.

22   Herbert J. Rose, 'Nvmen inest: "Animism" in Greek and Roman Religion', *The Harvard Theological Review* 28.4 (1935): 237–57.

23   Ibid., 240–41.

thology was imported from the Greeks. In fact, animism is a global feature of human understanding before and even after the introduction of organized religion or philosophy. Even today in Japan, trees, houses, and many ordinary objects are considered to embody a spirit and are treated with due respect. As Francis Cornford has argued, ancient Greek philosophy did not break away from animistic belief but developed alongside it.[24] Something similar may have happened with Buddhism and Shintoism in Japan.

Restall Orr, who is a British neo-druid, animist, priest, poet, and author, wrote an enchanting, semi-academic book in 2012 titled *The Wakeful World*, asking 'what nature is'.[25] From her rich experience of natural religion she declares panpsychism to be the philosophy of animism.[26] She declares that 'the animistic thesis is not just based upon rational arguments but informed too by the profound and visceral experience of integration'.[27] She articulates a profound understanding of the mindedness of all things when she states that 'everything in nature is awake, both perceiving its environment and with a sense of its own being'.[28] Is panpsychism a rebirth of animism and ancient philosophy?

The Catholic Church has rejected pantheism since the Middle Ages. Returning to Patrizi, his aspiration was to reinvigorate Catholic Christianity through an infusion of Platonic philosophy, mathematical theory, and a new 'universal philosophy' of nature. His work was however banned and placed on the Papal Index in 1595. Other Renaissance philosophers have entertained similar notions of an ensouled cosmos, but Giordano Bruno took a step further and proclaimed the universe to be infinite and eternal; for this view he was burned at the stake in 1600.[29] If panpsychism was an ancient view of the world, its Italian rebirth was short-lived. Seen as a growing threat by the Vatican, in 1864 pantheism was formally condemned by Pope Pius IX in his Syllabus of Errors. But recently, in 2015, Pope

---

24   Francis M. Cornford, *From Religion to Philosophy: A Study in the Origins of Western Speculation* (Princeton: Princeton University Press, 1991): xvii.

25   Emma Restall Orr, *The Wakeful World: Animism, Mind and the Self in Nature* (Alresford: Moon Books, 2012).

26   Ibid., 104.

27   Ibid., 153.

28   Ibid., 272.

29   Skrbina, *Panpsychism in the West*, 67–76.

Francis published the Encyclical *Laudato si'*, quoting the words of a canticle by Saint Francis of Assisi (1181–1226), who saw the presence of God in all nature—from flowers to fields of corn, vineyards, stones, beauteous meadows, tinkling brooks, sprouting gardens—and thus treated everything with the greatest reverence.[30] If any thinker in Christendom comes close to promoting panpsychism, it is Saint Francis. The Vatican Encyclical of 2015 quotes his canticle in the title and text, saying:

> Our common home is like a sister with whom we share our life and a beautiful mother who opens her arms to embrace us. 'Praise be to you, my Lord, through our Sister, Mother Earth, who sustains and governs us, and who produces various fruit with coloured flowers and herbs.' This sister now cries out to us because of the harm we have inflicted on her by our irresponsible use and abuse of the goods with which God has endowed her. We have come to see ourselves as her lords and masters, entitled to plunder her at will.[31]

With the rise of the mechanistic worldview in the 17th century, panpsychism disappeared from the academic agenda, although panpsychist ideas appeared in the works of individual philosophers and poets, for example, Baruch Spinoza, Gottfried Leibniz, Johann Wolfgang von Goethe, Friedrich Schelling, Gustav Fechner, William Wordsworth, John Keats, Percy Shelley, Henry David Thoreau, and Walt Whitman. In the 19th century, panpsychism reached its zenith, and for the sake of brevity I will refer the reader to David Skrbina's excellent study.[32] Instead, let me focus on the psychologist Carl Gustav Jung (1875–1961), who re-introduced *psyche* to the academy in the language of depth psychology, as the 'collective unconscious.'[33]

---

30   Ibid., 61, 223.

31   Vatican, *Encyclical Letter Laudato Si' of the Holy Father Francis on Care for Our Common Home* (2015).

32   Skrbina, *Panpsychism in the West.*

33   See for example, C.G. Jung, *The Structure of the Unconscious* (1916), Collected Works VII (Princeton: Princeton University Press, 1953).

Unus Mundus

Jung connected his analytical psychology with alchemy, and 'individuation' with the production of the *lapis philosophorum*.[34] In alchemy Jung found, as in a reservoir, 'the most enduring and the most important mythologems of the ancient world'.[35] The goal of analytical psychology, individuation, is approached through the technique of active imagination, engaging with archetypal images beyond the aesthetic, by acting out in word and deed with paint, music, and whatever comes to hand, to enable the transition of the patient to an attitude of inner certainty and self-reliance.[36] This, however, is only the first step in a lifelong struggle, which aims at the union with something the alchemists called the *unus mundus*, or 'one world'.[37] Jung himself followed this path, engaging with his imagination through *The Red Book*[38] and having visions of the *hieros gamos* (sacred marriage) later in life. For the alchemist all matter had a divine, mental aspect. In his last book, *Mysterium Coniunctionis,* Jung equated Gerhard Dorn's (c. 1530–1584) alchemical concept of the *unus mundus* with a union of opposites, 'the potential world of the first day of creation, when nothing was yet "in actu," i.e., divided into two and many, but was still one'.[39] Jung thinks the concept of the *unus mundus* can be traced back to Philo Judaeus and Plotinus.[40] David Fideler beautifully summarises Plotinus' *Ennead* IV. 4.32, thus: 'The source of the universe was unlimited, ineffable, and of infinite power, overflowing like a fountain, giving birth to Nous, which in turns gives birth to the World Soul, which gives birth to Nature, as links in an unbroken chain.'[41]

---

34 C.G. Jung, *Mysterium Coniunctionis: An Inquiry Into the Separation and Synthesis of Psychic Opposites in Alchemy*, second edition, trans. R.F.C. Hull (Princeton: Princeton University Press, 1970), xiii–xv.

35 C.G. Jung, *Alchemical Studies: V. The Philosophical Tree*, trans. R.F.C. Hull (Princeton: Princeton University Press, 1967), 274.

36 Jung, *Mysterium Coniunctionis*, 531.

37 Ibid., 534.

38 Carl G. Jung, *The Red Book*, ed. Sonu Shamdasani (London: Norton, 2009).

39 Jung, *Mysterium Coniunctionis*, 534.

40 Ibi.

41 David R. Fideler, *Restoring the Soul of the World: Our Living Bond with*

Because Jung's starting point was a psychoanalytical practice, his use of the word *psyche* is in general not associated with anything beyond the human soul. However, later in life Jung collaborated with the physicist Wolfgang Pauli and expanded his view of the collective unconscious and the archetypes beyond the human sphere, presenting the concepts of 'synchronicity' and the *unus mundus* in their joint publication *Naturerklärung und Psyche*.[42] In 1954 he wrote: 'the common background of microphysics and depth-psychology is as much physical as psychic and therefore neither, but rather a third thing, a neutral nature which can at most be grasped in hints since in essence it is transcendental.'[43] This sounds like neutral monism, and so I propose that one could consider the later Jung as a panpsychist. He was also aware of the analogy of his ideas with Eastern philosophy, as he compares the alchemist's encounter with the *unus mundus* to 'the *unio mystica*, or *tao*, or the content of *samadhi*, or the experience of *satori* in Zen, which would bring us to the realm of the ineffable and of extreme subjectivity where all the criteria of reason fail.'[44] As David Clarke has argued, the Buddhist saying that 'the Buddha nature is in all things' is consistent with panpsychism.[45]

The collaboration of Jung and Pauli resulted in an exchange of ideas, Jung expounding his concept of synchronicity and Pauli analysing the impact of archetypal images on the formation of the scientific theories of Johannes Kepler.[46] Pauli argued that Kepler's—and his own—pioneering insights arose from the unconscious, especially as archetypal material in dreams, and not from conscious reasoning. Jung went a step further and proposed that archetypes were patterning both the mental *and* the material aspects of reality, connected through the acausal principle of synchronicity.[47] In 1970 Marie-Louise von Franz presented her research based on Jung's

Nature's Intelligence (Rochester, VT: Inner Traditions, 2014), 66.

42   C.G. Jung & Wolfgang Pauli, eds., *Naturerklärung und Psyche: Synchronizität als ein Prinzip akausaler Zusammenhänge* (Zurich: Rascher-Verlag, 1952).

43   Jung, *Mysterium Coniunctionis*, 538.

44   Ibid., 540.

45   David S. Clarke, *Panpsychism and the Religious Attitude* (Albany: SUNY Press, 2003), 154.

46   Jung & Pauli, eds., *Naturerklärung und Psyche*.

47   Jung, *Mysterium Coniunctionis*, 464–65.

ideas of the archetypes of natural numbers as the path towards the *unus mundus*, connecting Pythagorean and Taoist insights.[48] Number, connecting mind and matter, makes a good case for a panpsychist approach to music and poetry.

Panpsychist philosophers often quote the findings of quantum physics to support the view that mental aspects can be ascribed to inorganic matter, because subatomic particles appear to react to the presence of an observer.[49] In that sense, mental qualities become a primal aspect of *all* matter, and the source of consciousness is positioned in the whole universe. The relativity of space and time at the subatomic and cosmic level that the physicists encountered seemed to support a parallel to the often unexplainable properties of the human mind. As Skrbina relates, philosophers with panpsychist leanings like Henri Bergson, Alfred Whitehead, Charles Hartshorne, Thomas Nagel, Kenneth M. Sayre, and David Chalmers have reflected on these new insights of physics.[50] Recently Ervin László has attempted to integrate all these concepts with his book *Science and the Akashic Field: An Integral Theory of Everything.*[51] The Sanskrit *Akasha* can be equated with the Stoic æther, a fluid pervading the whole cosmos. Theosophy uses 'Akashic records' to refer to an ethereal compendium of all knowledge and history, and László uses the term 'Akashic Field' to indicate the 'quantum vacuum', a term contemporary physics uses for empty space that is at once 'a swirling cauldron of virtual particles flickering into and out of existence'.[52] László seeks to posit a common source for cosmic energy and information, standing for the 'old' matter and mind. Freya Mathews has recently written a paper in which she explains why all these attempts to support the view that mental aspects can be ascribed to inorganic matter have not been very successful in establishing panpsychism as a philosophical paradigm. She argues that panpsychism does not

48   Marie-Louise von Franz, *Number and Time: Reflections Leading Toward a Unification of Depth Psychology and Physics*, trans. A. Dykes (Evanston: Northwestern University Press, 1974).

49   Fideler, *Restoring the Soul of the World*, 191.

50   Skrbina, *Panpsychism in the West*, 157 ff.

51   Ervin László, *Science and the Akashic Field: An Integral Theory of Everything* (Rochester, VT: Inner Traditions, 2004).

52   J. Linn Mackay, 'The Collective Unconscious and the Akashic Field', *Jung Journal* 1.2 (2007): 6.

appeal to the dominant Western philosophical tradition of *reflection*, but rather to a different mode of cognition, one that resembles the strategy of *engagement* of the Chinese wisdom tradition, based on 'wu wei', martial arts, and Taoism.[53] In my words: panpsychism needs to be lived.

FOR LOVE OF MATTER

Can we say that panpsychism is a both a philosophical theory *and* an experience of the nature of things? Panpsychism as an experience of ensouled nature is often found in poetry, especially in the late 19th century. Poetry seems to be better equipped to express holistic experiences of nature than academic prose. However, in the 1960s nature as a topic was back on the academic agenda with the rise of ecological philosophy and environmental ethics, not for sentimental reasons. In 1966 the ecologist Lynn White Jr. gave a talk entitled *The Historical Roots of Our Ecological Crisis*, blaming Christianity as 'the most anthropocentric religion the world has seen' for encouraging the exploitation of nature.[54] He thought that the Church's declaration that mankind had a divine right of dominion over nature both pre-dated and underlay the mechanism and materialism of the Industrial Revolution. It was this separation from nature that White thought allowed for the Darwinian model of consciousness as emerging from matter.[55] For the adherents of the Gaia hypothesis, formulated by James Lovelock in the 1970s, the earth is a self-regulating, complex system that helps to maintain the conditions for life. Among the supporters of the Gaia hypothesis, the biologist Rupert Sheldrake stands out as an advocate of the 'filter model' of consciousness, and panpsychism as a scientific paradigm.[56] Another avenue towards panpsychism opened up with the publication of Morris Berman's *The Reenchantment of the World*, which laments the loss of a participating consciousness with the advent of the mechanistic worl-

---

53   Freya Mathews, 'Why Has the West Failed to Embrace Panpsychism?' in *Mind That Abides: Panpsychism in the New Millenium*, ed. David Skrbina (Amsterdam/Philadelphia: John Benjamins, 2009), 314–60.

54   Skrbina, *Panpsychism in the West*, 226.

55   Restall Orr, *The Wakeful World*, 279.

56   Sheldrake, 'Setting Science Free from Materialism', 211–18.

dview.[57] In this tradition stands Freya Mathews. Her panpsychism is ecological philosophy, but with ethical consequences, showing a new way of engaging with nature.

Mathews claims that 'the environmental crisis is a symptom of deeper issues facing modern civilisation arising from the loss of the very meaning of culture. To come to grips with this crisis requires a change in the metaphysical premise of modernity.'[58] The old view that the universe is made out of dead matter has to go. 'The materialist view of the world that is a corollary of dualism maroons the epistemic subject in the small if charmed circle of its own subjectivity, and it is only the reanimation of matter itself that enables the subject to reconnect with reality' claims Mathews in her recent book *For Love of Matter*, which can be read as a manual for reconnecting with this reality.[59] Below I summarise some of the arguments from her book.

Mathews does not see the human body as 'an object, in the manner of a statue, for instance, but rather a process, a system, in dynamic equilibrium with its environment [...] Mind is not a mysterious entity in its own right but the reflexive, purposive aspect of a self-directive, self-realising system'.[60] The mind as a self-realising system is clearly inspired by nature, as expressed in the metaphor of the acorn growing into the oak tree. In this connection she often uses the term *conatus*. It goes back to Stoic ὁρμή and means something between self-moving, self-preservation, the will to live, and self-organisation. Aristotle called the soul an *entelecheia*, meaning 'that which has its end in itself' or 'the vital force that directs an organism toward self-fulfilment': an acorn has an inner urge to become an oak.

Mathews understands *conatus* in Spinoza's sense as the endeavour of all things to persist in their own being, the will to self-preservation, self-maintenance, and self-increase.[61] *Orexis* she defines as 'a condition of longing of self for contact with the real, the impulse to reach out to world, desire for contact and connection with the

57   Morris Berman, *The Reenchantment of the World* (Ithaca: Cornell University Press, 1981).

58   Freya Mathews, *Personal website* (2016).

59   Mathews, *For Love of Matter*, 44.

60   Ibid., 54.

61   Ibid., 48, 73.

other-than-self'.[62] 'The panpsychist avoids both egoism and self-ab-
negation by following the orectic impulse as the path of the self.'[63]
'The actual goal of life however, from a panpsychist point of view, is,
not release from suffering, not salvation nor redemption, but poten-
tiation, the sizzling charge that accrues from contact with the live
subjectivity of all that is. The refinement of the orectic impulse—
the impulse to reach out to world—from its basic appetitive form
through to its ultimate flowering in eros is the spiritual path that
panpsychism appoints'.[64]

Eros thus holds a central position in Mathews' thought. 'As
a source of energy, eros is a creative force, and hence a force for
self-realization' she says.[65] Her favourite myth is 'Eros and Psyche',
as told by the Platonic philosopher Apuleius (125–180 CE) in *The
Golden Ass*. 'Psyche sets out to win eros as an attitude, an orientation, a way of being in the world, an aspect of herself.'[66] To Mathews,
the myth bears out the idea that, 'if we are receptive to the messages of the psychically activated world, it will guide us in developing
our capacity for erotic engagement, because it is in its own interest
for the world to do so'.[67] 'It is only in the context of a panpsychist
world that the self can expect to find the poetic signals and clues,
in any given situation, that will enable her to navigate that situation
in an erotic manner.'[68] To Mathews, the story of *The Golden Ass* expresses the evolution from crude animism to a panpsychist spirituality, expressed by the final initiation of Lucius into the mysteries
of Isis. Panpsychism is the quest for 'spirituality in the service of
eros, for support and wisdom needed to fulfil the responsibilities of
conscious life'.[69]

Mathews makes a strong statement in favour of re-enchantment
in *For Love of Matter*. She urges engagement, using poetry and song:

From a panpsychist viewpoint, the aim is not to theorize

---

62   Ibid., 61, 73.
63   Ibid., 61.
64   Ibid., 111.
65   Ibid., 107.
66   Ibid., 116.
67   Ibid., 143.
68   Ibid., 141.
69   Ibid., 151.

the world, but to relate to it, and to rejoice in that relationship. For this we need practices of invocation and response—ritual practices, for instance, recovered and adapted from the great treasure houses of traditional religious forms. But the premier modes of address and celebration are surely poetry and song. A culture of encounter is a culture of poetry and song, poetry and song salvaged from their commodification as products of the entertainment and literary industries, and restored to their rightful place as participative arts of everyday life. All human praxes, at both collective and individual levels, can be transformed into on-going conversation with an increasingly animated and responsive world through the mediation of song. To talk with the world in this way, to translate the mundane into the dream language of the poetic order, is truly to sing the world up, and to attune ourselves to the inexhaustible layers of its own unconscious-but-simultaneously-all-conscious song. The point is not to explain the world, but to sing it.[70]

Can Mathews' panpsychism help to re-enchant the academy? Her ideas connect ancient and modern philosophy, East and West, myth and reason, nature, art and science, psyche and matter. They make philosophy come alive and integrate the arts, and indeed she is advocating scholarship 'with soul in mind'. C.G. Jung advocated the active use of the imagination in psychotherapy; its subsequent use as a scientific method can be seen as a contribution to the enrichment of scholarship by Jung and those who followed in his footsteps, for instance James Hillman, Thomas Moore, and John Dirkx. Mathews is, however, stepping beyond the imagination, into action.

Panpsychism is one way of suggesting a wider holistic paradigm within which to consider the nature of the reality we all inhabit. But there are many other contending philosophies, and they all like to enter the academic curriculum. To get into the academy Freya Mathews' panpsychism has—so to speak—to climb in through the bathroom window. But once inside, she can open the front door for her friends and turn the place into a temple of wisdom.

---

70   Ibid., 88.

SELECT BIBLIOGRAPHY

BUCKE, R. Maurice. *Cosmic Consciousness: A Study in the Evolution of the Human Mind*. Mineola: Dover Publications, 2009. Original 1901.

CLARKE, David S. *Panpsychism and the Religious Attitude*. Albany: SUNY Press, 2003.

FIDELER, David R. *Restoring the Soul of the World: Our Living Bond with Nature's Intelligence*. Rochester, VT: Inner Traditions, 2014.

HANEGRAAFF, Wouter J. *New Age Religion and Western Culture: Esotericism in the Mirror of Secular Thought*. Albany: SUNY Press, 1998.

HUXLEY, Aldous L. *The Doors of Perception*. Harmondsworth: Penguin Books, 1971.

IRWIN, Lee. 'A World Full of Gods: Panpsychism and the Paradigms of Esotericism' in *Esotericism, Religion, and Nature*, edited by Arthur Versluis, Claire Fanger, Lee Irwin, and Melinda Phillips, ASE series 2, 27–51. Lansing, MI: Michigan State University Press, 2010.

JUNG, C.G. *Mysterium Coniunctionis: An Inquiry into the Separation and Synthesis of Psychic Opposites in Alchemy*. Collected Works XIV. Translated by R.F.C. Hull. Princeton: Princeton University Press, 1970.

KELLY, Edward F., E.W. KELLY and A. CRABTREE, eds., *Irreducible Mind: Toward a Psychology for the 21st Century*. Lanham: Rowman & Littlefield, 2007.

MATHEWS, Freya. *For Love of Matter: A Contemporary Panpsychism*. Albany: SUNY Press, 2003.

_____. 'Why Has the West Failed to Embrace Panpsychism?' in *Mind That Abides: Panpsychism in the New Millennium*, edited by David Skrbina, 314–60. Amsterdam/Philadelphia: John Benjamins, 2009.

RESTALL Orr, Emma. *The Wakeful World: Animism, Mind, and the Self in Nature*. Alresford: Moon Books, 2012.

SHAW, Gregory. 'The *Chôra* of the Timaeus and Iamblichean Theurgy'. *Horizons* 3.2 (2012): 103–29.

SHELDRAKE, Rupert. 'Setting Science Free from Materialism'. *Explore: The Journal of Science and Healing* 9.4 (2013): 211–18.

SKRBINA, David. *Panpsychism in the West*. Cambridge, MA: MIT Press, 2005.

PART TWO

Re-enchanting the Curriculum

Docere, Delectare, Movere

Soul-learning, Reflexivity and the 'Third Classroom'[1]

ANGELA VOSS

INTRODUCTION

'It is as if we can study everything about religion, except what makes it fiercely religious'[2] observes Rice University religious studies professor Jeffrey Kripal. Well, what *does* make religion fiercely religious?[3] Should this highly-charged, sensual, devotional, or emotive impulse indeed find a place in academic studies?

In this chapter I will direct the theme of re-enchanting the academy towards an exploration of 'fierce religiousness', not only in relation to the study of spirituality, but also as an intrinsic part of all experiences which make us aware of a deeper, mysterious, or extraordinary dimension of reality, experiences which we may label paranormal, visionary, erotic or inspirational. Such an intuitive or imaginative apprehension of something other than the consensus

---

1 *Docere, delectare, movere* (to teach, delight and move) were the three aims of the orator as stated by Cicero (*Orator*, 46 BCE). 'The Third Classroom' is a term coined by Jeffrey J. Kripal in *The Serpent's Gift* (Chicago: Chicago University Press, 2007, 23). I would like to thank Jocelyn Lloyd for his detailed review of this chapter.

2 Jeffrey J. Kripal, *Comparing Religions* (Chichester: Wiley Blackwell, 2014) xiv.

3 The word 'religious' has a dual etymology: *religare*, to 'bind back' (as in Lactantius, *Divine Institutes*, IV, xxviii) and *religere*, to 'recover' (as in Augustine, *City of God* XIII). In both cases, it suggests the idea of a return to a former condition, and I am interpreting it here in the sense of an intuitive realisation or experience of awe, longing, piety, or reverence in relation to a numinous 'other' or alternative condition of reality, rather than a formal adherence to a specific tradition.

norm can be shocking, even life-changing, and may arise from engaging deeply with texts, images, and music which are explicitly
concerned with awakening a mysterious and elusive sense which we
could term 'sacred'.[4] Narratives such as scripture and poetry, cultural
mythologies, or the symbolic writings and images of our esoteric
wisdom traditions (for example Kabbalah, astrology, alchemy, or
magic[5]) all carry this potential because they speak in figurative language in order to evoke *meaning* through engaging the imagination.
But they also require *interpretation* through engaging the rational
mind, and therefore carry great potential for bringing intuitive apprehension and critical analysis into a harmonious relationship. I
want to show that moments of awe, love, desire, or awakening do
not have to be left outside the classroom, but can give rise to a learning process which is hermeneutically rich and personally transformative. Indeed, I find connections here with both contemporary
explorations of the cultivation of spirituality and wisdom in higher
education,[6] and with the transpersonal branch of the transformative

4   Kripal defines 'the sacred' as 'a particular structure of human conscious-
     ness that corresponds to a palpable presence, energy, or power encoun-
     tered in the environment'. It is a 'third thing' beyond faith or piety, which
     is not to be identified with 'the faith-claims of the religious traditions'. *Au-
     thors of the Impossible: The Paranormal and the Sacred* (Chicago: Chicago
     University Press, 2010), 9, 254. For an example of this kind of sudden in-
     sight in relation to astrological symbolism, see Maggie Hyde, 'The Judder
     Effect: Astrology and Alternative Reality', *The Astrological Journal* (2001),
     43.5, 48–53.

5   'Magic' is a ubiquitous yet difficult term to define, as it covers a variety of
     activities from the creation of illusions, to spell-making, working with the
     hidden forces of nature, and ceremonial and spiritual ritual. For a survey
     of the many types of magic practised in early modern Europe, see Brian
     P. Copenhaver, *Magic in Western Culture, from Antiquity to the Enlighten-
     ment* (Cambridge: Cambridge University Press, 2015).

6   Elizabeth J. Tisdell asserts that 'spirituality is about how people construct
     knowledge through largely unconscious and symbolic processes' and sug-
     gests that it is 'always present (although often unacknowledged) in the
     learning environment'. See *Exploring Spirituality and Culture in Adult and
     Higher Education* (San Francisco: John Wiley & Sons, 2003), xi; Wilma
     Fraser and Tara Hyland-Russell define wisdom as 'a stance of openness
     embracing possibility and multidimensionality…Wisdom is broader in
     scope than cognitive knowing and includes aspects of the sacred, divine,
     intuitive and experiential' in 'Searching for Sophia: Adult Educators and

learning movement,[7] and I would suggest that the principles I will discuss could apply to *all* human learning contexts, insofar as they might aim to achieve a balanced relationship between the representation of knowledge as information, and its living presence as an internally realised truth.

THE POWER OF SYMBOL

Timothy Scott has remarked that 'symbolic interpretation has become a practice to be studied rather than a mode of study itself',[8] due, as we shall see, to the Enlightenment project of stripping away all non-rational or 'subjective' elements from what was deemed to constitute positive knowledge.[9] However, the metaphorical language of mythic narrative presents multi-levelled possibilities of interpretation. For example, the Jewish and medieval Christian methods of fourfold exegesis provide a framework for the reader to move from literal, to allegorical, to tropological or moral,[10] to anagogic or mys-

---

Adult Learners as Wisdom Seekers', *New Directions for Adult and Continuing Education* 131 (Autumn 2011), 26; see also Wilma Fraser, 'Searching for Sophia: seeking wisdom in adult teaching and learning spaces' (PhD diss., Canterbury Christ Church University, 2013).

7   Transformative learning, arising from the work of Jack Mezirow, can be briefly defined as 'a process of examining, questioning and revising [our] perceptions of our experiences' (Edward W. Taylor, Patrician Cranton and Associates, eds., *The Handbook of Transformative Learning* [San Francisco: Jossey Bass 2012], 5). I am referring here to the depth-psychological and transpersonal perspectives on TL as promoted by writers such as John M. Dirkx, Robert D. Boyd, J. Gordon Myers, and Rosemary R. Ruether, as opposed to the social/political strand instigated by Paolo Freire.

8   Timothy Scott, 'Symbolic Exegesis, Cosmology, and Soteriology' (paper presented to the 3rd Annual *Alternative Expressions of the Numinous* conference, University of Queensland, 15th–17th August 2008), 2.

9   On the radical epistemological shift that took place during the 17th–18th centuries, see Iain McGilchrist, *The Master and his Emissary* (New Haven, CT: Yale University Press, 2009), 330–51. Positivism states that reason and logic, as interpreters of empirical evidence, are the only sources of truth.

10   From *tropos*, meaning 'turn'. Tropological thus means a 'turn of the soul', a change in viewpoint, understanding or action.

tical readings of scripture,[11] and similarly in the Western esoteric traditions (which in the main derive from Pythagorean and Platonic teachings) the symbol is seen as embodying meanings which allow the understanding to move from the concreteness of the particular instance to more universal or archetypal resonances.[12] Ritual contexts also provide for this transition from the literal, embodied presence or action to the revelation of meaningful insight, and participation in ritual as a methodological approach is certainly more widely recognised in anthropology than in religious studies or history.[13] With a hermeneutic approach to discourse or practice, participants can create meaningful narratives which amplify the literal sense, for as C.G. Jung observed, 'whether a thing is a symbol or not depends chiefly upon the attitude of the consciousness considering it'.[14] The meanings can never be ultimate, for readers will locate themselves at different places on the spectrum; for some, literal or historical meanings will dominate, for others, allegorical significances will be seen, and for yet others, the material in hand will instantiate a significance that may impel them to change in some way, through evoking a profound emotional connection between themselves and the nar-

---

11   See H. Flanders Dunbar, *Symbolism in Medieval Thought and its Culmination in the Divine Comedy* (New Haven, CT: Yale University Press, 1929). On the application of the four senses hermeneutic to the learning process, see Angela Voss, 'A Methodology of the Imagination', *Eye of the Heart Journal* 3 (2009): 37–52.

12   See Peter Struck, *Birth of the Symbol: Ancient Writers at the Limits of their Texts* (Princeton: Princeton University Press, 2004). For example, in the Hermetic rituals of statue magic, a statue of a deity was seen in four different ways: as a stone object, as a *representation* of the deity, as an *imitation* of the deity, and finally as fully embodying the deity and thus alive. Further on this topic, see Angela Voss, 'The Secret Life of Statues', in *Sky and Psyche*, eds. N. Campion & P. Curry (Edinburgh: Floris Books, 2006), 201–27.

13   See for example David Luke & Jack Hunter, eds, *Talking with Spirits, Ethnographies from Between the Worlds* (Brisbane: Daily Grail Publishing, 2014). In contrast, the historian Wouter Hanegraaff maintains that the scholar cannot achieve knowledge of the ecstatic state of 'divine frenzy' by entering into it (Wouter Hanegraaff, 'The Platonic Frenzies in Ficino', in *Myths, Martyrs and Modernity* (Leiden: Brill, 2010), 567.

14   C.G. Jung, 'Psychological Types', in *The Collected Works of C.G. Jung*, Vol. 6 (Princeton: Princeton University Press, 1976), 51.

rative that they have never glimpsed before. Perhaps rarely, a state of being may be induced in which they feel at one with a greater reality or presence, however it may be named.

In my career in H.E.,[15] I have observed a pervasive tension between sacred and secular domains of knowledge, with 'the sacred' assumed to be the concern of theology and religious studies rather than a *quality of relating* to any beloved activity or subject or study. No doubt for historical and doctrinal reasons, I have also experienced tension between theological perspectives and the field of esoteric philosophy, for the fields of magic, divination, the paranormal, and paganism (in short, New Age philosophy and practice) are often still regarded with suspicion from orthodox monotheistic viewpoints.[16] I hope to show, however, that it is possible (and desirable) to find an intellectual space where all expressions of a religious sense, spiritual agency, or revelatory wisdom can be brought into a comparative focus, and examined through the lens of *reflexivity*. Creative methodologies, arts practice, and personal journaling may all provide opportunities for a symbolic 'turn' to take place as the student not only learns *about* wisdom traditions (in all their variety) but also *from* them.

From the perspective of the modern rationalist, the realisation of symbolic truth (such as in divinatory or ritual practice, or in a powerful synchronicity[17] or dream), will remain forever foreign, impossible, curious. Gary Tomlinson, in *Music in Renaissance Magic*, demonstrates the problem when he claims that the modern scholar simply cannot cross over to the other side where magic 'works' but

---

15 I have directed two Masters' programmes in Canterbury, UK: 'The Cultural Study of Cosmology and Divination' (University of Kent, 2006–2010) and 'Myth, Cosmology and the Sacred' (Canterbury Christ Church University, 2014–present).

16 Geoffrey Cornelius has addressed the problem of divination in relation to both monotheistic and Enlightenment positions in 'Field of Omens, A study of Inductive Divination' (PhD diss., University of Kent, 2010), 2–22, 23–49.

17 Synchronicity, as defined by C.G. Jung, is a meaningful coincidence, which carries import for the individual in some way as it evokes archetypal patterns, and aids in the individuation process. See C.G. Jung, *Synchronicity: An Acausal Connecting Principle* (repr. London: Routledge & Kegan Paul, 1955).

can only sit uncomfortably on the fence, acknowledging that indeed it did work 'for the (historical) other'.[18] Similarly Peter Struck and Sarah Iles Johnston expose a common assumption of post-Enlightenment scholars that somehow 'we know better' than our forebears regarding the ontology of spiritual intelligence:

> Whatever our ancient sources may claim about the greater powers that enabled it to work—gods, demons, the cosmos itself—divination is an utterly human art, behind which one can glimpse not only the rules that participants have developed for its engagement, but also the rules by which participants assume (or hope) that the world works.[19]

Geoffrey Cornelius comments 'The question of provenance reveals our ultimate concern with respect to divination; there is nothing that goes beyond this question, and how we approach this concern testifies to our own attitude to divination and to the divine. Post-Kant, no modern rationalist conceives that there could be other than one respectable answer'.[20] He points out that there is no 'finally secure basis' for such an assertion to be assumed as a self-evident truth, and that it reminds us just how firmly the Enlightenment project cut the telephone wires, as it were, between men and gods.

One cannot help but want to give such scholars a shove, to propel them right over Tomlinson's fence into a world where the symbols of magical or divinatory ritual, of dreams and visions, do indeed 'work', here and now, as perhaps the most effective and powerful tools of all with which to unlock the imaginative powers of mind—indeed one only has to turn to depth and transpersonal psychology to see this in action.[21] The scholars will land, according to Iain McGilchrist, in

---

18   Gary Tomlinson, *Music in Renaissance Magic* (Oxford: Oxford University Press, 1989), 247.

19   Peter Struck and Sarah Iles Johnston, eds, *Mantike: Studies in Ancient Divination* (Leiden: Brill, 2005), 10–11.

20   Cornelius, 'Field of Omens', 190.

21   C.G. Jung and James Hillman being the key sources, their work on myth, symbolism, and 'active imagination' developed by writers such as Marie Angelo, Roberto Assagioli, Robert Boznak, Joseph Campbell, James Elkins, Patrick Harpur, and Thomas Moore. I should also mention Henry

the world of the right hemisphere, and it is to his thought-provoking conclusions that I now turn.

The two eyes of the soul

McGilchrist, neuroscientist and English literature scholar, provides us with a monumental overview of the fundamental duality of human cognition in his 2009 book, *The Master and His Emissary*.[22] He observes that 'the divided nature of our reality has been a consistent observation since humanity has been sufficiently self-conscious to reflect on it',[23] and beginning with the fact that the human brain is physically divided in two, he explores how this characteristic can be taken as a grand metaphor for the way Western culture over the last 2,000 years has demonstrated two distinct, and often adversarial, ways of knowing. This is not an ungrounded metaphor, for as a neuro-scientist McGilchrist demonstrates empirically how the human brain really does work in two different ways, according to the specific functions of the right and left hemispheres. However, it is important to emphasise that as the book is primarily about the power of this metaphor to reveal what happens when these two modes become unbalanced, it is the *meaning* of the duality with which McGilchrist is chiefly concerned. As he concludes, 'if [the divided mind] turns out to be "just" a metaphor, I will be content. I have a high regard for metaphor. It is how we come to understand the world'.[24]

The idea that there are two orders of reality (variously termed divine and human, spiritual and material, mental and somatic), reflected in two distinct parts or 'eyes' of the soul, is indeed an ancient one, first articulated in the philosophical canon by Plato in his

---

Corbin, Mircea Eliade, and Gershom Scholem, contributors to the *Eranos* conferences at Ascona along with Jung, who sought to re-empower the symbolic sense within comparative religion. See Hanegraaff, *Western Esotericism and the Academy: Rejected Knowledge in Western Culture* (Cambridge: Cambridge University Press, 2012), 295–313; Steven Wasserstrom, *Religion after Religion: Gershom Scholem, Mircea Eliade, and Henry Corbin at Eranos* (Princeton: Princeton University Press, 1999).

22   See fn. 9 for details.

23   McGilchrist, *The Master*, 461.

24   Ibid., *The Master*, 462.

'divided line' and 'cave' allegories.[25] Here, Plato posits two worlds: that of intellect (*nous*) and reason (*episteme*), and that of opinion (*doxa*) and sense perception (*æsthesis*). Intellect in this sense is not the domain of abstract thought as we might see it today, but a deeply intuitive connection of the soul with a source, or ground of all being termed the One (for which the sun is the supreme symbol). On this intuitive faculty, reason depends, being the capacity for discursive knowledge and ethical understanding. The knowing of the intuitive intellect is called *gnosis*, which as it has come to be understood through the study of Western esotericism, can be characterised as 'a kind of intuitive, nondiscursive, salvational knowledge of one's own true self and of God'.[26] As such it is *primary*, beyond words, experiential, and essentially subjective and non-predictable, requiring *episteme* to articulate and interpret its insights.[27]

These two dimensions of knowing are also characterised by Plato as 'the same' and 'the different', and they are intrinsic to the universal mind, or soul, which informs both the world and the human being.[28] We must of course remember that neither Plato nor Aristotle use the term *imagination* (*phantasia*) for the gnostic glimpse through the veil, or the vision of the sun outside the cave.[29] For the elevation of the imaginative faculty to this role we await Philostratus (190–230 CE) and Plotinus (204–270 CE),whose definition of higher imagination as the capacity of the soul to receive images of transcendent truth and convey them through creative genius was to be so celebrated by Renaissance and Romantic artists.[30]

---

25   Plato, *Republic* VII, 509D–511E and 514A–520A.

26   Wouter J. Hanegraaff, 'Reason, Faith, and Gnosis: Potentials and Problematics of a Typological Construct', in *Clashes of Knowledge* (New York: Springer, 2008), 133.

27   Further on the nature of *gnosis*, see e.g. Dan Merkur, *Gnosis: An Esoteric Tradition of Mystical Visions and Unions* (New York: SUNY Press, 1993). Please note that I am not talking here about Gnosticism, a dualist form of early Christian belief which shunned the material world.

28   Plato, *Timaeus* 34C–35A.

29   For an overview of the classical understanding of imagination, see J.M. Cocking, *Imagination: A Study in the History of Ideas* (Abingdon & New York: Routledge, 1991), 1–26; Gerard Watson, *Phantasia in Classical Thought* (Galway: Galway University Press, 1988).

30   See Philostratus, *Vita Appollonii* 6.19; Plotinus, *Enneads* IV.31, V.8. On

Tim Addey has shown how Plato uses myth to lead the reader towards *gnosis*, from the understanding that a 'likely story', a
poetic or metaphoric narrative, presents truths through images
which evoke a deep memory of the soul's original participation in
the world soul.[31] Indeed Bernardo Kastrup maintains that there is a
deep level of reality which 'cannot be conveyed through any other
means—scientific or philosophical—but religious mythology' as it
is simply 'not amenable to words or equations'.[32] We also find this
distinction in the Sufi tradition.[33] The medieval philosopher/mys-
tic Ibn 'Arabi speaks of 'the two eyes of the soul' as 'the eye of reason' and 'the eye of revelation or imagination'. The former knows
through representation, abstraction, and theorisation, whereas the
latter knows through similitude, metaphor, and symbol.[34] Ibn 'Arabi also distinguishes between 'imitation' and 'realisation'. Imitation
is second hand or theoretical knowledge, learned through received
traditions such as the sciences. Realisation is intellectual knowledge
in the Platonic sense, through tasting or knowing for oneself, and
involves action; for 'knowledge without practice is not true knowledge'.[35] Thus an ethical dimension is involved in the realisation of
the symbol as meaningful in the world, for in the Sufi context, as in
the Biblical four sense hermeneutic, the meaning of the sacred text
is understood as pointing to a moral imperative to act on behalf of
self, others, or community.[36]

McGilchrist's project is to show how these two modes of knowing
are characteristic of the two hemispheres, and in a healthy human

---

neoplatonic imagination, see John Dillon, 'Plotinus and the Transcendental Imagination', in *Religious Imagination*, ed. John Mackey (Edinburgh:
Edinburgh University Press, 1986) 55–64, Cocking, *Imagination*, 27–48.

31 Tim Addey, 'Myth, the Final Phase of Platonic education' (http://www.
prometheustrust.co.uk/html/myth_-_philosophy.html).

32 Kastrup, *More than Allegory*, 10.

33 On Ibn 'Arabi's understanding of imagination, see William Chittick, *Imaginal Worlds: Ibn al-'Arabi and the Problem of Religious Diversity* (Albany:
SUNY Press, 2007).

34 Ibid., 71–72.

35 Ibid., 35.

36 Further on the 'tropological' and 'realised' senses of symbol interpretation
and their moral implications (particularly in relation to astrology), see
Cornelius, *The Moment of Astrology* (Bournemouth: The Wessex Astrolo-
ger, 2003), 292–302.

and society should work together (*episteme* being the 'emissary' to the Master's *nous*). But they have become divided to such an extent that reason is no longer in service to intuition, and has become an autonomous *logos* or *rationality*, 'a closed system which cannot reach outside itself to whatever it is that exists apart from itself'.[37] I cannot possibly do justice here to McGilchrist's monumental survey, but in short, he argues that human culture and civilisation have flourished when the cognitive functions characterised by the left hemisphere (analysis, abstraction, and scientific empiricism), have been in appropriate relationship to those of the right (imagination, intuition, holistic vision, religious sense). He shows, with exhaustive attention to historical and cultural detail, that since the Enlightenment period, the power of metaphor to lead the mind out of the 'hall of mirrors' of the left hemisphere towards 'meaning rather than fact, ambiguity rather than certainty' has been relentlessly undermined, if not blocked.[38] Metaphor has become mistrusted, rather than understood as a path to knowledge, and consequently the arts have become merely entertainment, and divinatory practitioners generally regarded as indulging in pseudoscience when they are not outright charlatans.

However, McGilchrist points out that metaphor, as a right hemispheric function, 'is in every sense prior to abstraction and explicitness', and the means by which genuine creativity is stirred.[39] 'All understanding', he says '*depends on choosing the right metaphor*' (my italics) because the metaphor we choose governs what we see. I will come back to this important observation, but let us note here that in terms of our great religious mythologies McGilchrist says 'any mythos that allows us to approach a spiritual Other, and gives us something other than material values to live by is more valuable than one that dismisses the possibility of its existence'.[40] Why? Because then it becomes a key to *gnosis*, freeing us from the confines of a life which, in McGilchrist's view, is only half-lived.

---

37   McGilchrist, *The Master*, 30.

38   Ibid., 438. He points out that we have inherited an Enlightenment view of metaphor which does not allow it to be a 'vehicle of thought', but regards it as a linguistic device which is either 'indirectly literal' or 'purely fanciful' and either way 'can have nothing to do with truth'. 332. See also 337.

39   Ibid., 179.

40   Ibid., 442.

McGilchrist does certainly not underestimate the importance of left hemispheric knowing, in that it 'is a wonderful servant'; it is just that it is 'a very poor master'.[41] The problem is that the left hemisphere works like a very successful propaganda machine which wants to lead us to believe that 'what it does is more *highly evolved* that what the right hemisphere does',[42] and this has led to its determination to overthrow all that it deems irrational, occult, or superstitious in terms of knowledge. 'Magic is the way that the left hemisphere sees powers over which it has no control' acutely observes McGilchrist,[43] whereas for the right hemisphere these powers are built into the fabric of the world and indeed may move the soul towards right action and self-understanding, as well as inspired artistic achievement.

What has this to do with transformative learning? McGilchrist gives us a model which, in my opinion, can be put to practical use. He emphasises, in interpreting Hegel, that creativity arises from imaginal perception, reflection, and analysis, dependent on the flow and co-operation between the two hemispheric functions:

> What is offered by the right hemisphere to the left hemisphere is offered back again and taken up into a synthesis involving both hemispheres. This must be true of the processes of creativity, of the understanding of works of

---

41   Ibid., 437.

42   Ibid.

43   McGilchrist, *The Master*, 311. We could perhaps characterise 'sorcery' and 'natural magic' as the extraordinary powers of mind viewed from the left and right hemispheres respectively. It is interesting to note that in his paper 'Magic' (http://www.academia.edu/25678359/Magic) (accessed 20/10/2016), Wouter Hanegraaff ends by warning the scholar against 'falling under its spell', falling prey to illusions which may become 'potent factors in the real world'. In my view, this statement demonstrates McGilchrist's very point, which is the problem faced by the rational mind when confronted by events or phenomena that are inexplicable from its point of view. Of relevance here also is Bernardo Kastrup's metaphorical observation that if we locate ourselves 'outside' mind we are the mercy of what appear to be 'impersonal external forces' whereas if we are *in* mind, taking a participatory stance, then we participate consciously in these forces and they are no longer a threat (Kastrup, *Materialism is Baloney: How True Skeptics Know there is no Death and Fathom Answers to Life, the Universe and Everything* [Winchester: Iff Books 2014], 70).

art, of the development of the religious sense. In each
there is a progress from an intuitive apprehension of
whatever it may be, via a more formal process of enrichment through conscious, detailed analytic understanding, to a new, enhanced intuitive understanding
of this whole, now transformed by the process that it
has undergone.[44]

Philosophy, says McGilchrist (if it is to be true to its name), follows
such a trajectory, for

It begins in wonder, intuition, ambiguity, puzzlement
and uncertainty; it progresses through being unpacked,
inspected from all angles and wrestled into linearity
by the left hemisphere; but its endpoint is to see that
the very business of language and linearity must themselves be transcended, and once more left behind. The
progression is familiar: from right hemisphere, to left
hemisphere, to right hemisphere again.[45]

Plato tells us that in the state of wonder, *eros* is born, the energy
that fires the soul with a passion to pursue its truth.[46] Just contemplating the night sky, he says, will incite a desire for learning,[47] and
this arousal of affective and erotic longing deeply informs the revival
of Neoplatonic philosophy in the Renaissance period (which Mc-
Gilchrist points to as an example of the creative collaboration of the
hemispheres).[48]

Something crucially important is happening here. In the act of
'returning' to the right hemisphere, which McGilchrist affirms is a
supreme act of creative imagination,[49] a third element is added to
the process of applying reason to intuitive understanding, which
partakes of, yet transcends, both hemispherical functions. We find

---

44 Ibid., 206.

45 McGilchrist, *The Master*, 178.

46 See Plato, *Phaedrus*, 246A–254E.

47 Pseudo-Plato, *Epinomis*, 986C–D, Plato, *Timaeus*, 47B–E.

48 McGilchrist, *The Master*, 298–329.

49 Ibid., 199.

this too in Plato, who provided for it in his creation of the world soul which is comprised of three parts: the same, the different, and a mixture comprising the two. In many traditions, the third eye is used as a metaphor for this enhanced vision,[50] which points to the inherent possibility of transcending dualism through seeing in a different way, produced by a co-operation of rational and noetic faculties. I would like to suggest that following McGilchrist's threefold epistemological unfolding is one way of re-enchanting our learning processes, in not identifying with either the right hemisphere's comfort zone (intuition and belief but no discrimination) or the left hemisphere's tunnel-vision (rational analysis but no intuitive sense), but pushing through to a *deeper* synthesis in which a new dimension of consciousness is born. Indeed, I experience McGilchrist's grand metaphor, in so far as it rests on scientific evidence *and* confirms what spiritual traditions have taught for millennia, as facilitating the very hermeneutic breakthrough that it advocates.

I will now take McGilchrist's model further by looking at the work of Jeffrey Kripal, whose vision of the 'third classroom' provides firm guidelines for how to create such a breakthrough in pedagogic context.[51]

THE GNOSTIC CLASSROOM

'The Human as Two is not just an ancient mystical doctrine. It is a universal neuroanatomical fact' states Kripal in an affirmation of McGilchrist's thesis, in his 2010 book *Authors of the Impossible*.[52] In his calling for a new pedagogy of the 'impossible', Kripal pushes methodological boundaries in the academic study of religion; that is, he refuses to be limited by either the faith approaches of theology or the explanatory models of rational critique and promotes a new kind of scholar who finds a third perspective, echoing McGilchrist's threefold relationship of hemispheres:

---

50   For example, Hinduism and Buddhism.

51   Kripal acknowledges his indebtedness to McGilchrist in *Comparing Religions*, 390.

52   Kripal, *Authors of the Impossible*, 265–66.

> An author of the impossible is someone who has gone beyond all of the dualisms of right and left, mystical and rational, faith and reason, self and other, mind and matter, consciousness and energy, and so on. An author of the impossible is someone who knows that the Human is Two *and* One.[53]

Furthermore, such writers, he says

> possess unusual powers of imagination, receptivity, discipline, and experience that allow them to enter religious worlds in a different way. For these scholars, academic method and personal experience cannot be so easily separated [...] They do not so much process religious data as unite with sacred realities, whether in the imagination, the hidden depths of the soul, or the very fabric of their psychophysical selves. In their subjective poles, these understandings become personally transformative, in their objective poles, they produce genuine insights into the nature of the phenomena under study. These are types of understanding that are at once passionate and critical, personal and objective, religious and academic. Such forms of knowledge are not simply academic, although they are that as well, and rigorously so. But they are also transformative, and sometimes soteriological. In a word, the knowledge of such a scholar approaches a kind of gnosis.[54]

What would a classroom which promoted such integrative scholarship look like? In *The Serpent's Gift* (2007), Kripal makes the distinction between what he calls the classrooms of 'faith' and 'reason', or 'sympathy' and 'doubt', in relation to his own discipline of religious studies.[55] The parallels here with the hemispheres are obvious, for the classroom of faith 'takes religious claims seriously and sympathetically' whilst that of reason 'proceeds on the assumption that all

---

53   Ibid., 270.

54   Kripal, *Roads of Excess, Palaces of Wisdom* (Chicago: Chicago University Press, 2001), 5.

55   Kripal, *The Serpent's Gift*, 22–24.

religious claims are not what they claim to be' and therefore require explanation or analysis according to various critical theories.[56] However, 'Let us never forget', he says, 'that many gifted individuals are quite capable of deriving reason from faith, and of fusing faith and reason into a deeper gnosis that appears to be much more radical and potentially transformative than any social-scientific or purely rational method.'[57] This deeper gnosis, he suggests, finds its place in a 'third classroom,' a 'luminous space', a classroom of 'gnostic epiphany' which is set apart from the 'real world' by its freedom of speech and intellectual daring.[58] He likens it to a 'meditative ritual space'[59] in which teachers and learners can embark on an intellectual adventure which seeks to place both faith and reason within a larger structural whole, as 'two poles of a deeper unity.'[60] Kripal lays out a radical methodological basis for his argument. He imagines the snake in the Garden of Eden as a heterodox 'wisdom figure' which could infuse scholarship with this gnostic impulse, an 'erotic, humanistic, comparative, and esoteric' wisdom which we can recognise within ourselves and act upon, in defiance of orthodox academic agendas.[61]

Kripal also clearly aligns himself with McGilchrist's plea for a return to metaphor as the language of the third classroom, and indeed in *Authors of the Impossible*, he upholds the mythic or metaphoric narrative as more conducive to our understanding of extraordinary human experience than theoretical models, because 'theological, mystical, and literary metaphors deliver far more imaginative impact. They are closer to the lived experience of things'.[62]

The Serpent's Gift prepares the ground for Kripal's latest book, *Comparing Religions* (2015) which offers a working syllabus for the journey through the classrooms of faith and reason to the gnostic emporium of what he terms *reflexivity*. Here we find the Platonic injunction to 'know thyself' reiterated in a bold new vision of transformative learning for the student of human culture. It is worth mentioning at this point that intuitive, autobiographical, and

---

56   Ibid., 23.
57   Ibid.
58   Ibid.
59   Ibid., 24.
60   Ibid., 13.
61   Ibid., 1.
62   Ibid., 258.

heuristic research methods, practice-based research, and the appeal to spirituality and mythopoesis in learning are all gaining hold in the transdisciplinary transformative learning movement situated in education and the social sciences, and these are all very healthy indications that the kind of hemispheric collaboration McGilchrist advocates is alive and well.[63] But Kripal is doing something different here, and it has to do with his suggestion that access to the third classroom is not democratic. This allies his project to the underlying rationale of the esoteric traditions, which situate 'gnostic' insight on a vertical trajectory of *initiatory* merit. Kripal clearly states that his curriculum is underpinned by a 'modal initiatory structure', stressing that '*the textual initiation, like any initiation, is not for everyone and so requires an initial taking of responsibility and a moral assent on the part of the student or reader*'[64] (my italics). He points to the 'existential risks' involved in having one's worldview deconstructed and challenged, and suggests that in general academic disciplines 'erase the sacred' through producing a whole series of signs which are 'much too certain of themselves' and hide or suppress their constructed nature. The preservation of the 'sacred sense' which imbues his writing, here as elsewhere, is what distinguishes it from the average textbook, as does his appeal to the erotic as an attractive force which draws us towards knowledge, towards what he terms 'the school of the more',[65] and in this he is faithful to Plato.

When the student reaches the third classroom, then, they are able to adopt a method 'which combines faithful and rationalist re-readings even as it moves beyond both'.[66] Seeing our many spiritual traditions and philosophies as beautiful, intricate stained glass windows, the student is led to perceive something else or more that is shining through, without taking one particular window as 'the truth' or analysing its components as opaque structures of the hu-

---

63   See for example, Peter Willis, Timothy Leonard, Anne Morrison, and Steven Hodge, eds., *Spirituality, Mythopoesis & Learning* (Mt. Gravat: Post Pressed, 2009); Rosemarie Anderson and William Braud, eds., *Transforming Self and Others through Research* (Albany: SUNY Press, 2011); Taylor, Cranton & Associates, eds., *Transformative Learning*.

64   Kripal, *Comparing Religions*, xii.

65   Ibid., 367.

66   Ibid.

man mind.[67] This 'genuinely new way of interpreting religion'[68] entails a double vision, which focuses on both 'culture and cognition' *and* 'the sun outside the cave'.[69] It is indeed this metaphorical sun outside which Kripal sees the purely 'rational re-readers' as denying, and which the 'reflexive re-reader' begins to see as the projective consciousness in which they themselves are participating. These gnostic researchers can easily move, amphibian-like, from outsider to insider, where 'looking at the looker'[70] in a reflexive flip allows for interpretation and criticality to emerge from a broader field of reference, one which embraces mystery, paradox, ambiguity, and wonder.

Kripal knows he is an academic heretic, and is proud of it. He is daring to leap over Tomlinson's fence, daring to open up to the right hemisphere in a world dominated for the past four hundred years by the agendas of the left. 'I no longer want to study mystical literature,' he announces, 'I now want to write it.'[71] In setting up this deepening, or liberation, of consciousness as an academic method, Kripal has inevitably provoked criticism from a more objectivist perspective, and it is worth digressing for a moment to see how this critique might inform us about the challenges of his project.

Kripal's Dutch colleague Wouter Hanegraaff[72] has offered a penetrating critique of *The Serpent's Gift*[73] and whilst I cannot examine this in detail now, I want to draw attention to some key points. Hanegraaff is a brilliant and keenly perceptive scholar who subscribes to a 'methodological agnosticism' in his historical scholarship of western esotericism.[74] He is a true scholar of the European scientific enlightenment, who in a new found spirit of freedom from religious authority, privileges what Geoffrey Cornelius has called an 'objectivist

---

67   Kripal, *Comparing Religions*, 391–92.

68   Ibid., 367.

69   Ibid., 391.

70   Ibid., 392.

71   Kripal, *The Serpent's Gift*, 15.

72   Hanegraaff is Professor of the History of Hermetic Philosophy and related currents at the University of Amsterdam.

73   Wouter Hanegraaff, 'Leaving the Garden (In Search of Religion): Jeffrey J. Kripal's Vision of a Gnostic Study of Religion', *Religion* 38 (2008): 259–76.

74   Ibid., 262 fn 5; *Esotericism and the Academy: Rejected Knowledge in Western Culture* (Cambridge: Cambridge University Press, 2012), 357.

mode that is at once empirical and analytic'.[75] Cornelius has pointed out that 'one of [this mode's] primary tasks is to complete the
overthrow of the authority and meaningfulness of symbolism' as a
method in its own right. From this perspective, Kripal is described
as a 'religionist', a term which is explained in Hanegraaff's book *Esotericism and the Academy: Rejected Knowledge in Western Culture.*[76]
Here Hanegraaff postulates a clear distinction between what he
calls 'historiography' and 'religionism', and says 'we are dealing with
two types of reasoning that are internally consistent but mutually
exclusive', insisting that there is no common term between them.[77]
His 'methodological agnosticism' upholds empirical and historical
verification as an ideal, surveying texts, trends, and influences in
a dispassionate and distanced gaze which is never self-referencing,
avoids all value judgements and intuitive hunches, and is impec-
cably thorough. This approach, in service to what Hanegraaff calls
'the truth of history',[78] is primarily that of the modern academy. Re-
ligionists on the other hand pursue the 'impossible dream' of 'the
history of truth', in basing their studies on theological, metaphysical
or psychological premises and searching for 'eternal and universal'
truth in historical sources.[79] I would observe that Hanegraaff's re-
ligionists (for example, C.G. Jung, Rudolf Otto, Mircea Eliade, or
Henry Corbin) acknowledge and participate in a worldview revealed by the texts they study, respond in a reflexive, imaginative,
and intuitive way and understand that something is in fact at stake
here for themselves, and indeed all human beings.

Interestingly, Corbin, whom Hanegraaff singles out as an ex-

---

75   Cornelius, *Field of Omens*, 24.

76   A brief definition of (western) esotericism would be a path of spiritual
      development towards a higher consciousness which sees nature and cos-
      mos as metaphor or symbol, and therefore as keys to unlocking a deep
      wisdom inaccessible to the rational mind. These traditions are rooted in
      the Gnostic, Hermetic, Neoplatonic, and Hellenistic world of the first
      centuries CE. Such paths do not require 'exoteric' religious forms, and
      have been traditionally repressed, hidden, or the preserve of heterodox
      spiritual movements. See Nicholas Goodrick-Clarke, *The Western Esoter-
      ic Traditions* (Oxford: Oxford University Press, 2008).

77   Hanegraaff, *Esotericism*, 301.

78   Ibid., 257–367.

79   Ibid., 296. For a full discussion of 'the history of truth' see 5–76.

treme 'religionist',[80] also claims the impossibility of reconciling two distinct epistemological domains when he laments 'angelology and sociology must remain forever foreign to one another',[81] that is, that there is a fundamental disjunct between human and divine sciences. We could frame the former as a horizontal trajectory that follows the progress of history, and the latter as a vertical one which seeks to lead the reader both to deeper knowledge of themselves and to the subjects at hand. But such a move, Hanegraaff suggests, cannot and should not announce itself as a *method* of studying religion as it is rather 'a religious and normative (meta)discourse about the nature of religion'.[82] In his opinion, scholars 'are in no position to make statements about ontology',[83] and he considers Kripal's gnostic study of religion to be 'based upon personal beliefs or preferences and not on "knowledge" in any scholarly sense'.[84]

In seeking to redeem 'gnostic' knowing in the academy (which traditionally has high stakes, as it facilitates liberation or salvation of the soul),[85] Kripal is clearly going against the grain of such enlightened liberal scholarship, but in my view there is a deeper question to be raised. In polarising 'methodological agnosticism' and 'religionism', Hanegraaff is creating a distinction which simply would not be made in the third classroom, as from the 'reflexive' position, it is impossible to abstract oneself from the 'ontological underpinnings' of one's own research orientation which are subjected to scrutiny. Kripal is contrasting the kind of religious 'truth claims' which result, (at best) in a lack of comparative awareness, and (at worst) in fundamentalism, blind faith, and violence,[86] with an intellectual sensibility which arises from understanding the value of religious metaphors to point *beyond* their individual contexts towards some unknown source of consciousness. If, as Kripal suggests, our minds are like filters, then it behoves us to move between the analysis of

---

80   Ibid., 301–02.

81   Henry Corbin, 'Divine Epiphany and Spiritual Birth in Ismailian Gnosis' in *Man and Transformation* ed. Joseph Campbell (New York: Pantheon, 1964), 158.

82   Hanegraaff, 'Leaving the Garden', 269.

83   Ibid., 270, fn. 19.

84   Ibid., 271.

85   Kripal, *The Serpent's Gift*, 4.

86   Ibid., 69.

these filters *and* what is coming through.[87]

As we have seen, for Kripal this reflexive move is the key to the door of the third classroom. I do not think, as Hanegraaff claims, that he is suggesting that the gnostic scholar is superior, although ironically Hanegraaff himself could certainly seem to be claiming such for his own agnostic position *vis-à-vis* the study of religion.[88] Rather, Kripal is trying to articulate the *change of register* that occurs with the shift to a right-hemisphere approach, not to 'convince us of some "new worldview"'.[89] Conviction and argument only happen in the classroom of reason, where 'the transcendent' or 'divine' become concepts alienated from both imagination and experience. Kripal urges scholars to break free from such a narrow vision by *locating* themselves beyond a conceptual way of thinking. Of course he cannot provide a 'precise ontological status or psychological structure' for the 'larger complexly conscious field' that starts manifesting in the altered states of consciousness studied, or even entered into, in the third classroom.[90] This is not the kind of language recognised by the right hemisphere. But the *images* of such a complex field can be contemplated, and *interpreted* from a variety of perspectives.

It is undoubtedly tricky, for from within the watertight world of the left hemisphere those who attempt to integrate emotional, intuitive or imaginative insights into their teaching or research often seem to be sacrificing rigour and accuracy, and indeed may lose their voices altogether, appearing dumb, stumbling, incoherent or woolly in the laser-sharp precision of the other's critical gaze.[91] It is to Kripal's great credit that he is never guilty of this, and indeed he enchants his readers through a quite brilliant gift of rhetorical elegance and humour. But perhaps the trickiest obstacle of all to negotiate in the modern academy is that of 'initiatory' knowing, a kind of knowing that is simply not a 'given' for all students. Kripal's gnostic researcher has an intuitive understanding of the difference between literal and symbolic, rational and imaginal modes of exploring religious experience which enables him or her to recognise the unique moment of resonance of metaphoric meaning as *qualitatively differ-*

---

87   Kripal, *Comparing Religions*, 391–92.

88   Hanegraaff, 'Leaving the Garden', 271.

89   Ibid., 273, fn. 26.

90   Hanegraaff, 'Leaving the Garden', 274; Kripal, *The Serpent's Gift*, 164.

91   McGilchrist, *The Master*, 184–89.

ent from theoretical understanding. This can only be glimpsed *to the extent to which* there is a desire to engage in the first place. From the agnostic point of view of course, such a knowing can only ever be a 'claim' to knowledge, despite the fact that the gnostic does *not* claim anything, nor reach out to appropriate some assumed truth which can never be proved in left hemisphere terms. On the contrary, he or she lets go of all claims, all judgements of good, bad, true or false, right or wrong, in an openness of spirit to something unnameable, unclaimable, undefinable yet possibly life-changing.[92]

THE TRUTH OF RELIGIOUS MYTH

My final author is philosopher and scientist Bernardo Kastrup, who is an extraordinarily lucid and penetrating thinker. Clearly indebted to (and endorsed by) Kripal,[93] he deconstructs materialist world-views in a cogent and intelligent argument in favour of the primacy of consciousness, or 'mind at large'. Identifying with 'essentialism'[94] as his metaphysical position, Kastrup may at times appear a little too dismissive of other speculations on the—possibly ultimately un-knowable—nature of reality. However, in *More Than Allegory* he ad-dresses directly the question of mythic or metaphoric knowing, and wrestles with the nature of the 'truth' that arises from that elusive 'aha!' moment of insight or realisation with a clarity and creativity that I have not found elsewhere.

Chittick quotes the Sufi tenet that 'verified and realised knowl-edge carries with it the self-evidence of certainty',[95] and the question of this 'truth' arising in what is popularly called the 'power of now' is a central theme of *More Than Allegory*. Like Kripal, Kastrup calls for a deeper awareness of the nature of consciousness itself as not being limited to the human brain, but as filtered through human imagi-nations to produce the images and stories that make up our great religious and symbolic mythologies and religious philosophies.[96]

---

92   See Kripal, *The Serpent's Gift*, 23–24; *Comparing Religions*, xii–xiii.

93   See Kripal, 'Introduction' to Kastrup, *More Than Allegory*, 1–9.

94   Essentialism, for Kastrup, is the assumption that consciousness is nondu-al, primary, and the ultimate source of all that is.

95   Chittick, *Imaginal Worlds*, 35.

96   Kastrup, *More Than Allegory*, 51.

True religious myths, says Kastrup, remind us of a dimension of ourselves that is transcendent but often estranged, projected outwards as superhuman 'others'.[97] Like Plato he speaks of the soul as a symbol of a timeless reality, and 'faith' as being open to this reality as a prerequisite for transformation. 'Faith is the sincere *emotional* openness to transcendent truths connoted by a story, beyond the superficial literal appearances of the story's denotations' he says.[98] How interesting that Kastrup's description of sacred myths as 'the only pointers we have to a form of salvation'[99] echoes Socrates' injunction about the soteriological function of myth *if it is believed in*.[100] The implication in both cases being that 'faith' and 'belief' are far from subjective opinions but involve an inner commitment to a myth as true, that is, of direct relevance and import for the individual.[101]

Kastrup maintains that fables, religions, folklore, philosophical, and even scientific narratives are all stories by which we make sense of the world, but they are never universally applicable truths even though they may become the dominant narratives for whole societies. His point is that the living truth of these stories *only* emerges when they resonate with the reader's deepest intuitions, it simply cannot be imposed from without in any meaningful way.[102] Plato describes such a moment as a 'spark of understanding and intelligence' flashing out at the point when sympathy arises between the soul and the text.[103] The key to accessing this kind of insight, which I would

---

97   Ibid., 127.

98   Ibid., 49.

99   Ibid., 46.

100   Plato, *Republic* x, 614c; *Phaedo*, 114D.

101   Kastrup, *More Than Allegory*, 46–47. See also C.G. Jung, *Memories, Dreams, Reflections* (London: Routledge & Kegan Paul, 1963), 337: 'Myth [...] can conjure up other images [than a dark pit of nothingness] [...] helpful and enriching pictures of life in the land of the dead. If he believes in them, or greets them with some measure of credence, he is being just as right or wrong as someone who does not believe in them. But while the man who despairs marches towards nothingness, the one who has placed his faith in the archetype follows the tracks of life and lives right into his death. Both, to be sure, remain in uncertainty, but the one lives against his instincts, the other with them.'

102   Kastrup, *More Than Allegory*, 46–50.

103   Plato, *Seventh Letter*, 344. As a personal anecdote, I will mention here that this happened to me on first reading Plato's Allegory of the Cave at

associate with the tropological sense, is to fully and passionately enter one's chosen myth *as if* it were true, in an ultimate sense, whilst also knowing on an intellectual level that its truth points to something beyond and is therefore not to be taken literally, or at least not only literally.[104] It is as though one's intellect gives the heart permission to have faith, whilst at the same time standing outside and observing oneself giving assent to its metaphorical status. This is, I believe, what Kripal means by the 'reflexive researcher', and Kastrup illustrates this point with a trenchant comment:

> When the Christian myth is honoured by being *emotionally* taken *as if* it were the literal truth, Christians live lives of meaning and transcendent significance, escaping the madness of a materialist society and coming closer to truth. When it is *intellectually* taken to *be* the literal truth, countless innocent people die burning at the stake or at the point of the crusader's sword.[105]

When entered into in this way, its truth will lie in its mirroring of ourselves and our own inner worlds but also in pointing us towards the deeper meanings of these worlds, so that we may transcend the limited opinions and illusions that fill our everyday 'consensus reality'. Thus, in Kastrup's analysis, religious myths can bring a powerful glimpse of a transcendent order into everyday life, *and* allow us to know ourselves more fully. *More Than Allegory* ends with a contemporary myth which Kastrup has conceived in order to illustrate the potential of human beings to expand their current level of conscious awareness. Like Kripal, he posits three stages in this process of awakening. Firstly, the state of delusion, in which humans do not even realise that they are creating their own worlds within a vast field of imagination. Secondly, the sense of deception, where critical reasoning skills are used to 'see through the tricks' of the first stage (but which only serve to 'buy in' to the equally deceptive tricks of scientism or other explanatory worldviews). Thirdly, all these de-

---

university. This metaphor had the effect of shifting my worldview from one of radical atheism to an openness to other ways of knowing beyond the rational mind.

104 Kastrup, *More Than Allegory*, 52.

105 Ibid., 53.

ceptions are realised, and one sees *oneself* as a magician pulling the strings, consciously and deliberately entering into the intricate web of life on earth but knowing that one is simply an actor in a play.[106] This, I would add, is reflexivity.

CONCLUSION

In Kastrup's distinction between 'explanatory truth' and 'perceptual truth'[107] we find, it seems to me, an analogy with Hanegraaff's distinction between historiography and religionism, or Ibn 'Arabi's imitation and realisation, or McGilchrist's 'representation' and 'presencing'.[108] To quote Kripal, the student in the 'gnostic classroom' or 'school of the more' 'wants it both ways' precisely *'because the human being really is both ways'* (his italics).[109] Honouring this relationship within the academy means, I believe, not marginalising transcendent, intuitive, unitive, or sacred experiences as somehow apart from secular discourse, or as only the domain of religion. It means starting with one's own sense, memory or image of 'gnostic' insight, furthering the critical analysis and interpretation of such events within historical, cultural, and social contexts, and subjecting them to reflexive scrutiny. Finally, it means being able to situate the symbolic, ritual, or practice-based contexts (including reading) in which such 'fierce' insights occur within a wider framework of human being and consciousness, referring to interdisciplinary source material and a wide range of theoretical positions, but also recognising that, in the end, metaphor leads further than fact.

I'll end with McGilchrist, who points to the dangers of reducing or subjecting encounters of passion, of enthusiasm, of insight, which he attributes to the right hemisphere, to the dumbing analysis of the left. 'Our passions, sense of humour, all metaphoric and symbolic understanding, all religious sense' he says, are too easily 'denatured' by becoming objects of focused attention.[110] However, he continues, 'it is the faculty of imagination, which comes into being between

---

106　Kastrup, *More Than Allegory*, 229–30.

107　Ibid., 104–05.

108　McGilchrist, *The Master*, 191–94.

109　Kripal, *Comparing Religions*, 392.

110　McGilchrist, *The Master*, 209.

these two hemispheres, which enables us to take things back from the world of the left hemisphere and make them live again in the right. It is in this way, not by meretricious novelty, that things are made truly new again.'[111]

I believe that such an integrative methodology, as a path of both re-enchantment and *knowledge* in academic study, can provide a space for a deep healing to take place whose ripples will spread far beyond the classroom. It can allow students to be *both* fiercely religious, *and* discerningly critical, and may even lead them to radically change their lives and the lives of others in service to the raising of consciousness in our conflict-ridden world.

Select bibliography

CHITTICK, William. *Imaginal Worlds: Ibn 'Arabi and the Problem of Religious Diversity*. Albany: SUNY Press, 2007.

CORNELIUS, Geoffrey. 'Field of Omens: A Study in Inductive Divination'. Unpublished PhD thesis, Canterbury: University of Kent, 2010.

HANEGRAAFF, Wouter. *Esotericism and the Academy: Rejected Knowledge in Western Culture*. Cambridge: Cambridge University Press, 2012.

_____. 'Leaving the Garden (in Search of Religion): Jeffrey J. Kripal's Vision of a Gnostic Study of Religion.' *Religion*, 38 (2008): 259–276.

KASTRUP, Bernardo. *Materialism is Baloney: How True Skeptics Know there is no Death and Fathom Answers to Life, the Universe, and Everything*. Winchester: Iff Books, 2014.

_____. *More Than Allegory: On religious truth, myth and belief*. Winchester: Iff Books, 2016.

KRIPAL, Jeffrey J. *Roads of Excess, Palaces of Wisdom*. Chicago: Chicago University Press, 2001.

_____. *The Serpent's Gift*. Chicago: Chicago University Press, 2007.

_____. *Authors of the Impossible: The Paranormal and the Sacred*. Chicago: Chicago University Press, 2010.

_____. *Comparing Religions*. Chichester: Wiley Blackwell, 2014.

---

111   Ibid., 199.

McGILCHRIST, Iain. *The Master and his Emissary*. New Haven, CT: Yale University Press, 2009.

PLATO. *Republic, Phaedrus*.

SCOTT, Timothy. 'Symbolic Exegesis, Cosmology, and Soteriology'. Paper presented to the 3rd Annual *Alternative Expressions of the Numinous* conference, University of Queensland, 15th–17th August 2008.

STRUCK, Peter. *Birth of the Symbol: Ancient Writers at the Limits of Their Texts*. Princeton: Princeton University Press, 2004.

TOMLINSON, Gary. *Music in Renaissance Magic*. Oxford: Oxford University Press, 1989.

Stepping into Sacred Texts

How the Jesuits Taught Me to Read the Bible

ROBERT BOWIE

THIS CHAPTER WEAVES TOGETHER several elements around the question of how public education should teach students about sacred texts. The first element is education research since 2000, which raises critical questions about an undue emphasis on the use of proof texts in exams. This emphasis distorts the impression given of the role of sacred texts in religion. The second element which illustrates the degree of variance is a recounted experience of using Ignatian spiritual exercises with secondary age students. This involved deep learning and encounter with a sacred narrative, and contrasts radically with the utilisation of texts in external exams. Methods of experiential religious education (hereafter RE) which had come to focus in the 1990s had sought to respiritualise the study of sacred texts in British RE, and there were clearly attempts in the 1980s and 1990s to develop a different educative approach in schools. These observations about curriculum development in RE constitute a kind of classroom *participatory turn* similar to that observed in university studies of religion and spirituality. This turn challenges norms in academic learning and offers important insights into the developments in school studies.[1] Questions to do with the nature of the study of religion and sacred texts and the kind of learning that is privileged seem pertinent across the university/school boundaries.

---

1   Jorge Ferrer & Joseph Sherman, eds., *The Participatory Turn: Spirituality, Mysticism, Religious Studies* (Albany: SUNY Press, 2008), 1–78.

WHAT SHOULD PUBLIC EDUCATORS TEACH
PEOPLE ABOUT MAKING SENSE OF SACRED TEXTS?

There is today a mass availability of sacred texts, with higher than ever levels of literacy and an internet age which provides increasing access to translations. Globally, religion remains prominent in public life. These writings have longevity. Their ancient origins and modern applications demand scrutiny. How and why have these texts lasted and continued to be a factor in life? I would argue that their worthiness of study is easier to justify than their omission from the curriculum, which would constitute the opposite of education—a choice *not* to learn, venture, or enquire. These ancient words have had such a profound influence on human life throughout the ages, that surely they warrant *hermeneutic* enquiry.

But why try to educate people in the process of making sense of such texts? Religious education might be construed as an opportunity to disseminate the meanings, to illuminate what knowledge the texts have for the masses, but for many years RE has had an ambition that students should interpret texts. However, given the mysteriousness of sacred texts in their traditions, and the peculiarity of the methods by which such texts may be investigated within religion, is such interpretation feasible, or indeed proper in plural and diverse classrooms, if the process of interpretation involves a spiritual dimension? Perhaps students should not be expected to make meaning from texts. Better to create a *second order study*—a tempting route to avoid the difficulties of engaging with sacred texts, where commitments to traditions of religious enquiry may require exclusivity. Easier then, to look only at how other people make meaning from the texts (how does a human being use a text to be an inspiration for an action, an attitude, or a belief?) rather then enter into a direct project to encounter the text itself. This *second order study* dominates the religious education curriculum in exam-level English state schools as students discuss texts that might inspire Christians to campaign against abortion, to permit or prohibit divorce, to allow or abolish capital punishment, or to uphold a belief in one thing or another. Public education in England teaches children that sacred texts are sources for behaviours, attitudes, actions, beliefs and ultimately ways of life, and that their significance is found in what they cause people to do and believe. This is in part due to an emphasis on philosophy and ethics which leads the focus towards moral judgement, and the function of a text as a reason for that judgement. But such readings imply a causal relation between the source and the result of the impact of the source. This relation dominates the study of religion and texts at schools which affects the 284,000 students in English state schools who take Religious Studies qualifications at secondary-school exam level.[2] There is also a historical legacy for RE in English schools: a fear of a confessional imposition that used to be levelled on all children, even those in schools with no religious foundation or character.

However, this *second order study* sidesteps the first order enquiry —the enquiry into sacred texts, the step into the possibility that they offer meaning, revelation, enlightenment, or encounter. In fact, the *second order study* shackles RE to a subset of social studies. This is valuable in itself, but specifically avoids the genesis factor—the element that *leads to* this *second order study*, and means that the heart of religious experience, the possibility of an inner encounter or direct revelation, is relegated and moved out of sight. This problem is well illustrated through many research undertakings over the last twenty years, a few of which I will use as examples.

RESEARCH ON THE BIBLE IN RELIGIOUS EDUCATION CLASSES

There are problems with the way Christianity is taught in state-funded secondary schools in England. Ofsted, the body commissioned to examine teaching and learning in secondary schools, repeatedly raises concerns that the teaching of Christianity, as they observe it in classrooms, leaves pupils with a poor understanding of the religion. Ofsted published a number of religious education subject reports in 2007, 2010, and 2013 which note some examples of good teaching of Christianity, but an overall 'teaching about Christianity [was] one of the weakest aspects of RE provision'[3]. The handling of sacred texts in RE lessons is a key area of concern, but other research has delved into this matter revealing it is part of a deeper issue.

---

2   (www.jcq.org.uk/examination-results/gcses).

3   Ofsted, *Religious Education: Realising the Potential* (London: HMSO, 2013), 9.

The *Biblos* project (1996–2004), based at Exeter university, observed that the Bible was disappearing from RE and perceived as a text only relevant to committed Christians. It had no value of illumination or inspiration of wisdom for others, with teachers reluctant to address it. Researchers found that biblical meanings were often secularised at classroom level—spiritual meanings were set aside so learners struggled to achieve a theological understanding.[4] Students were also often ambivalent to the Bible, and researchers found that secular interpretations were made of the text. For example, a parable might be interpreted as a carrier for a common moral message with more mysterious, provoking, or controversial meanings evaded. The *Biblos* research reports suggest teachers would tend towards these common messages.[5]

More recently Julia Ipgrade's work has reconfirmed some of the *Biblos* findings. She observed a preference for seeing how texts applied, or manifested themselves in the world, rather than proclaimed kinds of religious understanding. She discovered that students were more amenable or receptive to the manifestations of issues in wider life, than the proclamation of truths linked to theological understandings.[6] In the classroom, the purpose of looking at the text is to see how it reflects life; the text points to the world, it does not point to anything revelatory beyond the world. It does not speak *to* the human experience but only *of* the human experience. In the study of the Christian Gospels this renders the concept of 'Good News' somewhat irrelevant.

In a major study, funded by the Government, Jackson (et al.) scrutinised resources used to support students in RE. It found these resources were not detailed or profound enough in historical and

---

4   Terence Copley, Rob Freathy & Karen Walshe, *Teaching Biblical narrative* (Exeter: University of Exeter Press, 2004).

5   Terence Copley, Rob Freathy, Sarah Lane, Karen Walshe, and Claire Copley, *On the Side of the Angels: The Third Report of the Biblos Project*. (Exeter: University of Exeter Press, 2004); Terence Copley, *Echo of Angels: The First Report of the Biblos Project* (Exeter: University of Exeter Press, 1998).

6   Julia Ipgrave, 'From Storybooks to Bullet Points: Books and the Bible in Primary and Secondary Religious Education', *British Journal of Religious Education* 35.3 (2013): 264–81.

theological areas about Christianity.[7] They did not explain different approaches to interpreting the Bible—single interpretations of
Christianity were presented to the exclusion of others. In some cases
theological concepts were vague or badly handled, leaving readers
more confused than when they started.

These problems in British public education get worse as children
progress through the schooling system and are embedded into the
educational ecology of government policy, examination boards,
publishers, and their resources. *Does Religious Education Work?* was
a multidimensional study of RE,[8] examining practices linked to the
use of textbooks and public exams. The exams required key texts to
be learned and these were written about in textbooks (sometimes
by senior examiners). The textbooks contained assurances that their
content was precisely what the exams required. This created a closed
ecology of the examination system and the resource for the exam
which led to an *exam version* of the religion which students sometimes specifically referred to and distinguished from their *real* encounter with religion. The research also found students articulating
scepticism about the textbook authors' representation of religion.
Sophisticated attempts at deeper learning from the texts were sur-
plus to requirements, sometimes added by teachers but not required,
expected, or encouraged by the exams.

Perhaps the most widely identified and criticised practice is the
use of proof texts in learning. *Does Religious Education Work?* found
examples of isolated quotations being learned in order to justify
views, something identified by Ofsted in 2007 which was observed
as leading to 'standard, mechanistic responses rather than thoughtful engagement with the issues'.[9] The learning of textbook quotations
for examination purposes was the topic of a close study by David

---

7   Robert Jackson, Julia Ipgrave, Mary Hayward, Paul Hopkins, Nigel Fan-
      court, Mandy Robbins, Leslie Francis and Ursula McKenna, *Materials
      used to Teach about World Religions in Schools in England* (London: DCSF,
      2010), 99.

8   James Conroy, David Lundie, Robert Davis, Vivienne Baumfield, L. Phil-
      ip Barnes, Tony Gallagher, Kevin Lowden, Nicole Bourque and Karen
      Wenell, *Does Religious Education Work? A Multi-dimensional Investiga-
      tion* (London: Bloomsbury Publishing, 2015).

9   Ofsted, *Making Sense of Religion* (London: HMSO, 2007), 14.

Horrell and Anna Davis,[10] who focused on the topic of religion and the environment and saw how 'proof-texting' to linked Biblical texts was used as the reason for certain Christian beliefs—for instance, a duty of care to the environment. They concluded that religious education 'runs the risk of reducing Biblical texts to points of reference that support some aspect of Christian belief, without inviting consideration of the diversity of contemporary Christian perspectives and the extent to which that diversity stems in part precisely from different, often competing, interpretations of Biblical texts.'[11]

Most recently, evidence of the impact of GCSE question structures has come from research by Trevor Cooling, Beth Green, Andrew Morris, and Lynn Revell.[12] They found that even in schools which chose to set exam papers focussed on scripture (such as St Mark's Gospel), there were difficulties, caused in part by the exam's approach which encouraged for-and-against arguments to be outlined in student answers. Proof texts were used as a key tool for these debates, to provide reasons for viewpoints, which became central to the clash between oppositional views within religion, or the clash between atheistic and religious opinions. One teacher, when discussing assisted dying, found that her approach was directed towards the exam specification, and the types of question and answers it encouraged. She said: 'a Christian wouldn't necessarily sit there and go "fors and against". We'd actually look at what the Bible would say and the actual meaning and how we talk to people and how we discuss issues with people, looking at it from that angle, rather than the clinical "fors and against."'[13] This black and white approach was leading pupils to imagine that Christian ethics and Christians' use of the Bible were mainly concerned with defeating opponents in academic arguments about values.

---

10   David G. Horrell & Anna Davis, 'Engaging the Bible in GCSE and A Level Religious Studies: Environmental Stewardship as a Test Case', *British Journal of Religious Education* 36.1 (2014): 72–87.

11   Horrell & Davis, 'Engaging the Bible', 76–77.

12   Trevor Cooling, Beth Green, Andrew Morris, & Lynn Revell, *Christian Faith in English Church Schools: Research Conversations with Classroom Teachers* (Oxford: Peter Lang, 2016).

13   Cooling, Green, Morris, and Revell, *Christian Faith in English Church Schools*, 79.

The *Biblos* study found that a more positive attitude towards the Bible was associated with a greater level of Biblical literacy. It also found that RE was the main source of Biblical knowledge, and the only context in which every child in public education in the UK is inducted into 'theological' discourse about Biblical narratives. RE frames how students come to understand what sacred texts are used for, except that what they learn they are used for has more to do with the structuring of exams and the cultivation of exam-ready text books, than a deep study of the meaning of the texts. There is a general narrowing of learning opportunity through the age phases of school education. Texts may offer an insightful narrative through which people may be inspired to live meaningful lives, but far too often researchers found that the texts are taught as serving other purposes—such as providing reasons for action or feeding oppositional debates—or overplayed with secularised meanings. The scope of learning is then reduced and what is being learned is distorted. The more profound encounter (and potential entry points to encounter) that religious people experience with these sources of wisdom is not sufficiently well explored and consequently, key aspects of religious life are badly treated. Education that views sacred texts as tools in a battle to win arguments places conflict at the heart of what evaluation of religion is supposed to be. Conflict studies replace deep enquiry. The role of sacred texts in prayer, worship, in meditation, or as narrative sources of living wisdom pass out of sight. This should be a major focus of study in making sense of why texts might come to impact on other dimensions of life, and how people engage with those texts to experience profound insights that are deeper than win/lose debates.

LEARNING THROUGH STEPPING INTO THE NARRATIVE

The room has four people: three students and a tutor, who is also a Jesuit priest. It is a living room, not a formal classroom. A candle is burning on a table between them. The tutor begins some stilling exercises similar to the kind used in meditation, mindfulness, and relaxation techniques. The exercises contain elements of silence, a focus on the senses (what you can hear and feel), and breathing. This is taking place after a busy school day. The atmosphere in the room is calm. The students are asked to set aside thoughts and emotions from the day and if those thoughts and emotions return to the mind they are to be acknowledged and set aside once more. There is a focus on settling of the mind and feelings, pushing aside influences, and an openness to whatever might come.

Then comes a narration. The tutor describes a scene: a hot sun, a dry sandy road, a lively village with a crowd surrounding some-one. The narration begins voyeuristically but there is a transition into an imagined setting. The language shifts from the third person to the first person. The students are invited to locate themselves in the scene. The emphasis on feelings that were related to the room and surroundings, is now placed on the narrative—the hot sun and the excited crowd. The tutor invites the students to imagine the feel-ings of the characters in the story, and imagine the scene from their perspective. Questions are asked: 'How do you feel? Do you want to see him? Do you want him to see you?' These are not to be an-swered aloud but simply pondered. The narrative slips into a more familiar reading from a Gospel (Luke 19:1ff.) after which more open questions are asked: 'Do you want to say something to him? How do you feel when he calls your name? How might you respond to what he says?' This is a recollection of mine from the late 1980s in a Jesuit secondary school in England.

Sometimes when writing about how texts are handled, and discussing the pedagogical theory and practice of a particular ap-proach, it is easy to make assumptions about what is conveyed by a phrase like 'Ignatian spiritual exercise', but I have tried here to give a clear example by describing it. This is a form of Bible reading where listeners actively step into the story. It is an internally imag-ined reading which provokes questions. This need not necessarily lead to a discussion about what a text might mean or even what it might mean for you or me, but it is a moment when the minds and feelings of the listeners are provoked in an inter-textual encounter. It reaches deeply within the person and beyond the immediate lo-cation of the room, through the imaginal framing in the mind. It does not prescribe a meaning, a result, a transferred piece of knowl-edge that could be easily written down. It is experiential and no written account or recollection, even this one, can do full justice to the moment.

The method used is based on a spiritual exercise practised by Christians, developed by a religious order called the *Society of Jesus*, or as they are commonly known, the Jesuits. The practice is part of a process of discernment, a method through which one sets aside the immediate layers of emotion and feeling and thought, in search of a deeper listening and response. It comes from a text written in the 16ᵗʰ century, the *Spiritual Exercises* which were written by the former Spanish knight and founder of the Jesuits, Ignatius of Loyola in 1548.[14] The exercises described a process of contemplation and meditation using imagination and involving all of the senses. A few words from Ignatius himself gives a strong flavour of the method:

> Here it is to be noted that, in a visible contemplation or meditation—as, for instance, when one contemplates Christ our Lord, Who is visible—the composition will be to see with the sight of the imagination the corporeal place where the thing is found which I want to contemplate. I say the corporeal place, as for instance, a Temple or Mountain where Jesus Christ or Our Lady is found, according to what I want to contemplate.[15]

The exercises have been practised since the 16ᵗʰ century within the Order but have become more widely used in modern times. They were made popular in the English-speaking world by the Jesuit Gerard W. Hughes in a modern classic of spiritual guidance.[16] Most recently they have been made even more accessible through a daily podcast called *Pray as you go*.[17] This includes music and a short reading followed by open questions which invite the participant to think reflectively about what provocation, feeling, or thought arises as a result of the exercise. I have encountered forms of this exercise run by school tutors, university chaplains, and retreat leaders, and

---

14   Ignatius of Loyola, *The Spiritual Exercises of St. Ignatius of Loyola,* trans. Fr. Elder Mullan, S.J. (1548; New York: P.J. Kennedy and Sons, 1914).

15   Ignatius of Loyola, *The Spiritual Exercises,* 26.

16   Gerard W. Hughes, *God of Surprises* (London: Barton, Longman and Todd, 1985).

17   *Pray as you go* is a short 'podcast': a daily downloadable audio meditation which has a Biblical reading that is introduced through music and reflective questions. It is designed to be listened to by commuters on their way to work or by people who have busy lives; an interpretation of the Ignatian Spiritual Exercises for the modern age.

now through the podcast with my mobile phone. This kind of en-quiry into a text is quite different from the mode of study that young people will encounter in their public education. In this method the listeners are invited to step into the narrative, to become a part of it and take on the surroundings and emotions of the narrative. Here the text is not treated as a source of the past which gives reasons for actions, but as a way of connecting to a different kind of knowl-edge, which is likely to produce very different sorts of responses in comparison to the kinds of questions that ask for what a quotation might mean, or how this quotation might cause a Christian to act in a certain way. These moments are provocative, mysterious and un-predictable. There is a sense of being *with* the text in a mystical prac-tice, through which a deeper insight into both the divine and the self can be accessed in the mind—opening up the possibility of an active imagination approach.[18] There is no explicit doctrinal requirement or confession expected of the listener, except an open attentiveness, a willingness to step into the narrative.

I am not arguing here that all public education should teach sa-cred texts using this particular method, but rather to illustrate the extent of the divergence between one common kind of exploration of sacred texts within a spiritual practice, and the kind of study of sacred texts that seems to be increasingly common and normative at exam level in public education. The two are drifting apart and a student who has been educated in religious studies at secondary school level might indeed find the kind of practice described above incomprehensible. The kind of learning she may have experienced would do little to prepare her for this kind of activity, and is unlikely to help her make sense of this kind of activity. Ethical and philo-sophical debates about questions of religion are valuable elements of a curriculum, but they do not exhaust the study of religion and nor do they give insights into the power of sacred texts in the lives of

---

18   There is a long tradition of Christian engagement of texts using spiritual methods that might be categorised as 'active imagination' methods. *Lec-tio divina* (Latin for 'divine reading') is a traditional Benedictine practice of scriptural reading, meditation and prayer dating from the 6th century with roots going back even further. It is intended to promote communion with God and to increase the knowledge of God's Word. For a modern account of the practice see David Foster, *Reading with God: Lectio Divina* (London: Bloomsbury, 2005).

those who live through and with them.

IMAGINAL EDUCATION IN SCHOOLS AND THE PARTICIPATORY TURN OF ACADEMIA

What is the learning objective? What is the aim? What is the learning outcome? Applying these kinds of questions to Ignatian spiritual exercises is difficult. It is not that there is no objective, no knowledge, no impact, but that these things are nuanced, personally discerned, layered and possibly will continue to be processed over many years. The *practice* is arguably as important as any 'outcome', and certainly my own experiences of this technique continue to trigger significant thoughts despite the passage of nearly thirty years. I can still remember particular meditations, particular experiences and encounters from my youth, which I continue to reflect on and interpret. No end of term test or quiz can possibly capture what was learned in those moments. The insights gained or emotions conjured speak to the deeper mysteries and require a different order of language than that deployed in, for example, proof text reasoning. The contrast between these experiences and the sort of thing commonly depicted and encouraged in examinations on religious studies is clear. The example illustrates the divergence between how texts are studied and taught, and the practice of meditative immersion in narratives from Christian life.

Historically, RE in England has been sensitive to the kind of knowing and learning that takes place in these spiritual readings of text. The book, *New Methods in RE Teaching: An Experiential Approach* by John Hammond, David Hay, Jo Moxon, Brian Netto, Kathy Raban, Ginny Straugheir and Christ Williams,[19] introduced a method of religious education that saw limitations in the kind of learning that concentrated on external and public phenomena of religion. The method instead provided exercises and techniques designed to help students learn about someone else's experience of the world. This required a very serious study of how a person under-

---

19   John Hammond, David Hay, Jo Moxon, Brian Netto, Kathy Raban, Ginny Straugheir & Christ Williams, *New Methods in RE Teaching: An Experiential Approach* (Harlow: Oliver and Boyd, 1990).

stands their own inner experience, and they consider this spiritual dimension of RE as important as the social and political dimensions. The practices and activities in the book use many of the techniques I described in my example of Ignatian spirituality (some appear in Gerard Hughes' *God of Surprises*), the focus of those activities being an appreciation of the inner world of the student as a stepping stone to appreciating the inner world of human beings as a whole. Instructions in the book, which was designed as a tool for teachers to use in the classroom, includes specific guidance on stilling, and a variety of dramatic and meditative readings including guided visualisations and dramatised activities designed to sensitise pupils to different experiences and cultivate empathy. These were organised to introduce and induct students and then build on the development of a range of skills to help them move into deeper, more complex experiential activities. They were not wedded to a particular tradition, and the vast majority of the activities were structured so as not to reference a specific religious narrative. This kind of experiential approach to religious education is offering a kind of learning that is far from that which religious studies exams require.

The observations made by the scholars such as Jorge Ferrer and Jacob Sherman in their book *The Participatory Turn: Spirituality, Mysticism, Religious Studies*, charted the *participatory turn* in academic religious studies. In their account *the turn* seeks to raise new questions that previous modes of study had omitted, and I suggest that the situation in the RE school curriculum in England reflects many of the traits that they observe. Ferrer and Sherman observe that previous methods of academic study focus on linguistic and conceptual studies of religion, asserting public language over private experience, and leaving mystical experience and mystical language aside. The focus of the study of religion was located in the realm of signs, rather than belief, inner states, and religious experiences. An analytical branch of this kind of academic study sees religions as a conceptual framework reflecting the focus on arguments and reasons for arguments, attitudes, and practices in the kind of study of religion required for public exams for schools. Ferrer and Sherman wrote, 'In the disenchanted world of post/modernity, the sacred has been de-transcendentalized, relativized, contextualized, and diversified but, most fundamentally, assimilated into linguistic expression'.[20] The sacred is linguistified, the philosophy of the sign is pre-eminent.

Ferrer and Sherman both identify and argue that the participatory turn seeks to problematise Western epistemological frameworks and recognise culturally specific criteria that determine what counts as valid knowledge. This realises 'a multiplicity of valid ways of knowing and the consequent challenge to the very idea of universal reason now exposed as being (conveniently) shaped by the assumptions of the Enlightenment project—a challenge issued by feminists decades ago'.[21] A key feature of their general criticism is that new categories are used to classify and explain the focus of study, categories of learning or hallmarks of knowledge which are asserted over and in place of categories that emerge from the spiritual traditions themselves. In so doing, religious studies removes religious phenomena from the context of their social embodiment and resituates them within conceptual universes of our own designing. This is characteristic of the criticism made by researchers investigating the use of the Bible in schools, where non-religious secularised accounts, explanations, and meanings are offered as the sole keys to interpretation.

Just as the authors of *New Methods in RE Teaching: An Experiential Approach* sought to more deeply appreciate the inner world, so Ferrer and Sherman identify increasing numbers of Western scholars who are 'coming out' as spiritual practitioners. They urge a move towards evaluating all knowledge claims '—etic and emic, insider and outsider, rational and transnational, naturalistic and supernaturalistic—through validity standards of both dominant and marginal Western and non-Western epistemologies in whatever measure may be appropriate according to the context of the enquiry and the type of knowledge claims'.[22] They argue that through a revaluation of emic epistemologies, extralinguistic variables (e.g., supernatural entities, spiritual energies, archetypal principles) are constitutive elements and real referents of religious knowledge and experience. They suggest the participatory turn requires an affirmation of the immanence of the sacred and the resacralisation of everyday life, together with the use of embodied religious experience to significantly shape the visionary imagination and language of the practitioner,

---

20   Ferrer & Sherman, *The Participatory Turn*, 6.

21   Ibid., 8.

22   Ibid., 10.

mystic or scholar. The goal of enquiry becomes ontological transformation and relation, and religious texts are resacralised.

Accompanying these themes of the participatory turn, is an explosion of interest around spirituality studies in which self-implication and transformation are constitutive methodological elements, and which challenge the trope that metaphysical claims of truth should be properly understood as statements about language. They also challenge studies that consider any metaphysical referent or transcendental signifier to be impossible and inaccessible, or which claim that the study of religion should take on an agnostic and supposedly neutral position, with the supernatural bracketed out or denied from the very beginning.

The turn offers an alternative mode of learning. *Participatory knowing* is creative multidimensional cognition, a fascination with the mysterious and an emphasis on feeling, intuition, and æsthetic experience incorporating the whole of human attributes into the study of religion for personal edification and the attainment of more reliable or comprehensive knowledge about religious phenomena. As Ferrer and Sherman suggest,

> The more human faculties participate in spiritual knowing, the greater the dynamic congruence between inquiry approach and studied phenomena and the more grounded in, coherent with, or attuned to the ongoing unfolding of reality and the mystery will the gained knowledge potentially be. [...] [M]ultidimensional cognition is connected to the participatory emphasis on spiritual creativity [...] Contemporary participatory approaches, we suggest, seek to enact with body, mind, heart, and consciousness a creative spirituality that lets a thousand spiritual flowers bloom.[23] However, this does not entail an uncritical approach. Spiritual visions may be illusory and '[P]articipatory study of religion needs to be hermeneutically critical of oppressive, repressive, and dissociative religious beliefs, attitudes, practices, and institutional dynamics.'[24]

---

23   Ibid., 41.

24   Ibid., 42.

It is clear how these proposals, arising from the academic discipline of Religious Studies, can be related to the teaching of RE in schools. A project of seeking to re-enchant the academy in some way, which here could mean the resacralisation or re-spiritualisation of learning, is not restricted to universities but forms part of a wider education issue. If over 280,000 students in England are introduced to the study of religion (at upper secondary level) through a framework that distances or discounts forms of learning that are central to practices of religious and spiritual traditions, then the project of developing academic practices at university, with many of those same students, will face great challenges. It will first need to de-indoctrinate students from the lesson that serious *higher* study precludes these kinds of learning.

CONCLUSION

The discussion of the *participatory turn* in academia frames the account of school RE in England. The debate that now sees new developments in academic practice, challenging the discourse of what is proper academic study, mirrors the oscillations in school curricula between spiritualised and more positivistic approaches to learning, and also between a focus on the signs of religion and the focus on what it is that religion seeks to discern and be. It is an illustration of the porous borders between academia and schooling.

The educational research considered here does not paint a comprehensive picture of everything taking place in RE classrooms, but it does show an increasing emphasis on a narrowing approach to learning in RE, as students prepare for and take externally recognised exams. *Proper* or *higher* study of religion becomes increasingly focused on the use of texts in arguments, to prove or disprove beliefs, to justify or challenge practices, attitudes and behaviours, in an argumentatively-framed conceptual educational ballpark. Spiritual forms of learning do not register and are implicitly viewed as antithetical to real *academic* learning. There are a number of probable reasons for this. First, the kind of spiritual activities and learning described in this chapter would probably attract accusations of indoctrination at a time when publicly-funded English schools are under increasing pressure to demonstrate they are doing all they can to help children resist radicalisation. The popular suspicion with which religion is viewed could be one reason for the argumentative and propositional approach to studying religion. This suspicion confuses spiritual development with a narrowing radicalisation. Second, any spiritual forms of learning would be subject to the criticism of being irrational. This is because of an overly prescriptive conception of knowledge that reduces religious phenomena to matters of human nature and history exclusively, and learning as transmission of propositional facts. The idea that aspects of human life cannot be adequately explained by reason, or that there is something more, or genuinely fantastic, is out of the question.[25] This approach would also undermine forms of learning in the arts and music.

The kind of study found at exam level distances pupils from the methods used in spiritually sensitised forms of learning, such as the methods used to step into texts and encounter the narrative through feeling and imagination. Those who advocated experiential religious education in the late 1980s and early 1990s were aware of this problem, and sought to find an approach to learning that was framed in terms of a greater awareness of the students' inner world and therefore the possibility of becoming sympathetic to the inner worlds of other people. Though their insights did not go on to shape RE qualifications, they do seem to have identified the demand for the kind of learning that is popularly understood through the mindfulness meditation movement—a movement that is present in English schools. I am convinced that it is possible for the kinds of reflexive, imagination-engaged spiritual learning that are practiced by religious traditions to be recognised and explored in many different school contexts, as a much needed counterweight to the current approach propagated through the exam culture.

Select bibliography

Cooling, T., B. Green, A. Morris, and L. Revell, *Christian Faith in English Church Schools: Research Conversations with Classroom Teachers*. Oxford: Peter Lang, 2016.

---

25   Jeffrey J. Kripal describes this as the distinction between rational re-readings and reflexive re-readings, with the latter leaving open the possibility of something beyond the rational account, in *Comparing Religions* (Oxford: Wiley Blackwell, 2014), 366ff.

COPLEY, T., *Echo of Angels: the first report of the Biblos project*. Exeter: University of Exeter Press, 1998.

_____., R. FREATHY, S. LANE, K. WALSHE, and C. COPLEY, *On the Side of the Angels: The Third Report of the Biblos Project*. Exeter: University of Exeter Press, 2004.

_____., R. FREATHY, R. and K. WALSHE, *Teaching Biblical narrative*. Exeter: University of Exeter Press, 2004.

CONROY, J., D. LUNDIE, R. DAVIS, V. BAUMFIELD, P. BARNES, T. GALLAGHER, K. LOWDEN, N. BOURQUE, and K. WENELL, *Does Religious Education Work? A Multi-dimensional Investigation*. London: Bloomsbury, 2015.

FERRER, J. & J. SHERMAN, eds. *The Participatory Turn: Spirituality, Mysticism, Religious Studies*. Albany: SUNY Press, 2008.

FOSTER, D., *Reading with God: Lectio Divina*. London: Bloomsbury, 2005.

HAMMOND, J., D. HAY, J. MOXON, B. NETTO, K. RABAN, G. STRAUGHEIR, and C. WILLIAMS, *New Methods in RE Teaching: An Experiential Approach*. Harlow: Oliver and Boyd, 1990.

HORRELL, D. and A. DAVIS., 'Engaging the Bible in GCSE and A Level Religious Studies: Environmental Stewardship as a Test Case'. *British Journal of Religious Education* 36.1 (2014): 72–87.

IPGRAVE, J., 'From storybooks to bullet points: books and the bible in primary and secondary religious education'. *British Journal of Religious Education* 35.3 (2013): 264–281.

JACKSON, R., J. IPGRAVE, M. HAYWARD, P. HOPKINS, N. FANCOURT, M. ROBBINS, L. FRANCIS, and U. MCKENNA, *Materials used to Teach about World Religions in Schools in England*. London: DCSF, 2010.

IGNATIUS OF LOYOLA. *The Spiritual Exercises of St. Ignatius of Loyola*, translated from the autograph by Father Elder Mullan, 1548. New York: P.J. Kennedy & Sons, 1914.

OFSTED. *Religious Education: Realising the Potential*. London: HMSO, 2013.

Enchanted Engineering

Reintegrating the Roots

LISA MCLOUGHLIN

> Technology does nothing to dispel the shadows at the edge of
> things. The ghost-story world still hovers at the limits of vision,
> making things stranger, darker, more magical, just as it always
> has [...][1]

BEGINNING TO COURT ENCHANTMENT, maybe I imagine a story.
I am sitting in a pool of moonlight in a stone circle. I feel the
power of the moon, and the stars are familiar to me. I put a wooden
stake carefully in the ground, moving it as its shadow crosses the
centre. Later a new stone will take its place...I am an engineer; my
secrets are writ in the language of stone.

Anything built on the physical plane is created by an engineer.
Engineers seek the elegance they see in the rest of nature—planes
shaped like eagle rays; adhesives that mimic gecko feet; robots that
move like snakes. To engineer is to attempt to be as efficient and
beautiful as the rest of the world, to find our place and meet our
needs within the universe's flow. Engineers spend three to five years
training so that what they call into being can be right: the right size,
the right material, the right purpose. This seeking of rightness, of fit,
makes engineering a hunt for answers to big questions in discrete
projects, a hunt for the truths of natural law and of where humans fit
into the scheme of things.

We engineers do this according to what we are taught: an incli-
nation towards order, expressed in our own language of maths and

---

1   Neil Gaiman, 'Ghosts in the Machines', *The New York Times*, 31st October
2006.

graphics. If the universe is a web, then engineers wish to be the spider at the centre, spinning radii at regular intervals, and neatening up the place. At first glance, this does not appear very enchanting. But within this process of ordering, of alignment, is an implicit understanding of the world as disordered, chaotic, haunted by the underlying tangle of roots. Engineering, like art, like shamanism, is a method of engaging with this tangle, bringing it into our reality, and manifesting it in a more tangible form.

> 'In all chaos there is a cosmos, in all disorder a secret order'.[2]

> 'The most complex object in mathematics, the Mandelbrot Set [...] is so complex as to be uncontrollable by mankind and describable as "chaos"'.[3]

> '[...] the test of a first-rate intelligence is the ability to hold two opposed ideas in the mind at the same time, and still retain the ability to function.'[4]

Philosophy and mathematics both assert there is order even in what we have come to think of as the very definition of disorder: chaos. 'Enchantment' is just another word for this whole chaotic large-scale tangle and the spirit that resides there. The trick of accessing and finding our way through the disorder, and allowing our processes to become enchanted by them is to experience and acknowledge the tangle both as chaos and as source of order simultaneously.

Design is a process whereby the hidden order of the chaotic tangle is traced and re-instantiated to create something new. Acknowl-

---

2   C.G. Jung, 'The Archetypes and the Collective Unconscious', in *The Collected Works of C.G. Jung*, vol. 9, pt. 1, ed. Sir Hubert Read, Michael Fordham, Gerhard Adler, trans. R.F.C. Hull (New York: Pantheon Books, 1959), 32.

3   Charles A. Fink, 'Opportunities for Broadening Brain Functioning While Modeling Cybernetic Dynamics', in *12th Proceedings of the International Association for Cybernetics* (Namur: International Association for Cybernetics, 1989), 485.

4   F. Scott Fitzgerald, 'The Crack-Up', in *The Crack-Up*, ed. Edmund Wilson (New York: New Directions, 1993), 69.

edging that the concepts of chaos and of pattern exist simultaneously, we thread a pathway that emphasises a chosen aspect of nature's
tangled whole and becomes a design. The design born this way is
not artificial, not superimposed upon nature from an incom-
patible culture, but is rather an authentic expression of nature
brought into being via contact with her roots, and so existing in
harmony with her.

Thus, good design is neither the stamp of an outside pattern upon
the natural resources of the world, nor the distillation of chaos into
an over-simplification that dissolves its link to its source. Rather, it
is a path navigated through nature's tangled complexity. It leaves
the surrounding enchanting chaos intact, yet highlights aspects
of the existing fractal pattern within it. Through design, this pat-
terned aspect becomes an instantiation of the energy of the whole
in material form.

The product, what we can see of engineering, the tip of the ice-
berg so to speak, is the ordered form—the I-beam, the truss, the
grid, the arch. But if the design is successful, enchantment can still
be seen in the whole: Canterbury Cathedral, the Mayan pyramids,
and Angkor Wat. Not only did the inspiration for these great designs come from the tangled roots of enchantment, not only did the
process of creating them require communication with that source,
but these creations are among the most beautiful ways humans have
found to manifest enchantment in this world, on this plane. The engineering process and its creations stand in the midst of the material
and the ethereal as the link that unites spirit, intellect, and structure,
that allows humans to work in concert with the universe's flow, and
to speak a common language with the natural world. Engineering is
nothing less than how we as ephemeral beings interact concretely
with the land and with our gods.

Animistic philosophical theories explain how material connects
with human beings in a united natural-cultural concept. An example is Jane Bennett's vibrant matter which posits an actor-network
in which matter has an innate impetus. Bennett names this 'thingly'
power,[5] the ability to interact, to enact, to act. Eduardo Kohn, in
How Forests Think, goes further, describing the connection between
humans and the rest of the world as semiotic, 'the world beyond the

---

5   Jane Bennett, *Vibrant Matter: A Political Ecology of Things* (Durham:
      Duke University Press, 2010), xiii.

human is not a meaningless one made meaningful by humans'.[6]

A true connection to the material world means the ability to interpret its animation, channel it in a way that is compatible with the universe's natural expression, yet serves the needs of humans, the specifications that necessitate design. Engineering is powerful, mystical, full of possibilities to integrate spirit with the physical plane. But within the academy, that is neither the way it is practised nor taught.

Engineering education

Engineering can be envisioned as a four-part process consisting first of accessing the roots, the spark of creativity that resides in nature's chaos; second, meshing what comes out of that with the existing society (a sort of conversation between the individual problem as framed by its designer and with the larger natureculture[7]); third, manifesting that idea into a physical design; and fourth, revising and using the design over time as it evolves along with the larger whole. Creating a building, or any other physical object in the world, follows this process. The process can be modelled as tracing in reverse the historical development of our scientific understanding of the universe and its laws. First, a design starts with creativity in chaos—something indefinable, something that lives in a different reality plane where quantum laws of physics and chaos make outcomes uncertain. Then, the creative impetus leaves the realm of endless possibility to our everyday reality plane, well-described by predictable Newtonian physical laws. In passing from the mysterious and manifesting into the ordinary, you could say the idea is drawn down into this world as a design. Here it is built, embodied, and so finally exists as a fixed point in space. Then time brings the flow of the animal, vegetable, mineral, and energetic worlds for it to effect and be affected by.

---

6   Eduardo Kohn, *How Forests Think: Toward an Anthropology beyond the Human* (Berkeley: University of California Press, 2013), 72.

7   'Natureculture' is a term developed by Donna J. Haraway to query the dualism of human activity and natural activity. See e.g.: Donna J. Haraway, *Simians, Cyborgs, and Women: The Reinvention of Nature* (New York: Routledge, 1991), passim.

To use a more socialscience-based theoretical progression, these steps from quantum to Newtonian physics could also be described as moving from premodern multiple frameworks and truths, through modernism which uses a fixed spatial reference and one capital 'T' Truth, to postmodernism with its dynamic space-time and relative frames of reference. Yet for many engineering educators and the university systems they create, engineering is stuck in modernism.[8]

There is something in engineering that makes it especially susceptible to being co-opted by modernity. The middle part of design—the manifestation of ideas in the physical plane—is most easily accomplished using Newtonian physics. One of the shortcuts inherent in this methodology is to assume that there are forces and influences on an object that are negligible. In order to solve a system in this mundane, everyday physics, we are required to draw a box around it and cut it off from the whole. We know this is not an entirely accurate or true representation. In a quantum universe it is impossible, and yet we do it, for the sake of manifesting tangible objects in what most of us consider the real world. This boxing, this disassociation, is an inherently violent process that denies both the roots from whence an idea comes and its connections to most other ideas and objects in the world—the essential design steps that come before and after it. And the problem is that this one, middle step in the process—the instantiation of a physical design—is itself used as a shortcut to stand for all of what engineering is. It is all most people think of as engineering, and it has become all we teach. This curtails the engineering process, excising what should be the first step—access to creativity—and in so doing it disconnects the process of engineering from its roots, from the philosophy that binds it to seek truth in nature. Nature's truth is the existence of infinite possibilities. By focusing on only one part of the engineering process, the part that separates out one possibility from all the rest, engineering education denies the existence of this larger potentiality and our creative role as engineers within it.

Engineering is no more free from the philosophy behind it than any of the liberal arts or social sciences. But because we teach in isolation only a portion of all that engineering encompasses, the rest is invisible, and this anæmic, mechanical, and most prosaic portion alone has become reified as engineering.

---

8   See Gary Lee Downey, 'Low Cost, Mass Use: American Engineers and the Metrics of Progress', *History and Technology* 23 (2007): 289–308.

CREATIVITY

The invisible-ness of the creative part of engineering, the step where an idea is educed from the enchanted world, has long concerned philosophers from all disciplines including engineering and its predecessor natural philosophy. One such philosopher and mathematician, Sophie Germain (1776–1831), wrote:

> [...] a stroke of genius, a stroke of eloquence, in the sciences, in *les beaux arts*, in literature, pleases us for one and the same reason: it reveals to our eyes a crowd of connections as we have never seen before. We find ourselves completely transported into a higher region, where we discover an unanticipated order of ideas or sentiments; the pleasure of the surprise moves our soul; it renders spontaneous homage to her benefactor; and this homage itself is once and again for the mind a new pleasure.[9]

Germain's writings tend to emphasise the underlying Truth as a fractal-like pattern, an eloquent tangle. To this she adds that creativity is truth-seeking and an undertaking that crosses disciplines, the processes of uncovering truth being the same for poets and mathematicians.

Can creativity be taught? We can no more teach this part of engineering than we can teach this part of poetry, an undertaking no doubt more ably addressed in other contributions to this collection. If we were to try to encourage creativity's reintegration into the definition of engineering, there are two aspects that might prove fertile to explore: experience and community. Poets, their brains trained to fluidity, have a much better understanding of the importance of a culture of exploration and communality. Their discipline, in setting itself up as an anti-discipline, has an element engineers lack: the rambling across neatly laid out fields of the countryside, the academy, and intellect. Poets train themselves in the flexibility essential to dipping down into enchantment and bringing back, like pollen, the inspiration to create. Their cultural mores purposely encourage this

---

9   Sophie Germain, *Considerations Generales sur L'Etat des Sciences* (Paris: Paul Ritti, 1879), 100. (Author's translation.)

need: the requirement to let one's brain off the leash and experience a meadow gambol, and the commingling of oneself with likeminded others whose creativity rubs against one's own, friction creating fires of enlightenment. But somehow engineers, in taking on the requirement of mathematical discipline as their unique contribution to the academy and the larger world, have forgotten the creative aspects of their work that link them with all who seek to devise something new. We have come to differentiate ourselves from the other innovators via discipline, and have become stuck in that one part of our role. And because we cannot explain creativity logically, in steps, we in the sciences—so fond of our lab instruction sheets—decline to teach it, or even discuss it. Thus, it remains a necessary part of the process of design whose acquisition is assumed to predate a student's entry to an engineering programme, and is left aside, outside the very definition of what we do.

NATURE'S PHILOSOPHY

> 'When into the womb of time everything is again withdrawn chaos will be restored, and chaos is the score upon which reality is written.'[10]

This failure to address and nurture an essential part of engineering design, to connect the remaining steps of design with the roots from which it should come, is at the root of the inadequacy of academic engineering education. That is, leaving out enchantment leaves us with a definition of engineering that boils down to rote, a well-defined list of simple actions unmoored from the philosophies that guide them.

It is this unmooring of engineering from principles that has created a void in which designs, and the process of their creation, have lost touch with their enchanted roots. Designs are created through people, who are products of their societies. So the structures we build are physical expressions of what we can imagine—the supercollider, the Berlin Wall, the space station—these are our desires and our fears, our morals and our beliefs manifested, and in turn they affect for better or worse—or both—the civilisation into which they

---

10   Henry Miller, *Tropic of Cancer* (New York: Grove Press, 1961), 2.

manifest. By excising the link between designers and the enchantment that underlies the natural world, we are left with only the cultural values of natureculture to influence design. Instead of nature's enchantment, roots reach into poisoned fracked bedrock, into the plastic trash gyre, into the spilled layer of oil between oceanic thermoclines. The problem, and one reason engineering is blamed for all our social ills, is that in our times our desires have been corrupted. We are no longer, if we ever were, a moral people. Drones that kill at a distance, ovens of mass murder, ever more efficient means of poisoning the earth as we violently extract oil and gas so we can use that to pollute the skies as well. This is not our finest hour. The sympathy between modernism's search for one capital 'T' Truth—which requires truth to be cut out from context and become universal—and the stage within instantiating a design that requires an isolating box to be drawn around the problem, creating a simplified version of physical reality, has been dangerous for us as a society and for the discipline of engineering in particular. It has caused people to lose touch with the complicated truths, and the source of those truths—nature. Good design requires creativity, requires access to the roots, to enchantment. If the connection to enchantment is lost, our designs manifest as stunted and broken, mirroring their designers' souls.

A holistic training programme would take into consideration the entire system of how enchantment flows through the conduit of the designer and out into the world. This would help develop within the engineer a moral centre in tune with nature. It is the very opposite of what we are doing now.

RE-ENCHANTING THE ACADEMY

I believe in intuition and inspiration [...] Imagination is more important than knowledge. For knowledge is limited, whereas imagination embraces the entire world, stimulating progress, giving birth to evolution. It is, strictly speaking, a real factor in scientific research.[11]

---

11   Albert Einstein, 'On Science', in *Cosmic Religion with other Opinions and Aphorisms* (New York: Covici-Friede, 1931), 97.

Re-enchanting engineering education would involve reconnecting the engineering process, and engineers themselves, to nature's enchanted roots. We could call this connection creativity, or genius, or being a shaman. Currently we don't know how to teach this, so we just leave it out. Completely. But there is hope because engineering has a portal for creativity built in: design. Da Vinci was a designer, an engineer, and artist strongly and positively creative, and therefore in touch with enchantment—the ultimate engineer. How do we help students use the portal of design to reconnect with creativity and the nature-based philosophy from which it flows?

Before we answer that question, we need to address what has become the elephant in the room for engineering education: are or should or can engineers truly be designers? Engineering education theorists debate, clandestinely, whether the important tasks of both interpreting the needs of our society and concretely manifesting these solutions should be left to what some consider basically walking calculators.[12] Certainly, formal engineering education has reduced the amount of philosophical and theoretical thinking in any field but mathematics to its ugly bare minimum. Science and engineering, once labelled Natural Philosophy, as currently taught are no longer natural, and no longer philosophy.

Yet currently engineers' jobs are to design. If you accept that however imperfect and short the education process is, engineers must somehow be prepared to become designers, then the question becomes how best to get them there. Note that we are still not dealing with creativity, even less enchantment, because we still do not know how to teach that. We are only talking about keeping open the place within the engineering education that could hold these concepts: design.

Context

To create a good design, the engineer has to imagine how this idea might fit into a system of naturalcultural thought: i.e., what does this design say and do in the world? Is it a bridge? A wall? Does it make the world a better place? Students' theories and actions around how

---

12   Gary Lee Downey, 'What is Engineering Studies For? Dominant Practices and Scalable Scholarship', *Engineering Studies* 1 (2009): 55–76.

to relate to natureculture do not begin and end when they enrol in an engineering programme, but in engineering education we pretend they do. We teach engineering ethics as if it were isolated from every other ethical decision people make. Attempting to create a sort of engineering profession bubble further isolates engineering from the natural world, discouraging access to any existing creativity in the students.

Problem Based Learning (PBL) is engineering education's most prevalent attempt to put design into social context applications.[13] The chosen real-world problems or made-up problems, whose roots are rarely considered, reflect the values of the professors and/ or their institutions. Schools of engineering in the United States and elsewhere in the world have close ties to industry and the military.[14] While some instructors may interject a guilt-ridden, patriarchal, self-reflexive, postcolonial sort of concern with the otherly-advantaged, the trend for design classes within engineering schools is towards business start-ups, i.e., making money not (necessarily) positive change.[15]

At best, PBL is helping to expand the role of design in the engineering education curriculum, but I find it deeply unsatisfying in its inability to address three issues. Firstly, it leaves unexamined the roots of the problems it carves out and attempts to solve, that is, it neglects to engage the philosophy behind the designs funded by corporate and military interests. This is related to the second issue, also to do with design parameters: In the context of 'problem solving' it leaves no room for anything not practically oriented. Thirdly, PBL

---

13   J.R. Savery, 'Overview of Problem-based Learning: Definitions and Distinctions', *Interdisciplinary Journal of Problem-Based Learning* 1 (2006): 9–20.

14   Donna Riley, 'Engineering and Social Justice', *Synthesis Lectures on Engineers, Technology, and Society* 3 (2008): 1–152.

15   This statement is based on my experience reviewing proposals for the National Science Foundation. Important alternative efforts exist. Within these counter-culture efforts lies hope for the future of engineering education. See e.g., the journal *Engineering Studies*, and G. Catalano, C. Baillie, D. Riley, and D. Nieusma, 'Engineering, Peace, Justice and The Earth: Developing Course Modules', paper presented at the American Association for Engineering Education Annual Conference and Exposition, Pittsburgh, PA, June 2008 (https://peer.asee.org/3484Engineering and Social Justice).

lacks a robust interpretation of the role of creativity in design. Most often taking the form of unstructured group 'brainstorming', it relies too much on what students bring to the table, their own pre-existing, pre-developed creative abilities, and because our educational systems allow for very little expression and no guided development of creativity as a collection of related skills, these abilities tend to be inadequate. I have no complete solution for improving creativity among engineering students, but I suggest that we begin by recognising our inadequacies in addressing the dialectic between creativity and philosophy. We could at least allow students opportunities to use and strengthen those abilities, benefiting both the students themselves and the field of engineering as a whole.

How would we create these opportunities? Over the history of engineering education globally, the importance of teaching design—and attempts to teach it—wax and wane. PBL is our most wide-spread attempt to date to teach design, and throughout the undergraduate curriculum its practice is increasing as at present design is considered important, and known to be insufficiently taught. Can we, within the current system of engineering education, reconnect engineering design with the enchanted creative roots from whence a nature—not culture—based philosophy comes? My experience with non-traditional engineers in a PBL setting indicates that if this linking were to become possible it would need to occur on two levels. On a macro-scale we would need to demonstrate to students the link between science and technology, and 'the rest of society', that is, make explicit the philosophical beliefs behind societies as a whole as well as engineering designs so that these influences in students' own work would be made visible. On the individual level, we would need to help students link engineering (being an engineer) to the rest of their life stories. We would have to make room within the definition of engineering for everything students bring to it, including their definitions of self, creativity, and philosophical beliefs. Ideally, these two levels would work together and the student would maintain a personal connection to the roots of creativity, and channel what is found there into a nature-based guiding philosophy.

The movement within engineering education that comes closest to this type of re-enchantment is focused on social justice.[16] I think it is not a coincidence that this movement reintegrates passion and

16   See, for example, Caroline Baillie, Alice L. Pawley, and Donna Riley, eds.,

philosophy with design. It is fuelled by aspects of engineering that were purposely excluded during the Enlightenment when Natural Philosophy became science.

MULTIPLE POOLS

So who could do this robust, rooted, enchanted engineering? There is a lack of agreement among engineering educators that good design is possible among the student population that is currently drawn to engineering. Boxing students into narrow roles before we have explored their and our capabilities is a mistake that engineering educators make on a large scale. Essentialism abounds in this field that confidently expects to become more diverse by simply admitting students with similar educational and socio-economic backgrounds and goals but different skin tones, genders, and sexual orientations. The capabilities of all students are largely untested in part because we have only recently come to understand that shortcomings among graduates lodge partially in the professoriate and institutional levels. Engineering as a discipline, with its myth of meritocracy, was slower than most to come to the realisation that good teaching matters. Despite research showing that students' performance in PBL is tied to a professor's proficiency, some have asked if maybe the answer is not to teach engineers to reason and create, but to teach creative people to engineer? This is a great way to sidestep the question of how to teach creativity and design. As with PBL it relies on whatever creativity students arrive with. It recognises that some students are more creative than others, and further it assumes those students are non-engineering majors.

Putting aside the obvious problem of shifting the burden to enhance creativity elsewhere, I like the idea of letting engineering out of the box and sharing these skills and content with students from all disciplines. If we were all maths literate, the technical aspects of building would be easy enough for everyone to pick up. Part of the key to pursuing this solution would be to break down the barriers between disciplines so that those who dig deeply into one subject can commune with and cross-fertilise those who wander among

---

Engineering and Social Justice: In the University and Beyond (West Lafayette: Purdue University Press, 2012), passim.

them in an interdisciplinary way. We need to encourage both these types of scholars and facilitate sharing of information. While I do not subscribe to this multiple pools theory as a complete solution to the lack of designers, it does contain an important kernel of truth relevant to this discussion: individually, it has become impossible to go both deeper into the exponentially expanding literature within one field, and wider across disciplines.

Engineering has sought to divide and divide again into smaller sub-disciplines, each time getting further away from integrated design rooted in the complexities of nature. I submit that addressing the explosion of content within a discipline requires a diffused approach: not a modern hierarchy, but a post-modern web. Currently we teach engineering—we teach everything—by trying to stuff into each head all the engineering or discipline x they will ever need, and then hoping they need it. But while this promotes deep specialisation it reduces the likelihood of interdisciplinary and of creative work, at least within the single individual. So this method is untenable as knowledge grows. Instead, we could focus on students learning to design (a variation on the learn-to-learn approach), and teach content on a need-to-know (or 'invent-as-necessary') basis. In a way, this is already happening on a small scale within engineering education with design teams. Teams are the norm now because individually we have outgrown the capacity to hold and sort all we need to know to imagine and manifest good design on a complex scale. Shifting engineering educational emphasis from content to the process of design shifts the focus toward creativity and a philosophical tangle of natural roots.

As elsewhere in the academy, we have come to realise that there is more in heaven and earth than one person's knowledge can encompass in one lifetime. Whether we see the solution as involving students from outside the discipline of engineering, or change within the field itself, we recognise that dividing engineering education and the world into static, exclusive disciplinary turfs by content is no longer tenable. So what should one person do?

Multiple paths

My answer is that it does not matter. On the individual scale it is impossible to choose 'and' not 'or', but collectively we could. Razing academic disciplinary silos, interjecting a little chaos into the modern hierarchy, we could let each individual walk their own path through the forest, and then the world will be known as a whole—just not by any one individual. It would be inefficient and fun. If we let go of the myth of moving forward in lockstep and learned to value instead the unique voice of each designer in the same way that poets measure worth by innovation and authenticity it could even be tenable. Encouraging individualised paths from the beginning of a student's educational career with their creativity and connections to nature intact would attack the problem at the root. Loosening the stranglehold of the single military-industrial philosophy that binds both content and processes within university engineering programmes would free students of the obligation to graduate as identical, certifiable walking calculators, and would create the opportunity for other underlying philosophies to enter engineering and guide research questions and the processes that we use to formulate and solve them. Students supported in pursuing their own interests throughout their educational career would retain a multitude of more nature-based rather than culture-based philosophies with which to guide their design work. Using the portal of design at the individual and cultural levels, we could reconnect engineering and engineers with the creative philosophy embedded in nature and her tangled roots.

Organically, this approach is already manifesting itself in our society. The maker movement is an especially fascinating engineering example. Makers are engineers who approach the discipline in a playful and cooperative way. Like artisans they seek to use design as an expression of the relationship between themselves and their passions. As such, they remain in touch with their creativity, and some, undoubtedly, channel enchantment.

Student-led, curiosity-based learning as opposed to a structured one-size-fits-all discipline-based prescribed curriculum are solutions that lead to independent, passionate learners who follow unique paths. Ignoring the lines between academic fields, rather than one track, one major, in this 'forest' model each person maps her own way. There will be deep experts to serve as resources to others. There will be interdisciplinary designers who wander and create. There needs to be room for both, and at all levels of learning. Facilitated by easy access to information, we can stop memorising steps and knowledge and start analysing them together in context sooner. Models already exist for encouraging interdisciplinarity.

Childhood education programmes like Montessori, and accredited but non-traditional colleges such as Hampshire College (Amherst, Massachusetts, USA) where students create their own majors, allow students freedom to roam. Deep immersion in one area remains a model for graduate work in the sciences where students apprentice to mentors to become single-subject experts. Opportunities to follow these models through lifelong learning could be provided within or outside the current formal academic system.

FLEXIBILITY OVER FIXED CREDENTIALS

It is essential that we find a way to allow engineers to stay in touch with the passion for creativity we are all born with, not least because we do not know how to teach it once it has been lost. Currently we test this out of students in obeisance to a corporate need for credentialing and measurement. Instead, we need to encourage and nurture passion and educe creativity, providing tools to make dreams and designs into reality. The backlash against career-oriented programmes like engineering by the liberal arts and humanities is one way the academy is reaching for this goal by asserting that they create the kind of thinkers who can flexibly learn to do whatever is needed of them. Cyclically, engineering too argues we should create 'flexible engineers' who can adapt to changing requirements. Unfortunately, the requirements are still and ever-more under the control of large corporate-government structures that do not take nature into account. Because of the link between creativity and a nature-based guiding philosophy, questioning these requirements is essential to the project of promoting creative engineers. To do this we will need to dismantle the corporate structure that requires everyone to bend their time and effort to the process of making money. Or, if that is too large a tack, we need to at least convince our fellow educators that there are some things that cannot be quantified—a rather difficult row to hoe in engineering education in particular. Within engineering education, solutions are elusive due to the methodological incompatibility of credentialing with freedom (and anything that cannot be quantified). Yet it is the unquantifiable, the access to the enchanted roots that we need, to be really good at what we do.

This emphasis on credentialing and on corporate needs is why

recruitment efforts for 'non-traditional' engineers fail. Students
with less of an economic or other stake in the status quo do not see
how engineering is relevant to their individual and naturalcultural
goals, and they don't see places for their whole selves in the engineering process. One such student of mine who had come to major
in engineering from a vocational high school,[17] derided engineers as
rule-following idiots. He, like many makers, wanted to be an inventor. An inventor, he told me, was in touch with his passion, and used
only those rules he needed. This student desperately wanted to go to
MIT[18] but unfortunately his shunning of rules included the rules of
mathematics, physics, and the grading system that valued only his
mastery of a pre-determined sub-set of these subjects' contents. This
is how engineering loses students with a love of design. We teach
only the non-creative parts of the design framework, and pretend
passion and creativity just happen when they need to. Passion and
creativity walk out the door to other majors, or like my student, back
out to the 'real world' where he works peacefully, at his own pace in
the obscurity of his garage.

Forest paths

Is there any way that we can retain students with creativity and/or
a nature-based design philosophy in the academy? Not using current methods alone. We have failed to make the connection between
creativity and the rest of design, and we allow corporations and the
military to tell us why we engineer. By equating design with only
the prosaic part of what is a complex, holistic process, we promote
this stunted view of engineering. Without the connections to enchantment, inspired, ethical design is hard to come by. In turn, the
construction of cultures in harmony with, and in service to nature
is also absent.

Engineering disciplines are conservative and have resisted the
introduction of less structured design opportunities into the undergraduate curriculum. With their emphasis on quantitative method-

---

17   A vocational high school is not college preparatory but trains students for
      hands-on, technician-level jobs.
18   Massachusetts Institute of Technology, an elite engineering college
      in the USA.

ology they will continue to resist in-depth exploration of the ill-defined concept of creativity outside the context of 'problem solving'. Promoting more creativity in engineering education has been slow, labelled as too 'soft', and shunted into ethics and diversity sub-disciplines of engineering education rather than the re-imagining of the discipline as a whole it could bring about.

An alternative to internal, stepwise change is a paradigm shift in which new individual pathways are created. The spate of technology-based humanitarian organisations is one example of how inspired engineering concepts escape the academy and spill out into the world. The emergence of engineering-related programmes with an emphasis on nature, such as environmental science, and science and technology studies, outside the confines of accredited engineering schools, is an example of how the academy is stretching to share engineering concepts including design with other less rule-bound disciplines. Engineering, as the ability to link the material world and our cultural values, cannot be confined to traditional rule-bound schools of engineering. Enchanted engineering, a process rooted in creativity and resulting in built pieces of material culture in the physical world belongs not in the mass-populated hallways of engineering schools but in lonely enchanted holloways throughout and outside the academy.

SELECT BIBLIOGRAPHY

BENNETT, Jane. *Vibrant Matter: A Political Ecology of Things.* Durham: Duke University Press, 2010.

BAILLIE, Caroline, Alice L. Pawley, and Donna Riley, eds. *Engineering and Social Justice: In the University and Beyond.* West Lafayette: Purdue University Press, 2012.

CATALANO, G., C. BAILLIE, D. RILEY, & D. NIEUSMA. 'Engineering, Peace, Justice and The Earth: Developing Course Modules'. Paper presented at the American Association for Engineering Education Annual Conference and Exposition, Pittsburgh, PA, June 2008 (https://peer.asee.org/3484Engineering and Social Justice).

DOWNEY, Gary Lee. 'Low Cost, Mass Use: American Engineers and the Metrics of Progress'. *History and Technology* 23 (2007): 289–308.

EINSTEIN, Albert. 'On Science'. In *Cosmic Religion with other Opinions and Aphorisms*. New York: Covici-Friede, 1931.

FINK, Charles A. 'Opportunities for Broadening Brain Functioning While Modeling Cybernetic Dynamics', *12th Proceedings of the International Associate for Cybernetics*. Namur, Belgium: International Association for Cybernetics, 1989: 483–486.

GAIMAN, Neil. 'Ghosts in the Machines'. *The New York Times*, 31st October 2006.

GERMAIN, Sophie. *Considerations Generales sur L'Etat des Sciences*. Paris: Paul Ritti, 1879.

HARAWAY, Donna J. *Simians, Cyborgs, and Women: The Reinvention of Nature*. New York: Routledge, 1991.

JUNG C.G. 'The Archetypes of the Collective Unconscious'. *The Collected Works of C.G. Jung*, vol. 9, pt. 1, edited by Sir Hubert Read, Michael Fordham, and Gerhard Adler. Translated by R.F.C. Hull. New York: Pantheon Books, 1959.

KOHN, Eduardo. *How Forests Think: Toward an Anthropology Beyond the Human*. Berkeley: University of California Press, 2013.

SAVERY, J.R. 'Overview of Problem-based Learning: Definitions and Distinctions'. *Interdisciplinary Journal of Problem-Based Learning* 1 (2006): 9–20.

On the Margins of the Academy

Séances, Sitter Groups, and Academics

JULIA MOORE

INTRODUCTION AND DEFINITIONS

In this chapter I want to look at three sets of people who experimented with the séance format, led by Kenneth Batcheldor (in the United Kingdom), George and Iris Owen (in Canada) and Montague Ullman (in the USA). In slightly different ways, each of the three sets of people might be said to have communicated with something or someone in séances. In each case I will talk about, for example, Batcheldor's *group*, because they worked with other people. I want to look at what each of the groups did, and how it related to academia.

I am interested in what I call the experimental séance. Séances, or attempts to communicate with the dead, have a longish history, intertwined with the history of spiritualism. Séances were particularly popular in Victorian times, but interest in them remains, as witnessed by the number of films featuring attempts to communicate with the undead.[1] Often, people who take part in séances do so believing that they are contacting dead people, or perhaps believing that the whole thing is nonsensical or fraudulent, and that people who think they are contacting the spirits of the dead are stupid, misled, or mistaken. The *experimental* séance is one in which the participants are interested in what is happening, do not assume that what happens is always down to fraud or deliberate deception, do

---

1   See, for example, the films *Séance on a Wet Afternoon*, directed by Bryan Forbes (London: Rank Organisation, 1964); *Séance*, directed by Mark L. Smith (Burbank: Snowfall Films, 2006); *Ouija*, directed by Stiles White (Universal City: Universal Pictures, 2014).

not necessarily assume that they are contacting the spirits of dead people, but are interested in the ontology and/or epistemology of the event. Participants in experimental séances approach what they are doing in an experimental spirit, although their experiments do not generally adhere to the conventions of the scientific experiment.

Just as participants in the experimental séance do not have to have firm beliefs about the nature of what is happening, one does not have to hold any beliefs about the ontological status of the phenomena generated in experimental séances to follow this discussion, apart from believing that something happened.

In the following I will sometimes also talk about the paranormal, which I define as hypothesised processes 'that in principle are physically impossible and outside the realm of human or animal capabilities as presently conceived by conventional scientists'.[2] Batcheldor used the term 'sitter group' to designate the people taking part in an experimental séance,[3] and if I use the term, that is what I take it to mean.

THE EXPERIMENTAL SÉANCE AND ACADEMIA

When I was starting to look at Batcheldor, the Owens, and Ullman and what they did, I realised that their experiments all took place outside of the academy; either before they entered academia, after they retired, or as a recreation separate from their working life. This struck me as quite interesting. Was there any reason why they did what they did when they did? Was there anything about academia which meant it was not the ideal arena to take part in séances? What is the relationship between the séance and academia? Is it important what the relationship is? Are they really from utterly different worlds, or do they overlap? I think the difference is partly to do with the different types of language which characterise each domain. Speaking in a séance is not the same as speaking—and writing—in

---

2   Stanley Krippner and Harris L. Friedman, *Debating Psychic Experience: Human Potential or Human Illusion?* (Santa Barbara: ABC-Clio, 2010), 217.

3   Kenneth J. Batcheldor, 'Contributions to the Theory of PK Induction from Sitter-group Work', *Journal of the American Society for Psychical Research* 78 (1984): 105–22.

academia. I am summarising some of the differences between the two worlds like this (TABLE 1):

ACADEMIA	SÉANCE
Veracity	Missing the mark, falsehood
Language denotational, referential	Language metaphorical, symbolic, present
Sincerity	Insincerity, duplicity, fraud
Truth	Lies, falsehood, dissemination
Seriousness	Lightheartedness, play
Institutional	Personal
Distance, neutrality	Taking part, getting involved, not neutral
Hierarchy, power, command	Margins, marginalised, powerless
Clarity, understanding	There is nothing to understand
Writing	Speech
Sense/reference/referent	
Truth as correspondence	Truth as (some) coherence
The classroom	The art studio
The mind, cognition, logic, thought	The body, experiential, experience
Light, day	Dark, night, darkness
Validity, reliability	Invalid, unreliable
Fact, factual	Fiction, imaginary
	Parody, camp
	Ambiguity
Sense	*Delire*,[4] nonsense

I am aware, of course, that this is a somewhat contentious set of oppositions. Although I claim that the things in the left hand column are applicable to academia, and the ones in the right hand column to the séance, of course things in the right are embraced by academia,

---

4   A form of discourse which exists on the 'borderline between sense and nonsense [...]' and which 'questions our most common conceptions of language'. See Jean-Jacques Lecercle, *Philosophy Through the Look-*

and things in the left might be claimed by the séance. And the oppositions, set out in pairs, are not even always opposites. To make things worse, surely no one would claim all the things in the left column are always true of academia, no more than anyone would claim that all the stuff in the right column is true of any one séance. But still. There is something, somewhere in the lists, and in the lists compared with each other, which captures a flavour of the differences between academic enterprises and séance-related ones.

In the rest of this discussion, I am going to look briefly at what each of the three groups did. I am then going to look at what George Hansen has said about the paranormal, particularly his idea that it resists institutionalism, and use that as a way of framing the three groups. I should mention that none of the people I am discussing really talked about the relationship between what they did (séances) and the academic world. So I do a bit of extrapolation and guessing.

Kenneth J. Batcheldor

Kenneth J. Batcheldor (1921–1988) was a clinical psychologist who worked in UK hospitals. He became interested in investigating séances after a dinner party in 1964 when the guests decided to have a go at table tipping. Although nothing happened at the first session, they heard loud bangs at a subsequent session. Batcheldor became fascinated by the phenomena, and went on to hold over 200 sitter group sessions between 1964 and 1965, with some interesting results.[5] After retirement at 55, he was able to devote more time to his investigations. The phenomena his group witnessed were macro-psychokinesis (macro-PK) events. That is, events where the mind (or something) apparently causes matter to move without the intervention of the body, where such events are large enough to be visible to the eye.[6] Batcheldor's phenomena included table turning, noises (raps, bangs), and apports (objects which appear, apparently out of

---

ing-Glass: Language, Nonsense, Desire (Abingdon: Routledge, 2016), 6.

5   Kenneth J. Batcheldor, 'Report of a Case of Table Levitation and Associated Phenomena', Journal of the Society for Psychical Research 43 (1966): 339–356.

6   Pamela R. Heath, The PK Zone: A Cross-cultural Review of Psychokinesis (PK) (New York: iUniverse, 2003), xxv.

nowhere). As Batcheldor commented: 'sittings which started off as tableturning but which led to moderately spectacular phenomena including ostensible total levitations and movements without contact have been taking place at Exeter since April 1964'.[7]

Batcheldor and academia

The question I started with was about the relationship of experimental séances to academia. Batcheldor was not, in fact, an academic. And I haven't so far found out any details of his career as a psychologist, so I am unclear what role the academy played in his working life. However, from his writings I get a sense of his having been steeped in psychological theory, particularly behaviourism, and that he understood the mechanics of academic writing. His writings also demonstrate, more so than the Owens, for example, an interest in theorising about the subject, and doing so not in a crackbrained anything goes sort of way, but in a way which is dense, complex, and precise (though sometimes confusing).[8] And I think it is fair to say that clinical psychology, as a discipline, is steeped in theory in a way that other things one can do for a living are not.

Batcheldor's theory

Batcheldor was much more interested in *how* his group produced table tipping, noises, raps, bangs, and apports than he was interested in *what* they were. He came to believe that no special mediumship ability was needed, but rather that anyone, given the right circumstances and patience, could experience these things. His interest was primarily in how to create the right circumstances to produce macro-PK events. There were different aspects to creating the right circumstances. On the one hand, the group had to cultivate the right atmosphere, partly by keeping the same conditions during regular meetings (dark or dim light, comfortable, relaxed, enjoyable) and partly by developing the appropriate mental

---

7   Kenneth J. Batcheldor, 'Macro-PK in Group Sittings: Theoretical and
     Practical Aspects', (unpublished manuscript, Exeter, 1968), 1–101.

8   Ibid.

attitude (curious, flexible, neither too sceptical nor too firmly a be-
liever, light hearted, patient, interested). The group should also avoid
certain attitudes: doubt, an overly 'scientific' (by which I think he
means 'very sceptical') mind set, the idea that testing of hypotheses
was taking place, the expectation of failure and the need to explain
what was witnessed. On the other hand, to help manifest genuine
phenomena, Batcheldor thought that fraud, trickery, and deception were necessary. So he, or a designated person, would e.g., push
the table, and this would subsequently lead to phenomena which
appeared genuine.[9]

What did Batcheldor make of all this?

Batcheldor's main interests then, were in producing phenomena
and writing about the best conditions for generating phenomena.
He was not particularly interested in the ontology of the phenomena, he was not interested in whether they were signs of something,
nor interested in what they might be signs of. He certainly seems to
think that the phenomena are in some way a function of the people
present in the sitter group, and that there is some sort of causal relationship between the group and the phenomena. Indeed, the optimum conditions for generating phenomena through the right sort
of attitude and manipulation of expectation preoccupy him.[10]

He also did not really think about why all this happened for him
after he had retired. Perhaps he just had more time on his hands
to experiment and interpret the results of his experiments. He did
speculate that famous mediums are sometimes 'outsiders', and he
links that to something he noticed in his groups, that people like to
scapegoat one member of the group as responsible for the phenomena. He said: 'ordinary people simply find difficulty in believing that

9   Batcheldor, 'Report of a Case of Table Levitation'; Batcheldor, 'Macro-PK
     in Group Sittings', 1–101; Kenneth J. Batcheldor and Colin Brookes-Smith,
     Manual of Advanced Psychokinetic Procedures (London: Society for Psy-
     chical Research, 1970); Kenneth J. Batcheldor, 'PK in Sitter Groups', *Psy-
     choenergetic Systems* 3 (1979): 77–93; Kenneth J. Batcheldor, 'Contribu-
     tions to the theory of PK induction'; Kenneth J. Batcheldor, 'Notes on the
     elusiveness problem in relation to a radical view of Paranormality: Erra-
     tum', *Journal of the American Society for Psychical Research* 88 (1994): 292.

10   Batcheldor, 'Macro-PK in Group Sittings'.

they may have supernormal capacities [...] it is easier to attribute the phenomena either to supernatural entities or [...] to the odd man out [...] to anyone other than ourselves'.[11] We will make more of this connection of paranormality with the outsider figure later on.

What do we make of this?

Batcheldor was, in a way, very influential, and in a way not. To the extent that there exist sitter group experiments after him, they tended to be influenced by Batcheldor's method.[12] Although he was not an academic as such, he worked in a way which suggests that the academic approach was important to him, that a scientific method was important, and that theory was important. In fact, although theory was important to Batcheldor, it was important in a way which started to undermine itself.

Batcheldor's theory is about undercutting the method of scientific experiment, undermining the stance of the detached observer, rejecting the position of doubt, using fraud and lies at the heart of investigation. What is interesting about Batcheldor is that he both embraces the scientific method and yet also says that one has to throw away the assumptions of science to get anywhere in sitter groups. This connects with some of George Hansen's ideas, as we will see later. What is also interesting is that, through the work he did with Brookes-Smith, Batcheldor's method has inspired studies which are driven by the need to produce statistically valid and reliable results,[13] rather than the ambivalent, participatory, experiential direction Batcheldor seems to have mapped out in his suggestions about cheating, fraud and collaboration. Batcheldor stressed the need to join in, enjoy the quasi-experiment and suspend disbelief in order to get results: not very scientific.[14]

---

11   Ibid., 35.

12   See, for example Robert L. Bourgeois, *Psychokinesis and Contact with an Artificial Spirit: A Replication of the Philip Phenomena* (New Hampshire: Franklin Pierce College, 1994).

13   See, for example, Lance Storm and Colin Mitchell, "'Are you there, Spenser?" Attempts at PK by Committee in a Séance-like Situation', *Australian Journal of Parapsychology* 3 (2003): 3–19.

14   Batcheldor, 'Macro-PK in Group Sittings', 1–60.

THE OWENS

George Owen (1919–2003) was a lecturer in genetics, and mathematics at Cambridge, writing about mathematics, statistics, genetics and population theory. His wife, Iris (1916–2009), was a nurse. They lived in the UK until 1970, when they emigrated to Canada. George Owen had been invited to direct parapsychology research at the New Horizons Research Foundation, in Toronto, an organisation founded to promote research on the fringes of science and disseminate information about such research. They were also involved in the Toronto Society for Psychical Research.[15]

George Owen became interested in poltergeist phenomena (writing a book, *Can we Explain the Poltergeist?* in 1964), and in the question of how many of the cases of poltergeist activity were faked and how many were genuine. He felt that at least some of the phenomena had objective reality. The activity for which the Owens were perhaps best known was the 'Philip' experiment. The Owens thought that paranormal phenomena could be created by the unconscious mind. Wanting to test this idea, they decided, with other members of the Toronto Society for Psychical Research, to create a fictional character Philip, who had lived in the 17th century in England, and used séances to communicate with him.[16] They worked as a group to imagine Philip, giving him a personality, deciding on his appearance, when he lived, and what happened to him when he was alive. Philip had a complicated personal life, his marriage was not satisfying, and he fell unhappily in love with a gypsy girl. The process of developing 'Philip' was longwinded, taking months. They started with a character sketch of Philip, then elaborated his story, and drew pictures of him to help establish a mental image of him. Initial attempts were unsuccessful.[17]

---

15   See Christopher M. Moreman, *The Spiritualist Movement: Speaking with the Dead in America and Around the World* (Santa Barbara: ABC-Clio, 2013); Debra Barr and Walter Meyer zu Erpen (www.islandnet.com/sric), *vide*: Owen, A.R.G. (1919–2003) and Iris M. Owen (1916–2009).

16   Barr and zu Erpen, *vide*: Owen, A.R.G. (1919–2003) and Iris M. Owen (1916–2009).

17   Iris M. Owen and Margaret H. Sparrow, 'Generation of Paranormal Physical Phenomena in Connection with an Imaginary "Communicator"', *Journal of the New Horizons Research Foundation* 1 (1974): 6–13; Iris M.

The group experimented for a year, meeting once a week ('Stage 1'), placing their hands on a table and concentrating on developing a force of energy through meditation. They believed that their group would produce a physical manifestation of Philip, but this did not happen immediately. Owen and Sparrow suggest that the initial method made it difficult to see Philip as an entity that belonged to the group as a whole. The Owens then used some of Batcheldor's recommended methods as a way of overcoming the failure of Stage 1. For example, they used Batcheldor's idea of creating an 'atmosphere of jollity and relaxation' which they interpreted as singing songs, telling jokes, and bantering with the table.[18]

The change in method in Stage 2 was successful. Soon there were rappings, communications, noise. They also experienced table movements (the table started flinging itself around the room and developing what they thought of as its own personality). Stage 2 was marked by successful communications with Philip. Some of the phenomena were witnessed by scientists and researchers. The group asked Philip questions, and reported a sense of a definite personality, which mostly matched the personality they had created together. However, sometimes his answers were at odds with the character the group had developed. The group thought that the change in methods was the reason for success, but it is also possible that the bonding that occurred during Stage 1 was necessary to the success in Stage 2.[19]

The Owens' relationship to academia

As is clear from the above, the Owens had been immersed in aca-

---

Owen, '"Philip's" Story Continued', *Journal of the New Horizons Research Foundation* 2 (1974): 14–20; Iris M. Owen, 'Continuation of the Philip Experiment', *Journal of the New Horizons Research Foundation* 2 (1976): 3–6; Iris M. Owen and Margaret H. Sparrow, '"Philip's" Fourth Year', *Journal of the New Horizons Research Foundation* 2 (1977): 11–15.

18 Owen and Sparrow, 'Communicator', 6–13; Iris M. Owen and Margaret Sparrow, *Conjuring Up Philip, An Adventure in Psychokinesis* (New York: Harper & Row Publishers, 1976); Owen, '"Philip's" Story', 14–20; Owen, 'Continuation', 3–6; Owen and Sparrow, 'Fourth Year', 11–15.

19 Owen and Sparrow, 'Communicator', 6–13; Owen, '"Philip's" Story', 14–20; Owen, 'Continuation', 3–6; Owen and Sparrow, 'Fourth Year', 11–15.

demia. George Owen continued to work in mainstream academia, teaching statistics and biostatistics part-time at the University of Toronto.[20] Perhaps it is most accurate to see their Philip experiments as situated on the margins of academia. Interestingly, the accounts given by Iris Owen in the *Journal of the New Horizons Research Foundation* are not particularly academic: they are easy to read and anecdotal, without much in the way of theory or references. There is none of the agonised pondering and trying to develop a coherent theory of what is going on that is found in Batcheldor, for instance, nor any of the statistics-heavy approach you often find in post-Rhine investigations of the paranormal.

The Owens' conclusions

The Owens had a number of ideas about what they were doing and the best way to achieve results like this (although they did not theorise extensively, as Batcheldor did). For example, Owen felt that the results they achieved should be repeatable by any group determined enough. They also felt that six to eight people was the optimum number for groups. There is some ambiguity about what the Owens thought about the ontology of Philip. On the one hand, their starting point was that poltergeist phenomena, for example, were a product of the unconscious mind. However, they were members of the United Church of Canada and believed in an afterlife.[21] To add to the confusion, Iris Owen stated in an interview in 2006 that she had never been convinced by survival evidence, as some other explanation of the phenomena was always available.[22]

What do we make of this?

The thing that most interests me about the Owens' work with Philip is that they created a fictional character who communicated with

---

20   Barr and zu Erpen, *vide:* Owen, A.R.G. (1919–2003) and Iris M. Owen (1916–2009).

21   Ibid.

22   Owen and Sparrow, 'Communicator', 6–13; Owen, '"Philip's" Story', 14–20; Owen, 'Continuation', 3–6; Owen and Sparrow, 'Fourth Year', 11–15.

them. How could that not be interesting? What I like about Philip is the way he starts to undermine the distinction between fiction and fact, subjectivity and objectivity. One common-sense way of understanding the world is that there is a complete distinction between the subjective and the objective. But the Owens' work seems to question this, because they created a fiction which then had an objective reality. Is this to say that the power of their imagination made Philip a really real thing, who was objectively there? Or is it rather to suggest that the distinction between what is really there, the objective, and what is in our heads, our talk, our imagination, the subjective, is erroneous. This idea that the paranormal undermines commonly accepted binary distinctions is also found in Hansen.[23]

It also seems relevant that only when the Owens, following Batcheldor, embraced light-heartedness as a method, gave up on seriousness and started to play did Philip start to communicate. That seems important, though it is tricky to articulate why.

Montague Ullman

Montague Ullman (1916–2008) was a psychologist, psychoanalyst and parapsychologist, and was director of the Department of Psychiatry at the Maimonides Medical Centre (New York), one of the first laboratories designed to investigate sleeping, dreams, and telepathy. During his working life he wrote over eighty papers and a number of books. The story I want to tell about Ullman is not a story about what he did after he retired. Rather, it is about what he and some friends did before he entered psychology and academia.

When Ullman was a teenager in New York, he and a group of friends held séances in which they got in touch with a spirit guide, Dr Bindelof, and, while thus communicating, also experienced a variety of seemingly paranormal phenomena. These included the production of photographs from unexposed negatives, table movements (tilting, violence, movement around the room), knocks, intelligent responses via table, photographic, materialisation and healing. The séances took place between 1932 to 1934, with Dr Bindelof making his first appearance in 1933. Dr Bindelof, it was claimed, had

---

23   George P. Hansen, *The Trickster and the Paranormal* (Bloomington: Xlibris, 2001), 273–368.

been a medical doctor, and seemed to enjoy handing out advice on health problems. He also did a little healing.[24]

Ullman says:

> What we witnessed over this period was the gradual and ultimately climactic unfolding of almost the full gamut of psychical phenomena as such phenomena were known and defined by writers on the subject in the 19th and early 20th centuries. The developmental sequence began with equivocal movements, tilting of the table, and knocks and ultimately went to such startling phenomena as the table moving about the room and actual levitation, photographs taken without exposure of the plates, and messages appearing on paper with no one holding the pencil, purportedly written by someone who had died years before.[25]

Ullman's relationship to academia

Obviously, this all predated Ullman's academic career. Perhaps this experience influenced Ullman in his career, or perhaps he took part in the séances, and cared about them enough to write about them afterwards, because he was already interested. I do not think that is really the point. I think the main thing is that it all took place outside academia.

In the document where Ullman describes the séances, he includes a number of interviews with other participants, and this format means you get multiple perspectives on the events: some of them, for example, saw Dr Bindelof as an unconscious projection who fulfilled a need for a father figure. Ullman himself felt that while this was a contributing factor, there remained elements

---

24   Montague Ullman, 'The Bindelof Story, Part I (of 4)', *Exceptional Human Experience* 11 (1993), 11–28; Montague Ullman, 'The Bindelof Story, Part 2', *Exceptional Human Experience* 12 (1994), 25–32; Montague Ullman, 'The Bindelof Story, Part 3', *Exceptional Human Experience* 12 (1994), 208–22; Montague Ullman, 'The Bindelof Story, Part 4', *Exceptional Human Experience* 13 (1995), 32–42.

25   Ullman, 'Bindelof Part 1', 12.

which could not be explained entirely in terms of psychodynamic processes. Ullman's group was much more easy-going and free-form in its methodology than either Batcheldor or the Owens, or indeed compared with other paranormal researchers of the séance. There is none of the intricate choreography of the Scole group, for example, nor the carefully articulated theoretical underpinnings of Batcheldor (except perhaps in Dr Bindelof's theories of energy, force, and otherworldly metaphysics). Ullman, I think, was far too enchanted by the workings out of the group's life stories, and the sheer excitement of what happened in the séances to be much bothered by theory. Ullman is particularly interested in the enjoyment of the experience: he talks about 'the excitement, the fun, the moments of fear, the passion and commitment'.[26]

What do we make of this?

I find Ullman's Bindelof story interesting, not just because of the descriptions of the séances and how the group went about them, but also as a story of friendship and what happened to the group over the years. There is something rather melancholy about it, and touching. It is also interesting because there is a strong sense of the liminality of adolescence, the feeling that the participants were between two worlds. What also comes across particularly strongly is the participants' commitment to the séances, the enjoyment they found in them, and the sense of being party to the very beginning of a series of complex life-stories as a group of friends develop shared lives through gossip, significant events, histories, and layering. This strong sense of collaboration, friendship, and group work seems somehow important in the story of Dr Bindelof.

ACADEMIA VERSUS THE SÉANCE: YES, BUT...

I have offered the above as examples of the way in which academia and the séance are both linked and also mutually exclusive. In each of the cases, the séance experiments happened outside academia, but were conducted by people with a strong link to academia, theory,

---

26   Ibid., 11.

and scientific experiment. However, it could be argued that academia does accommodate the séance (and the paranormal) for the following reasons (numbered for clarity):

(1) There is a long history of parapsychology, from SPR through Rhine on to Bem, and others.

This is true. The paranormal is the subject of a number of academic journals including the *Journal of Parapsychology*, and *Parapsychology*. There are a huge number of laboratory experiments and other analyses of the paranormal. However, the stance of these is predominantly one in which scientific testing, statistics, and quantitative methods are used to prove or disprove hypotheses about micro-PK, for example using random number generation. Other quantitative studies exist in other disciplines, e.g., psychology, but these are often reductive and/or dismissive. For example, Joel Royalty suggests that paranormal belief is associated with defects in critical thinking, and Michael Persinger suggests that there is a link with delusion and misinterpretation of stimuli.[27] Mediumship is reduced to a function of something else, while belief in the paranormal has been linked with fantasy-proneness.[28]

(2) Academia has discussed the séance. For example, language studies have looked at the séance and mediumship in terms of the performativity of the medium.[29]

This is true, but again there is a tendency to assume that the séance is primarily about something else, or that the activity is often fraudulent.

(3) Anthropology and religious studies have started to look at the paranormal. For example, Jack Hunter's journal *Paranthropology* aims to take the paranormal and anomalous experience seriously, using rigorous academic standards to offer new perspectives and ex-

---

27   Joel Royalty, 'The Generalizability of Critical Thinking: Paranormal Beliefs Versus Statistical Reasoning', *The Journal of Genetic Psychology* 156 (1995): 477–88; and Michael A. Persinger, 'The Neuropsychiatry of Paranormal Experiences', *The Journal of Neuropsychiatry and Clinical Neuroscience* 13 (2001): 515–24.

28   Harvey J. Irwin, 'Fantasy Proneness and Paranormal Beliefs', *Psychological Reports* 66 (1990): 655–58; Harvey J. Irwin, 'A Study of Paranormal Belief, Psychological Adjustment, and Fantasy Proneness', *Journal of the American Society for Psychical Research* 85 (1991): 317–31.

29   Robin Wooffitt, *The Language of Mediums and Psychics: The Social Organization of Everyday Miracles* (Aldershot: Ashgate Publishing, 2006).

panding beyond a philosophically naïve materialism. Scholars such as Hunter, Jeffrey Kripal, Fiona Bowie, and Angela Voss are doing undoubtedly important work in this area.[30]

This is true. And this raises an interesting question about research methods, which I'll come back to later.

(4) There is some consideration of the séance in art, and to some extent in institutionalised art (art that is related to art schools, academia and/or universities).

This is also true. Artists like Jeffrey Vallance, based in the USA, and Susan Hillier and Sarah Sparkes, from the UK, explore these phenomena. But art's relationship with academia is perhaps less than straightforward, and it is only recently that there has emerged an idea of practice-based research. Perhaps the séance is more like art practice than it is like anything else, and as such needs research methods which expand what is considered to be research in this field. To reiterate a theme touched upon earlier, it might be necessary to look more closely at the role played by writing in the practice of the séance. This is something Hansen's analysis considers.

George Hansen

George Hansen has worked professionally in parapsychology labs including the Rhine Research Centre (North Carolina) and the Psychophysical Research Laboratories (Princeton, New Jersey), is a professional magician, and has been involved in sceptical groups in the USA. In the following I'm primarily interested in his *The Trickster and the Paranormal*.

---

30   See for example: Fiona Bowie, 'Building Bridges, Dissolving Boundaries: Towards a Methodology for the Ethnographic Study of the Afterlife, Mediumship and Spiritual Beings', *Journal of the American Academy of Religion* 81.3 (2013): 698–733; Jack Hunter, *Why People Believe in Spirits, Gods and Magic: An Introduction to the Anthropology of the Supernatural* (Exeter: David & Charles, 2012); Jeffrey Kripal, *Authors of the Impossible: The Paranormal and the Sacred* (Chicago: University of Chicago Press, 2010); William Rowlandson and Angela Voss, eds., *Daimonic Imagination: Uncanny Intelligence* (Newcastle upon Tyne: Cambridge Scholars Publishing, 2013).

Hansen, reflexivity, subjective-objectivity, and the trickster

In *The Trickster and the Paranormal*, Hansen uses a theory of the trickster to explain paranormal phenomena. As discussed before, attempts to explain the paranormal have often been framed in a scientific context. However, what I particularly like about Hansen is that he draws upon a range of other disciplines for his explanation, including anthropology, structuralism, poststructuralism, semiotics, and literary criticism. One key element of all these approaches is that they are both reflexive and also question the assumptions sometimes made between what is 'really real' in the world, and what is a product of human subjectivity. I think, for Hansen, as for some phenomenologists and other philosophers, there is no clear-cut ontological distinction between what's objective and what's subjective. There is also nothing definitive to be said about reality, except that it is shifting and constantly changing. This is embedded in his ideas about the trickster and the paranormal:

> Psi, the paranormal and the supernatural are fundamentally linked to destructuring, change, transition, disorder, marginality, the ephemeral, fluidity, ambiguity, and blurring of boundaries. In contrast, the phenomena are repressed or excluded with order, structure, routine, stasis, regularity, precision, rigidity, and clear demarcation.[31]

Hansen uses the notion of the trickster, then, as an emblem of all that is ephemeral, fluid, and blurred, and as a way of connecting the disparate theoretical frameworks he draws upon. The trickster is found in different parts of the world, across different eras, and in different textual places (folklore, literature, mythology). The trickster can take different forms: animal, human (both, neither), and partakes in some or all of a set of characteristics which include disruptiveness, overt sexuality, nonconformity, deceptiveness, irrationality, being illogical, being puzzling, nonlinearity, and antistructure:

> In short, the paranormal and supernatural are ambiguous and marginal in virtually all ways: socially, intel-

---

31   Hansen, *The Trickster*, 22.

lectually, academically, religiously, scientifically, and conceptuality.[32]

The trickster, cultural structures, and the outsider

For Hansen, the paranormal is inextricably linked to cultural structures, and the trickster figure reveals the extent to which we take culture for granted when we are embedded in it. When cultures change, interest in the paranormal increases. Equally, when individuals are ambiguously situated in, or out of, a culture, paranormal phenomena are manifested. Outsider figures are more prone to have paranormal powers, and those with paranormal powers are often those outside cultures. As we saw with Batcheldor, fakery is at the heart of the paranormal, and insincerity, fraud, and duplicity generate true wonders. For Hansen, the paranormal is inherently and always outside the institution, including but not limited to the academic institution: while ghosts, UFOS, etc. have 'temporarily captured intense popular interest, that has never been translated into financially viable, stable institutions that directly elicit or engage the phenomena'.[33]

The trickster and academia

Hansen explicitly applies his theory to the academic world. Drawing upon Weber, he suggests that because academia is primarily concerned with the rational and rationalisation, 'it is there that we find the greatest incomprehension of, and antagonism to, the paranormal'.[34] The process of rationalisation has led to bureaucracies in which power is encoded and made impersonal, and in which magic is eliminated. Actually, Hansen thinks that magic is not eliminated, it is rather shunted to the margins, that is, seen as something that people without power do; or written off as fiction. Hansen is perhaps interested in some movements associated with anthropology and literary criticism because they undercut the rationalist enter-

---

32   Ibid., 24.

33   Ibid., 23.

34   Ibid., 25.

prise and say that all texts are important, not just ones which have a referential, truth telling role. For Hansen, magic is inherently connected with meaningfulness. Hansen also seems to be saying that for most of rationalist academia, the mechanics of meaning are taken for granted (though hopefully not in philosophy departments): 'In most rational discourse [...] the problem of meaning is banished from consciousness'.[35] Most discourse of this sort assumes that there is a 'clear, unambiguous connection between a word and its referent, between a signifier and its signified'.[36] This is also an assumption of the unproblematic existence of objective reality. Hansen holds this to be a process whereby magic is banished from the world.

For Hansen, the deconstructionists and postmodernists, through challenging this view of language, also offer a way to overturn the notions of rationality and objective reality which, he thinks, are the frame in which academia exists: 'Both deconstructionism and psi subvert the rational, and there are similar, important consequences to both.'[37]

As an aside, the physicality of his book seems to express something of the liminality and tricksterishness of the paranormal. It is not quite right. It looks something like a parody of an academic book, or like one that has taken the conventions of academic publishing and done them in a way that is slightly off-key. This is not really just an aside. The physicality of books and of academia is important, for reasons which I cannot really go into here.

Conclusion

So, how can we summarise what Hansen says, and how does it relate to our original questions about academia, the séance and what Batcheldor, the Owens, and Ullman did?

Hansen seems to be saying that:

¶ Academia = bureaucratic, rational, institutionalised power
¶ Academia = language is not a problem, meaning is not a problem, objective reality is not a problem

---

35   Ibid., 27.
36   Ibid., 27.
37   Ibid., 27.

- ¶ The paranormal is associated with the outsider/liminality/powerlessness/the excluded/the trickster
- ¶ The paranormal is linked with fraud, trickery, lies, insincerity
- ¶ The paranormal should be understood through a process of problematising language and meaning, as postmodernism/deconstructionism did, and therefore:
- ¶ Academia and the séance are mutually exclusive.

Which partly explains why Batcheldor only got interested in séances after he retired, and why the Owens did the same, and why Ullman did his séancing as an adolescent. This I suppose raises the question of whether academia might accommodate the séance, whether this would be a good thing (and why), and how it might do so. This can be answered in different ways (although there is not really space to go into them here in any detail). One way academia might accommodate the séance is the way it already does, to the extent it already does, by studying it at a distance. Another way is to take the new(ish) anthropology route as evidenced by Jack Hunter's *Paranthropology*, and use approaches developed in ethnography and participative research, so that one's research is not about looking at something from outside but about being part of it. I think a third way is to bring the things associated with the séance into academia, perhaps by looking at what the concept of research as practice, developed in the creative arts, might mean.[38] Of course, this raises the question of why academia might want to accommodate the séance. My instinct is that by bringing séance things (the dark, lots of silence, the uncanny) into the bright light of academic worlds, we might inch a little nearer to lost enchantments.

---

38 The presentation upon which this essay is based was originally envisaged as having two parallel streams, one functioning as an academic presentation and one functioning, through illustrations, as a sort of Rorschachian ink blot, where there is more showing going on and not too much saying, and where the presentation is as much performance as lecture. The original idea was to raise a question about which stream of the presentation best answered the original question, and why.

Select bibliography

Batcheldor, Kenneth J. 'Contributions to the Theory of PK Induction from Sitter Group Work'. *Journal of the American Society for Psychical Research* 78 (1984): 105–22.

———. 'PK in Sitter Groups'. *Psychoenergetic Systems* 3 (1979): 77–93.

———. 'Report of a Case of Table Levitation and Associated Phenomena'. *Journal of the Society for Psychical Research* 43 (1966): 339–356.

———., and Colin Brookes-Smith. *Manual of Advanced Psychokinetic Procedures*. London: Society for Psychical Research, 1970.

Hansen, George P. *The Trickster and the Paranormal*. Bloomington: Xlibris, 2001.

Owen, Iris M. 'Continuation of the Philip Experiment'. *Journal of the New Horizons Research Foundation* 2 (1976): 3–6.

Owen, Iris M. '"Philip's" Fourth Year'. *Journal of the New Horizons Research Foundation* 2 (1977): 11–15.

———. '"Philip's" Story Continued'. *Journal of the New Horizons Research Foundation* 2 (1974): 14–20.

———., and Margaret Sparrow. *Conjuring Up Philip, An Adventure in Psychokinesis*. New York: Harper & Row , 1976.

———., and Margaret Sparrow. 'Generation of Paranormal Physical Phenomena in Connection with an Imaginary "Communicator"'. *Journal of the New Horizons Research Foundation* 1 (1974): 6–13.

Ullman, Montague. 'The Bindelof Story, Part I (of 4)'. *Exceptional Human Experience* 11 (1993): 17–28.

Ullman, Montague. 'The Bindelof Story, Part 2'. *Exceptional Human Experience* 12 (1994): 25–32.

———. 'The Bindelof Story, Part 3', *Exceptional Human Experience* 12 (1994): 208–21.

———. 'The Bindelof Story, Part 4'. *Exceptional Human Experience* 13 (1995): 1–12.

PART THREE

*Re-enchanting
the Mind*

The Salutogenic Imagination

ANITA KLUJBER

'Imagination, realm of enchantment!'[1]
—XAVIER DE MAISTRE

THE SENSE OF COHERENCE AS AN ATTRIBUTE OF THE IMAGINATION

The *Re-enchanting the Academy* conference addressed the need to cultivate transformative forms of learning, such as enchantment and the imagination, in education. There was a general agreement among conference participants that enchantment and the imagination are mutually arising, inseparable experiences. Simon Wilson pointed out that they are near-synonyms.[2] Patrick Curry explained the essence of their relation in a profound statement: 'The imagination is the primary organ of perception that enables you to realise enchantment.'[3] The consubstantiality of enchantment and imagination can be discerned in their vital power, which Simon Wilson described as 'a manifestation of life itself'.[4] This enlivening energy

---

1   Xavier de Maistre, *Voyage Around My Room. Selected Works of Xavier de Maistre*, trans. Stephen Sartarelli (New York: New Directions, 1994), 77.

2   'Enchantment [...] has close synonyms, such as imagination, inspiration, transfiguration, enspiritment, ensoulment, Eden, Paradise, love'. Simon Wilson, 'Clutching the Wheel of St Catherine, or, A Visit to a Re-Enchanted College', in the present volume, 53–66.

3   Patrick Curry, 'The Enchantment of Learning and "The Fate of our Times"' (audio recording of paper presented at the Re-enchanting the Academy conference, Canterbury Christ Church University, 25th September 2015. Oral statement from the speaker's response to questions following his paper: see https://youtu.be/omnG5t6Bolo), at 1.02 h., *vide*: 'conference materials Re-Enchanting'.

4   Wilson, 'Clutching the Wheel', 53–66. Many creative artists describe the state of inspiration as being united with the creative energy of the universe.

produces an immediate uplifting feeling and a long-term soul-shaping effect. This chapter is concerned with the lasting impact of the imagination, arguing that imaginative experiences constitute a transformative learning process, whereby the mind is conditioned to detect and construct coherence, and when this creative habit of mind is carried over to life, it helps us to cope with challenges, find meaning, and create harmony. Samuel Taylor Coleridge believed that this tendency to unify is 'a necessity of the human mind', an organic process that facilitates 'connection of parts to a whole', exhibiting the 'living power' of the imagination.[5]

Meaning-oriented convergence, whereby discrete entities are drawn together into unity and resonate with each other in harmony, is one of the ways in which one can experience the creative energy of life. The unifying nature of imaginative perception originates from the instinctive human desire for connection. Constructive mind-work that is carried out with a loving attention is always accompanied by a sense of wonder that arises from participating in bringing order and beauty to life.[6] Order is connectedness; it is based on the principle of attraction, sharing the structure of love.[7] Simon Wilson discusses the interrelation of love, enchantment, imagination, and the vital power of life in his chapter. He describes the life force in terms of a mandalic centre, a point of convergence, from where enchantment emanates, and he correlates this with love.[8] With reference to Empedocles, W.B. Yeats distinguishes the unifying, centripetal power of life from the centrifugal energy, calling these 'Concord' and 'Discord', i.e., 'Love' and 'War', respectively.[9] In this chapter, I shall explore the unifying faculty of the mind as an attribute of the imagination, arguing that the life-enhancing effect of the imagination may be explained by its relational, synthesising nature, its

---

5   Samuel Taylor Coleridge, *Coleridge's Shakespearean Criticism*, ed. T.M. Raysor (London: Dent, 1960), 197.

6   Aristotle correlates order and beauty: '[A] beautiful object [...] must [...] have an orderly arrangement of parts'. Aristotle, *Poetics*, ed. Richard Koss, trans. S. H. Butcher (Mineola: Dover, 1997), 14.

7   An enchanting poetic account of love as the organising principle of cosmic dance is Sir John Davies, *Orchestra: or a Poeme of Dauncing* (United States: Hardpress, 2012).

8   Wilson, 'Clutching the Wheel'.

9   W.B. Yeats, *A Vision* (London: Papermac, 1981), 67–68.

rootedness in the cosmic principle of love.

It is a widely held opinion that enchantment and the imagination promote emotional, moral, and intellectual development as well as health.[10] Ralph Waldo Emerson believed that 'the imagination is not a talent of some men, but is the health of every man'.[11] In response to this statement, James E. Miller comments: 'Imagination is the health of the society, the endurance of civilization, the survival of the world. If we are to save the world, we must begin by saving that which makes the world a world—the human'.[12] These words bring J.R.R. Tolkien's statement, the motto of this conference, to mind: 'Enchantment is as necessary for the health and complete functioning of the Human as is sunlight for physical life'.[13] W.B. Yeats observes that the imagination has a therapeutic power. He notes: '[M]agical simples [...] do their work [...] by awakening in the depths of the mind where it mingles with the Great Mind, and is enlarged by the Great Memory, some curative energy', and he pointed out that 'this great mind and great memory [are] evoked by symbols'.[14] Simon Wilson refers to Yeats scholar T.R. Henn, who succeeded in activating the revitalising energy of the imagination through archetypal symbols, '[opening] his students to [the] life-giving experience of literature'.[15] C.G. Jung provides substantial evidence that engagement with archetypes by means of the active imagination initiates a transformative and healing process.[16]

---

10   Laura Shannon, a speaker at the conference, gave a wonderful example of the lasting effect of enchantment. She explained that dance as a form of the active imagination promotes the healing of the body and the soul, and even the memory of having danced has this health-boosting power when it is not possible to dance. See also Laura's chapter in this volume.

11   Ralph Waldo Emerson, 'Poetry and Imagination', in *The Collected Works of Ralph Waldo Emerson*, vol. 8, ed. Glen M. Johnson and Joel Myerson (Cambridge: The Belknap Press of Harvard University Press, 2010), 30.

12   James E. Miller, 'Imagination and the Health of Everyman', *College English* 32.5 (1971): 570.

13   J.R.R. Tolkien, *Smith of Wootton Major*, ed. Verlyn Flieger (London: HarperCollins, 2005), 101, quoted in Patrick Curry, 'Enchantment and Modernity', *Philosophy, Activism, Nature* 12 (2012): 82.

14   W.B. Yeats, 'Magic', in *Essays and Introductions* (London: Macmillan, 1961), 50, 28.

15   Wilson, 'Clutching the Wheel'.

16   C.G. Jung, 'The Tavistock Lectures: On the Theory and Practice of An-

Owing to Jung's pioneering work, the value of the imagination is being increasingly recognized and its transformative power is being harnessed in creative art therapies.[17] A growing number of educators are drawing on Jung's insights into the beneficial role that the imagination plays in promoting personal growth towards wholeness, and are integrating Jungian techniques into their holistic pedagogical approaches.[18] However, educational institutions still tend to be reluctant to integrate the cultivation of the imagination into the curriculum on a regular and systematic basis. This chapter is an attempt to take a step towards removing this obstacle by arguing that regular imaginative activity is conducive to a constructive approach to life, which benefits intellectual and emotional development as well as health. In order to validate this argument, I will refer to Aaron Antonovsky's research in the field of medical sociology and discuss his ideas in a larger interdisciplinary context. Antonovsky discovered that constructive thinking, which enables us to organise our experiences and perceptions, is the key factor in promoting and maintaining physical and mental health.[19] He referred to this quality of mind as the 'sense of coherence',[20] and he collected quantifiable data which indicate that a strong sense of coherence boosts health and improves the quality of life. I shall contend that it is exactly

alytical Psychology. Lecture V,' in *The Collected Works of C.G. Jung*, vol. 18, ed. Sir Herbert Read, Michael Fordham, Gerhard Adler, and William McGuire, trans. R.F.C. Hull (London: Routledge & Kegan Paul, 1977), 169–82 (par. 390–415), esp. 173 (par. 401).

17   Joan Chodorow, 'Post-Jungian Contributions', afterword in Joan Chodorow, ed., *Jung on Active Imagination* (Princeton: Princeton University Press, 1997), 177–79.

18   See, for example, Raya A. Jones, Austin Clarkson, Sue Congram, and Nick Stratton, eds., *Education and Imagination. Post-Jungian Perspectives* (London: Routledge, 2008); Darrell Dobson, *Transformative Teaching: Promoting Transformation Through Literature, the Arts, and Jungian Psychology* (Rotterdam: Sense Publishers, 2008); and Inna Semetsky, ed., *Jung and Educational Theory* (Chichester: Wiley-Blackwell, 2013).

19   See Aaron Antonovsky, *Health, Stress, and Coping* (San Francisco: Jossey-Bass, 1979), passim; and Aaron Antonovsky, *Unraveling the Mystery of Health: How People Manage Stress and Stay Well* (San Francisco: Jossey-Bass, 1987), passim.

20   Antonovsky acknowledged that it was his wife Helen 'who proposed the term "the sense of coherence"'. Antonovsky, *Unraveling*, xiii.

this quality of mind, the sense of coherence, the ability to generate meaning by making connections, which is strengthened by enchantment and the imagination. Creating space for these transformative experiences in education would be an effective way to boost the life-enhancing faculty of the sense of coherence because the human mind naturally carries over its skills and general orientation from one domain of experience to another.

Imagination and enchantment are commonly regarded as advanced coherence-generating acts.[21] Emerson describes the imagination as 'the impulse to search resemblance, affinity, identity'.[22] Coleridge regards the imagination as an esemplastic, unifying power,[23] 'the greatest faculty of the human mind [...that] acts chiefly by producing out of many things [...] a oneness',[24] a 'synthetic and magical power [... that] forms all into one graceful and intelligent whole'.[25] He believed that the synthesising power of the imagination is so great that it can embrace reason. In his words, the imagination is 'a reconciling and mediatory power, which, incorporating the Reason [...] gives birth to a system of symbols'.[26] Similarly, the imagination is shown to contain reason in William Wordsworth's last book of *The Prelude*, where the poet also links this psycho-cosmic power to love:

> This spiritual Love acts not nor can exist
> Without Imagination, which, in truth
> Is but another name for absolute power

---

21   Patrick Curry draws attention to the relational nature of enchantment. With reference to Saul Bellow, he distinguishes 'disenchanting division', or lack of coherence, from enchanting synthesis. He notes: 'the concrete magic of enchantment [...] is truly transgressive, because it fuses what modernity tries to keep chastely apart'. Patrick Curry, 'The Enchantment of Learning and 'the Fate of our Times', in the present volume, 33–51.

22   Emerson, 'Poetry and Imagination', 3.

23   See Samuel Taylor Coleridge, *Biographia Literaria*, ed. George Watson (London: Dent, 1975), 161–67.

24   Coleridge, *Coleridge's Shakespearean*, 188.

25   Coleridge, *Biographia*, 174.

26   Samuel Taylor Coleridge, *The Statesman's Manual, or The Bible the Best Guide to Political Skill and Foresight* (London, 1816), 35.

And clearest insight, amplitude of mind,
And reason, in her most exalted mood. (ll.188–192)[27]

Shelley correlates imagination and love on the basis of their connective nature, attributing empathy to both.[28] He also points out
that the imagination is 'the creative faculty, which is the basis of all
knowledge.'[29] He defines the imagination as 'the principle of synthesis', which he distinguishes (but does not separate) from reason, the
'principle of analysis', only to bring the two together as an inseparable pair: 'Reason is to imagination as the instrument to the agent, as
the body to the spirit, as the shadow to the substance.'[30] In a similar
vein, C.S. Lewis writes: '[R]eason is the natural organ of truth; but
imagination is the organ of meaning. Imagination [...] is not the
cause of truth, but its condition.'[31] Wallace Stevens offers yet another
explanation: 'reason is simply the methodiser of the imagination.
It may be that the imagination is a miracle of logic and that its ex-
quisite divinations are calculations beyond analysis.'[32] In an essay
on Stevens, Northrop Frye remarks: 'The imagination contains reason and emotion.'[33] Likewise, Patrick Curry notes that 'reason and
reasoning should be included within the purview of enchantment

---

27   William Wordsworth, *The Prelude: A Parallel Text*, ed. J. C. Maxwell (Lon-
       don: Penguin Books, 1971), 521.

28   'The great secret of morals is love [...] A man, to be greatly good, must
       imagine intensely and comprehensively; he must put himself in the place
       of another [...] The great instrument of moral good is the imagination'.
       Percy Bysshe Shelley, 'A Defence of Poetry', in *The Complete Works of Per-
       cy Bysshe Shelley*, vol. 7, ed. Roger Ingpen and Walter E. Peck (London:
       Ernest Benn Limited, 1965), 118.

29   Ibid., 134.

30   Ibid., 109.

31   C.S. Lewis, 'Bluspels and Flalansferes: A Semantic Nightmare', in *Selected
       Literary Essays*, ed. Walter Hooper (Cambridge: Cambridge University
       Press, 1969), 265.

32   Wallace Stevens, 'Imagination as Value', in *Collected Poetry and Prose*, ed.
       Frank Kermode and Joan Richardson (New York: The Library of Ameri-
       ca, 1997), 738.

33   Northrop Frye, 'The Realistic Oriole: A Study of Wallace Stevens', in *Fa-
       bles of Identity: Studies in Poetic Mythology* (New York: Harcourt, Brace &
       World, 1963), 240.

and the imagination.'[34] Matthew Del Nevo attributes the integration of rational and imaginative mental processes to enchantment. He writes: 'Scientific thinking and poetic thinking are surprisingly harmonized by the work of enchantment.'[35] Albert Einstein praised the all-embracing power of the imagination in an unhesitating statement: 'Imagination is more important than knowledge. For knowledge is limited, whereas imagination embraces the entire world, stimulating progress, giving birth to evolution. It is, strictly speaking, a real factor in scientific research.'[36] C.G. Jung also understood the imagination in a broad way. He pointed out that 'every good idea and all creative work are the offspring of the imagination.'[37] Jung discovered that the active imagination promotes the integration of different aspects of the psyche, and that this is crucial to mental and physical health.

These are just a few observations chosen at random to establish the point that the imagination and enchantment nurture relational thinking, which can grow into a highly developed sense of coherence that involves the integration of left-hemisphere analysis and right-hemisphere synthesis. Aaron Antonovsky's research confirmed that the sense of coherence is a fundamental health-promoting life skill, a perceptual orientation that is responsible for 'seeing the world as ordered rather than chaotic.'[38] Wallace Stevens attributes this ordering process to the imagination, contending that we use this ability of the mind in everyday life. He points out that 'the imagination is the power that enables us to perceive the normal in the abnormal, the opposite of chaos in chaos,'[39] asserting that 'the imagination pervades life.'[40]

---

34   Curry, *vide*: 'conference materials *Re-Enchanting*', at 1.01.26 h.

35   Matthew Del Nevo, *The Work of Enchantment* (New Brunswick: Transaction Publishers, 2011), 17.

36   Albert Einstein, *Einstein on Cosmic Religion and Other Opinions and Aphorisms* (Mineola: Dover, 2009), 97.

37   C.G. Jung, 'The Problem of Types in the History of Classical and Medieval Thought', in *The Collected Works of C.G. Jung*, vol. 6, ed. Sir Herbert Read, Michael Fordham, Gerhard Adler, and William McGuire, trans. H.G. Baynes, revised R.F.C. Hull (1971, repr. London: Routledge, 1989), 63 (par. 93).

38   Antonovsky, *Unraveling*, 92.

39   Stevens, 'Imagination as Value', 737.

40   Ibid., 732.

CONVERGING PERSPECTIVES ON COHERENCE, MEANING, AND PURPOSE

Aaron Antonovsky devoted his research to the question of why some people stay healthy in potentially damaging circumstances while other people who face similar negative stressors are unable to cope. Trying to understand the origin of health, therefore, he called the orientation of his research *salutogenic*, to distinguish it from pathogenic approaches that deal with the origin and treatment of disease. The word 'salutogenesis' contains the Latin root *salus* and the Greek word *genesis* (origin). *Salus* refers to safety, health, greeting, salvation, and it is also the name of the Roman goddess of health and prosperity.[41] Thus, a healer from the world of imagination greets us when we deal with the concept of salutogenesis.

Antonovsky summarises his main discovery as follows: 'the central thesis of the salutogenic model is that a strong SOC [sense of coherence] is crucial to successful coping with the ubiquitous stressors of living and hence to health maintenance.'[42] He regarded this sense of coherence as 'a dispositional orientation rather than a personality trait,'[43] a quality of mind that is built up and shaped through life experiences.

While Antonovsky's main concern is the effect of life situations on one's sense of coherence, he also mentions that the imagination has relevance to the salutogenic model. He writes: 'When one searches for effective adaptation of the organism, one can move beyond post-Cartesian dualism and look to imagination, love, play, meaning, will, and social structures that foster them. Or, as I would prefer to put it, to theories of successful coping.'[44] In this statement, Antonovsky brings together imagination and love, identifying them as salutogenic acts. I will explore this idea further by correlating Antonovsky's findings with the observations of others.

---

41   Charlton T. Lewis and Charles Short, *A Latin Dictionary* (http://www.per-seus.tufts.edu/hopper/text?doc=Perseus:text:1999.04.0059:entry=salus), *vide*: 'salus Latin Charlton'.

42   Antonovsky, *Unraveling*, 164.

43   Ibid., xvii.

44   Ibid., 9.

Antonovsky distinguishes three main components of the sense of coherence: comprehensibility, manageability, and meaningfulness.[45] I shall give a brief survey of these abilities and point out that they are inherent in Jung's concept of active imagination.

Antonovsky defines *comprehensibility*, the cognitive component of a sense of coherence, as follows:

> Comprehensibility [...] refers to the extent to which one perceives the stimuli that confront one, deriving from the internal and external environments, as making cognitive sense, as information that is ordered, consistent, structured, and clear, rather than as noise—chaotic, disordered, random, accidental, inexplicable.[46]

Jung too was aware that the ability to comprehend internal and external stimuli and their interrelations contributes to health, and he found that the imagination plays a crucial role in this process. He insisted that quieting consciousness is just the first phase of active imagination. Once the unconscious is given freedom to express itself and evoke enchantment, a conscious, reflective examination of the emerging contents must ensue in order to achieve a healthy integration of the unconscious and consciousness. Jung refers to this process as the constructive, synthetic method, as distinct from what he calls the concretistic, reductive approach.[47] He explains: 'Constructive treatment of the unconscious, that is the question of meaning and purpose, paves the way for the patient's insight into that process which I call the transcendent function.'[48] Jung attributes the healing power of the imagination to the transcendent function, 'the collaboration of conscious and unconscious data'.[49] He uses the active imagination as a psychotherapeutic method to heal emotional

---

45   Ibid., 15–19.

46   Ibid., 16–17.

47   C.G. Jung, 'The Transcendent Function', in *The Collected Works of C.G. Jung*, vol. 8, ed. Sir Herbert Read, Michael Fordham, and Gerhard Adler, trans. R.F.C. Hull (London: Routledge & Kegan Paul, 1960), 73–77 (par. 145–152). Jung, 'Definitions', in *Collected Works*, vol 6, 423–29 (par. 702–714).

48   Jung, 'The Transcendent Function', 75 (par. 147).

49   Ibid., 82 (par. 167).

dysfunction. The aim of his constructive method is to make meaningful connections, often with the help of myth, in order to bring coherence into apparently illogical and confusingly obscure expressions of the unconscious. As a result of this constructive approach, Jung explains, products of the unconscious 'acquire a more ordered character; they become dramatically composed and reveal clear sense-connections'.[50] The Jungian active imagination is, then, a mental intervention that strengthens the sense of coherence by conditioning the mind for actively participating in making its own products and perceptions comprehensible. According to Antonovsky, 'to experience, time again, things that fit together, unknowns that are explained to one's satisfaction, and ordered patterns strengthens one's sense of comprehensibility'.[51] Jung showed that the mind can be trained to make this happen; in other words, comprehensibility can be strengthened intentionally by undertaking experiences in which the mind actively shapes its own products, turning relative chaos into a network of sense-connections, which reveals meaning and purpose.

Antonovsky identifies *manageability* as the instrumental-behavioural component of the sense of coherence, defining it as 'the extent to which one perceives that resources are at one's disposal which are adequate to meet the demands posed by the stimuli that bombard one'.[52] Manageability is a strong inner trust in one's ability to use one's resistance resources when facing challenges and difficulties in life. Antonovsky distinguishes a number of 'generalized resistance resources' of internal and external origin, such as optimism, self-esteem, knowledge-intelligence, social connectedness, financial stability, education, etc.[53] We could add that the imagination can also function as a resistance resource as it involves trust in the ability of the mind to transform itself and its perceptions in its search for meaning. Jung explains that regular practice of constructive thinking increases self-reliance; this implies that the active imagination is a psychological skill that contributes to manageability. Jung believed that by learning how to integrate unconscious material into consciousness, one can develop a life-skill that prepares one to cope

---

50   Ibid., 77 (par. 152).

51   Antonovsky, *Unraveling*, 113–14.

52   Ibid., 17.

53   Antonovsky, *Health*, 98–122.

with future challenges. He writes:

> The avowed purpose of [voluntary involvement in fan-
> tasy-processes] is to integrate the statements of the un-
> conscious, to assimilate their compensatory content,
> and thereby produce a whole meaning which alone
> makes life worth living and, for not a few people, possi-
> ble at all. [...] [O]nly one who has risked the fight with
> the dragon and is not overcome by it wins the hoard, the
> 'treasure hard to attain.' He alone has a genuine claim to
> self-confidence, for he has faced the dark ground of his
> self and thereby gained himself. This experience gives
> him faith and trust, the *pistis* in the ability of the self
> to sustain him, for everything that menaced him from
> inside he has made his own. He has acquired the right
> to believe that he will be able to overcome all future
> threats by the same means. He has arrived at an inner
> certainty which makes him capable of self-reliance, and
> attained what the alchemists called *unio mentalis*.[54]

This is a concise explanation of how the constructive nature of active imagination facilitates integration of the personality, and how this process strengthens inner certainty and self-reliance, in other words manageability.

In the first sentence of the quotation above, Jung writes about the drive to 'produce a whole meaning which alone makes life worth living'. This is a perfect formulation of what Antonovsky calls *mean-ingfulness*, the motivational component of the sense of coherence. Meaningfulness is an emotional orientation, which complements the cognitive nature of comprehensibility. Antonovsky explains:

> Formally, the meaningfulness component of the soc
> refers to the extent to which one feels that life makes
> sense emotionally, that at least some of the problems
> and demands posed by living are worth investing ener-
> gy in, are worthy of commitment and engagement, are

---

54   C.G. Jung, 'The Conjunction', in *The Collected Works of C.G. Jung*, vol. 14, ed. Sir Herbert Read, Michael Fordham, and Gerhard Adler, trans. R.F.C. Hull (London: Routledge & Kegan Paul, 1963), 531 (par. 756).

> challenges that are 'welcome' rather than burdens that one would much rather do without. [...] [W]hen [...] unhappy experiences are imposed on [...] a person, he or she will willingly take up the challenge, will be determined to seek meaning in it, and will do his or her best to overcome it with dignity.[55]

From a Jungian perspective, the search for meaning or meaningfulness is the key catalyst of psychological development. Jung emphasised that the transcendent function involves the attempt to discover and construct meaning: 'aesthetic formulation needs understanding of the meaning, and understanding needs aesthetic formulation. The two supplement each other to form the transcendent function.'[56] The transcendent function is, then, an imaginative act; it involves transcending oppositions by allowing unconscious contents to constellate and to be observed by, and integrated into, conscious awareness. In this process, emotion-centred meaningfulness and meta-cognitive comprehensibility work together to achieve wholeness. When right-hemisphere and left-hemisphere brain activities are integrated in such a way, the whole capacity of the mind is used, and this enhances well-being.

Daniel J. Siegel's applied neurobiological research provides supportive evidence for the importance of promoting integration in the brain at all stages of personal development.[57] Since the discovery of neuroplasticity, we have scientific proof that profound mental-emotional experiences can actually shape the structure of the brain as new connections are made between neurons and different brain functions are co-ordinated. Siegel explains this process in an easily accessible way, contending that experiences and states of mind affect the function and structure of the brain.[58] He draws attention to the educational and developmental benefits of integration:

> We want to help our children become better integrated so they can use their whole brain in a co-ordinated way. For example, we want them to be *horizontally integrat-*

---

55   Antonovsky, *Unraveling*, 18–19.

56   Jung, 'Transcendent', 85 (par.177).

57   See Daniel J. Siegel, *Mindsight* (London: Oneworld, 2011), 64–76.

58   See ibid., 38–44.

ed, so that their left-brain logic can work well with their right-brain emotion. We also want them to be *vertically integrated*, so that the physically higher parts of their brain, which let them thoughtfully consider their actions, work well with the lower parts, which are more concerned with instinct, gut reactions, and survival [...] [A]n integrated brain is capable of doing much more than its individual parts could accomplish alone [...] As a result, [children] will thrive emotionally, intellectually, and socially. An integrated brain results in improved decision making, better control of body and emotions, fuller self-understanding, stronger relationships, and success in school. And it all begins with the experiences parents and other caregivers provide, which lay the groundwork for integration and mental health.[59]

Nurturing the imagination serves exactly this purpose: it promotes integration by harmonising different functions of the brain.

The practical aspects of Siegel's research involve utilising everyday parenting situations as opportunities to develop integration in the brain. This, he points out, leads to an integrated life, which he describes using the ancient Greek term *eudaimonia* that he defines as 'living a life of meaning, compassion, equanimity, and connection'.[60] The *Re-enchanting the Academy* conference brought together scholars who are united by the same goal, to move life towards eudaimonia, using an alternative route, the path of enchantment or imagination.

The coherence-oriented mental process is regarded as the neurotypical cognitive processing style, as distinct from fragmented perception, which Uta Frith and Francesca Happé describe as 'weak central coherence', a deficit in integrating details into a coherent, meaningful whole and comprehending global meaning. Weak central coherence characterises individuals with autistic spectrum disorders, who, however, have an atypical local processing bias, an

---

59   Daniel J. Siegel and Tina Pane Bryson, *The Whole Brain Child* (London: Robinson, 2012), 6–10.

60   Daniel J. Siegel, *The Mindful Therapist. A Clinician's Guide to Mindsight and Neural Integration* (New York: W.W. Norton, 2010), xxiv.

enhanced ability to perceive local details.[61] Bruce Mills relates the concept of central coherence to Romantic theories of the imagination, emphasising that it is this integrative mental process that leads to a sense of purpose and larger meaning.[62]

I referred to the findings of Antonovsky, Jung, Siegel, Frith, Happé, and Mills to provide plausible explanations for the observation that the imagination has salutogenic benefits due to its integrative and constructive nature. The 'sense of coherence' is comparable with integration and with the perception of 'sense-connections' and 'central coherence'. These concepts are rooted in the common understanding that coherence-oriented mind-work is essential for generating and maintaining a sense of purpose and meaning in life. These perspectives can shed light on a neglected potential of the humanities, increasing the weight of the argument that enchantment and the imagination can have *lasting* beneficial effects because they promote integrative comprehension.

THE SALUTOGENIC IMAGINATION IN EDUCATION

So far, we have established that the sense of coherence is salutogenic, and we argued that the imagination, which boosts one's sense of coherence, is bound to be salutogenic also.

I have devoted a large section of this paper to placing the imagination into an interdisciplinary context as I hope that the quantifiable evidence provided by biopsychosocial investigations of constructive mind-work may further the endeavour to create space for the training of the imagination in education. In presenting the imagination as a salutogenic act in education, we are clearly not trying to practise therapy but we are preparing relatively healthy individuals for life by boosting their sense of coherence.

Antonovsky explored the dynamics of the sense of coherence

---

61   Uta Frith, *Autism: Explaining the Enigma*, 2nd edition (Oxford: Blackwell, 2003). The book contains a chapter on 'The Enchantment of Autism', 17–33. Francesca Happé and Uta Frith, 'The weak coherence account: Detail-focused cognitive style in autism spectrum disorders', *Journal of Autism and Developmental Disorders* 36.1 (2006): 5–25.

62   Bruce Mills, 'Autism and the Imagination', in *Autism and Representation*, ed. Mark Osteen (New York: Routledge, 2008), 117–32.

over the lifespan, and concluded that 'in the period of early adult-hood [...] one's location on the SOC continuum becomes more or less fixed'.[63] He developed this controversial stability hypothesis in his first book, *Health, Stress, and Coping,* and he devoted a whole chapter in his second book to refining it, but his main argument remained essentially the same.[64] If his suggestion that the level of one's sense of coherence is usually established 'by the end of the first decade or so of one's adulthood',[65] is right, then it would be vitally important to put more emphasis on improving the coherence-generating faculty in the critical period, within the framework of education, instead of just hoping that life will provide relevant experiences. It would be desirable to foster the imagination and its meta-cognitive appreciation at all levels of education with the explicit purpose of improving the sense of coherence. This is a salutogenic approach that is beneficial for anyone, not just to those in need of therapy.[66]

I conjecture that with the aid of the imagination, one's sense of coherence could be improved at any stage of life, even in late adult-hood. This could be a significant contribution to Antonovsky's research.[67] Jung's success in using the active imagination as a psy-chotherapeutic method in adult life points into this direction. Research into the neuroplasticity of the adult brain also presents promising results.[68]

Antonovsky conducted his research passionately, with a sense of wonder that led him to new insights. He tested his hypotheses empirically, but all aspects of his research, including the scientific approaches, were fuelled by what he calls an 'enchantment with the mystery of health'.[69] He demonstrated integrative thinking by placing his model of salutogenesis in the context of what he saw as

---

63   Antonovsky, *Unraveling,* 107.

64   Ibid., 89–127.

65   Ibid., 119.

66   For this reason, I avoid using the word 'bibliotherapy' for the salutogenic branch of applied literature.

67   This hypothesis was supported by psychotherapists and other participants of this conference following the oral presentation of this paper.

68   Denise C. Park and Gérard N. Bischof, 'The Aging Mind: Neuroplasticity in Response to Cognitive Training', *Dialogues in Clinical Neuroscience* 15.1 (2013): 109–19.

69   Antonovsky, *Unraveling,* xvii.

'an emerging central problem in all of science, the mystery of the transformation of order out of chaos'.[70] Bringing order into chaos is, of course, an act of the creative imagination. It has always been a central preoccupation of the arts and humanities. This concept thus establishes the possibility of a productive communication between different but complementary areas of knowledge, generating a sense of coherence within an interdisciplinary framework.

Antonovky was aware that the concept of the sense of coherence can bridge the fields of science and the arts. He identified a range of new directions towards which the salutogenic model opens up a path.[71] In this survey, he refers to an article written by the psychologist E.E. Sampson,[72] in which the author makes an interdisciplinary connection between physics and literary criticism. Antonovsky summarises the main point as follows:

> Sampson sees Derrida's contribution in literary criticism as pointing precisely in the same direction as nonequilibrium theory in physics. Only if we view literature as totally open-ended, multiple-meaning texts, with reading as a dialogue over time between text and reader, with no absolute fixed textual reality, can coherence and order be approached.[73]

There is a general agreement amongst readers and scholars of literature that coherence and order emerge through the reader's active imaginative involvement in the construction of meaning, both in intratextual and intertextual contexts. The attempt to make sense of imaginative literature stimulates the constructive faculty of the mind, which is also beneficial in other domains of experience. It is gratifying to find this idea in an embryonic form in Antonovsky's discussion of 'Issues for Further Exploration', where he brings poet-

---

70   Ibid., xvii, 163. Antonovsky explicitly stated that his model 'suggested the possibility of integrating a considerable body of seemingly disparate findings and ideas': ibid., xiii.

71   Ibid., 163–87.

72   E.E. Sampson, 'The Decentralisation of Identity: Toward a Revised Concept of Personal and Social Order', *American Psychologist* 40 (1985): 1203–11. Quoted in Antonovsky, *Unraveling*, 167–70.

73   Antonovsky, *Unraveling*, 169.

ry and life into a metaphorical relation:

> [God] may be a poet. His works are full of allusion, illu-
> sion, question, contradiction, open-ended alternatives,
> puns, despair, and love. Yet we can seek to understand a
> poem. My own work has been devoted to studying the
> ways human beings cope with the reality of the poem
> that is social existence. Clearly, other scientists are en-
> gaged in parallel endeavors. Is it too grandiose an ambi-
> tion to set as a goal moving closer to an integrated theo-
> ry that proposes how any system copes with its reality?[74]

Antonovsky intuitively rediscovered the archetypal idea that life
is structured like a poem. This idea implies that in trying to make
sense of a poem, one is practicing a mental-emotional skill that promotes one's ability to cope with life. It is the imagination that we use
in making sense of poetry and other forms of art, and we can use
the same faculty to make sense of life. It was probably his 'enchantment with the mystery of health'[75] that enabled Antonovsky to see a
reflective relation between the semantic complexity of a poem and
the dynamics of social existence. This is an example of how imaginative thinking enables one to grasp meanings and connections that
are beyond the reach of non-imaginative forms of knowledge. The
parallel which Antonovsky draws between life and poetry implies
that we can improve the life skill of a sense of coherence by dealing
with poetry, and, by extension, with any product of the imagination.

THE SALUTOGENIC POTENTIAL OF LITERARY EDUCATION

In discussing the salutogenic impact of the imagination, it is in-
structive to refer to Northrop Frye's pioneering attempts to harness,
for its mind-shaping and life-enhancing power, the potential of literary education to improve the imagination. Frye recognised that
the imagination is 'the constructive power of the mind',[76] the ability

---

74 Ibid., 170.

75 Ibid., xvii (my italics).

76 Northrop Frye, *The Educated Imagination* (Bloomington: Indiana Uni-

to transform experience, mainly by connecting diverse entities into coherence, order, and unity.[77] Throughout his career, Frye emphasised that 'the end of literary teaching is not simply the admiration of literature; it's something more like the transfer of imaginative energy from literature to student'.[78] He was, of course, familiar with the English Romantics' view of the imagination,[79] and he was also fascinated by Wallace Stevens' poetic and theoretical reflections on the imagination.[80] Common to all of them is the understanding that the imagination is not limited to the domain of art; it shapes all aspects of human experience.[81] Through imaginative activity, we develop a constructive orientation that has an effect on how we relate to other people and how we live our lives. Frye regarded the imagination as 'pure construction, construction for its own sake',[82] but he also emphasised that the ultimate value of such an exercise in constructive thinking is that it transgresses the domain of art. He wrote: 'The constructs of the imagination tell us things about human life that we don't get in any other way',[83] and he maintained that the transfer of 'imaginative energy *to our own lives* [...] is the aim of all education in the arts'.[84] He praised the imagination for its broad impact. He wrote: 'we use our imagination all the time [...] [O]ur imagination is what our whole social life is really based on [...] In practically ev-

---

versity Press, 1964), 119.

77   'The [...] imagination begins [with] arresting [...] a flow of perceptions without and of impressions within. In that arrest there is born the principle of form or order [...] Stevens follows Coleridge in distinguishing the transforming of experience by the imagination from the re-arranging of it by the "fancy," and ranks the former higher.' Frye, 'Realistic Oriole', 240.

78   Frye, *Educated*, 129.

79   Northrop Frye, *A Study of English Romanticism* (New York: Random House, 1968).

80   Frye, 'Realistic Oriole', passim.

81   William Blake's seminal statement sums it all up: 'The Imagination is not a State: it is the Human Existence itself.' William Blake, 'Milton a Poem in 2 Books', in *The Complete Poetry and Prose of William Blake*, ed. David V. Erdman, rev. ed. (Berkeley: University of California Press, 2008), 132, line 32.

82   Frye, *Educated*, 119.

83   Ibid., 124–25.

84   Northrop Frye, *The Stubborn Structure. Essays on Criticism and Society* (London: Methuen, 1970), 65 (my italics).

erything we do it's the combination of emotion and intellect we call imagination that goes to work'.[85]

Furthering the endeavours of Frye and his adherents,[86] this paper advocates a pedagogic strategy of employing imaginative literature (including myth) as a means of transformative learning. I wish to raise awareness that professionally guided interpretation of products of the imagination is an enjoyable and effective way to enrich the soul and promote integration in the brain. A teaching strategy that is concerned with developing an integrative habit of mind by involving students in a participatory and reflective exploration of enchantment and the imagination is likely to have a positive impact on life. I have used this approach to teaching literature and myth in higher education for ten years, and the results are promising. The majority of students report that what they have experienced through their exploration of the imagination continues to have a positive impact on their learning journey as well as on their lives. This educational orientation ties in with other transformative approaches such as reflective learning, experiential learning, metacognition, mindfulness, and contemplative pedagogy.

Philosopher Matthew Del Nevo urges the need to integrate enchantment into education in order to compensate the soul-damaging tendency of the dominant competitive, business-oriented mentality of our culture. He presents literature as a route that can lead to enchantment, and he extends this claim to art in general: 'Art [...] gives us something, and one of the gifts it can bring—that of enchantment—is a gift of great importance. It is life-enriching. Yet we cannot experience enchantment unless we have receptive ability,

---

85   Frye, *Educated*, 134–35. Similarly, Patrick Curry points out that enchantment is not a temporary escape into another realm, but an orientation that affects the quality of all aspects of our lives. He writes: 'Wonder [...] shows us the imaginal not as altogether somewhere else, another realm, but at the very heart of our ordinary, normal, carnal lives'. Curry, 'The Enchantment of Learning', 33–51.

86   Alan Bewell, Neil ten Kortenaar, and Germaine Warkentin, eds., *Educating the Imagination. Northrop Frye Past, Present, and Future* (Montreal: McGill-Queen's University Press, 2015); Deanne Bogdan, *Re-Educating the Imagination: Towards a Poetics, Politics, and Pedagogy of Literary Engagement* (Portsmouth: Boynto/Cook Publishers, 1992); Kieran Egan, *An Imaginative Approach to Teaching* (San Francisco: Jossey-Bass, 2005).

and this is where culture and education come in'.[87]

Del Nevo distinguishes three main forms of enchantment: reflective reading, attuned listening, and absorbed gazing,[88] and he points out that 'these activities, which are commonly regarded as, if not a waste of time, something you do in your spare time, are in fact [...] absolutely important for every one of us. That is why education that does not have them at its heart is no education at all'.[89]

Patrick Curry distinguishes the same three modalities of enchantment—hearing, watching, and reading—in his chapter, and he discusses these activities in relation to metaphor, which he regards as 'the life-blood of learning'.[90] His view is congruent with the main argument of my paper; after all, metaphor is a creative synthesis whereby one thing is perceived and described in terms of another. Metaphor is perhaps the most compact manifestation of a sense of coherence that emerges through the relational nature of imaginative perception. The 'A is B' structure of metaphor captures a complex mental process whereby two entities are distinguished and united at the same time, epitomizing the crucial moment of creation, the transformation of chaos into condensed meaning.

The attempts to move enchantment and imagination towards the centre of education often involve an acknowledgement of the timeless relevance of ancient wisdom. Enchanters of old had a vital role and a highly respected status in pagan societies, where the life-enhancing power of the imagination was recognised intuitively. C.G. Jung's in-depth psychoanalytic research has confirmed that the ancient intuition about the healing power of the imagination is a valid form of knowledge. Jung observed that this natural wisdom is on the decline, and he drew attention to the damaging psychological consequences of this process. He notes: 'The matrix of a mythopoeic imagination [...] has vanished from our rational age.'[91] Consequently, Jung explains, 'the psyche of civilised man is no longer a self-regulating system'.[92] Jung utilised the inborn potential of

---

87   Del Nevo, *Work of Enchantment*, 2.

88   Ibid., 6–7.

89   Ibid., 161.

90   Curry, 'The Enchantment of Learning'.

91   C.G. Jung, *Memories, Dreams, Reflections*, ed. Aniela Jaffé, trans. Richard and Clara Winston (London: Collins, 1969), 213.

92   Jung, 'The Transcendent Function', 79 (par. 159).

the imagination in his therapeutic method of active imagination. In Jungian psychotherapy, the patient deals with the contents of their own unconscious mind in a constructive way, and a similar approach can be adopted in bibliotherapy and transformative reading, where the products of someone else's imagination are used to stimulate the reader's constructive imagination. In the process of guided interpretation, readers are encouraged to reflect on their changing responses to the text in question, as this makes them aware of the development of their own sense of coherence.

Jung conducted his pioneering research into the active imagination in 1913–1916.[93] More than a decade earlier, W.B. Yeats also observed the decline of the imagination-oriented attitude, and was concerned about its damaging effects. He lamented 'the slow perishing through the centuries of a quality of mind'[94] that is characterised by a natural openness to magic, enchantment, and the imagination. Yeats refers to these mental faculties as 'the greater energies of the mind'[95] that give rise to 'our most elaborate thoughts'[96] and allow us to catch glimpses of 'visions of truth in the depths of the mind'.[97] What he means by 'visions of truth' are spontaneous discoveries of transpersonal, archetypal wisdom in states of magical enchantment. Yeats's main concern was how to 'cast a glamour, an enchantment, over persons of our own time'[98] when 'our education [...] has made our souls less sensitive'.[99] He proposed that enchantment and the imagination can be re-awakened through the arts. He traced the origin of poetry and music to enchantment, acclaiming their enduring power to enchant. He wrote: 'Have not poetry and music arisen, as it seems, out of the sounds the enchanters made to help their imagination enchant, to charm, to bind with a spell themselves and the passers-by? [...] [T]he musician or the poet enchants and charms and binds with a spell his own mind when he would enchant the mind of others.'[100] He pointed out that 'in the making and in the understand-

---

93 Chodorow, *Jung on Active Imagination*, 1.
94 Yeats, 'Magic', 28.
95 Ibid., 37.
96 Ibid., 40.
97 Ibid., 28.
98 Ibid., 42.
99 Ibid., 41.
100 Ibid., 43.

ing of a work of art, and the more easily if it is full of patterns and symbols and music, we are lured to the threshold of sleep',[101] into a semi-conscious state, when enchantment can happen as 'the mind is liberated from the pressure of the will and is unfolded in symbols'.[102] What he describes here is, of course, the image-producing activity of the unconscious mind, which plays such a crucial role in the Jungian active imagination. As Jung stressed the importance of exploring latent sense-connections in spontaneous products of the imagination, so did Yeats take delight in the convergence of seemingly disconnected elements in works of art. He wrote:

> All sounds, all colours, all forms, either because of their preordained energies or because of long association, evoke indefinable and yet precise emotions [...]; and when sound, and colour, and form are in a musical relation, a beautiful relation to one another, they become, as it were, one sound, one colour, one form, and evoke an emotion that is made out of their distinct evocations and yet is one emotion. The same relation exists between all portions of every work of art.[103]

The 'musical relation' Yeats discusses here is a poetic experience of a sense of coherence that emerges through a resonance that is perceived by the imagination.

At the core of the concept of enchantment, there is song, and song is resonance, a primordial vibrational form of connection. Resonance is also the sense of harmony felt when we form loving relationships, and when coherence crystallises in the mind. Poetry sings enchantment into being by the power of resonance, the meaning-generating intersection of images and ideas, which we perceive as unity or a sense of coherence. Yeats' concept of 'musical relation' resonates with Thomas Carlyle's opinion that the harmony of poetic coherence is essentially a musical experience. In his words:

---

101   W.B. Yeats, 'The Symbolism of Poetry', in *Essays and Introductions*, 160.

102   Ibid., 159.

103   Ibid., 156–57.

> A *musical* thought is one spoken by a mind that has penetrated into the inmost heart of the thing; detected the inmost mystery of it, namely, the *melody* that lies hidden in it; the inward harmony of coherence which is its soul, whereby it exists, and has a right to be here, here in this world. All inmost things, we may say, are melodious; naturally utter themselves in Song. The meaning of Song goes deep [...] All deep things are Song. It seems somehow the very central essence of us, Song [...] The primal element of us; of us, and of all things. [...] Poetry, therefore, we call *musical Thought*. The poet is he who *thinks* in that manner [...] See deep enough, and you see musically; the heart of Nature *being* everywhere music, if you can only reach it.[104]

It is enchantment through which you can reach the heart of nature. The meaning of song, or 'musical Thought', does, indeed, go deep because it leaves a lasting impression on the soul.

The poet Denise Levertov praised the song-like quality of poetic thought and language and their soul-shaping effect. She noted: 'When words penetrate deep into us they change the chemistry of the soul, of the imagination'.[105] Levertov observed the vital power of the imagination in the integrative effect of poetry. She wrote:

> The poem has a social *effect* of some kind whether or not the poet wills that it have. It has a kinetic force, it sets in motion [...] elements in the reader that otherwise would be stagnant. And that movement, that coming into play of the otherwise dormant or stagnant element, however small, cannot be without importance if one conceives the human being as one in which all

---

104   Thomas Carlyle, 'The Hero as Poet', in *The Works of Thomas Carlyle*, ed. H.D. Traill (Delhi: Facsimile Publisher, 2015), 83–84; cf. 'The lack of a unifying intelligence [...] is associated [...] with a lack of music'. Denise Levertov, 'Great Possessions', in *The Poet in the World* (New York: New Directions, 1973), 91.

105   Levertov, 'The Poet in the World', in *Poet*, 114.

the parts are so related that none completely fulfills its
function unless all are active.[106]

It is the vital power of enchantment and imagination that brings
about this salutogenic orchestration of all aspects of the human
being. Simon Wilson explains this process with reference to René
Guénon: 'Illumination and enchantment takes place in our heart,
from which it radiates through our whole being.'[107] He emphasises the importance of being in touch with the life-giving, unifying,
archetypal centre of being, which, he states, 'we carry [...] around
in [...] our own interior Centre, in the form of our heart'.[108] Carlyle
refers to this mandalic centre as the song at 'the heart of Nature',
which, he points out, is also 'the very central essence of us'.[109] Carlyle's 'musical Thought', the centripetal, converging mind-work that
produces a sense of coherence through semantic resonance, is only
possible through enchantment, when the thought process is conducted by the love in one's heart. Friedrich Schlegel regarded this
love-driven organising act as the quintessence of poetry and mythology, their transformative power that allows us to recognise that
'the highest beauty, indeed the highest order is yet only that of chaos,
namely of such a one that waits only for the touch of love to unfold
as a harmonious world'.[110] What he describes here is, of course, the
salutogenic imagination infused with the connective energy of love.

Diverse source materials have been orchestrated in this paper to
bring the sense of coherence alive and to approximate the concept
of musical thought. For the final note, I borrow Wordsworth's sum-
mary of *The Prelude* to let our backward glance at this chapter be
embraced by a poetic utterance:

---

106   Levertov, 'A Testament and a Postscript 1959–1973', in *Poet*, 6.
107   Wilson, 'Clutching the Wheel'. Wilson is referring to René Guénon, *Sym-
      bols of Sacred Science*, trans. Henry D. Fohr (Hillsdale: Sophia Perennis,
      2004), 406.
108   Wilson, 'Clutching the Wheel'.
109   Carlyle, 'Hero as Poet', 83–84.
110   Friedrich Schlegel, 'Talk on Mythology', in Burton Feldman and Robert
      D. Richardson eds., *The Rise of Modern Mythology 1680–1860* (Blooming-
      ton: Indiana University Press, 1972), 310.

Imagination having been our theme,
So also hath that intellectual Love,
For they are each in each, and cannot stand
Dividually. (ll. 206–9)[111]

Select bibliography

ANTONOVSKY, Aaron. *Health, Stress, and Coping*. San Francisco: Jossey-Bass, 1979.

_____. *Unraveling the Mystery of Health. How People Manage Stress and Stay Well*. San Francisco: Jossey-Bass, 1987.

CARLYLE, Thomas. 'The Hero as Poet'. In *The Works of Thomas Carlyle*, edited by H.D. Traill, 78–114. Delhi: Facsimile Publisher, 2015.

CHODOROW, Joan, ed. *Jung on Active Imagination*. Princeton: Princeton University Press, 1997.

CURRY, Patrick. 'The Enchantment of Learning and "the Fate of our Times"', in Angela Voss and Simon Wilson, eds., *Re-enchanting the Academy*, 33–51. Auckland: Rubedo Press, 2017.

DEL NEVO, Matthew. *The Work of Enchantment*. New Brunswick: Transaction Publishers, 2011.

EMERSON, Ralph Waldo. 'Poetry and Imagination'. In *The Collected Works of Ralph Waldo Emerson*, vol. 8, edited by Glen M. Johnson and Joel Myerson, 1–42. Cambridge: The Belknap Press of Harvard University Press, 2010.

FRYE, Northrop. *The Educated Imagination*. Bloomington: Indiana University Press, 1964.

HAPPÉ, Francesca and Uta FRITH. 'The Weak Coherence Account: Detail-focused Cognitive Style in Autism Spectrum Disorders'. *Journal of Autism and Developmental Disorders* 36.1 (2006): 5–25.

MILLS, Bruce. 'Autism and the Imagination'. In *Autism and Representation*, edited by Mark Osteen, 117–32. New York: Routledge, 2008.

SIEGEL, Daniel J., and Tina Pane BRYSON. *The Whole Brain Child*. London: Robinson, 2012.

STEVENS, Wallace. 'Imagination as Value'. In *Collected Poetry and Prose*, edited by Frank Kermode and Joan Richardson, 724–39.

---

111   Wordsworth, *Prelude*, 521.

New York: The Library of America, 1997.

WILSON, Simon. 'Clutching the Wheel of St Catherine', or, A Visit to a Re-Enchanted College', in Angela Voss and Simon Wilson, eds., *Re-enchanting the Academy*, 53–66. Auckland: Rubedo Press, 2017.

YEATS, W.B. 'The Symbolism of Poetry'. In *Essays and Introductions*, 153–64. London: Macmillan, 1961.

Enrichment and Enchantment

The Poetic Heritage of the Western Esoteric Tradition

JUDITH WAY

BOTH THE WISDOM TRADITION of the Celtic bardic cycle of poems and the Western esoteric literary tradition yield a 'store of ancient verse'[1] and are inlaid with the 'mystic import of words'.[2] This
treasury of enchantment is contained and supported by the warp
and weft of myth, which is indispensable to poetry, and the function
that poetry serves as a sublime conduit of wisdom. In this sense,
tradition is as Kathleen Raine describes:

> that whole body of canonical symbolic language in
> which such metaphysical knowledge is enshrined, and
> in which the prophets, theologians, poets, and artists
> have transmitted through the ages.[3]

Through tracing the lines of transmission within this tradition, it
is evident that poetry has a long appointed role in the drama of
enchantment and disenchantment which characterises the flux of
consciousness through time. Raine attributes to poetry the art of
preserving the perennial wisdom 'when this has been all but lost by
churches and by philosophers'.[4] Indeed there is evidence in Robert
Graves' book *The White Goddess* of the ancient Celtic Welsh minstrel
poets disguising their mythic heritage in deliberately 'pied' language

1   Robert Graves, *The White Goddess* (London: Faber and Faber, 1961), 20.

2   John Matthews, *Taliesin* (London: The Aquarian Press, 1991), 120.

3   Kathleen Raine, *Blake and Antiquity* (London and Henly: Routledge &
    Kegan Paul, 1979), 101.

4   Kathleen Raine, *Defending Ancient Springs* (Suffolk: Golgonooza Press,
    1985), 110.

in order to perpetuate their tradition due to the dominant culture of the unsympathetic Christian church.[5] Furthermore Graves describes a parting of ways from the ancient Celtic bardic tradition by the court bards who eschewed their mythic origins and 'were prohibited from writing imaginative narrative' in order to please the courts and the prevailing cultural demands.[6] Once the mythic tap root was cut, Graves insists that their work became a 'barren poetic code'.[7] It is through the interdependence and relationship of myth, and imagination and symbol that the relationships of enrichment that foster enchantment takes place.

> Enchantment produces a Secondary World into which both designer and spectator can enter, to the satisfaction of their sense while they are inside; but in its purity it is artistic in desire and purpose.[8]

According to Tolkien's definition, 'enchantment seeks shared enrichment, partners in making and delight not slaves';[9] setting enchantment apart from intentional magic, which would be seeking a change in the Primary world, for the engagement of personal power. It is through the imagination that the Secondary world may be entered, and through his theory of the subcreative power, this ability to create and enchant can be known as a divine gift.[10] In accordance with primary reality, the subcreative power of enchantment can reveal in moments the gleam or echo of original blueprint,[11] a chiming forth of the primary truth of reality; within the subcreated world, which unites the subcreation with the primary reality. Here primary reality and the primary world are not the same thing. Primary reality refers to the idea of a God created world in which humans are made: and not only made, but made in image and likeness of a Maker,[12] so the primary reality bears the hallmark of that maker, in

---

5   Graves, *The White Goddess*, 80, 39.

6   Ibid., 80.

7   Ibid., 19.

8   J.R.R. Tolkien, *On Fairy Stories* (London: Unwin Paperbacks, 1975), 54.

9   Ibid., 55.

10   Ibid., 57.

11   Ibid., 70.

12   Ibid., 54.

its laws and truths. The primary world, is the established and sub-jective sense of reality as it is agreed upon and maintained through habituated common belief and practice. It can be likened to 'consen-sus reality', a term introduced by Bernardo Kastrup in *More than Al-legory*.[13] Consensus reality describes the outer realm, a construct of agreed ideas which are shared across a body of people. He defines it as subject to sensory impressions and ideas, and in a continual state of flux, being influenced by perception and myth. Thus this primary world can be altered, through enchantment, or disenchantment, as be the case. Tolkien speaks of the penalty of appropriation; which can disenchant objects of perception through acquisition.

> the things that are trite, or [...] familiar, are the things we have appropriated legally or mentally. We say we know them. They have become like the things which once attracted us by their glitter and colour, or their shape, and we laid hands on them, and then locked them in our hoard, acquired them, and acquiring ceased to look at them.[14]

It is through language that this appropriation can take place, as lan-guage wields a subcreative power of its own. 'The incarnate mind, the tongue, and the tale are in our world coeval'.[15] Through their interdependence, language, the mind, and myth form a trinity of enrichment which can yield the subcreated fruit of the enchanted tree. When these relationships of enrichment break down, then they may not produce enchantment, but their influence upon each other remains. Language and definition have an inexorable part in forging the narratives which inform consensus reality. The modern defini-tion of poetry in the Oxford online dictionary could be seen to be participating in the appropriation which Tolkien describes above: 'a literary work in which the expression of feelings and ideas is given intensity by the use of distinctive style and rhythm'.[16]

This definition meets the demands of description within the

---

13   Bernado Kastrup, *More than Allegory* (Alresford: Iff Books, 2016), 15.

14   Tolkien, *On Fairy Stories*, 59.

15   Ibid.

16   Oxford Dictionaries, 2016 (https://en.oxforddictionaries.com/definition/poetry).

agreement of a modern consensus reality, in which a definition will serve to identify and locate what one thing is from another; but when weighed in the balance of the poetic heritage of the Western esoteric tradition, it reveals a deep inadequacy of acknowledgement of origin and import, and a disinheritance of tradition.

MYTHIC TAPESTRIES

> Three things that enrich the poet: Myths, poetic power,
> a store of ancient verse.[17]

This fundamental triad cited by Graves, originates in the *Red Book of Hergest*, the 13ᵗʰ century collection of poems from the Celtic bardic tradition, and celebrates the integral relationships of enrichment within the poetic art. Myths, the poet, the muse, tales, and symbols of the tradition, are the constituents of this ancient recipe.[18] In his book *The White Goddess* Graves insists upon the definition of myth as 'verbal iconograph',[19] distilling its meaning to its image making function, and discarding the accumulated association of fantasy with which myth has been *appropriated* over time. This distinction implies something intrinsic about the interrelationship between word and image and the mythic dimension that together they create. This dimension is perceived through the imagination; the place where word and image converge. Kastrup defines myth as a translation code; a code established by the sensory impressions forming a mental narrative in order to make meaning of reality.[20] Myths function within traditions as means of establishing symbolic interpretations of wisdom and knowledge. Graves speaks of the ancient bardic tales as explanations of ritual and religious theory, corresponding to scriptures.[21] Of the same tradition, Matthews speaks of the seers, 'endowed with extra human capacities', who as the custodians of

---

17   Graves, *The White Goddess*, 20.

18   Ibid., 21.

19   Ibid.

20   Kastrup, *More than Allegory*, 19.

21   Graves, *The White Goddess*, 60.

this sacred wisdom were required to recite it for the functioning of the Celtic societies.[22] When a myth loses the context of its tradition and meaning-making function, it can become implausible;[23] it may no longer participate in achieving the 'inner consistency of reality' which Tolkien describes as necessary for true Secondary belief.[24]

However, as Kastrup describes, the myth-making capacity does not recede or cease to act without the scope of symbolic systems of knowledge or wisdom: it continues to draw meaning, even from a limited basis. The result is the hollowing out of implausible religious myths and the establishment of deprived myths.[25] A deprived myth is a translation code of reality, but the depth of the meaning from which it derives its form is limited, as it does not draw from a coherent or deep symbolic syntax. The growing predominance of deprived myths in the modern world, issued from the forge of capitalism and commerce, are the likes of—money equals happiness, sex equals power, and the celebrity as nobility. As deprived myths operate within a shallow context, there is a limited scope for interpretation of meaning, or for accessing the imagination in pursuit of a symbolic hermeneutic. They enforce a currency of deprived meaning, which utilises the inherent meaning-seeking function in human nature, and yet short circuits its capacity to derive depth of meaning through contact with symbolic and mythic material. This reinforces conceptual nihilism, as the narratives are obviously flimsy, and so consensus reality appears essentially meaningless.

In reclaiming the word myth from its appropriated associations with fantasy, and acknowledging its inherent role in consciousness, myth can be recognised as an indispensable part of the way humans relate to their world and their lives. In redressing a modern criticism of mythology, Tolkien refutes Max Müller's view that mythology is a disease of language, but asserts that like all human things it may become diseased.[26] The effect of the deterioration of the symbolic lexicon from its mythic origins is summarised by Graves, as he comments unflinchingly upon the degradation of modern cultural perception.

22   Matthews, *Taliesin*, 125.
23   Kastrup, *More than Allegory*, 49.
24   Tolkien, *On Fairy Stories*, 49.
25   Kastrup, *More than Allegory*, 19.
26   Tolkien, *On Fairy Stories*, 27.

> Nowadays is a civilisation in which the prime emblems
> of poetry are dishonoured. In which serpent, lion, and
> eagle belong to the circus tent; ox, salmon, and boar
> to the cannery, racehorse and greyhound to the betting
> ring, and the sacred grove to the sawmill.[27]

This lamentation equates the loss of perception of the symbol with its concurrent demise or destruction within the primary world. Poetry and the symbols that it enshrines have traditionally been integral to the benefit of a people and their culture, as in the case of the Celtic bardic tradition.[28] When this is lost or compromised, the demise is not restricted to the cultural loss of the poetic form alone: the loss is prolific and accountable at the level of perception and experience, for it is apparent that the relationships of consciousness, myth, and symbol are interdependent with perception and impact on the reality that they describe. When the mythic fabric is disregarded, the symbolic depth of perception is compromised, and humanity flounders to derive deeper meaning for existence. Into antiquity poetry and prophecy has been a long-standing theme. In the Celtic bardic tradition, Chadwick asserts that poetic inspiration and the entire mantic art 'was developed and elaborated to a degree for which we know no parallel.'[29] Shelley recalls the Roman name for poet was *vates*, which also meant seer, diviner, prophet:[30] both these details confirm that this association was wholly established within these ancient cultures, and not merely a matter of esoteric, or fringe material. It is in the word 'seer' that the essence of this role translates, for the idea of the poet as a prophet bound to predictions of time and futurity is not helpful for comprehending what this association truly implies. It is the ability to *see*; to be able to interpret symbolically, and to participate in the atemporal sphere of the imagination. The glimpses given are not of the future, but are visions from a perceptual location in the imagination; they are the gleam of primary reality glimpsed in the subcreated enchantment. The art of the poet is to

---

27   Graves, *The White Goddess*, 14.

28   Matthews, *Taliesin*, 4.

29   Ibid., 178.

30   Percy Shelley, *A Defence of Poetry* (New York: W.W Norton & Company, 1993), 755.

communicate from this place through the symbols of the tradition, establishing the ground for a flow of inspiration and interpretation that can be seen to characterise the type of motion within this atemporal sphere. In this way enriched relationships between symbolic data and mythic context are enabled through the nexus in the imagination where word and image converge. It is in this space that another encounter[31] is facilitated, between *knower* and *known*, and through this, wisdom is gleaned and *seen*.

POETRY AND PROPHECY: AHISTORICAL CONTINUITY WITHIN THE WESTERN ESOTERIC TRADITION

> The symbolic language of neo-Platonism [sic] is a thread woven throughout European art and poetry; the language may at times be forgotten, yet we cannot call it dead; for the visions it describes are, as Blake says 'Permanent in the Imagination'; the beauty and meaning of such symbols is unageing.[32]

This woven thread designates the subtle strand of the perennial wisdom tradition: despite not being exoterically known, its founding members 'were as reputable as Plato and Plotinus'.[33] Blake's incorporation of this thread, and his symbolic craftsmanship in developing its proliferations within his poetry and art, reveal that it is in the liminal atemporal sphere that artistry and prophecy converge. In his book *Restoring Paradise* Arthur Versluis suggests that a characteristic of the Western esoteric literary tradition is that its mode of transmission is *ahistorical* and unbound to time, place, person, and region. It is unified by 'an insistence upon gnosis',[34] and recognised by the revelatory potential within art and poetry that can be found in certain masterpieces. In this tradition, there is no direct master and disciple lineage, but transmission of gnosis takes place in the 'field of the imagination'.[35] Versluis describes a deep symbolic

---

31 Arthur Versluis, *Restoring Paradise* (Albany: SUNY Press, 2004), 25.

32 Raine, *Blake and Antiquity*, 8.

33 Ibid., viii.

34 Versluis, *Restoring Paradise*, 22.

35 Ibid.

presence within the literature or poetics as being 'hieroeidetically charged'.[36] It is the potency of this charge, encountered in the field of the imagination which allows the symbolic data of the tradition to be relayed through gnosis and inner revelation, and this is facilitated by the enchanted art of the poet. This is exemplified through Raine's study of Blake's poetry in respect of its roots in the Western esoteric wisdom tradition, where it is possible to see how he concurs with the foundational triad of antiquity in utilising the relationships of enrichment: the store of ancient verse, myths, and his own poetic power.[37]

ENGRAVING IN THE IMAGINAL

In her book *Blake and Antiquity*, Raine excavates the symbolic foundations of Blake's mythic vocabulary and finds them to be ardently faithful to the perennial wisdom tradition. As the source of Western esoteric tradition, the symbols laid down by these ancient forefathers form the original touchstones from which, she argues, Blake extrapolates his themes:

> From his reading of Porphyry and Plotinus he came to recognise in the works of poets already known to him the same symbols, endlessly recreated and clothed in beautiful forms. Thus he was able to extend his field of allusion and to introduce themes and images taken from many sources without destroying the unity of his symbolic structure.[38]

Through tracing the symbols back to their origins, Blake was able to understand their codified essences and then to expand upon his themes by incorporating their timeless and eternal wisdom within his poetry. By heeding their deep import he fuses together symbolic material in bringing forth his prophetic poetry. To describe it as a mere literary form would be to gloss over the deeper seams of philosophy and alchemy that are embedded into the worlds he creates

---

36   Ibid., 25.

37   Graves, *The White Goddess*, 20.

38   Raine, *Blake and Antiquity*, 17.

through the word. He was engaged in a quest which, Versluis argues, was shared by a broad range of artists and poets that participate in this lineage, and whose mission was

> to restore alchemy in the word, to create a new magic through poetry, since the old magic was so apparent-ly gone. The attraction of all these poets was not only their literary ability but also, and perhaps more, in their successive attempts to reintroduce the Hermetic vision of the world, of which magic and alchemy are inevitability a part.[39]

Versluis includes Blake with Pico, Bruno, Wordsworth, Coleridge, Shelley, Nerval, Novalis, Yeats, Rimbaud, Baudelaire, and Hugo in this summation. Raine names a succession of artists that are dis-tinguished by their work possessing 'a reality, coherence, climate, and atmosphere of its own':[40] these are Shakespeare, Dante, Dürer, Fra Angelico, Claude, and Michelangelo. There is an implication through the line of influence that these artists and poets have upon each other that there *is* a mode of transmission at work, as Versluis suggests, and that the evidence of it is visible in the actual fruits of their works, and the way the symbolic content can be seen to collab-orate within the field of the imagination. This motif of collaboration echoes the idea of 'shared enrichment' which Tolkien finds char-acteristic of enchantment.[41] The 'reality' that their work possesses is not forged by literary technique or artistic prowess alone, but by their ability to transmit something that is tangibly *other*, and yet possesses similitude.

Raine locates Blake's overarching theme as his 'prophetic urgen-cy to preach to the English nation a return to spiritual vision lost since the Renaissance'.[42] According to Raine the *Book of Thel* consti-tutes 'the philosophy of Alchemy as the solution to the problem of duality'.[43] Blake's purpose is manifold: while he expounds a symbolic re-visioning of a philosophy or a symbolic system, he also indicates

---

39   Versluis, *Restoring Paradise*, 5.

40   Kathleen Raine, *William Blake* (London: Thames and Hudson, 1970), 7.

41   Tolkien, *On Fairy Stories*, 55.

42   Raine, *Blake and Antiquity*, 99.

43   Ibid., 71.

the hermeneutic required to restore the loss of the Renaissance vision or the loss of Spiritual Vision, in his own words. In his exegesis of the *Mundus Imaginalis*, Henry Corbin states that it is not a theory: it is an initiation to vision.[44] Similarly, Blake's poetry is an invitation to prophetic topographies; where the mode of perception is through the imagination. Within the invitation to view imaginatively, is also the explanation of how the faculty has been compromised, relayed in mythic form, in order that the reader may find their orientation point within this visionary landscape and in their own consciousness.

> Blake's prophecies are addressed, specifically to the English nation, the Giant Albion. Vala, Milton, and Jerusalem all tell of the fall of the national mind into the 'deadly sleep' of the scientific philosophy of Bacon, Newton, and Locke; and our prophet calls the sleepers to awaken to the vision of eternity.[45]

The closed western gate of the city of Albion, representing its soul, indicates the disinheritance of Eden. This annexing of man's inherent nature is due to the false belief that matter is separate from mind. The materialist philosophers and believers are the 'only heathen who have ever been so blind as to "bow down to wood and stone"'.[46] It is through a return to this vision in the imagination that the western gate can be opened. While man insists upon a merely literal perception, founded only in sense perception of concrete materialism, perception is bound to the realm of idolatry and Eden is lost. It is in the breaking from the literal and linear mode of conception that the movement into the field of the imagination occurs. In this way Blake describes the situation of consciousness and offers a remedial orientation through the potent symbolic data that is mapped out within his work. This 'prophetic urgency'[47] is the call to awaken perception into imaginative vision.

In the warp and weft of mythic threads in his work, Blake not

---

44   Henry Corbin, *Alone with the Alone* (Princeton: Princeton Paperbacks, 1998), 93.

45   Raine, *Blake and Antiquity*, 96.

46   Ibid., 100.

47   Ibid., 99.

only drew from the Neoplatonists in philosophy and image, he also blended into his iconographic vocabulary Christian images and symbols and the Greek myths. Blake is a master craftsperson of his moment, merging apparently differentiated streams into a comprehensive message that is radically progressive and yet representing those 'Portions of Eternity'.[48] Blake's reworking of myth to serve his theme, and dexterity for incorporating different strands of tradition and religion, has a unifying quality, which points into the world of imagination and beyond. It punctures time by delivering strands of perennial wisdom into the climate of the zeitgeist; and in utilising these strands he rejuvenates the standard of the mythic and symbolic lexicon to date. His willingness to exercise this visionary zeal is what makes his art so profound, and beyond any suggestion of secondary representation, despite the latticing of ancient mythic symbology.

An example of the multifaceted symbolic resonances within his work is indicated by Raine, where she reveals the original description of Psyche's house given by Apuleius and shows how this resonates by similitude in the description of Vala's house by Blake. Later this image of Psyche's mansion is found again in the form of a Chapel from one of Blake's poems.[49] Far from being plagiarised reiterations of mythic material, there is a sense that the location resounds with a mythic permanence, as a hieroeidetically charged symbol. It garners potency in the imagination, through the presence of simultaneous references which reside in the same symbolic space. It is Vala's house, aspected in the myth of Cupid and Psyche, in order that the rich associations may pierce through and guide the inquirer in the symbolic interpretation. This artistry, yielding and enriching meaning, is almost musical at times: the echoes of symbolic associations chime at intervals and add depth and gravitas through resonance. It invokes harmonic perception, which is a characteristic of a symbolic hermeneutic, in which the same sound can be heard on several levels simultaneously.[50] Raine gives further examples of this in the myth of Cupid which is transparently present in the poem of Vala:

---

48   Ibid., 7.

49   Ibid., 30.

50   Henry Corbin, *Spiritual Body and Celestial Earth: From Mazdean Iran to Shi'ite Iran*, trans. Nancy Pearson (Princeton: Princeton University Press, 1997), 54.

'Where is the Lord of Vala? Dost thou hide in clefts
of the rock?' referring to Cupid who is mentioned in
Apuleius' myth 'O my dove, that art in the clefts of the
rock'.[51]

This incorporation of symbolic themes was always precise[52] and involved Blake's total immersion in the related symbolic materials. It has the effect of reinforcing the prevailing Western esoteric tradition as it gestures back along the lineage to the origin point of the symbol. This precision, a characteristic of his artistic and visionary capacity, and founded in his own established gnosis, demonstrates a means of perception which does not follow the linear or logical line. It also clearly indicates that while these nexuses are made in the imaginal zones, they are not arbitrary, nor deemed significant from a purely personal level, but they are revealing a greater depth of initiatic content that lies within the scope of perception. Through exposing the readers to such symbolic content, the mode of vision required is invoked: precisely what Blake is advocating in his prophetic cry for the soul of Albion to awaken. It follows that, without such a perception, the meaning of what is being described in Blake's prophecies will not be garnered by a cursory glance. If we consider Graves' pursuit of the meaning of Gwion's riddles,[53] what may appear like guesswork, or random summoning of mythic material, is actually a similarly precise manoeuvring of the imagination within the arcana of symbolic material towards resolution through interpretation. While Graves provides a good example of a true mythic hermeneutic in his scholarly pursuit, he reveals that the other side of the coin of interpretation is inspiration. As Graves admits, it was after 'a drop or two of the brew of Inspiration' that he was able to make sense of Gwion's riddle.[54] This movement between inspiration and interpretation demonstrates the mutable dialogue with the divine which is described in other spiritual hermeneutics, and is central to the poetic spirit.

---

51   Raine, *Blake and Antiquity*, 29.

52   Ibid., 36.

53   Graves, *The White Goddess*, 86.

54   Ibid., 30.

In Blake's vision, human language in all its forms and
the works of God are all facets of the same divine-hu-
man figure. The Divine Word and poetry lie at the very
heart of human life.[55]

A poet-prophet in this sense is the messenger of the Divine Word.[56]
Human language, seen in its divine aspect, requires a hermeneutic
which is able to transmute symbols into gnosis. Cheetham describes
ta'wil,[57] via Corbin, a mode of perception and interpretation which
sees that the hermeneutic of the soul is the alchemical process by
which the literal is transformed by the symbolic. The idolatry of the
materialist philosophers which Blake identifies becomes a potential
arena of emancipation through the return of spiritual vision. *Ta'wil*
and Blake's spiritual vision are the 'means by which idols are trans-
muted into icons'.[58] Prophecy taken in a literal sense, of a prophet
who tells the future, entails a linear view of time and is a reified and
static concept which fails to grasp the nuances of interrelationship
between poetry and prophecy. Emerson warns:

> The quality of the imagination is to flow and not to
> freeze [...] Here is the difference betwixt the poet and
> the mystic, that the last nails a symbol to one sense,
> which was a true sense for a moment, but soon be-
> comes old and false.[59]

It is through the motion of this supple conduit that the wisdom
threads are able to move transparently through time and persons to
participate in this ahistorical lineage. Walt Whitman, who Harold
Bloom suggests in his introduction to *Leaves of Grass* is Blake's

---

55   Tom Cheetham, *All the World an Icon* (Berkeley: North Atlantic Books,
      2012), 88.

56   Ibid.

57   *Ta'wil* is a hermeneutic made evident in the West by Henry Corbin, who
      derived his sense of it from the Shi'ite tradition. It is the metaphorical
      reading of reality, which transmutes the literal appearance in order to ex-
      perience the underlying reality of the soul. It facilitates a return to the true
      dimension of seeing of the soul, through the imagination.

58   Cheetham, *All the world an Icon*, 92.

59   Ibid., 96.

Albion,[60] and has similar Neoplatonic allegiances, describes the fruition of beauty, and its interconnectivity with a primary reality.

> The fruition of beauty is no chance of hit and miss [...]
> it is as inevitable as life [...] it is exact and plumb as
> gravitations from the eyesight proceed another eyesight
> and from the hearing process another voice eternally
> curious of the harmony of things within man.[61]

Suggested here is the process by which the baton in the ahistorical lineage of the Western esoteric tradition is seamlessly and naturally passed through these inherent principles of harmony and their urge to proliferate. It is possible to hear in Whitman's poetry the voice of Blake's Jesus the Imagination; the living representation of the redeemer, describing this process of symbolic translation and reiteration through time.[62] As the embodiment of Blake's prophetic works, he gives voice and dimension to something previously revealed in the lineage. It is as if the ultimate prophetic poet lies beyond the scope of one life, and the 'living shapes that move from mind to mind'[63] reveal this wisdom tradition. Echoes of Taliesin;[64] Graves,[65] and the transmigration of souls,[66] shimmer through Whitman's mystical conclusion to *Leaves of Grass*.

> Great is life [...] and real and mystical [...] wherever
> and whoever: great is death [...] sure as life holds all
> parts together, death holds all parts together. Sure as the
> stars return after they merge into the light, death is as
> great as life.[67]

---

60   Walt Whitman, *Leaves of Grass* (New York: Penguin Books, 2005), xviii.

61   Ibid., 12.

62   Ibid., 50.

63   Tolkien, *On Fairy Stories*, 56.

64   Matthews, *Taliesin*, 55.

65   Graves, *The White Goddess*, 24.

66   Transmigration of Souls is a theory with its origin in the Celtic tradition: Matthews, *Taliesin*, 30.

67   Whitman, *Leaves of Grass*, 160.

Emerson's essays and Whitman's verse brought forth a new spirit in America rooted in the Western esoteric tradition.[68] The presence of their vision at the beginning of a new era ('Emerson invented the American Religion, Whitman incarnated it')[69] supports the Romantic idea that regards poetry as a provoker and creator of consciousness.[70] In *A Defence of Poetry*, Shelley unites this idea with the figure of poet as prophet and proclaims that poets are 'the unacknowledged legislators of the world'.[71]

Metaphorical hijack

If poetry has been long esteemed for its profound impact and role in transmission of subtle wisdom, then how have we gained such a modern definition, that centres solely on its literary role and emotional influence? In his vast and ground breaking work, *The Master and His Emissary*, Iain McGilchrist maps the journey of the evolution of consciousness with his thesis that it is a power struggle between the different hemispheres of the brain that characterises and influences certain epochs in history. Consensus reality is informed and sculpted by the predominance of one hemisphere or the shift from one to another. The pivotal moment in which the word became separated from its mythic root with the image is found as the Renaissance transitions to the Enlightenment period, and it is to this moment and consequent alteration in perception that Blake's prophetic poems are addressed. According to McGilchrist this is a moment where the right-brain influence is superseded by a left-brain predominance. Through this translation, the comprehension of the image through the imagination, and the veracity of the mythic form, is lost in favour of the esteemed code of literalism which accompanied the Age of Reason:

> Images become explicit, understood by reading a kind
> of key, which demonstrates that the image is thought of
> simply as an adornment, whose only function is to fix a

---

68 Raine, *Blake and Antiquity*, 5.

69 Whitman, *Leaves of Grass*, x.

70 Cheetham, *All the World an Icon*, 96.

71 Shelley, *Defence of Poetry*, 755.

meaning more readily in the mind—a meaning which could have been better stated literally. This anticipates the Enlightenment view of metaphor as an adornment that shows the writers skill, or entertains, or aids flagging attention, rather than an indispensable part of understanding.[72]

The conceptual legacy of the Enlightenment constitutes much of the materialist and nihilist bedrock of modern conceptual thought, in which art has become a commentary on life rather than integral to life. Metaphor, meaning to carry over, is an indispensable part of understanding when it is understood that meaning may need to traverse or bridge a gap, or be transmitted from realm to realm. If metaphor is purely a literary device, then the notion of a symbolic hermeneutic is lost in the collapsing of spaces which were once to be bridged. This is a symptom of the departure of language from the 'enchantment of the body'.[73] McGilchrist sees metaphor as the means by which language remains interconnected, and in relationship to the world. When the left brain's dominant tendency demands a literal language 'mind loosens its contact with reality and becomes a self-consistent system of tokens'.[74] It becomes a topsoil that no longer identifies with its root system, and disinherits its origins. While the left hemisphere of the brain entails a narrowing of view in order to calculate and stratify, it has to necessarily occlude the larger interconnected vista of the right brain, the domain of tradition and the collective. In this way it has been seen to 'neuter the power of art',[75] as well as seeking to eradicate intuitive context and primordial meaning in order to maintain control.[76]

Robert Svoboda is explicit concerning the evolution of language and its impact upon tradition. In his article 'Speaking Truth: The Art of Sacred Speech' he draws attention to the four modes of human speech that are distinguished in the ancient Tantras. These four modes, which are nuanced by the different levels of perception

---

72   Iain McGilchrist, *The Master and His Emissary* (New Haven, CT: Yale University Press, 2012), 318.

73   Ibid., 120.

74   Ibid., 126.

75   Ibid., 442.

76   Ibid., 319.

and consciousness that they engage, are being jettisoned in the predominance of *vaikhari*, the speech of everyday language. Modern
culture, with its narrow priorities, demands the expansion of this
single linguistic nuance, and so the defining intentions of modern
culture proliferate as the form is translated and taught. The nuances
of speech which were direct lines to the perceptual states of pure
intention, the speech of contemplation, and speech beyond partic-
ularities are judged by the utilitarian principles of the everyday and
are discarded:

> Apply this inflexibility to a culture and you get the
> grammar of cultural imperialism [...] and you erase
> the experience of generations 'breathing from ancient
> times'.[77]

This linguistic monoculturalism, prevalent in the overriding use of
English worldwide, is dangerous as it weighs tradition in the balance that it finds, by the means of its own limited perception. It is
language and definitions which extrapolate these forms, redefining
according to a sole perspective, as can be seen with the modern definition of poetry. As ancient texts and traditions are reviewed by this
mode of appropriating, the value of their mythic content and metaphorical import is lost and their enriched meaning defies account.
This mode of perception is unable to acknowledge the full scope of
what it purports to describe, and yet insists on editing according to
its perspective. This is what Shelley refers to as the 'unmitigated exercise of the calculating faculty'[78] and it is this excess towards an arrogant certainty of view which McGilchrist refers to as the 'ultimate
hubris'.[79] Hubris in Greek tragedy always marks the turning point of
the individual back into the hands of Fate, a movement which tends
towards equilibrium again. Although language has evolved from
music and the original impulse to communicate and forge relationships, and thus has its origin in the right hemisphere of the brain,
through the evolution of the left-brain predominance it has forged
a new form:

---

77   Robert Svoboda, 'Speaking Truth: The Art of Sacred Speech' (www.drsvo-
     boda.com/resources/articles/speaking-truth-the-art-of-sacred-speech/).

78   Shelley, *Defence of Poetry*, 761.

79   McGilchrist, *The Master and his Emissary*, 459.

> Referential language, with its huge vocabulary and so-
> phisticated syntax, did not originate in a drive to com-
> municate, and from this point of view represents some-
> thing of a hijack.[80]

The sense of a metaphorical hijack, where such bifurcations of language are able to short circuit inherent meaning, is evident in the
modern dictionary definition of poetry. The rich associations with
tradition, art, and the sublime are not evident from this perspective.
The relationships of enrichment that support enchantment are invisible to this referential eye. The paradox is that poetry, a redeem-
ing force in consciousness, is interred within a cultural stasis by its
own definition. Through this definition of a literary form, there will
be a widespread assumption that poetry which fulfils those mild
conditions is in fact poetry, without an acknowledgement or even
comprehension of the great and epic works which constitute such
a living body of wisdom, and the vast dimensions of their import.
The cry for re-enchantment of modern vision lies at the crux of this
issue of definition, which demonstrates the active presence of disembodied language as a residual tideline of inheritance from the
Enlightenment period. A definition such as the modern one could
be argued in itself to constitute a deprived myth, as it forges a limited narrative about the subject, and it corrals the scope of meaning
into the smaller territories of 'literary' and 'feeling'. It provides a fine
example of the 'metaphorical hijack' which denotes the need for a
turning point in the haste to appropriate, and a redressing of definitions, language, and consciousness, in order to recover a heritage
which has not been altogether lost, but has yet to become *known*.

POETRY AND RE-ENCHANTMENT

In this call to re-imagine the definition of poetry, it becomes evident that poetry's family of origin, myth, imagination, and tradition
has also gathered some post-Enlightenment dust. As the lenses of
truth defined by literalism and historicism are due an upgrade, and
curiosity takes precedence over hubristic certainty, a rediscovery of
these elements in relation to their participation within this tradi-

---

80   Ibid., 125.

tion, and their relationships of enrichment, could be the means by which their true dimensions are discovered and valued. In the growing absence of a traditional culture, the Western world could benefit from acknowledging the ahistorical lineage which poetry evidences, and nourish the deprived cultural mythos with the sacred narratives that are found through such art; and the wisdom that can be gleaned through the marriage of word and image in the gateway of the imagination. This entranceway into a symbolic lexicon, resplendent with ancestral lore and the depths of the unconscious, need no longer be guarded by definitions of the esoteric. In blowing the dust off conceptual confinements, Jeffrey Kripal, speaking on the re-enchantment of the academy, suggests that re-imagining the humanities as consciousness coded in culture is a way forward.

> With respect to the study of religion, what if we stop trying to discipline reality into our depressing little materialist boxes, refigured the sacred as consciousness itself and looked again to extreme, uncanny, 'impossible' experiences as keys to human nature.[81]

The academy could take up the mantle of viewing tradition, not through the narrow confines of historical observation, nor from an acquisitive approach to knowledge, but as a means of re-discovering the inherent wisdom qualities of symbolic language, to rebuild the atrophied muscle of mythic hermeneutic. In order to do this, a shift in attitude would be required, recognising the need to rectify the pervasive hubristic tendencies to appropriate and assume which have shaped the current tides of language and definition. Accepting the 'uncanny and impossible' as keys to understanding would entail intuition no longer being assumed as unverifiable and therefore not academically sound. As the boundaries widen to include these aspects, and language is *re-embodied*, then the academy could be the means by which these inclusions are rigorously engaged and redefined. Kastrup calls for the need to recognise the validity of transcendent truths in the restoration of religious myths.[82] These are truths which speak to the unconscious mind, and are grasped intui-

---

81   Jeffrey Kripal, paper presented to the Re-enchanting the Academy conference, Canterbury, 25th–27th September 2015.

82   Kastrup, *More than Allegory*, 44.

tively. However, it is important to understand that the intuitive sense is to be engaged within the context of a symbolic system, a mythic narrative, and not to authorise a proliferation of subjective personal qualifications of experience as wisdom.

> It is conceivable that the comparative study of religion, as professionally done in academia, could help us recognize true religious myths by identifying the symbolic patterns typical of genuine intuitive insight [83]

If we look back into the past with the attitude of curiosity, then it is possible to see, in the example of traditional mystery schools, programmes of advanced scholarship which facilitated the continuation of the wisdom tradition. John Matthews writes of the long training of the ancient Bardic tradition, which involved a lifelong immersion in the 'alphabets, grammars, tales, poems, philosophies'[84] prior to engaging in composition of poetry. Such training and immersion in the symbols which related directly to the culture could be assumed to lead to the development of a highly attuned intuitive sense of the symbolic, and a genuine sense of intuitive insight. The 'mystic import of words'[85] that enlivened scholarship of that day refers to their hieroeidetic content, and therefore to their stimulation of the intuitive and imaginative faculty of interpretation.

Experience necessitates interpretation, whether that is through a disenchanted and dim set of conclusions and assumptions which form a narrative within the frame of those coordinates, or from coordinates whose length and breadth exceed the literal and accountable. The tendency of the conceptual mind is to reify, and make concepts static and brittle within the inescapable winds of change and flux. If the academy can integrate the spacious and fluid mediums of art and poetry, and celebrate their capacities in preserving and maintaining the essence of wisdom, then a flexibility and buoyancy can operate between scholarship, interpretation, and narrative and culture. Moving into a new territory, one that brings the jurisdiction of the left hemisphere predominance into an integrative movement that encompasses the qualities of the right brain, and acknowledges

---

83   Ibid., 54.

84   Matthews, *Taliesin*, 122.

85   Ibid., 120.

the importance of the unverifiable, the spacious, and the unknown, the ground of the Academy could be the cusp of regeneration in its facilitation of discussion and enquiry in exploring new topographies of consciousness. Re-enchantment is the re-acquaintance with something that was never lost, just occluded from view; and the subtle thread of the Western esoteric tradition, with its meandering conduit of inspiration and interpretation, serves as a tapestry of re-engagement, lest we forget.

In the refiguring of the sacred as consciousness, poetry—known as a conduit of consciousness, able to transmit different levels and nuances of perceptions, and to forge supple pathways for symbolic hermeneutics—would no longer be separated from its territory of sacred narrative, and its lands no longer disinherited. In the poetic dowry of word and image is the 'store of ancient verse', engraved with the venerable heritage of the lineage of poets and artists and interpreters, abiding in atemporal potential. Open for participation, which springs from acknowledgement, it awaits the moment for those with the eyes to see, ears to hear, and heart to know—to take the thread and keep on weaving.

Select Bibliography

Cheetham, Tom. *All the World an Icon.* Berkeley, ca: North Atlantic Books, 2012.

Corbin, Henry. *Alone with the Alone.* Princeton: Princeton University Press, 1998.

_____. *Spiritual Body and Celestial Earth: From Mazdan Iran to Shi'ite Iran.* Translated by Nancy Pearson. Princeton: Princeton University Press, 1997.

Graves, Robert. *The White Goddess.* London: Faber and Faber, 1961.

Kastrup, Bernado. *More than Allegory.* Alresford: Iff Books, 2016.

Kripal, Jeffrey. Paper presented to the *Re-enchanting the Academy* conference, Canterbury, 25th–27th September 2015.

Matthews, John. *Taliesin.* London: The Aquarian Press, 1991.

McGilchrist, Iain. *The Master and His Emissary.* New Haven, ct: Yale University Press, 2012.

Raine, Kathleen. *Blake and Antiquity.* London: Routledge & Kegan Paul, 1979.

_____. *William Blake*. London: Thames & Hudson, 1970.

SHELLEY, Percy. *A Defence of Poetry*. New York: W.W. Norton, 2013.

SVOBODA, Robert. 'The Art of Sacred Speech' (http://www.drsvo-boda.com/resources/articles/speaking-truth-the-art-of-sacred-speech/).

VERSLUIS, Arthur. *The Philosophy of Magic*. London: Arkana, 1986.

_____. *Restoring Paradise*. Albany: SUNY Press, 2004.

WHITMAN, Walt. *Leaves of Grass*. New York: Penguin Books, 2005.

The Fantastic Imagination

Sub-creating Tolkien's Middle Earth

BECCA S. TARNAS

INTRODUCTION

In the disenchanted heart of the 20th century, J.R.R. Tolkien gave words to a living myth, producing a work of artistic creativity rooted in the cultural symbols of the European mythopoeic tradition. Although *The Lord of the Rings* was criticised for being escapist, for not depicting the harsh realities of the modern world, Tolkien's narrative nonetheless became a cultural phenomenon, a work that broke through the disenchanted rationalism of its time and spoke to the souls of its readers. Tolkien's work answers the desire of soul to recognise the enchanted nature of our Earth and cosmos. In our contemporary world of commodified knowledge, desacralised landscapes, political division, isolated individualism, and ecospiritual crises, a body of work such as Tolkien's demonstrates the power of the imagination to re-enchant one's perspective, and to reveal the depth of spirituality and meaning inherent to this world.

The roots of Middle-earth extend deeply into the rich soils of our own world: to achieve this, Tolkien employed the powers of language, cartography, history, and legend. Yet, as the willing reader steps through the page into Middle-earth, the landscape and peoples one encounters seem to have a life of their own, as if a spark of vitality has been breathed by a divine Creator into the realm Tolkien wove from the resources of his own genius. Whether humanity was indeed given life and form by an ultimate Creator or not, humans have been endowed with the ability to create in our own right. Moreover, sometimes these creations seem to be gifted with their own life and may even seem to be as real as we are—nonetheless still residing within a secondary world accessible through the imagination. This world has been given innumerable names: the *mundus imaginalis*,[1] the world of the imagination, or as Tolkien called it at times in his own writings, Faërie.[2] Why some of our human creations are granted such life and others not is a mystery beyond my ability to fathom, but it could perhaps be that some are *meant* to have their own life and truth, an idea that Tolkien expresses in *The Lord of the Rings* through Gandalf, when he speaks to Frodo about Bilbo's finding of the Ring of Power:

> Behind that there was something else at work, beyond any design of the Ring-maker. I can put it no plainer than by saying that Bilbo was *meant* to find the Ring, and *not* by its maker. In which case you also were *meant* to have it. And that may be an encouraging thought.[3]

It may also be that Tolkien was *meant* to bring the mythology of Middle-earth into being through his writing, and as such it was given the authenticity and truth that so many feel when they traverse its woods and mountains, and converse with its inhabitants as they walk along their roads.

During the decades when he was crafting his Middle-earth *legendarium*, Tolkien often felt as though the mythology was not being made *by* him, but rather coming *through* him. In part to explain this experience, Tolkien described his composition of the tales of Middle-earth as a *sub-creation*, an intertwined outpouring of both invention and inspiration.[4] Tolkien's theory of imagination is closely related to the philosophical explorations of Samuel Taylor Coleridge: his delineations of the primary and secondary imagination, their relationship to each other, and an understanding of their ultimate source.[5] Exploring Tolkien's and Coleridge's philosophies of

---

1   Henry Corbin, 'Mundus Imaginalis, or The Imaginary and the Imaginal', trans. Ruth Horine, *En Islam Iranien: Aspects Spirituels et Philosophiques*, tome IV, livre 7 (Paris: Gallimard, 1971), 1.

2   J.R.R. Tolkien, *On Fairy-Stories*, ed. Verlyn Flieger and Douglas A. Anderson (London: HarperCollins, 2014), 27.

3   J.R.R. Tolkien, *The Fellowship of the Ring: The Lord of the Rings* (New York: Houghton Mifflin Company, 1994), 54–55.

4   Tolkien, *On Fairy-Stories*, 59.

5   Samuel Taylor Coleridge, *Biographia Literaria* (London: J.M. Dent & Co.,

imagination in relation to each other can provide a deeper understanding of this profound faculty, and give credence to what truths
the imagination is able to reveal.

THE REALITY OF THE IMAGINAL

As the philosopher and theologian Henry Corbin elucidates, for
most contemporary speakers 'the term "imaginary" is equated with
the unreal, with something that is outside the framework of being
and existing'.[6] Yet one may find quite the opposite: the imaginary,
or what Corbin calls the *imaginal*, exists not outside reality but in
the innermost place of our souls, and thus is internal and intrinsic to the outer world we call reality. Tolkien is an avid explorer of
this realm, which he sometimes calls Faërie, and seems to attest to
its reality in an almost offhand way in his essay *On Fairy-Stories*.[7]
Tom Shippey sees this as a sign that Tolkien is talking down to his
readers: 'Repeatedly he plays the trick of pretending that fairies are
real—they tell "human stories" instead of "fairy stories", they put on
plays for men "according to abundant records", and so on'.[8] While
Tolkien's remarks could certainly be interpreted that way, it seems
rather that Tolkien may actually be describing what he knows of
Faërie, as a genuine traveller in the perilous realm. Tolkien valued
viewing the world symbolically and mythically, perceiving reality
as a whole through the organ of the imagination.[9] As Peter Beagle
writes, 'I believe that Tolkien has wandered in Middle-earth' and
that he 'believes in his world, and in all those who inhabit it'.[10] For
Tolkien, Beagle, and many others, Middle-earth was not 'created, for
it was always there'.[11]

1906), 159–160.

6   Corbin, 'Mundus Imaginalis', 1.

7   Tolkien, *On Fairy-Stories*, 27.

8   Tom Shippey, *The Road to Middle-Earth: How J.R.R. Tolkien Created a
     New Mythology* (New York: Houghton Mifflin, 2003), 49.

9   Colin Duriez, *Tolkien and C.S. Lewis: The Gift of Friendship* (Mahwah:
     Hidden Spring, 2003), 178.

10   Peter Beagle, 'Tolkien's Magic Ring', in J.R.R. Tolkien, *The Tolkien Reader*
     (New York: Ballantine, 1966), xvi.

11   Ibid., ix.

Tolkien's own experience of writing was that he was 'recording what was already "there," somewhere: not of "inventing"'.[12] As Tolkien states in a letter to his son Christopher, 'the thing seems to write itself once I get going, as if the truth comes out then, only imperfectly glimpsed in the preliminary sketch'.[13] This has, of course, been the experience of countless artists over the centuries in moments of high inspiration. Norris Clarke writes of these creative experiences of artists: 'It felt, they say, as though they were tuned in or connected to some higher power which somehow took over and flowed through them'.[14] What this higher power may be, and how it relates to the imagination, can better be understood by contemplating Coleridge's philosophical delineations of primary imagination, secondary imagination, and fancy.

DELINEATIONS OF IMAGINATION

In his pivotal essay on imagination and the realm of Faërie, *On Fairy-Stories*, Tolkien lays out a theory of the creative imagination that, as has been observed by several Tolkien scholars, notably Verlyn Flieger[15] and Tom Shippey,[16] clearly echoes Coleridge's thoughts on the primary and secondary imagination. In Coleridge's immortal words: 'The primary Imagination I hold to be the living power and prime agent of all human perception, and as a repetition in the finite mind of the eternal act of creation in the infinite I AM'.[17] The primary imagination is that of the divine Creator, bringing the world as we know it into being. Thus all human perception finds its source in the primary imagination. Yet the primary and secondary imagination differ from each other only in degree and mode but not

12   J.R.R. Tolkien, *The Letters of J.R.R. Tolkien*, ed. Humphrey Carpenter, with Christopher Tolkien (New York: Houghton Mifflin, 2000), 145.

13   Ibid., 104.

14   Norris Clarke, 'The Creative Imagination: Unique Expression of Our Soul-Body Unity', in *The Creative Retrieval of St. Thomas Aquinas* (New York: Fordham University Press, 2009), 203.

15   Verlyn Flieger, *Splintered Light: Logos and Language in Tolkien's World* (Kent: The Kent State University Press, 2002), 24–25.

16   Shippey, *The Road to Middle-Earth*, 50.

17   Coleridge, *Biographia Literaria*, 159.

in kind. The secondary imagination is that same imaginative power as the primary, yet it is operating through the human being, 'co-existing with the conscious will'.[18] Owen Barfield, a friend of Tolkien's and a fellow member of their literary circle the Inklings, explored Coleridge's thought deeply in this area. Barfield explains that the primary imagination is an act of which we, as human beings, are not conscious, and when we are conscious of it as our own creative agency it becomes the secondary imagination.[19]

The secondary imagination 'dissolves, diffuses, dissipates, in order to recreate',[20] and 'struggles to idealize and to unify'.[21] As an extension of the primary imagination responsible for creating reality, the secondary imagination also has the ability to create reality, but of a different degree: imaginal reality. This is, for example, why Corbin chose the term *mundus imaginalis* to differentiate what is just 'made up' from 'the object of imaginative or imagining perception'.[22] This concept indicates that the product of the secondary imagination has a reality of its own, because its ultimate source, like reality, is the primary imagination, only it is shaped through the agency of the human being. Tolkien uses the term 'sub-creation' to refer to the product of the secondary imagination, because the result is created *under* an ultimate Creator.[23]

In addition to the primary and secondary imagination, Coleridge also writes of 'fancy', which is 'no other than a mode of memory emancipated from the order of time and space'.[24] Barfield notes that Coleridge seems not to have explicitly segregated fancy from imagination, for at times he appears to write of them differing entirely in kind, and at others in degree, comparable to the distinction between primary and secondary imagination.[25] The difference between the products of fancy, on the one hand, and imagination on the other, could be seen as the difference between something that is just 'made

---

18   Ibid.

19   Owen Barfield, *What Coleridge Thought* (San Rafael: The Barfield Press, 1971), 77.

20   Coleridge, *Biographia Literaria*, 159.

21   Ibid., 160.

22   Corbin, 'Mundus Imaginalis', 10.

23   Tolkien, *On Fairy-Stories*, 65–66.

24   Coleridge, *Biographia Literaria*, 160.

25   Barfield, *What Coleridge Thought*, 82.

up' and a living imaginal world, a true *mundus imaginalis*.

Tolkien himself addresses the differences between imagination and fancy in *On Fairy-Stories* and, although he does not refer directly to Coleridge, it is clear, as Shippey[26] and Flieger[27] both point out, that Tolkien is chiefly addressing Coleridge. While Tolkien has comparable, if not identical, definitions of these terms, as a philologist he disagrees with Coleridge's choice of names. Tolkien asserts that the image-making faculty is the imagination, and any difference in kind marked by Coleridge between fancy and imagination, Tolkien feels solely belongs to a difference in degree. What gives the 'inner consistency of reality'[28] to imagination, the same reality the product of Coleridge's imagination has, Tolkien calls 'art'.[29] Art conjoins with imagination to create the final result: sub-creation. The word Tolkien chooses to fully encompass imagination and the resulting sub-creative art, perhaps out of philological jest with Coleridge, is 'fantasy', an older form of the diminished word 'fancy'.[30] Tolkien acknowledged that 'fantasy, the making or glimpsing of Other-worlds,'[31] is difficult to achieve: in order to be true fantasy it must have an inner consistency of reality flowing through the sub-creator's imagination and into the secondary world.

A successful sub-creator brings forward a world which 'both designer and spectator can enter', a world that has its own laws by which it operates.[32] As long as every facet of the imaginal realm follows these laws, the inner reality of the world remains intact and the world is true.[33] Because of this, for Tolkien, it is essential that all stories about such secondary worlds are presented as truth—not as a dream, or some other unreal whimsical creation, because such a trope undermines the reality of what one encounters in that world.[34] For Coleridge, the richness of art is dependent on the unity provided by the secondary imagination: it will be 'rich in proportion to

---

26   Shippey, *The Road to Middle-Earth*, 50.

27   Flieger, *Splintered Light*, 24.

28   Tolkien, *On Fairy-Stories*, 59.

29   Ibid.

30   Ibid., 59–60; Flieger, *Splintered Light*, 24.

31   Tolkien, *On Fairy-Stories*, 55.

32   Ibid., 64.

33   Ibid., 52.

34   Ibid., 35.

the variety of parts which it holds in unity'.[35] The unity of Tolkien's Middle-earth is held together because each landscape, creature, and name has a consistency that he has forged into the very structure of his world. Furthermore, when the imaginal world is consistent with itself it creates for the reader what Tolkien calls 'Secondary Belief', or when fully realised, 'Enchantment'.[36] Thus it is as enchanted humans that we walk the glades and forests of Middle-earth.

What ultimately gives reality to secondary art is that it is consistent not only with itself, but also with what Tolkien and Shippey refer to as 'Primary Art'.[37] If the source of secondary art is the human imagination, the source of primary art is the divine imagination, what Coleridge calls the primary imagination. For Tolkien, primary art is synonymous with Creation, or Truth.[38] For a sub-created secondary world to be true then, it must echo the primary world, as Colin Duriez writes, capturing in its 'imaginative accuracy [...] some of the depths and splendor of the Primary World'.[39] Fantasy is crafted out of the primary world, just as the painter or sculptor's materials are drawn from nature.[40] But in the fantasy realm we are able to see these primary ingredients in a new way, once again marveling at the wonders of our own world.[41] Tolkien shows the overlap between our own world and Faërie when he writes:

> Faërie contains many things besides elves and fays, and besides dwarfs, witches, trolls, giants, or dragons: it holds the seas, the sun, the moon, the sky; and the earth, and all things that are in it: tree and bird, water and stone, wine and bread, and ourselves, mortal men, when we are enchanted.[42]

Faërie could then be seen as the real cosmos but without the human, or rather, without the *disenchanted* human. After all, as Beagle

---

35   Coleridge, quoted in Barfield, *What Coleridge Thought*, 81.

36   Tolkien, *On Fairy-Stories*, 64.

37   Shippey, *The Road to Middle-Earth*, 93.

38   Tolkien, *On Fairy-Stories*, 78.

39   Duriez, *Tolkien and C.S. Lewis*, 176.

40   Tolkien, *On Fairy-Stories*, 68.

41   Ibid., 67.

42   Ibid., 32.

remarks, the same forces that shape our own lives shape the lives of those in Middle-earth: 'history, chance, and desire'.[43] When we lead our lives in response to these forces, whether or not we find ourselves in Faërie depends on our level of enchantment, or our secondary belief.

ROOTS OF THE MYTHOLOGY:
INVENTION AND INSPIRATION

Tolkien's initial desire behind his decades of imaginative effort was to create a mythology for England, which he felt lacked a myth comparable to the great Norse and Greek traditions.[44] England did have the Arthurian legends, but these he felt did not suffice, in part because Christianity was an element of the narratives, and in part because they were not rooted in the ancient languages of England. Tolkien's objection to religion in myth is based on his sense that the contours of religious doctrine should only exist implicitly within fantasy, sunk deep into the morality and actions of the characters. He writes of the Arthurian myth that:

> it is involved in, and explicitly contains the Christian religion. For reasons which I will not elaborate, that seems to me fatal. Myth and fairy-story must, as all art, reflect and contain in solution elements of moral and religious truth (or error), but not explicit, not in the known form of the primary 'real' world.[45]

Like the religious element, language also plays a foundational role in the development of Middle-earth, rooted deeply into the world's symbolism and structures. To forge a world like Middle-earth, and bring it to the level of a mythology, Tolkien drew simultaneously on *invention* and *inspiration*, which seem to be the two major ingredients of sub-creation. Through *invention* he built up the world of Middle-earth from the myths, legends, and languages of Europe.

---

43   Beagle, 'Tolkien's Magic Ring', x.

44   Humphrey Carpenter, *J.R.R. Tolkien: A Biography* (New York: Houghton Mifflin, 2000), 97.

45   Tolkien, *Letters*, 144.

As Patrick Curry writes, Middle-earth 'was a co-creation, in part-nership with some very old and durable cultural materials'.[46] Yet it was *inspiration* that breathed life into the world Tolkien had shaped, imbuing it with unique characteristics and a vitality of its own.

In some ways, invention can be seen as related to Coleridge's no-tion of fancy, and inspiration to the imagination. Fancy is memo-ry disconnected from time and space, and can only draw on what has been consciously experienced.[47] 'Fancy is the *aggregating* pow-er', as Barfield writes, 'it combines and aggregates given units of already conscious experience; whereas the secondary imagination "modifies" the units themselves'.[48] On the other hand, inspiration, like imagination, almost seems to have a divine source that pours through the sub-creator and imbues the creation with life and indi-viduality. An example of the difference between fancy and imagina-tion, and invention and inspiration, can be seen in the race of Ents in Middle-earth. As invented by fancy, an Ent is just a talking tree, a rearrangement of the idea 'tree' by giving it the human property of 'speech'. The word 'Ent' comes from the Anglo-Saxon word *enta* un-covered by Tolkien in his philological research.[49] At this stage Ents are perhaps an interesting etymological find, something to pique one's curiosity, but as of yet certainly not a living being. But through the power of imaginal inspiration, the invented concept of Ent sud-denly comes alive as the bark-skinned Treebeard, also named Fan-gorn, the oldest living being to walk under the Sun. It is truly an enchanted transformation. Ents are bestowed life and step forth as a race of creatures, tree-herders, shepherds of the forests, with a long tragic history of their own, speaking in a slow, rhythmic language of names compiled over the Ages of the World.

FANCY AND ALLEGORY

Fancy, without the influence of imagination, has ties to another form of artistic creation, one which Tolkien said he 'cordially dislike[d]

---

46   Patrick Curry, *Defending Middle-Earth* (Edinburgh: Floris Books, 1997), 134.

47   Coleridge, *Biographia Literaria*, 160.

48   Barfield, *What Coleridge Thought*, 86.

49   Shippey, *The Road to Middle-Earth*, 131.

[...] in all its manifestations': allegory.[50] By having a prescribed intention—whether a moral, lesson, or message—or by telling an old story in the same configuration but with new names, allegory undermines the freedom of the reader to experience a story as an entity in itself, a self-contained reality. Great imaginative works cannot be reduced simply to a moral message or lesson, they have a life of their own, an inherent autonomy beyond the will of the author.[51] Allegory, by its very nature, undermines truth. Corbin draws out the difference between allegory and genuine 'Image' when he writes: 'Allegory [...] is a cover, or rather a travesty of something that is already known or at least knowable in some other way; whereas, the appearance of an Image that can be qualified as a symbol is a primordial phenomenon'.[52] A symbolic image cannot be exhausted, for the very nature of a symbol is that it presences what is absent. Symbolic works speak to the soul, and they open a doorway to the imagination as a way of knowing, as a way of revealing truth.

Despite his dislike of allegory, Tolkien did write at least one in his career, but it served the purpose of encouraging him to continue his work on *The Lord of the Rings*, and offered an image of his hope for the world of Middle-earth. This was the little tale 'Leaf by Niggle'. Niggle is a painter, and can be equated with Tolkien the writer, who spends his life working on a detailed painting of a tree:

> It had begun with a leaf caught in the wind, and it became a tree; and the tree grew, sending out innumerable branches, and thrusting out the most fantastic roots. Strange birds came and settled on the twigs and had to be attended to. Then all round the Tree, and behind it, through the gaps in the leaves and boughs, a country began to open out; and there were glimpses of a forest marching over the land, and of mountains tipped with snow.[53]

Shippey sees in the allegory that the leaf is Tolkien's first book *The Hobbit*, his tree *The Lord of the Rings*, and the landscape behind as

---

50   Tolkien, 'Foreword', in *The Lord of the Rings*, xv.

51   Duriez, *Tolkien and C.S. Lewis*, 186.

52   Corbin, 'Mundus Imaginalis', 10–11.

53   Tolkien, 'Leaf by Niggle', in *The Tolkien Reader*, 101.

all the other stories that make up *The Silmarillion* and fill in the vast-
ness of Middle-earth.[54] However, the most remarkable part of the
story is when it seems to leave the realm of allegory altogether. Niggle goes on a great journey, which is synonymous with death, and
after some time in a hospitalised form of purgatory, he is sent to an
oddly familiar country which he suddenly recognises:

> Before him stood the Tree, his Tree, finished [...] All
> the leaves he had ever laboured at were there, as he
> had imagined them rather than as he had made them;
> and there were many others that had only budded in
> his mind, and many that might have budded, if only he
> had had time.[55]

By stepping into an enchanted realm, Niggle's work becomes real,
the invented becomes the imagined, and he can stand in the shade
of his own tree. The tree, whether an allegory for *The Lord of the
Rings*, or for fairy-story in general, is aptly chosen: the philosopher
Gaston Bachelard writes of the tree as a symbol of the imagination,
an imagination with the gift to create worlds:

> The imagination is a tree. It has the integrative virtues
> of a tree. It is root and boughs. It lives between earth
> and sky. It lives in the earth and in the wind. The imag-
> ined tree becomes imperceptibly the cosmological tree,
> the tree which epitomizes the universe, which makes a
> universe [...][56]

Trees not only have high branches but also long roots, and the roots
of Tolkien's Middle-earth run deep, drawing nourishment from the
soil of our own primary world.

---

54   Shippey, *The Road to Middle-Earth*, 43.

55   Tolkien, 'Leaf by Niggle', 113.

56   Gaston Bachelard, *On Poetic Imagination and Reverie* (Putnam: Spring
      Publications, 2005), 85.

Myth sculpted from language

Like most cultural myths, Middle-earth is rooted in language, but unlike the ancient cultures in which stories and languages evolved simultaneously, Middle-earth is a philological re-creation, a laying of stonework far older than the hands that built it.[57] Tolkien was as well-equipped as any builder to undertake the task: as a philologist who taught at Oxford and Leeds, he knew some twenty languages to varying degrees, and during his lifetime invented another fourteen, as well as a variety of scripts.[58] He reconstructed words and names from almost forgotten linguistic origins, drawing on fragments of words from poems and texts that had once formed legends.[59] Tolkien writes in a letter to Milton Waldman about his Middle-earth mythology:

> These tales are 'new,' they are not directly derived from other myths and legends, but they must inevitably contain a large measure of ancient widespread motives or elements. After all, I believe that legends and myths are largely made of 'truth'.[60]

For Tolkien reconstruction was the work of invention, but as he would have known, the root of the word 'invention' comes from the Latin *invenire*, meaning 'to find'.[61] So for him invention certainly was not 'making up', but rather 'discovering', an experience he mentioned many times when reflecting on writing the mythology of Middle-earth. He was not only discovering the different names and languages in the primary world and reconfiguring them: he seemed also to be discovering Middle-earth itself, a complete world existing already in the primary imagination, coming into form through Tolkien's own secondary imagination.

---

57   Shippey, *The Road to Middle-Earth*, 57.
58   Ruth S. Noel, *The Languages of Tolkien's Middle-Earth* (Boston: Houghton Mifflin, 1974), 3–4.
59   Shippey, *The Road to Middle-Earth*, 48–49.
60   Tolkien, *Letters*, 147.
61   Shippey, *The Road to Middle-Earth*, 25.

In approaching *The Lord of the Rings*, Tolkien began with the map, which gave a solid foundation for the world before he and his characters embarked on their adventures. As in the primary world, the names of places on the map were crafted out of topographical or historical descriptions of those places; these, in turn, were then worn down into names used in other languages, but no longer holding a meaning beyond the given places.[62] Whether called Tookland, Nobottle, Wetwang, Dunharrow, Gladden, Silverlode, or Limlight, each place has its history within and outside of Middle-earth.[63]

The name Middle-earth itself, related to the Norse *Midgard*, actually came to Tolkien through an Old English poem called *Crist* by the Anglo-Saxon poet Cynewulf. Two lines particularly caught Tolkien's eye:

> *Eala Earendelenglabeorhtast*
> *offermiddangeardmonnumsended.*
>
> Hail Earendel, brightest of angels,
> Above Middle-earth sent unto men.[64]

Not only was the name Middle-earth present as *middangeard*, but the name Earendel stood out to Tolkien as well, a name which became Eärendil in *The Silmarillion*; Eärendil was the father of Elrond and bearer of the last Silmaril, the evening star most beloved by the Elves.

Tolkien's Elves and Dwarves are, in part, shaped by the legends and myths of immemorable age that pervade cultures across Europe.[65] Tolkien drew on many aspects of the lore of Elves and Dwarves, presenting both the peril and beauty of the Elves, the longevity and gold-mongering of the Dwarves.[66] His emphasis on spelling 'Elves' and 'Dwarves' in the ancient manner, as opposed to 'elfs' and 'dwarfs', further deepened their roots in history.[67] His invented languages were also based on the languages of Europe; the

---

62   Ibid., 101.

63   Ibid., 103.

64   Cynewulf, quoted in Noel, *The Languages of Tolkien's Middle-Earth*, 4.

65   Shippey, *The Road to Middle-Earth*, 57–58.

66   Ibid., 59–61.

67   Ibid., 56.

two Elvish tongues were his most developed vocabulary, with the more common Sindarin Elvish rooted in Welsh, and the High Elvish Quenya drawing on Finnish structures.

Because the Middle-earth *legendarium* was originally meant to be a mythology for England, Tolkien drew deeply from the waters of the Anglo-Saxon well: the Rohirrim were based in part on Anglo-Saxons, and the name Eorl is from a line of Old English poetry; other names such as Éomer and Éowyn, as well as the term éored for a troop of horses, all stem from the word *eoh* meaning 'horse'.[68] Tolkien even embedded linguistic changes in the history of Middle-earth itself. For example, before Eorl the Young brought the Rohirrim from the North to inhabit the Gondorian plains of Rohan, the names of Rohirric leaders had Gothic origins: Vidugavia, Vidumavi, Marhwini.[69] Only after they enter into allegiance with Gondor do the Rohirrim take on Anglo-Saxon names. Both the words 'Ent' and 'Woses' appeared in Old English poetry, and in Middle-earth the Rohirrim are appropriately situated between the Entish woods of Fangorn, and the Druadan Forest in which the Woses dwell to the South.[70]

THE BREATH OF PURE INSPIRATION

Tolkien's almost obsessive attention to detail touched every word he wrote in *The Lord of the Rings*, and he even attended to such particulars as the direction of the blowing wind and the cycling phases of the Moon. He wanted his readers to feel as though they had stepped into history.[71] All of his attention to the distinctions of locality, as Curry describes:

> contributes greatly to the uncanny feeling, shared by many of his readers, of actually having been there, and knowing it from the inside, rather than simply having read about it—the sensation, as one put it, of 'actually walking, running, fighting and breathing in Middle-earth'.[72]

---

68   Ibid., 20–21.

69   Ibid., 15.

70   Ibid., 131.

71   Carpenter, *J.R.R. Tolkien: A Biography*, 198–99.

72   Curry, *Defending Middle-Earth*, 27.

Beagle captures beautifully the interwoven intricacy of Middle-earth, the miniscule details discovered to invent it, and the natural reality they express when fused together as a unified whole: 'The structure of Tolkien's world is as dizzyingly complex and as natural as a snowflake or a spiderweb.'[73] Inspiration unifies the invented parts into an organic whole, thereby animating them. Tolkien writes in one letter, 'I have long ceased to *invent* [...] I wait till I seem to know what really happened. Or till it writes itself.'[74] In another letter, this one to W.H. Auden, Tolkien writes:

> I daresay something had been going on in the 'unconscious' for some time, and that accounts for my feeling throughout, especially when stuck, that I was not inventing but reporting (imperfectly) and had at times to wait till 'what really happened' came through.[75]

As Shippey observes, Tolkien seemed to labour at invention until he reached a moment when he could go no further. Somehow, in that moment inspiration would take over and life would fill the creation he had built: he would then be led into the adventure with just as much bewilderment as his literary companions.[76] It was, as Tolkien calls it, the 'fusion-point of imagination',[77] where invention and inspiration meet and something new is born.

The race of people that set Middle-earth most apart from all other manifestations of Faërie were not an invention drawn from European legends. They seemed to have arrived fully formed, already inhabiting their little northwestern corner of Tolkien's world. These were the Hobbits. As Tolkien writes on several occasions, the origin of Hobbits is unknown, even to themselves.[78] In the now well-known pivotal moment, Tolkien was grading exams one summer's day when he unexpectedly wrote on a blank sheet: '*In a hole in the ground there lived a hobbit*'.[79] As Shippey notes, Hobbits are

---

73   Beagle, 'Tolkien's Magic Ring', xi.
74   Tolkien, *Letters*, 231.
75   Ibid., 212.
76   Shippey, *The Road to Middle-Earth*, 104.
77   Tolkien, quoted in Shippey, *The Road to Middle-Earth*, 63.
78   Tolkien, *Letters*, 158.
79   Tolkien, quoted in Carpenter, *J.R.R. Tolkien: A Biography*, 175.

'pure inspiration' without a trace of invention to them.[80] Tolkien of course quickly gave them philological roots, connecting "Hobbit" to the Old English word *hol-bytla*, meaning 'hole-dweller'.[81] He went further, setting the Hobbits in an English style of life, seemingly far more modern than the rest of Middle-earth extending beyond the Shire. Even the names of the Hobbits have echoes of English culture; for example, the name Baggins recalls the English word 'baggins' meaning afternoon tea, or any food eaten in between meals, of which Hobbits are rather fond.[82] 'The implication', writes Shippey, 'is that the inspiration was a memory of something that could in reality have existed.'[83]

Hobbits, in many ways, are more human than the race of Men in Middle-earth, and offer us modern readers a window into their world. The Hobbits provided the link for Tolkien to connect the Elvish mythologies recorded in *The Silmarillion* to the world presented in *The Hobbit*; the result was, of course, *The Lord of the Rings*. Hobbits put 'earth under the feet of "romance"', and as readers we are invited to walk with them.[84]

LIGHT FROM AN INVISIBLE LAMP

While fantasy, as 'Sub-created Art', can be expressed through many artistic forms, Tolkien felt that it was 'best left to words, to true literature'.[85] Literature allows the imagination to flourish at every level, from the author writing it, to each individual reader imagining what the author presents in their own unique way. Tolkien writes: 'every hearer of the words will have his own picture, and it will be made out of all the hills and rivers and dales he has ever seen, but especially out of The Hill, The River, The Valley which were for him the first embodiment of the word.'[86] It is as though author and reader alike are drawing on an archetypal realm of the imagination, and

---

80   Shippey, *The Road to Middle-Earth*, 65.

81   Ibid., 66.

82   Ibid., 72.

83   Ibid., 67.

84   Tolkien, *Letters*, 215.

85   Tolkien, *On Fairy-Stories*, 61.

86   Ibid., 82, n E.

each of the images they produce of this world adds another layer of dimensionality, bringing it further into reality. As Tolkien also says: 'Literature works from mind to mind and is thus more progenitive'.[87]

When the imagination of the reader participates in a secondary world, the reader then becomes part of that world as well. Beagle writes of his experiences reading *The Lord of the Rings*: 'Something of ourselves has gone into reading it, and so it belongs to us'.[88] He goes on to say the book 'will bear the mind's handling, and it is a book that acquires an individual patina in each mind that takes it up, like a much-caressed pocket stone or piece of wood'.[89] The meaning of the work, as R.J. Reilly says, resides between the 'art work and the perceiving subject'[90] and ultimately lies, as Tolkien wanted, in the 'freedom of the reader'.[91] As readers we also become sub-creators of the secondary world, as our own imaginations lead us into our experience of it.

As Duriez expresses, and as a Roman Catholic Tolkien surely believed, our human ability to be sub-creators derives from our being made in God's image.[92] Tolkien confirms his belief in this when he writes in *On Fairy-Stories*, 'Fantasy remains a human right: we make in our measure and in our derivative mode, because we are made, and not only made, but made in the image and likeness of a Maker'.[93] Sub-creation is the imagining of God's world after God.[94] Yet sub-creative art can also enhance human life by expanding, in Clarke's words, the '*limited boundaries* of the real world in which we presently live by *creating something really new*, never experienced by humans before'.[95] Indeed, Tolkien writes that 'liberation "from the channels the creator is known to have used already" is the fundamental function of "sub-creation", a tribute to the infinity of His

87   Ibid.

88   Beagle, 'Tolkien's Magic Ring', x.

89   Ibid., xii.

90   R.J. Reilly, *Romantic Religion: A Study of Barfield, Lewis, Williams, and Tolkien* (Athens: University of Georgia Press, 1971), 196.

91   Tolkien, 'Foreword', in *The Lord of the Rings*, xv.

92   Duriez, *Tolkien and C.S. Lewis*, 72.

93   Tolkien, *On Fairy-Stories*, 66.

94   Duriez, *Tolkien and C.S. Lewis*, 198.

95   Clarke, 'The Creative Imagination', 205.

potential variety'.[96] For Tolkien, God was, in a way, creating Middle-earth through him, which may be why he felt like he was discovering a world already in existence.

In one of the last years of Tolkien's life he received a letter from a man, which Tolkien describes as follows: This man

> classified himself as 'an unbeliever, or at best a man of belatedly and dimly dawning religious feeling [...] but you [Tolkien], he said, 'create a world in which some sort of faith seems to be everywhere without a visible source, like light from an invisible lamp'. I [Tolkien] can only answer: 'Of his own sanity no man can securely judge. If sanctity inhabits his work or as a pervading light illumines it then it does not come from him but through him. And [...] you would [not] perceive it in these terms unless it was with you also.[97]

Beagle too was perceiving something of this quality of Tolkien's work when he wrote about the music that 'springs from the center of this world'.[98] Tolkien's living imagination, flowing from what Coleridge called the primary imagination, sprang up alive in the heart of Middle-earth. It was almost as though the story were asking to be written. For example, Tolkien had a recurrent dream of 'the Great Wave, towering up, and coming in ineluctably over the trees and green fields'.[99] He eventually wrote this vision into Middle-earth, giving it as a dream to Faramir, but also capturing it more fully in the 'Downfall of Númenor' in *The Silmarillion*. Interestingly, once he did write it, the dream ceased recurring. It was as though the dream, possibly

---

96   Tolkien, *Letters*, 188. This particular letter by Tolkien was in response to a fellow Catholic, Peter Hastings, who felt that a sub-creator should not diverge 'from the channels the creator is known to have used already', as Tolkien did when he wrote about the reincarnation of Elves. He continued in his response to Hastings to say: 'But I do not see how even in the Primary World any theologian or philosopher, unless very much better informed about the relation of spirit and body than I believe anyone to be, could deny the *possibility* of reincarnation as a mode of existence, prescribed for certain kinds of rational incarnate creatures'.

97   Ibid., 413.

98   Beagle, 'Tolkien's Magic Ring', xv.

99   Tolkien, *Letters*, 213.

coming from the primary imagination, needed to become a reality, and once revealed through Tolkien it could rest.

In the lecture Tolkien gave that eventually became *On Fairy-Stories*, he expressed his wish that one day the mythology of Middle-earth would be discovered to be 'true'.[100] He felt the possibility that all myths might exist in some realm other than our own.[101] Indeed, it was because of the link Tolkien saw between human creativity and divine making, that he felt 'all tales may come true'.[102] Many critics have accused *The Lord of the Rings* of being an escapist narrative, and not having a clear message for the modern world, but as Curry points out: 'It offers not an "escape" from our world, this world, but hope for its future'.[103] So indeed perhaps all myths may come true, and Middle-earth will take on a new reality in another realm not of space but of time, possibly a time we can imagine in our distant future.

At last, perhaps, we can return to the little allegory, 'Leaf by Niggle', better to understand what Tolkien meant by this hope that 'all tales may come true'. Niggle is joined in the country he painted by his neighbour Parish, who never much appreciated Niggle's painting when they had been alive together. Yet when Parish realises that it was Niggle who dreamt up the country they are now in he remarks:

> 'But it did not look like this then, not *real*,' said Parish.
> 'No, it was only a glimpse then,' said the man; 'but you
> might have caught the glimpse, if you had ever thought
> it worth while to try.'[104]

Whenever Tolkien uses the word 'glimpse' he frequently seems to be referring to the gleam of truth that shines through fantasy, whether it is in Niggle's story, in the preliminary sketches of his plots, or in his definition of fantasy as 'the making or glimpsing of Other-worlds'.[105] Tolkien believed that 'there is no higher function for

---

100   Carpenter, *J.R.R. Tolkien: A Biography*, 195; Tolkien, *On Fairy-Stories*, 79.

101   Reilly, *Romantic Religion*, 214.

102   Tolkien, *On Fairy-Stories*, 79.

103   Curry, *Defending Middle-Earth*, 33.

104   Tolkien, 'Leaf by Niggle', 117.

105   Tolkien, *On Fairy-Stories*, 55.

man than the "sub-creation" of a Secondary World'[106] because, as Shippey writes, 'it might be mankind's one chance to create a vision of Paradise which would be true in the future if never in the past'.[107] For Tolkien, the human imagination has the power to bring forth a new Paradise, because he saw the secondary imagination as an echo of God's imagination, and as it worked through him he felt he was ultimately doing the creative work of God.

CONCLUSION:
IMAGINAL KNOWING IN THE ACADEMY

Over the course of his lifetime, Tolkien witnessed a human civilisation ever more disconnected from the spiritual and ecological dimensions of our world. As a professor at the University of Oxford, Tolkien's literary creations and his professional life were always kept distinctly separate, a boundary clearly reflective of the cultural and educational milieu of his time that continues to be seen in academia today. Yet, a large part of what gives the sense of reality to Tolkien's Middle-earth is the way in which he used his philological skills, honed in his academic studies and career, to bring forth new languages, and therefore new peoples and stories to embody those languages. Tolkien's mythopoeic work continues to speak to each new generation that steps through its pages and enters the imaginal world of Middle-earth. Although the disconnection between industrial civilisation—and the disenchanted forms of education that continue to sustain it—and the ensouled nature of the cosmos continues to widen in our own times, works of the imagination hold a powerful antidote to bridging the gap.

Tolkien's writings, both those that are a product of the imagination—such as *The Lord of the Rings*—and those that reflect on the nature of imagination—such as *On Fairy-Stories*—are key texts that present an imaginal method of learning and can inspire a re-enchanted approach to the world. Although it would have been nearly inconceivable in Tolkien's own time and academic environment, his works are entering into the academy with greater frequency and are being taught in various forms at different levels of higher

---

106   Carpenter, *J.R.R. Tolkien: A Biography*, 195.
107   Shippey, *The Road to Middle-Earth*, 53.

education. Tolkien's creations speak not only to the mind but to the soul, and they can awaken one to an imaginal means of acquiring knowledge. World views are fundamentally shaped by one's education and learning communities, and diversifying the ways of knowing taught in the academy can profoundly shift world views—and thereby bring forth new worlds. Tolkien, like so many other creative artists, offers an example of how we can each become vessels, learning how to open ourselves as conduits for the primary imagination and channelling it into newly re-enchanted visions for the future.

Select bibliography

BARFIELD, Owen. *What Coleridge Thought*. San Rafael: The Barfield Press, 1971.

CARPENTER, Humphrey. *J.R.R. Tolkien: A Biography*. New York: Houghton Mifflin, 2000.

CLARKE, Norris. 'The Creative Imagination: Unique Expression of Our Soul-Body Unity'. In *The Creative Retrieval of St. Thomas Aquinas*, 191–208. New York: Fordham University Press, 2009.

COLERIDGE, Samuel Taylor. *Biographia Literaria*. London: J.M. Dent & Co., 1906.

CORBIN, Henry. 'Mundus Imaginalis, or The Imaginary and the Imaginal'. Translated by Ruth Horine. *En Islam Iranien: Aspects Spirituels et Philosophiques*, tome IV, livre 7. Paris: Gallimard, 1971.

CURRY, Patrick. *Defending Middle-Earth*. Edinburgh, UK: Floris Books, 1997.

DURIEZ, Colin. *Tolkien and C.S. Lewis: The Gift of Friendship*. Mahwah: Hidden Spring, 2003.

FLIEGER, Verlyn. *Splintered Light: Logos and Languages in Tolkien's World*. Kent: The Kent State University Press, 2002.

NOEL, Ruth S. *The Languages of Tolkien's Middle-Earth*. Boston: Houghton Mifflin, 1974.

REILLY, R. J. *Romantic Religion: A Study of Barfield, Lewis, Williams, and Tolkien*. Athens: University of Georgia Press, 1971.

SHIPPEY, Tom. *The Road to Middle-Earth: How J.R.R. Tolkien Created a New Mythology*. New York: Houghton Mifflin Company, 2003.

TOLKIEN, J.R.R. *The Hobbit*. New York: Houghton Mifflin, 1997.

———. *The Letters of J.R.R. Tolkien*. Edited by Humphrey Carpenter, with the assistance of Christopher Tolkien. New York: Houghton Mifflin, 2000.

———. *The Lord of the Rings*. New York: Houghton Mifflin, 1994.

———. *On Fairy-Stories*. Edited by Verlyn Flieger and Douglas A. Anderson. London: HarperCollins, 2014.

———. *The Silmarillion*. New York: Houghton Mifflin, 2001.

———. *The Tolkien Reader*. New York: Ballantine Publishing Group, 1966.

Engaging the Non-linguistic Mind

Re-enchantment Beyond Words

PAUL STEVENS

ENCHANTMENT IS SOMETHING which is almost impossible to define, yet we know it when we encounter it, or when we feel it is missing. This makes it hard to write about enchantment, and even harder to write about how we might go about *re*-enchanting anything. Yet this very difficulty is a clue to the nature of enchantment: it is mysterious, it is magical, it is all those things that the dominant worldview, so often influenced by Western science, is not. It is on the tip of our tongues yet we can only talk indirectly about it by referring to fairy tales and folklore, myth and metaphor. It is something which can only be understood by experiencing it, by feeling it in the way our bodies come alive, become part of a living, animated world.

Yet it is often something which academics banish to the depths of the unconscious or subconscious mind: that subliminal realm which we cannot directly experience, which can only partially affect our everyday experience. Enchantment thus becomes something we can only dream about, not real or meaningful in the waking world. This, I believe, is the wrong way to think about it. Instead, let us start by thinking about how we commonly visualise a mind. As an analogy, think of a mind as being a kind of surface, having an inside and an outside (see FIGURE 1).

The inside surface looks inwards, at all of the things we think of as being part of our interior world: subjective experiences, thoughts, feelings, sensations from the body. This side of the mind-surface is all about the self, and is seen as being the place where the sub- and unconscious reside. In other words, it is a realm of the imagination, of fluid fantasy and everything that is in some sense 'not real'. The outside surface looks outward, into the 'real' world of objective, shared experiences that happen in a rational, orderly manner. It is

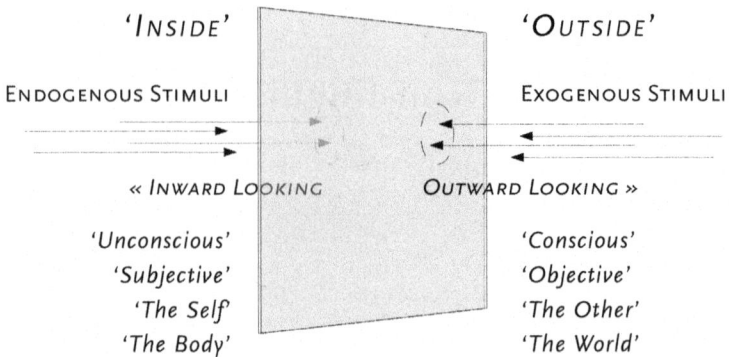

'INSIDE'   'OUTSIDE'

ENDOGENOUS STIMULI   EXOGENOUS STIMULI

« INWARD LOOKING   OUTWARD LOOKING »

'Unconscious'   'Conscious'
'Subjective'   'Objective'
'The Self'   'The Other'
'The Body'   'The World'

FIGURE 1:

Mind as surface.

the realm of the social, the other, where the conscious mind is pre-sumed to be dominant.

To this way of thinking, the mind-surface envelops the inner, private self. It is the boundary that separates real and unreal, the mundane world from the enchanted. It keeps us separate, discrete; autonomous, isolated entities moving through the world but not really a part of it. Endogenous stimuli (mostly seen as 'subjective') from the body, from the self, can only be felt by their effect on the inner side of the mind-surface; exogenous ('objective') stimuli can only register on the outer side of the mind-surface. Above all, each of us can never really know what it is like 'inside' another entity: what is within each mind, that enchanted realm beyond the boundary, is forever out of reach.

Yet what if this way of visualising the mind actually creates the separation? What if the two apparent sides of that mind-surface are actually just the two halves of a continuum, with what we thought of as being inside instead just being further away, harder to perceive, from the outside? In other words, what if what we thought of as an impenetrable boundary was instead just a corner we couldn't see around? A kink in the surface which we can iron out (see FIGURE 2)?

'OPEN OUT' & FLATTEN
THE MIND-SURFACE TO REMOVE
THE APPARENT INSIDE/
OUTSIDE SPLIT.

1

2

3

4

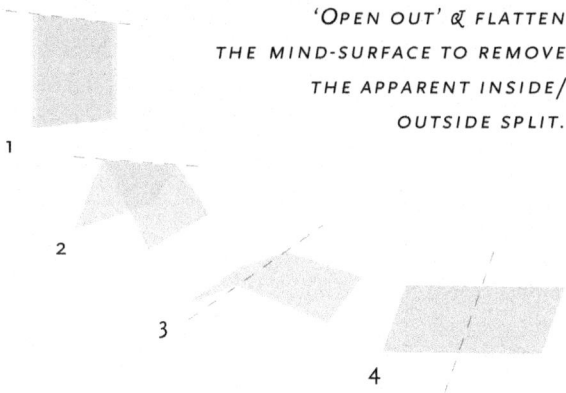

FIGURE 2:
Unfolding the mind-surface.

But, in this case, why was the 'inside' harder to perceive by those 'outside'? In what sense was it further away? Whatever we originally thought of as being 'inside' does undeniably have different qualities. We think of 'inside stuff' as being harder to talk about, more idiosyncratic, impossible to point to and say 'look, that's what I'm talking about!' So going back to our analogy of mind as a surface, albeit now a flattened-out surface (see FIGURE 3), we can re-conceptualise what endogenous and exogenous might mean.

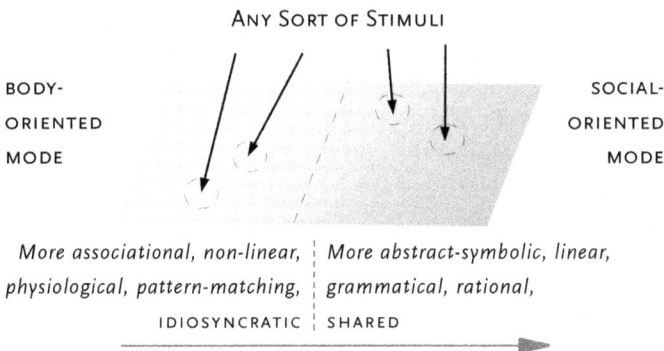

ANY SORT OF STIMULI

BODY-
ORIENTED
MODE

SOCIAL-
ORIENTED
MODE

More associational, non-linear, | *More abstract-symbolic, linear,*
physiological, pattern-matching, | *grammatical, rational,*
IDIOSYNCRATIC | SHARED

FIGURE 3:
Mind as a continuum.

Let's start with the 'outside', the source of exogenous stimuli. Whatever else we are, humans are social creatures. So much of our minds and bodies evolved to interact with others, and social-oriented behaviour is so dominant that we use it as the basis for our interactions with apparently inanimate objects too (if you disagree, I will leave it up to you to explain why people name and assign a gender to their boats, or why you were whispering encouragement to your car the last time you drove up that steep hill...). So it seems appropriate to re-label the 'exogenous' right-hand side of the diagram the *social-oriented* world, the realm of the other over which we have only indirect control.

That being the case, the 'endogenous' left-hand side of the diagram must be the realm of the self, that which we have at least some control over. An appropriate re-labelling would be the *body-oriented* world.

We can now see that it might be harder than we previously assumed to find a qualitative difference between stimuli originating from the 'outside' social-oriented world and the 'inside' body-oriented world; exogenous and endogenous are just labels we assign depending on *where* on the mind-surface those stimuli appear to arrive. Any boundary between the two is thus much more arbitrary than it first appeared. Immediately this has an appeal, as our everyday experience is often much more ambiguous than we like to admit. Did I really see something move, or just imagine it? Did I reply to what you said, or to what I thought you said? And, just by re-imagining the mind in this way, it implies that the enchanted realm is now only separated by a mere mist of perception rather than an impenetrable boundary.

Going back to those questions—why was what we originally saw as the 'inside' harder to perceive by others, and what might it mean that the left-hand side of the mind-surface was 'further away'?—we now have some answers. The left-hand side is body oriented: as each of our bodies differs due to genetics and experience, that end of your mind-surface will be idiosyncratic, shaped by the form of your body and especially by the complex network of interconnections between your neuronal cells that make up your embodied brain. It is not that that part of your mind is inaccessible per se; it is just that it is hard to communicate its nature to another person, and equally hard for that other person to interpret what you are saying in such a way that they can relate it to their own idiosyncratic 'inner' mind.

This is why that apparent boundary forms. It's a line marking 'here be idiosyncratic dragons'; a demarcation that, as we grow, we map out in implicit negotiation with others, soon learning at which point most people back off and think we are weird, or sharing too much, or 'have no boundaries'. The exact placement of your boundary will always have some flexibility depending on who you are with: further to the body-oriented left for those you have an affinity with, further to the social-oriented right for those you do not know or trust, and moving further back and forth depending on mood, confidence, and many other factors.

The reason it is so hard to communicate what is on the inner side of the boundary is that we tend to express things in language: a form of consensus communication that is firmly a part of the social-oriented world. As such, it is always going to convey only an approximation of what is occurring in the body-oriented world. Simply put, we can lose a sense of enchantment when we try to reify an experience by putting it into words: language shapes what we can express, even what we think, about an experience.[1] Words structure any experience, giving it cause and effect, placing it in the linear timeline of past-present-future, reducing the fuzziness and idiosyncrasy to recognisable (and so communicable) categories.

Yet, as we have all experienced at some point in our lives (often in childhood), the enchanted realm has subtleties and nuances that words cannot completely describe. Every experience is unique, with colours, shapes, smells, and sensations that are malleable, in constant flux, so delicate that paying them too much attention can bring about their dissolution. Some get closer than others in being able to articulate what it is like in an enchanted world. Poets play with words, breaking the rigidity of grammar to hint at what is behind those words. This happens at the expense of clear understanding: for some, poetry revitalises memories of similar enchanted experiences, but for others it is simply word-play, seen as pretentious rather than an act of re-enchantment. Writers and effective teachers often turn to simile and metaphor, weaving tales of magic, of fantastical creatures or otherworldly lands. There is enchantment there, but it is distant, seen as a work of fiction (not 'real') or New Age philosophy (usually used to mean a pseudo-understanding at best). Music

---

1   Lera Boroditsky, 'How Language Shapes Thought', *Scientific American* 304 (2011): 63–65.

can get even closer, abandoning language all together to describe enchantment in the ebb and flow of a melody, shaped and paced by rhythm, emotion, and landscape intertwined in the pitch and timbre of the instruments.[2] Music can carry us away, back, within, transcending the boundary to speak directly to the body-oriented mind.

By considering these three areas—poetry, metaphor, and music—and looking at what qualities they share, we can find techniques to reliably bring enchantment back into academia, and perhaps to bring it back into everyday life as well.

HYPNOSIS

One of these techniques is exemplified by a phenomenon long associated with being enchanted: hypnosis. This can be defined as a 'state of consciousness involving focused attention and reduced peripheral awareness characterised by an enhanced capacity for response to suggestion'.[3] Yet it is not so much the state itself which is of interest here but the way in which that state is reached. Although there are diverse ways of achieving hypnosis, a typical procedure involves two main steps:

1.   The creation of a rapport between hypnotist and client; and
2.   A period of hypnotic 'induction'.

If performed satisfactorily, these result in the attainment of a 'trance' state (really an alteration in consciousness as per the definition above) wherein therapeutic change or self-development is more easily achieved. This state is one in which metaphor and associational logic are dominant. The client might experience the enactment of symbolic rituals, a meeting with their past or future selves, the shape-shifting of their body, or travelling in the blink of an eye to far-off lands, both fictional and real. While what they experience is not logical in terms of the social-oriented world, it is powerful,

---

2   See Daniel Levitin, *This is your Brain on Music* (London: Atlantic Books, 2006), 15–18.

3   This is a recent formulation, with wide consensus, from the website of the American Psychological Association's Society of Psychological Hypnosis (www.apadivisions.org/division-30/about).

and can bring about significant behavioural and attitudinal changes when they return to that everyday world. In short, they have
been enchanted.

So let us look at those two steps in more detail for indications of
what a (re-)enchanter might need to know. First of all, rapport can
be defined as 'sympathy, harmony between individuals, an emotional bond or connection'.[4] It is about feeling comfortable with each
other, engendering a reciprocal feeling of trust, a mutual agreement
to share an experience. While hypnosis is often perceived as the effect or influence *of* the hypnotist *on* the client, it is actually an interactive relationship between the two, with much of the effort being
on the part of the client. Indeed, a common maxim amongst hyp-
notherapists is that 'all hypnosis is self-hypnosis'; the hypnotist is
there to guide, to facilitate, to safeguard, and simply to accompany
the client while they go on a journey together into the inner realms
of the client's mind. Rapport is, in whatever context, about feeling
safe enough with someone to let them travel with you across that
self-imposed boundary on the mind-surface, knowing that they will
accept what you discover together without judgement or fear. As the
rapport grows, each journey can go deeper beyond the boundary,
making new, shared discoveries every time.

The first lesson for the (re-)enchanter is therefore to encourage
rapport with your intended companions. Be genuine. Make the attempt to show you might share a particular perspective, or at least
have empathy where perspectives differ. Have confidence in what
you say, whether in person or in print: you are offering a gift, not
asking permission! This requires trust on your part as well as theirs,
as you need to put your*self* back into your work, thereby exposing
parts of yourself that you might think of as being private rather
than public. There will always be the risk that you get hurt by rid-
icule or being patronised, but you may also make that connection
with another, or others: the first step in re-enchanting your work
and their world.

The second step is the induction. In hypnosis, this is seen as
the process by which an altered state of consciousness occurs in
the client, and, to some extent, where a complementary empathic
response occurs in the hypnotist as well. Typically, this induction

---

4   Les Brann, Jacky Owens, and Anne Williamson, eds., *The Handbook of
     Contemporary Clinical Hypnosis* (Chichester: Wiley-Blackwell, 2012), 89.

process will involve some form of relaxation and harmonisation of bodily responses. So, for example, the client might be taken through a progressive relaxation exercise, breathing deeply in a calm and comfortable manner while allowing each muscle group to relax systematically, all the way down from head to toe. The resultant state is then encouraged to deepen through the hypnotist's use of carefully chosen words and phrases, spoken with particular attention to tone and rhythm, intended to multi-sensorially evoke specific imagery. This should not be taken to mean that the relaxation need be passive. Equally effective would be a more dynamic procedure, where the client chants or dances their way into a state of narrowed attention, with the use of music or song, or other sensory stimuli that evoke the same kind of imagery through tone, rhythm or synæsthetic association.

So the second lesson for the would-be (re-)enchanter is to be aware of the manner in which you present your work, whatever the medium used. If speaking, then consider the tone of your speech. If you wish to speed up, elevate, excite your audience, raise your tone. To calm them down, go deeper, signify importance, lower your tone. This works best when it is complemented by the content, so match the tone to what you are describing: a decreasing, quietening tone if describing something which is shrinking, descending, slowing; an increasing, louder tone if describing something growing, rising, speeding up. If writing, create the same effect by association: in English, 'red' tends to be larger, more dangerous, angrier, closer than 'blue'; 'susurration' is 'heard' as calmer and quieter than 'roar'; 'faster' is 'heard' as speedier than 'slow'. Even the characters you might use in a written narrative can help: a female child will usually be 'heard' as saying something in a higher voice than a male adult, especially if you have previously primed your audience with a vivid description of these narrators.

Much easier to think about in relation to the written word, but just as important to verbal presentation, is the rhythm of delivery. Whether it is you speaking, or your writing, evoking an imagined voice in the reader's head, the rhythms can be used to change their perception of what you want to convey. Short words or hard consonants are rapid, punctuating bursts that rev up the percipient and focus their attention on you; longer, languid, alliterative words send your audience into a state of drifting reverie. Pauses especially can say more than the words themselves. They are:

CALMING

SLOWING

SPACE CLEARING

OFFERING TIME TO THINK

All of these approaches move us deeper across the mind-surface, taking us away from the social-oriented right side to the body-oriented left side. The words themselves remain on the right but the tones and rhythms in which they are spoken go deeper; they mimic the older, deeper 'language' of the body. Speeding up and slowing down heart rate and breathing. Mapping onto the highs and lows of activity in the brain. Reaching below the cognitive centres of language processing to resonate in the deeper limbic structures of emotion, memory, needs and desires, patterns that existed before we ever learned to speak or read.[5]

Once you have guided your audience towards an altered state of consciousness, then enchantment becomes easier. While maintaining the idea that the rhythm and tone of the words are often as important as the words themselves, you can now go further. In such a state, your audience is more open to seeing associations, to absorbing any metaphors used to explain and illustrate specific ideas, to the reality and efficacy of magical thinking. Previous beliefs are willingly put aside, allowing them to hear what you are saying and creatively assimilate this into their own personal worlds. This is indeed enchantment, and one in which your audience are willing, active participants. It is the difference between presenting *to* an audience, and inviting them to come *with* you on a shared journey allowing them to perceive things for themselves, and perhaps to reciprocally offer insights back to you.

NATURE

Another technique can be discovered through looking at the roots of *why* the kinds of patterns evoked by poetry, metaphor and music became so deeply embedded in our minds. This takes us into the

---

5   See Ellen Dissanayake, 'Prelinguistic and Preliterate Substrates of Poetic Narrative', *Poetics Today* 32 (2011): 55–79.

evolutionary history of humans, and the realms of ecopsychology: the study of the inter-relationship between humans and the rest of the natural world.[6]

For most of their evolutionary history, our human ancestors, like all other creatures on Earth, lived in environments that were modified only by the action of weather, vegetation, and the un-augmented action of living creatures. They were immersed in a world of natural patterns: shapes that were produced by relatively simple biological, chemical, and physical processes. While diverse, these patterns shared some common forms: they were *fractal*, having a self-similar geometry that arises from things growing and dividing, being weathered, disintegrating, decaying. Think of a fern leaf: the overall shape of the plant is repeated in each frond, and repeated again in the individual leaflets, and yet again in the subleaflets. These are fractal patterns that repeat as you 'zoom in' to higher magnifications. Rivulets of water in sand show the same patterns as rivers seen from space, as the path that lightning takes when it strikes, as the branching of trees or the blood vessels in your body. The natural world is composed of fractal shapes, fractal sounds, fractal textures. As humans are (though we often forget this) also a part of that world, we too are fractal: our bodies, our physiology, and our minds. We learn not just by adding new information, new knowledge, but by building on what has gone before. The patterns we learn as infants are expanded upon, linked together to form more complex yet still self-similar patterns as we grow through childhood; layers of yet more complex, self-similar patterns of behaviour and thought are added as we become adults. All that we were is implicit in who we now are, and in who we will become.[7]

As a result of this, we all respond favourably to fractal patterns whenever we encounter them in the world because they resonate with the fractals within our minds and bodies. We find such patterns and shapes easier to perceive, restful, calming. If we see a picture of trees, or waves on a beach, or mountains silhouetted against the sky, we are instinctively drawn to that image, tend to express a preference for it over other images that are less fractal (usually hu-

---

6   See Theodore Roszak, *The Voice of the Earth* (Grand Rapids, MI: Phanes Press, 2001), 14.

7   See Paul Stevens, 'Embedment in the Environment', *Perspectives in Public Health* 130 (2010): 265–69.

man made, urban scenes and objects). Similarly, we respond well to other modalities that are fractal: the sounds of birds singing and the wind blowing through leaves; the feel of flowing water, or of natural fabrics. It works even if we consciously think we don't like nature: our bodies still respond, becoming calmer, less excitable, more relaxed. Poetry, metaphor, music all mimic these forms, bringing the rhythms and patterns of nature into an all too often abstracted and nature-isolated human world.

What this means is that the environments in which we find ourselves affect us deeply, beyond the linear logic of the social-oriented world. Places that we would consider to be natural, especially wild places, give us more immersive, embodied, embedded experiences. The world becomes a bigger, more expansive place which we feel much deeper in the mind, further to the left of our mind-surface. Anyone familiar with folklore and fairytale will have noticed the preponderance of natural phenomena—fairy forests, mystical mountains, sun-dappled seas. The organic shapes and patterns of the natural world are themselves a fascinating path to enchantment.

So the final lesson for the (re-)enchanter is this: choose your place wisely. Think about—feel!—the buildings and spaces in which you learn, work, and give out your ideas. Ask yourself how they feel to be in, what emotions they engender, what associations you have with them. The kinds of emotions, sensations, intuitions you feel are likely to be the ones your audience will feel when they listen to or watch you, what they will subtly respond to when they read your work. If you can, choose a place of strength from which to present your work: a location in which you feel comfortable, a room with natural colours and textures, with window views of trees, or with lots of interior plants. If that isn't possible, then use natural imagery in your work: images of leaves and flower, naturalistic colours, organic decorations and symbols, words which evoke a sense of being connected to the natural world, and structures and patterns which are reminiscent of natural growth or, when appropriate, decay. Embed your message in a fractal kaleidoscope, implicitly contextualising the knowledge within a wider environment, and so enticing your audience to explore an enchanted world.

On some level, we have always known that enchantment is fundamentally about feeling connected to something. Even the primary dictionary definitions usually include terms like 'being attracted to' and 'holding your attention'.[8] There is a recognition that there are certain qualities, specific attributes, that we cannot help but be drawn to, and fascinated by. But beyond this, the idea that enchantment is about 'being under a spell' signifies that we are in a different state of being when enchanted, spell also meaning 'words held to have magic power'. We know that the right words, written or spoken, have the power to change the way we think and act. What this essay offers are some hints as to how you can choose and deliver those words in the most enchanting way.

SELECT BIBLIOGRAPHY

BRANN, Les, Jacky OWENS, and Anne WILLIAMSON, eds. *The Handbook of Contemporary Clinical Hypnosis*. Chichester: Wiley-Blackwell, 2012.

DISSANAYAKE, Ellen. 'Prelinguistic and Preliterate Substrates of Poetic Narrative'. *Poetics Today* 32 (2011): 55–79.

LEVITIN, Daniel. *This is your Brain on Music*. London: Atlantic Books, 2006.

ROSZAK, Theodore. *The Voice of the Earth*. Grand Rapids, MI: Phanes Press, 2001.

STEVENS, Paul. 'Embedment in the Environment'. *Perspectives in Public Health* 130 (2010): 265–69.

---

8   The Merriam-Webster dictionary, *vide:* 'enchantment'.

PART FOUR

*Re-enchanting
Nature and Body*

Toward Enchantment

Cultivating Nature Connection and Ecological Regeneration through Experiential Learning in Sustainable Agriculture

CHARA ARMON *&* JOAN ARMON

IN A TIME OF ECOLOGICAL CRISIS and deep concern about the future of life on Earth, our teaching and research explore how to guide undergraduate students to bring their hearts and bodies, not only their minds, to the work of helping to regenerate our ravaged natural world. Central questions in our work include: 'How can connection to and care for the natural world become a meaningful part of undergraduate education?'; and, 'How can we offer students opportunities to acquire knowledge and skills related to ecologically mindful living that empower them to move beyond despair, denial, or complacency regarding environmental degradation?' In response to our own and other scholars' concerns regarding how weakened human-nature relationship contributes to worldwide environmental crises and reduced human well-being, we teach humanities-based agriculture courses that immerse our students in viewpoints and experiences which portray humans as within and of the natural world rather than separate from it.

Although dismissive, exclusively intellectual, and materialistic attitudes are common responses to the natural world among our American undergraduate students, some seek opportunities to shift toward connected perspectives that recognise human dependence on, and perhaps interdependence with, the natural world. Students who are open to recognising modes of perception and values beyond the intellectual and materialistic, and willing to explore interacting with the natural world in a broader way, may experience what we term enchantment with nature and the human-nature relationship. Here we explore the unfolding of this enchantment. As we consider students' interest in connecting to the natural world, we draw upon the work of scholars such as Thomas Berry, who argued that our future relies on the human 'capacity for intimacy in our human-Earth relations' and that educators must 'see their purpose not as training personnel for exploiting the Earth but as guiding students toward an intimate relationship with the Earth'.[1]

Our students engage, both as a whole class and individually, in experiential fieldwork on farms and gardens on and off campus. We thus provide opportunities through humanities-based agricultural theory and practice for students to explore perspectives and actions that promote the well-being of humans and the many life forms with whom we share the planet. Fieldwork sites include urban, suburban, and rural farms and gardens, often those where economic and environmental injustices present pressing challenges. Through the combination of classroom learning and fieldwork, students encounter ways of perceiving the natural world that may be alternative or complementary to the intellectual and materialistic approaches that have dominated industrialised cultures for the past several centuries.

Some students begin their farm and garden fieldwork with scepticism or timidity, doubting their ability or desire to shovel manure, plant kale, confront insects, unearth carrots, or collect seeds, yet nearly all complete our courses expressing not only a sense of accomplishment and expanded knowledge, but heightened connection to the natural world. In their reflective writing we find reports of sensory engagement, insights into the natural world's intricacy and even sacredness, and hopefulness that regenerative agricultural practices can contribute to the flourishing of both people and planet. To understand our students' learning during their classroom study and fieldwork on sustainable farms, we evaluate trends in students' fieldwork logs and other writings through the lenses of *active care*, *kincentricity*, and *rewilding*. Each is a form of connection to nature. What we term active care develops as students tend soil, plants, animals, and people in pursuit of supporting life's flourishing.[2] Kincentricity, a term developed by anthropologist Enrique Salmón, emerges

---

1   Thomas Berry, *The Great Work: Our Way into the Future* (New York: Bell Tower, 1999), x.

2   Joan Armon and Chara Armon, 'Cultivating Intimacy with the Natural World: College Students' Care, Connection, and Regeneration in an Agriculture-Focused Humanities Course', *Journal of Sustainability Education* 9 (2015): [n.p]. Nel Noddings, *The Challenge to Care in Schools: An Alternative Approach to Education* (New York: Teachers College Press, 1992), 127, 134, 136, et passim.

as students become aware of reciprocal human-nature relationship and influence.[3] Students' experiences of what ecologist Marc Bekoff calls rewilding occur as they open their hearts to nature, perceiving with compassion.[4]

Our conceptual framework illuminates how students' experiences of active care, kincentricity, and rewilding may lead to the deep experience of what we here term enchantment. Through experiences of connection to nature, some students come to express enchantment with diverse life forms, natural systems, the work of caring for them, and the beneficial effects of such care on the human caregiver. We understand enchantment as a perspective or state that students potentially, but not assuredly, reach. Our working definition regards enchantment as a state of deep respect, wonder, awe and even love or reverence, for forces—in this case those of the natural world—that are dynamically larger than oneself and are in some way sacred.[5] Enchantment is always more than intellectual in its range and may develop from a combination of the intellect with other of our human ways of knowing the world, such as through the body, soul, or emotions. Our conceptualisation of enchantment is influenced by scholars who suggest that the fullest way for humans to encounter the natural world involves capacities in addition to our intellects.[6] As Thomas Berry wrote, 'The natural world demands a

---

3   Enrique Salmón, *Eating the Landscape: American Indian Stories of Food, Identity, and Resilience* (Tucson: University of Arizona Press, 2012), 21, 22, et passim.

4   Marc Bekoff, *Rewilding Our Hearts: Building Pathways of Compassion and Coexistence* (Novato: New World Library, 2014), 5. Bekoff's view of rewilding is related to, yet distinct from, other definitions of rewilding aimed at leaving areas of natural habitat to management by natural processes, as the Wilderness Foundation UK or the Rewilding Institute in the US describe.

5   Bekoff uses the term 'enchantment' differently than we do, seeing it as part of rewilding. See, for example, Bekoff, *Rewilding Our Hearts*, 5. We instead see enchantment as a state evolving from experience or awareness of active care, kincentricity, and rewilding.

6   Liberty Hyde Bailey, *The Holy Earth* (Berkeley: Counterpoint, 2015), 3–4. T. Berry, *The Great Work*, 55–57 et passim. Douglas Christie, *Blue Sapphire of the Mind* (New York: Oxford University Press, 2013), 3–5 et passim. Stephan Harding, *Animate Earth* (White River Junction: Chelsea Green, 2006), 26, 43. Robin Wall Kimmerer, *Braiding Sweetgrass: Indig-*

response beyond that of rational calculation, beyond philosophical reasoning, beyond scientific insight'.[7] Enchantment may be guided by what Wendell Berry calls 'an old intelligence of the heart', not excluding the intellect or its rational capacities, yet prioritising the heart's emotional and spiritual awareness.[8] What we find to be important in defining enchantment is the mode of perception of feeling along with thinking; as Harding elaborates in his discussion of the appeal of concepts of Gaia, many people 'feel disillusioned with the now clearly outdated deterministic world-view which they see as needing to be superseded by a more holistic approach'.[9] Enchantment is one way to conceptualise a profound experience of contact with the natural world that elicits responses such as respect, reverence, wonder, and love.

The concept of enchantment opens our understanding of our students' descriptions of their experiences during fieldwork on sustainable farms. Our student Amy's fieldwork reflections, for example, evince her experience of enchantment:

> There is something about being in touch with the earth that I find very soothing and life giving, especially with planting, because it gives me the feeling that I am a part of creating something. Something that I really honestly don't understand [...] often the most meaningful and important things are unknowable. Surprisingly, I am rather comfortable with my uncertainty of the natural world; the mystery further contributes to its beauty [...] There was so much we all were able to teach each other [during fieldwork], so much that we learned from the land, from the native plants and the way they grow, from the birds and squirrels and other little animals

---

enous Wisdom, Scientific Knowledge, and the Teachings of Plants (Minneapolis: Milkweed Editions, 2013), 232–40 et passim. Joanna Macy and Molly Young Brown, *Coming Back to Life* (Gabriola Island: New Society Publishers, 1998), 58–59.

7   T. Berry, *The Great Work*, 54.

8   Wendell Berry, 'Some Further Words', in *New Collected Poems* (Berkeley: Counterpoint, 2012), 362.

9   Harding, *Animate Earth*, 57.

roaming around us while we worked. We learned how
to live in connectedness.[10]

The significance of enchantment is both the experience of it for its
own sake, as it draws on diverse human capacities of responding to
the world, and its potential to elicit a commitment to interact with
the natural world and other people in ways that contribute to the
regeneration and flourishing of life on Earth.

Pedagogical & research approaches

Voices from three sources shape our pedagogical approaches. First are
voices of the natural world, which students discern through physical,
emotional, intellectual, and spiritual perceptions during farm fieldwork and silent sitting in nature. In valuing students' ability to encounter the voices of the natural world in multiple ways, we draw on
the work of scholars such as Stephan Sterling, who argues against our
ongoing 'privileging of cognitive/intellectual knowing over affective
and practical knowing',[11] Tewa Pueblo Indian Gregory Cajete who
articulates indigenous ecological education that is understood not
by objectivity but by subjectivity experienced within a cultural context as 'an intimate and complex set of inner and outer place-orient-
ed environmental relationships',[12] and ecologist-philosopher David

---

10   Amy's statements are reminiscent of the thought of agricultural scientist
     and cultural commentator Liberty Hyde Bailey, who wrote in 1915: 'Man
     listens in the forest. He pauses in the forest. He finds himself. He loses
     himself in the town and even perhaps in the university. He may lose him-
     self in business and in great affairs; but in the forest he is one with a tree,
     he stands by himself and yet has consolation, and he comes back to his
     own place in the scheme of things.' Bailey, *The Holy Earth*, 106.

11   Stephen Sterling, 'Sustainable Education: Towards a Deep Learning Re-
     sponse to Unsustainability', *Policy and Practice: A Development Education
     Review* 6 (Spring 2008): 64. Robin Wall Kimmerer shares Sterling's con-
     cern about the need for a whole-person approach to perceiving nature;
     see *Braiding Sweetgrass*, 47, 123.

12   Gregory Cajete, 'Indigenous Education and Ecology: Perspectives of an
     American Indian Educator', in *Indigenous Traditions and Ecology*, ed.
     John Grim (Cambridge: Harvard University Press, 2001), 620–21. For
     other discussions of the need to perceive the natural world in multiple

Abram, who advocates slipping 'beneath the exclusively human logic' to a logic of the senses.[13] Second are voices of diverse farmers
encountered via fieldwork trips, guest lectures, video-conferencing,
videos, and texts. American Indian elders tell of renewing ancient
knowledge of relationship with spirit-infused lands and lives; His-
pano elders describe nurturing children's rootedness to sacred place;
and Quechua elders explain preserving reverent relationship with
the Earth Mother. We also learn from Asian and African-American
farmers who are activists in organic, local, permaculture, and justice-oriented agriculture. The European-American farmers whom
students encounter practise varied organic approaches, often blend-
ing environmental and justice activism with knowledge of traditional and scientific innovations in sustainable agriculture.

Third, in our course readings, voices of interdisciplinary scholars raise questions regarding humanity's role on planet Earth, inter-relationships among humans and between humans and other
life forms, and how both science and spirituality guide our renewal
of the human-nature relationship and our attention to justice within
the human community. Our courses are informed by scholarship
from fields such as history, religion, ecology and humanities, sustainable education,[14] peace and justice, anthropology, and the agricultural sciences. While readings by scientists focus several discussions, most assigned readings present cultural topics relevant to
sustainable agriculture. Students read texts by indigenous authors
explaining a 'theology of place',[15] for example, or the agrarian essays of farmer and author Wendell Berry, who emphasises that '[l]
and that is in human use must be lovingly used; it requires intimate

---

ways, see Bekoff, *Rewilding Our Hearts*, 5, 19, et passim; and Gretel Van
Wieren, *Restored to Earth: Christianity, Environmental Ethics, and Ecological Restoration* (Washington: Georgetown University Press, 2013), 89–91.

13   David Abram, *The Spell of the Sensuous: Perception and Language in a
More-than-Human World* (New York: Pantheon Books, 1996), 268.

14   In Sterling's definition, sustainable education involves a shift in perception and values and is an educational paradigm that is '*relational*, [Ster-
ling's italics] engaged, ethically oriented, and locally and globally relevant'.
It is participatory, aiming for change in hearts and minds toward long-
term environmental vitality. Sterling, 'Sustainable Education', 64.

15   Gregory Cajete, *A People's Ecology* (Santa Fe: Clear Light Books, 1999),
3–6.

knowledge, attention, and care,[16] as well as perspectives and practices of permaculture farmers who blend scientific and traditional
approaches[17] and biodynamic farmers who ground agriculture in
creativity, freedom, individuality, and the sacred, as originated by
Rudolph Steiner.[18] We bridge perspectives from the sciences and
humanities with the ideas of scholars such as biologist Edward O.
Wilson, who has written of biophilia, humanity's propensity for
connecting to life in its diverse forms;[19] agricultural scientist Wes
Jackson, who writes that 'we must turn to nature to inform us, to
serve as a reference, must turn our thoughts to building a science
of ecology that reflects a consultation of nature';[20] and Mary Evelyn
Tucker and Brian Swimme, who, grounded in expertise in both the
humanities and sciences, ponder what it would mean for us to know
'how we belong and that we belong so that we enhance the flourishing of the Earth community'.[21] To learn how issues of social and
environmental justice are highly relevant to the topic of sustainable
agriculture, students examine sources depicting farming (in)justice
in various countries as related to poverty and environmental (in)
justice.[22]

Our grounded theory research methodology emerges from students' reflective writing before, during, and after outdoor experi-

---

16   Wendell Berry, *Bringing it to the Table* (Berkeley: Counterpoint Press,
     2009), 33.

17   Bill Mollison, *Introduction to Permaculture* (Tyalgum: Tagari Press, 1991).

18   Robert Karp, 'Biodynamics and the Dignity of the Farmer', *Biodynamics*
     276 (2011): 16–17.

19   Edward O. Wilson, *Biophilia* (Cambridge, MA: Harvard University Press,
     1984).

20   Wes Jackson, *Nature as Measure* (Berkeley: Counterpoint, 2011), 56. Likewise comparable is the statement by biologist Steve Pacala, who described
     to John Grim and Mary Evelyn Tucker his three-phase manner of studying nature: 'I observe, I cherish, and I conceptualize', thus suggesting how
     sensory, emotional, moral, or spiritual perception may function in dialogue with rationality. John Grim and Mary Evelyn Tucker, Ecology and
     Religion (Washington: Island Press, 2014), 33.

21   Brian Swimme and Mary Evelyn Tucker, *Journey of the Universe* (New
     Haven, CT: Yale University Press, 2011), 113.

22   Jill Harrison, 'Lessons Learned from Pesticide Drift: A Call to Bring Production Agriculture, Farm Labor, and Social Justice Back into Agrifood
     Research and Activism', *Agriculture and Human Values* 25 (2008): 163–67.

ential learning, course readings and discussions, and interactions with farmers, each other, and guest speakers. In addition to autobiographical and research papers, students write fieldwork logs, which serve as a tool to reflect on their farm or garden work site and its myriad life forms, describe learning arising from farm/garden tasks, and consider their physical, emotional, intellectual, and spiritual responses. The process of writing fieldwork logs or journals can effectively stimulate students' reflections on experiences and allow them to make connections to course concepts.[23]

Students' responses relevant to active care, kincentricity, and rewilding

As we evaluate our students' experiences through the lenses of active care, kincentricity, and rewilding, we observe that they may experience these types of nature connection physically, emotionally, intellectually, and/or spiritually. Elucidating all of the nuances among physical, emotional, intellectual, or spiritual experiences is not our main focus here, which is instead to show how students' overall learning can be understood via active care, kincentricity, and rewilding, but we note that we endeavour in our teaching to acknowledge, and enable students to acknowledge, the presence of multiple levels of experience and perception in the context of fieldwork. We think of students' physical perceptions as those that arise from the physical work and sensory stimulation involved in fieldwork tasks. Emotional perceptions are visible in the feelings students describe. We categorise as intellectual perceptions the concepts students analyse and evaluate, and connections they make to factual knowledge. Spiritual perceptions relate to shifts in awareness, connections students make to former or new beliefs, views of the natural world and its inhabitants as valuable, awe-inspiring, or sacred in ways beyond materialistic value, and expressions of personal oneness with or embeddedness in nature.

---

23   Janet Dyment and Timothy O'Connell, 'Assessing the Quality of Reflection in Student Journals: A Review of the Research', *Teaching in Higher Education* 16.1 (2011): 81–97. Our background knowledge and experiences as organic permaculture gardeners inform our analysis and interpretation of students' written responses. In quoting from students' writing, we use pseudonyms for the names of students and the farms on which they work.

Active Care

Active care entails tending plants, people, animals, and ecosystems to promote their flourishing.[24] We offer the term to represent students' frequent uses of words such as 'care' and 'caring' in their fieldwork logs. We define it as the work students perform to promote the well-being of plants, animals, land, and people, often in a protective and even tender manner. Students' farm tasks include planting, weeding, composting, mulching, harvesting, readying produce for sale, building farm structures, and interacting with farm animals. Rather than emphasising the more common approach of learning only through reading, talking, or writing about phenomena, we seek to engage students in also physically acting upon and with phenomena. As students engage physically with the natural world via active care, they also may experience emotional and/or spiritual engagement: for example, partnership with a seed they plant and observe as it responds with foliage, flower, and fruit allows students to explore a sense of loving connection, as does freeing vegetables or blueberry bushes from weeds or contributing to the production of chemical-free food for local families.

Students' desire to cultivate and support the well-being of plants, animals, and the systems of the natural world, as well as their own and peers' well-being, inspires mindful and connected farm or garden work. A student whose fieldwork site was a prison garden observed the impact that active care for plants had upon prisoners. Rather than their common violent behaviours, Stephanos recalled prisoners' gentleness with greenhouse plants they had been tending all winter:

> The plants were so delicate and fragile but to see these inmates with them was interesting. Keep in mind that all these men have tattoos, and look very rough and tough. But when they got around these plants all that went out the window, they acted like they were handling small children[,] they were so delicate with them.

Stephanos discovered that actively caring for plants, while tending

---

24   Armon and Armon, 'Cultivating Intimacy', n.p.; Noddings, *Challenge to Care*, 127, 134, 136, et passim.

vegetables and flowers for donation to people living in low-income neighbourhoods, stimulated some prisoners' memories of childhood garden and farm experiences and revealed their 'wealth of knowledge'. Stephanos reflected on the significance of prisoners' active care when he noted that, through creating opportunities for prisoners' engagement in plant care, '[w]e are taking their negative energy and frustrations and shaping them into something beautiful'.

Students notice that caring agriculture also requires attention to animals. Olivia stated: 'Today I learned about how careful and aware farmers have to be of all the living creatures on their farm. For instance, we were using a long hoe-like tool to weed the herbs, [and] we discovered a little wild bunny hiding in between the plants. If we had not been observant, we would have significantly hurt the bunny with our sharp, forceful weeding tools'.

When our students write about their opportunities to engage in active care in gardens and on farms, they often express awareness of how a commitment to active care of natural systems can be embodied through certain types of agricultural decisions. Caroline explained this when she recalled that a farmer with whom she worked discussed how the selection of tools impacts on the amount of damage done to the soil, while Giulia explained her new awareness that caring agricultural priorities have broad consequences: 'By placing the weeds [we cut] back around the plants, we were replenishing the soil with nutrients so that the foods grown are healthier for a human than those grown in nutrient deficient soils. In this respect, this farming practice rewards both the land and the human beings living in harmony with nature'.

Ava, a student who wrote that she struggles with anxiety, articulated an experience of active care for nature as a form of care for her own well-being: 'There is something about playing (or working) in the dirt, about physically touching the earth that is so calming, grounding, refreshing [...] To be reminded of how nature itself can balance everything back out was so incredibly restorative and healthy for me'. Students also demonstrate awareness of how active care can be attentive toward not only plants, but also toward other people, as expressed by Shea:

> I really enjoyed this experience with classmates as we were intentional with the plants and with each other. In classrooms you are separate and physical touch is not

common, but in the garden our hands met as we placed plants in the hands of others [...] Touching and being intentional with the plants, we delicately planted them so that they could sustain life.

Some students write about how experiences of active care open them into enchanted states. Kallie, a student who spends her free time in somewhat stressful advocacy for citizen awareness regarding the dangers of a local nuclear waste site, expressed how active care transported her into what we deem a state of enchantment. She voiced her experience of a state of wonder in the following words:

Next, I added soil to the makeshift pots and added the seedlings. I spent 3 hours doing this and completely lost track of the time. The repetitive task of moving dirt and feeling it in my hands was very relaxing [...] The sounds struck me the most because they were so peaceful. Her backyard garden transported me out of suburbia and into a secluded outside environment. I could have been in a meadow somewhere if I had shut my eyes.

Kincentricity

The work of active care opens awareness to inter-relationships among people, plants, animals, ecosystems, and the systems of the planet as a whole. To understand more deeply our students' growing awareness of inter-relationship and inter-dependence, we rely on Salmón's term, kincentricity, which describes reciprocal human-nature relationships and influences.[25] In Salmón's words, 'the human niche is only one of a myriad of united niches that work together to continue the process of *iwigara*: the interconnectedness and cycling of all there is'.[26] Writing particularly of the Rarámuri tribe of which he is a member, Salmón continues: 'The Rarámuri view themselves as participants in their natural community [...] Rarámuri understand that they are a part of the land, that they were placed here as caretakers of their land, and that they are directly responsible for the

---

25   Salmón, *Eating the Landscape*, 21–23.
26   Ibid., 156.

health of the Creator, who works hard each day to provide for the land and its inhabitants'.²⁷ Another voice for kincentric thinking is Wendell Berry, who approaches interconnectedness through discussion of what he terms 'context'. Berry writes:

> It has become increasingly clear that the way we farm affects the local community, and that the economy of the local community affects the way we farm; that the way we farm affects the health and integrity of the local ecosystem, and that the farm is intricately dependent, even economically, upon the health of the local ecosystem [...] we are farming in the world, in a webwork of dependences and influences more intricate than we will ever understand.²⁸

Many of our students are pleased to find writers such as Salmón and Berry contributing to current agricultural conversations in ways that leave room for deliberate, mutually beneficial human interactions with the natural world.

In their fieldwork, students consistently have been fascinated by experiencing farming that acknowledges and respects inter-relationship. Beatrice observed the animals on a farm surrounded by residential properties and, struck by her new awareness of how a farm's systems inter-relate with one another and with local environments, she wrote:

> Because [these farmers] don't use [herbicides], runoff of those chemicals doesn't reach the water supply to the community, or the other animals on the farm. The pigs are kept right by the blueberry field and Swiss chard field, and [if herbicides were used] they would be drinking water and digging through soil that has been affected by that runoff.

For Beatrice, human-nature influences and relationships are honoured through the planful, harmless approaches of sustainable, small-scale agriculture. Julianna, a student involved in animal

---

27   Ibid., 157.
28   W. Berry, *Bringing it to the Table*, 89–90.

rights, also evaluated a day of fieldwork through a kincentric lens:

> Today's fieldwork very much brings home Wendell
> Berry's emphasis on the holistic connection between
> all living things and the land, as well as how critical
> knowledge of this interconnectedness is to being a
> good farmer; good, not only in the sense of skilled, but
> justice-oriented and able to see the entire picture. One
> must not only see the farm through a specialized lens,
> but must be able to have the foresight to understand
> that each alteration of nature and the land will have its
> own consequences.

Later Julianna offered a summation of her own commitment to what
we deem kincentric thinking: 'it is necessary to be conscious of the
connection between the people, the animals, and the land [...] Even
the tiny creatures that live off of the land have to be considered in order for farming to be dignified and justice-oriented, in my opinion'.
These and other students repeatedly express appreciation as they observe ways of farming that allow nurturing treatment of the vital in-
ter-connections that are crucial to life's flourishing. Demonstrating
insight into the kincentric relationships that occur among people
and between people and the land, Victoria wrote:

> I gained insight into how environmentally conscious
> farming brings people together. Not only do these
> farmers have relationships with the plants and fields as
> they take the time to physically go and nurture them,
> but they create amazingly close relationships with the
> many people they encounter between all of the out-
> reach activity, volunteers, and workers. Everyone bene-
> fits from this type of farming—the farmers themselves,
> the people eating the food, the animals that live on the
> farms, and the produce itself feels healthier and happier
> in such a caring atmosphere.

As Victoria summarised, 'the organically run farm is just one big
life cycle'.

Many students remark on the reciprocal benefits humans and the natural world receive from kincentric approaches to farming. The ways in which sustainable farming nurtures communities of people, plants, and animals seem to inspire some students' experiences of enchantment. Focusing on how fieldwork enabled her sense of connection to and among the Earth, farmers, classmates, and the local community, Amy recollected days of farm work using words that call to mind our understanding of enchantment:

> Maybe it was the sun and fresh-air, maybe it was getting our hands dirty and feeling a physical connection to the earth, or maybe it was inspiration from the farmers with whom we met, but regardless, something significant happened on those days when we ventured outside off campus. There was suddenly a sense of community among us that we as a class gained by joining in and helping in the larger community [...] For me, a feeling of hopefulness characterizes my experiences with our fieldwork this semester.

Christian, an engineering student who worked on a small inner-city farm, similarly seems to have experienced the feelings of respect or wonder that we see as characterising enchantment. He wrote: 'Maple Creek Farm is a place of true beauty in my mind. A place where the earth and the community come together to give each other the things that they need and work in harmony to allow one another to flourish'.

We invite students to critique all aspects of our courses, emphasising that respectful agreement and disagreement alike are welcome. During the first weeks of the course, Lilleth, a psychology major, was a vocal critic of readings and guest speakers. Later she expressed her own shift in thinking:

> [A]s much as I tried I couldn't just accept that all lives (amoeba, cats, fish, cows, alligators—you name it) matter equally [...] Kimmerer made points that called out what was missing from my connection to the world: basic communication and respect [...][29] She suggest-

---

29   See Kimmerer, *Braiding Sweetgrass*.

ed doing what [urban farmer] Deb practices which is talking and listening to plants [...] Only when I saw other organisms around me in terms of kinship did I really become excited about learning about them [...] Out of this, I noticed that I started feeling more empathy towards animals, plants, and people. Deep down inside I wanted to know them and for them to thrive because we are interconnected [...] I had to radically change my life style in as many ways as possible.

Rewilding

Ecologist Marc Bekoff has coined the term 'rewilding' to refer to the process of opening our hearts to compassion and empathy toward the natural world.[30] Bekoff explains, 'Re-wilding our hearts is about becoming re-enchanted with nature.'[31] In Bekoff's view and our own, a heart-based, loving connection to the natural world is the most potent impetus for treating it caringly. As Bekoff asserts and our students experience, rewilding is an interactive process, 'a transformative exploration that centers on bringing other animals and their homes, all ecosystems, back into our hearts.'[32] As an interactive and reciprocal process, rewilding may draw upon our imaginal and intuitive capacities as we ponder the lives of other creatures in the natural world and 'imagine their point of view', including 'the Earth's perspective', and thus enhance our ability to make wise decisions about our impact on the world.[33]

Some of our students experience rewilding through compassion, as evidenced in a statement written by Kimberly, an aspiring teacher, after reading Kimmerer's book, *Braiding Sweetgrass*. Kimberly writes that:

> The Indigenous people embodied this message in every way of life, including how they treated the landscape. They never saw themselves as caretakers, rather, as co-

---

30   Bekoff, *Rewilding our Hearts*, 4, 56.

31   Ibid., 5.

32   Ibid., 13.

33   Ibid., 6, 7.

existing individuals with respect for the other. This reminds me of how important it will be as a teacher to
promote the message of compassion in my classroom.
Arguably, this is the most important concept I could
ever teach. I am reminded by this article that not only
does compassion extend to our fellow humans, but also
to nature and our ecosystems.

Other students' writing evinces experiences of respectful empathy
with nature that epitomise Bekoff's description of rewilded hearts as
those that are open to and enchanted with nature. Cristina, a student
who grew up in a highly urbanised borough of a major northeastern
city, expressed some discomfort with the outdoors, and experienced
farm work for the first time in our course, wrote of how her interactions during weeding grew into an empathetic awareness of the soil,
animals, and plants with whom she worked:

Squatting down with my hands in the dirt and sun on
[my] back I felt a peace within. I was able to forget about
the stress of school work, the stress of my future, and as
I looked around I saw my friends and classmates quietly
contemplating the peace and the intimacy of farming.
We worked in silence pulling, weeding, and thinning
and then my thoughts ran. I thought about the soil and
the animals that moved around with the disorder of my
presence. I thought about the soft dirt and its ability to
move into my shoes, under my nails, and how for me it
was a thing I'd wash away later, but for the plants it was
life, nutrients, and comfort [...] For a second I had no
problems, it was just me and the beets.

Cristina's descriptions of her fieldwork link with Bekoff's statement
that 'By rewilding, we get past the false dualisms of us and them,
humans and animals, civilization and nature. Rather, we see and
cultivate a close and reciprocal interrelationship built on peace,
compassion, empathy, and love'.[34]

Other students focus on sustainable farmers' respect for the land,
which often results from regarding nature as a source of wisdom.

---

34   Ibid., 19.

Ilene wrote, 'As I talked to the farmers about how each thing worked or why they chose to use each piece of equipment, or what crop they would plant where, I realised [...] the way they listened to the land'. Students frequently write about their observations of the attitudes and actions toward nature of farmers who have what we might call 'rewilded hearts'. We share Bekoff's sense that rewilding is a healing response to the unwilding of modern industrialisation. Bekoff explains: 'As we unwild, we lose compassion and empathy for other beings and for nature as a whole. We do not understand that landscapes are alive, vibrant, dynamic, magical, magnificent, and interconnected'.[35]

When we observe indications of rewilding in our students' writing, we note the excitement and wonder they convey. Albert wrote:

> At the end of our work, we found a baby owl that was injured and taking shelter in the garden beds. It was there the whole time we were working and never got frightened. It's almost as if it knew that the garden was for everybody, and we wouldn't hurt it. Emit called animal control to come help it as we were leaving.

Increasingly open to the presence of other-than-human creatures in farm and garden settings, Albert later stated:

> People generally view insects and other animals with fear of how they can harm them, and not how those animals help them. Most people are terrified of a bee sting, but do not rejoice in how nothing around us would be possible without them. I believe the best lesson that I learned [...] is that people are too selfish when they try to view the world, and the only way to understand the truth is to try to view the world from other people's and animals' eyes.

Rewilding for Keera meant accepting an insect as a guide during silent sitting outdoors:

> I started focusing on a moth and imagining that it was a

---

35   Ibid., 35.

> guide to the garden. So maybe intellectual learning isn't always the most important thing to do in the moment. I think this experience strengthened my resolve in protecting nature, and in my belief that other life forms are just as sacred as ours.

As these students' writing demonstrates, garden and farm experiences can stimulate the rewilded awareness that the natural world is full of living systems and creatures that are our partners in existence on Earth. Students' responses reveal that observing or experiencing rewilding may convey learning that is at once spiritual, emotional, and intellectual. As students gain awareness of human embeddedness in and connection to the natural world beyond intellectual, scientific analysis, they explore what it is to have a rewilded heart. When their rewilding involves the meditative and peaceful wonder Cristina expresses, the deep respect Ilene describes, the respectful wonder Albert felt at the baby owl's presence, or the acceptance of an insect guide that Keera experienced, then the possibility of seeing the world through other-than-human eyes emerges. The concept of enchantment helps to illuminate the depth of these experiences.

ELICITING EXPERIENCES OF ENCHANTMENT

What are the results of students' experiences of active care, kincentricity, and rewilding and the enchantment they may elicit? Student fieldwork logs suggest that many students discover significant shifts in perspective through their fieldwork. Through participating in and observing active care, kincentricity, and rewilding, our students experience types of connection to nature that, for many of them, elicit experiences of enchantment. Our definition of 'enchantment' views it as a state of respect, reverence, wonder, or awe that inspires a desire to honour something beloved, mysterious, and sacred, and we observe it in students' statements about their explorations within sustainable agriculture. Enchantment, however, is a destination toward which we can only offer our students opportunities to move. Our courses are an invitation. A minority of student writing reflects primarily descriptions of what the students experience physically and observe intellectually, reflecting paradigms dominant in our educational systems and culture. We regard enchantment as a field into which a majority of our students enters; some students travel toward it; others do not show written evidence of it.

Native American botanist Robin Wall Kimmerer describes ecologically restorative acts as 'ceremonies of practical reverence'.[36] Although people who are grounded in a spiritual understanding of agriculture may easily approach agricultural work as a ceremony of reverence for life and land, merging work and reverence from the beginning, our students' experience is more likely to be one in which bodily work with the land occurs and then may elicit a reverent enchantment. As students move further into opportunities to practise care for the natural world, many enter into a level of relationship to nature that surpasses the physical provision of active care and moves into the more emotional and spiritual experience of kincentricity, rewilding, and enchantment. Beyond the anxiety-producing facts about climate change and ecosystem demise which they encounter in some courses and the media, students welcome experiences of the restorative possibilities that call for their bodily, emotional, and spiritual participation, not only their intellectual knowledge; allow them to voice the enchantment they may feel; and also offer grounds for hope.

Our students' writing reflects how encounters with enchantment may produce new life commitments to love, respect, honour, and tend the mysterious, complex, and beloved natural world. Although we are not conducting a longitudinal study of our students' post-graduate choices, we note that over the past five years approximately two dozen of our students have chosen to spend their first year after college working in areas related to agriculture, environmental protection, and food justice. A large majority of our students express plans to integrate long-term, small-scale food production into their lives in some way, identifying desires such as retaining close connections with the natural world, enjoying fresh and healthy foods they grow themselves, providing pollinator habitats, and maintaining a personal connection with nature. Salmón helps to explain the shift many of our students seem to experience when he writes of how 'the idea of *iwigara*', which he defines as 'the interconnectedness and cycling of all there is', 'becomes an affirmation of caretaking responsibilities and an assurance of sustainable subsistence and harvesting [...] This knowledge is a reflection of a way of being or [...] a way

---

36   Kimmerer, *Braiding Sweetgrass*, 249; see also 195.

of life. This is not so much a lifestyle [...] but just being. It is not a movement that can be joined, but rather a resilient worldview [...]'[37] Students' writing suggests that through agricultural fieldwork they can become aware of, and then enchanted by, possibilities for ways of living that are not just 'sustainable' but deeply founded on the respect, love, reverence, and awe of enchantment, and potentially the protective impulse that may arise from it.

ENCHANTMENT AND ITS INFLUENCES

Active care, kincentricity, and rewilding are all entry points into enchantment: each can restore us as humans as we endeavour to restore the natural world and our relationships to it. Our aim is to add to students' intellectual learning the experiential, participatory encounters with the natural world that open pathways to heart-centred, life-sustaining connection and care. Students' reflections on their fieldwork suggest that in offering them experiences relevant to active care, kincentricity, and rewilding, we may contribute to enchanting their minds, their bodily experience, and their hearts, and potentially thus contribute to re-enchanting the academy and the larger culture. In the context of our work with students, re-enchanting the academy means exploring the natural world in ways that have the potential to revitalise their connection to and care for the natural world, themselves, and other people. Re-enchanting the academy, in our view, thus means being advocates for a wiser balance of human intellectual, physical, emotional, and spiritual capacities within the context of undergraduate education and scholarly research. If, as this book topic presumes and as we believe, academia is in need of an enchantment or re-enchantment that integrates or re-integrates aspects of other-than-intellectual discourse into our customary intellectual approaches, then experiential learning within the context of sustainable agriculture (and, surely, in other contexts that similarly engage students' whole-person capacities) can be seen as a vital entry point to re-enchantment within the academy and also within our human existence on Earth. In the presence of courses that successfully interweave intellectual, physical, emotional, and spiritual evidence and experience, we hope that the academy may

---

37   Salmón, *Eating the Landscape*, 161.

become more amenable to honouring a diversity of experiences and inclinations as valid, perhaps eventually closing the door to an era of learning in which intellectual rationality alone has defined higher education and excluded other modes of learning and perception. We intend for our courses to offer students the possibility of becoming enchanted by the potential for multi-faceted human relationships to one another, other life forms, and our planet, rather than only the intellectual and often distant relationship common in recent centuries. When we repeatedly find that students express appreciation for undergraduate learning that acknowledges their experiences as people with active bodies, compassionate hearts, and reverent souls, as well as curious intellects, their appreciation enhances our conviction of the value of this balanced approach to learning.

Working within the existing academic structure of classroom-based education, how can we continue to create bridges between the academy's standards and the integrated approaches we believe to be crucially important? Attentiveness to students' multidimensional responses can guide the integrated approaches faculty choose to embed in our courses as we co-create expanded notions of pedagogy, content, and ways of learning in higher education. Students' reflective responses, such as an entry James composed after silent sitting outdoors, reveal the value they gain from diverse learning experiences: 'Mentally, like physically, I felt still. My attitudes and feelings fluctuated during the hour, but were largely feelings of oneness, of acceptance, of love. In nature I am always struck by the beauty, simplicity, and intricacy [...]' Commenting on the significance of agricultural fieldwork, James continued with his reflection, writing specifically for those who have not experienced this type of work:

> I would tell them that there is a distinct energy and emotional response when listening to, working with, and learning from the Earth's soil and plant life [...] I think that the world would truly be a better place if everyone had this experience. Our knowledge of the land and of the life it produces will be (and always has been) extremely important to the quality of human life.

In James' account of feeling mentally and physically still in a fruitful pause; of experiencing energy and emotions, such as oneness and love, that cannot be defined in intellectual terms alone; and of learning from the life system of plants and animals, not only from other humans, we find reminders of what students may value, and what can be offered to them, even within classroom-based academic coursework. Both students' and our own desires for a flourishing existence can guide us to move toward re-enchantment. Stephan Harding suggests that this transition may be less remote than one might think. Harding explains, 'My own practices as a deep ecology educator have shown me that for most of us deep experience lies just below the surface of everyday awareness, and that a slight shift of context can easily make it visible'.[38] Although a re-enchanted academy may not yet be visible, we value Harding's intimation that re-enchanted awareness is accessible through shifts in context that need not be dramatic. When we reflect on the depth of perspective our students appear to gain from one semester of coursework, we conclude that alternative contexts may kindle vibrant nature connection and regeneration when educators welcome students' engagement of their whole-person capacities. Enchantment is then within reach.

Select bibliography

ARMON, Joan, and Chara ARMON. 'Cultivating Intimacy with the Natural World: College Students' Care, Connection, and Regeneration in an Agriculture-focused Humanities Course'. *Journal of Sustainability Education* 9 (2015): n.p.

BAILEY, Liberty Hyde. *The Holy Earth: The Birth of a New Land Ethic*. Berkeley: Counterpoint Press, 2015.

BEKOFF, Marc. *Rewilding our Hearts*. Novato: New World Library, 2014.

BERRY, Thomas. *The Great Work: Our Way into the Future*. New York: Bell Tower, 1999.

BERRY, Wendell. *Bringing It to the Table*. Berkeley: Counterpoint Press, 2009.

_____. *New Collected Poems*. Berkeley: Counterpoint Press, 2012.

CAJETE, Gregory. 'Indigenous Education and Ecology: Perspectives of an American Indian Educator'. In *Indigenous Traditions and Ecology: The Interbeing of Cosmology and Community*, edited by

---

38   Harding, *Animate Earth*, 50–51.

John Grim, 619–38. Cambridge, MA: Harvard University Press, 2001.

———. *A People's Ecology: Explorations in Sustainable Living.* Santa Fe: ClearLight Books, 1999.

GRIM, John, and Mary Evelyn TUCKER. *Ecology and Religion.* Washington: Island Press, 2014.

HARDING, Stephan. *Animate Earth: Science, Intuition and Gaia.* White River Junction: Chelsea Green, 2006.

KIMMERER, Robin Wall. *Braiding Sweetgrass: Indigenous Wisdom, Scientific Knowledge, and the Teachings of Plants.* Minneapolis: Milkweed Editions, 2013.

MACY, Joanna, and Molly Young BROWN. *Coming Back to Life: Practices to Reconnect Our Lives, Our World.* Gabriola Island: New Society Publishers, 1998.

NODDINGS, Nel. *The Challenge to Care in Schools: An Alternative Approach to Education.* New York: Teachers College Press, 1992.

SALMÓN, Enrique. *Eating the Landscape: American Indian Stories of Food, Identity and Resilience.* Tucson: University of Arizona Press, 2012.

SWIMME, Brian Thomas, and Mary Evelyn TUCKER. *Journey of the Universe.* New Haven, CT: Yale University Press, 2011.

WILSON, Edward O. *Biophilia: The Human Bond with Other Species.* Cambridge, MA: Harvard University Press, 1984.

'How do you Breathe?'

Duoethnography as a Means to Re-embody
Research in the Academy

LAURA FORMENTI & SILVIA LURASCHI

DUOETHNOGRAPHY IS A RECENT, creative method of collaborative inquiry in qualitative research, aimed at fostering dialogic
imagination and celebrating a critical appraisal of multiple voices.[1]
This makes it an amazingly effective way of re-enchanting academic life, by activating a process of reciprocal exploration, recognition
and celebration of *differences*: knowing, indeed, is not about searching for one (mono-logic) truth, or creating a master story, since it
entails dynamic tensions, dilemmas, competing representations and
definitions, hence an evolving ecology of ideas that cannot be easily reduced to one view, or trivialised. Duoethnography is based on
currere, i.e., a transformative view of curriculum: by telling stories
of the past, it brings awareness of the present and opens possibilities
for the future. How does it work? Two people of difference—here,
a professor and a doctoral student—assist each other in reciprocal
narrative writing and critical reading; the exchange of texts becomes,
for some time (in this case, one year), a way of re-conceptualising
the researchers' experience of a phenomenon. Duoethnography has
been used to investigate a range of diverse issues, such as sexual orientation, racism, mourning, democratic teaching, migration, friendship. We used it to explore the experience of breathing, its meaning
as a metaphor of the neglect of the body in the academy, and the
effects it has on people's lives and learning. Duoethnography helped
us to engage with each other in a dialogic process, to interrogate our
frames and preconceived views,[2] to learn from each other. Percep

---

1   Richard D. Sawyer and Joe Norris, 'Duoethnography. A Retrospective 10
     Years After', *International Review of Qualitative Research* 8 (2015): 1–4.
2   Richard D. Sawyer and Joe Norris, *Duoethnography* (New York: Oxford

tions and representations are the objects of this research method; we show, in this chapter, how they are tied to root narratives and how they transformed in the process of dialogic inquiry.

Duoethnography can be considered as a way of re-enchanting qualitative research by involving the researcher in a critical process of self-interrogation. The process of normalisation and trivialisation that is haunting qualitative methods, not least by the increase of pre-structured, pseudo-objective forms of data collection, triangulation, analysis, creates in fact forms of distance and alienation of the inquirer from inquiry. To us, research becomes trustworthy when it entails the researcher's reflexivity, when it is explicitly tied to human life and experience, and recognises the epistemological challenge intrinsic to the 'impossibility of representing another person's views.'[3] The goal of duoethnography is to promote reciprocal reflexivity, and to build more complex and inclusive ideas about the social construction and conceptualization of experience. It is a means of composing life histories with embodied experience and aesthetic representation, and of fostering transformative learning.[4] This study took the form, then, of an embodied, personal, and reciprocal search, involving the telling and writing of our life experience within and outside academia, and a combining of our experiential data with other subjects' data, with academic and common sense theories, and practical knowledge.

'HOW DO YOU BREATHE?' EMBODIED RESEARCH IN THE ACADEMY

24th July 2014. Bicocca, Building U6, Fourth floor, Recess 1461, 9:00 AM. Laura is beating her keyboard with two fingers, her shoulders are stiff. 'Hi Laura, how are you?' Silvia's voice awakens her to the here-and-now. Her head turns away from the screen, to meet Silvia's gaze. She bursts out with: 'Not well. Too much pressure, too many things to do. I'm gasping. I feel air-hungry.' Silvia's big eyes grow bigger from surprise. 'Don't tell me! I also feel like I'm holding my breath. Why? Does

---

University Press, 2013): 98–101.

3   Sawyer and Norris, 'Duoethnography. A Retrospective 10 Years After', 1.

4   Jack Mezirow, *Transformative Dimensions of Adult Learning* (New York: John Wiley and Sons, 1991), passim.

academic life doom us to this?' Some days after, an exchange of emails starts a shared inquiry: 'Let's think about this breathing thing. It seems urgent to me to understand this feeling. Next autumn we could begin a duoethnography. Shall we dance?'

This is how our journey into the body, breathing, and the meaning of our living within a university began. The search is not finished yet: we present here some understanding of the complexity of this theme, and the issues involved, by illustrating our exploration during one academic year. Duoethnography is the enactment of a dialogue; it also aims to involve the reader in dialogue. So, we invite you—the Reader—to join us in the movement of breathing and knowing. Inhalation, exhalation, with two short pauses in the middle. Try it, three to four times. Eyes shut. Gently, and lovingly listening to your body. Now. The quaternary structure of breathing—in/pause/out/pause—is a metaphor of knowing itself, as a circular process between subject and object. We also used it to shape our writing.[5] So, please, follow us in this cyclic movement.

First cycle: Experience

[INHALE] *We began our exploration by telling and writing stories of our embodied relationship with academia. For Silvia, the aim of the narration is to highlight her past and present experience as a student, while Laura is interested both in her past experience as a student, and in her present life as a professional academic. The stories we gathered in our exchanges (two of them are presented below) reveal strategies of adaptation to a world that does not appear to be built to welcome the needs of a living organism. The body is silenced and neglected. Institutional power is exerted on it, hence on subjectivity, freedom, creativity,*

---

5   Since knowing is understood here as an ongoing conversation, the paper's layout gives a typographical (analogic, æsthetical) representation of the different *voices* that are entailed by our conversation: Silvia's and Laura's narrative (individual voices) are set as *italicised paragraphs*; the coordinated co-authorship voice ('we') is set as a regular paragraph; other authors' voices are set as indented block quotes. We also ask questions to the reader set in *ITALICISED SMALL CAPITALS* as an invitation to add his/her own voice, by writing, telling to someone, or simply taking some time to think.

and the possibility of expressing oneself. The hidden curriculum of academia silences the body by asking people to keep it quiet, still, to control it, to render gestures uniform; however, the body is still there, all the time, and sometimes it speaks, or shouts out.

> HOW MANY HOURS DO YOU SPEND IN THE UNIVERSITY, ON A DAILY, WEEKLY, MONTHLY, YEARLY BASIS? WHEN, WHERE AND HOW ARE YOU SITTING, OR STANDING UP, WALKING, LYING DOWN, SPEAKING, AND LISTENING? ARE YOU INVOLVED IN AIMLESS, FUN, RELAXING, EMBODIED ACTIVITIES, INSIDE AND OUTSIDE THE UNIVERSITY? HOW MANY HOURS A DAY, A WEEK, A MONTH, A YEAR? HOW DO YOU BREATHE?

[EXHALE]—*A memory of the body in my academic experience.*

SILVIA—*In the big, crowded Aula Magna, the professor is sweeping his blue velvet sleeves through the air; his sparkling eyes behind the glasses accompany his telling of the genealogy of power in Ancient Greece. I sit in front of him, listening, left leg crossed over the right, apparently comfortable, but after one hour I realise how cramped the purple armchair feels, so I close my eyes. I am now running across the Athenian plain.*

A latecomer takes the seat next to me, I open my eyes and see my colleague Sergio: running shoes, shorts, and a sweat-soaked t-shirt. An aficionado of education, he cycles three times a week through the city, from his sport sciences department, to follow the open lectures in Philosophy of Education.

I shift position, and place both my feet on the floor. Through the soles, they seek contact with the ground. Sergio's gym outfit connects with the old professor's movements. I realise that I badly need to move, to learn.

LAURA—*I was in my office alone, scrolling through emails, and all l of a sudden I felt SO tired and drowsy that I couldn't just keep going on. My eyes only wanted to close. Arms felt heavy. My head swayed. My whole body was desperately longing to lie down, and take a rest. No chance to make it obey my commands. I felt so angry and embarrassed, self-deceived. I tried with a coffee. Useless. To sleep was the only reasonable thing to do. So I locked the door from inside (what if someone came in and found me in that odd situation?), then put my head on the desk (vaguely reminded of myself doing the same at three, when attending preschool), and gave up to the powerful imperative of my "other" will.*

DO YOU LISTEN TO YOUR BODY? WHAT DOES IT TELL OR ASK YOU? HOW DO YOU ANSWER?

[A]s for our bodies, we retain just sufficient proprioceptive sensations to coordinate our movements and to ensure the minimal requirements for biosocial survival—to register fatigue, signals for food, sex, defecation, sleep; beyond that, little or nothing [...] [O]ur capacity even to see, hear, touch, taste and smell is so shrouded in veils of mystification that an intensive discipline of unlearning is necessary for anyone before one can begin to experience the world afresh, with innocence, truth and love.[6]

[There is] a larger entity, call it A plus B, [...] achieving a process for which I suggest that the correct name is practice. This is a learning process in which the system A plus B receives no new information from outside, only from within the system. The interaction makes information about parts of A available to parts of B and vice versa. There has been a change in boundaries.[7]

HOW MUCH EMBODIED AND IMPLICIT LEARNING IS EN-TAILED BY OUR WAYS OF LIVING IN ACADEMIA?

Second cycle: every difference tells a story

[INHALE] *This paper is the outcome of a shared desire—a necessity indeed—to become more reflexive about the body, and to understand the role of embodied relationships in academic life. We are aware of the differences between us due to roles, status, attitudes, and personal*

---

6   Ronald D. Laing, *The Politics of Experience* (New York: Pantheon Books, 1967), 26.

7   Gregory Bateson, *Mind and Nature: A Necessary Unity* (New York: Bantam Books, 1979), 153.

experience in the university, as well as to our learning biographies. We belong to different generations, different historical times. We have a different perspective on, and knowledge of the institution, Laura as an established member of it, Silvia as a newcomer, who is still learning the conventions of academic life. We have a different temporal horizon: Silvia will soon finish her doctorate, and maybe leave, while Laura could stay within the academy until retirement. Silvia's status is that of a learner, hence it is expected from her to transform, to change. Laura does not have an explicit learner status; in fact, professors are not expected to represent themselves as lifelong and lifewide learners. Hence, our perspectives and constraints are not the same. As 'researchers of difference'[8] we need to define what kind of difference 'makes a difference'[9] for us, in this research; so, we re-visited our lived experience by using auto/biographic writing, all along the path, to illuminate our embodied relationships in different situations, our values and actions, the accidents and problems we met, as well as the discoveries and creative solutions we found for ourselves. This narrative exploration, using sensitive and aesthetic (embodied) writing, enabled us to narrate to each other what the academy meant for us.

THE UNIVERSITY AND I: WHAT DOES IT MEAN FOR ME TO BE HERE? WHERE IS MY OWN ENCHANTMENT ROOTED?

What we are suggesting is a change in the nature of reflection from an abstract, disembodied activity to an embodied (mindful), open-ended reflection. By embodied, we mean reflection in which body and mind have been brought together. What this formulation intends to convey is that reflection is not just on experience, but reflection is a form of experience itself—and that reflective form of experience can be performed with mindfulness/awareness. When reflection is done in that way, it can cut the chain of habitual thought patterns and preconceptions such that it can be an open-ended reflection, open to possibilities other than those contained in one's current representations of

---

8   Sawyer and Norris, *Duoethnography*, 4.

9   Gregory Bateson, *Steps to an Ecology of Mind* (New York: Ballantine Books, 1972), 10.

the life space. We call this form of reflection mindful, open-ended reflection.[10]

[EXHALE]—*My motives for being in the academy.*

SILVIA—*Doing a* PHD *is a privilege for me, a long unspoken desire that became reality. During my whole academic life, breadwinning activities kept me away from participating in lessons every day. However, as may happen to non-traditional students, the books I was reading and some fortunate meetings with teachers opened windows in the walls. Today, as a doctoral student, I am researching the learning process, and reflecting on my own, and on how it affects others around me. I am learning how to do research. And above all I have discovered the pleasure of asking questions.*

To reach the university, I travel by train with commuters headed to Milan, from the area where I live, near the Swiss border. My first intention was to 'capitalise' on this time spent travelling by studying, but I discovered the beauty of 'wasting time' in daily exchanges with travellers. Their stories taught to me how many ways there are to live and learn.

Bicocca's campus is a complex of red concrete buildings, interspersed with a few heroic trees. They mark the seasons. Falling leaves signal the beginning of every new academic year. Last autumn I picked up a leaf and brought it to the PHD *students' room. I proposed a guessing-game to my colleagues: how many new seasons will we see here? Everybody laughed. Our future in research is not foreseeable.*

LAURA—*While I was discussing my doctorate thesis, nineteen years ago, my 15-day-old son was waiting outside, in his father's arms, to be breastfed. The president of the evaluation committee asked: 'Which outcome do you want to discuss? This one [the thesis], or the other one outside the door?' My answer was: 'They are indeed connected. My research is on learning biographies: life does not happen in hermetically sealed compartments. My identities as a scholar and a mother are linked.'*

Thank you Silvia, this research is excavating my memories, and helping me to become reflexive about my choice to be a researcher. I

---

10   Francisco J. Varela, Evan Thompson, and Eleanor Rosch, *The Embodied Mind: Cognitive Science and the Human Experience* (Cambridge: MIT Press, 1991), 27.

strongly feel, now, the necessity to rediscover my voice and unmask faces that are not my own.[11] *In my eyes, research was the realm of possibilities, and university a place for imagination. I was given the means (a doctorate bursary is an 'extraordinary privilege', as you told to me yesterday) to think, to reflect, to construct theories and practices that could transform me into a better person, and the world into a better world. The biggest hope of mine was to connect (my) education and life, learning, and care. I saw too much disconnection in the world of education, but I trusted the power of knowledge. My expectation, maybe naïve and overly ideological, was disrupted on many occasions, while I was chasing my way within the institution. But I never gave up. My penchant for stories was very hope-full, in the beginning; now I think, more ironically and critically, that stories cannot make a difference, unless you take into consideration and try to transform the context, the perspectives of meaning, and the relationships entailed by them.*

Just after my doctorate, I began a collaboration with a colleague (Ivano Gamelli, a former yoga teacher and drama expert, now a scholar in Body Pedagogy). We organised workshops aimed at connecting body and words in teaching and training. We invited participants to act, move, dance, breathe, sing, draw...and tell (as well as write) stories related to these experiences. I learned a lot in those years about the body, movement, aesthetical languages, by being a practitioner myself. We published papers and books on those experiences. But when we became faculty members, we needed to publish more academic texts, and there was a split. Outside the university I kept exploring—theatre, singing, Middle-Eastern dance, drawing, and more recently meditation. Within the university, I clothed myself in the academic conventions, and got absorbed by teaching, writing, and meetings!

Third cycle: space, time, freedom, rules

[INHALE] *Our dialogue based on the narration of experience enabled the nurturing in both of us of an awareness of the pervasive practices of silencing the body, in which we are constantly immersed. The fragments here reported are but a few examples of how collective space*

---

11   Elizabeth J. Tisdell, *Exploring Spirituality and Culture in Adult and Higher Education* (San Francisco: Jossey-Bass, 2003), 89.

and time are structured in everyday life within the university, how the body is disciplined in and by discourse, by forced positions and closed spaces, and how people's expected actions are mostly ruled by scripts, instead of deliberate choice. The autoethnographic description of experience—also entailing the analysis of artefacts, objects, furniture, buildings, repeated gestures, positions, and their effects on our minds—allowed us to re-embody our perceptions and representations of ourselves in academic life, and to enhance/interrogate the meaning that was hidden in some details. The ongoing material experience of sensing the body was weaved with the development of meaning, in this case through writing, that re-connects perceptions to memory and imagination, celebrating the metaphoric and symbolic in embodied experience. Our dialogue revealed the multiple messages that are constantly (and mostly unconsciously) exchanged between inside and outside, in the flux of perception and cognition. A stiffened position, for example, echoes a stiffened mind, or soul. Badly designed chairs, and buildings, force the users' bodies into unliveable, not sustainable shapes. The unconscious structure of higher education institutions becomes more visible, thanks to body awareness, and highlight anti-ecological structures.

THE UNIVERSITY AND I: WHAT COULD MY BODY SAY IF IT COULD SPEAK?

[EXHALE]—*My embodied narration of living in the university*
SILVIA—*The Human Sciences Department is on the fourth floor. In the elevator, with a rucksack on my shoulders and my lunchbox in another bag, space is tight: I hold my breath to allow three other people in. Silence fills the space. My mind already goes to the room or office I am heading to. I feel the tensions in my body: My head's weight stretches my neck forward, my lower jaw is tense, and my shoulders are blocked by the bag's weight.*

I do not have a 'fixed' place in the Department: lesson rooms change all the time and the PHD students' room is a shared space with five computer desks and two tables. In my bag, I have the keys to Laura's office, where I also share a desk with other colleagues. When I sit there, my back is forced to bend forward, to allow alignment of my sight to the screen. Besides, with one leg crossed over the other, the pelvis' weight lies more on the right ischium. So twisted, I do not feel comfortable. My ankle's adductor muscles are tense and my back lacks proper contact with the chairback. I am suspended.

The library is on the second floor. I go there when I need to 're-cover my centre'. I walk amongst those silent shelves, my eyes wide open, keeping a slow pace, lured by words and colours on the books' spines. Then, I stop in front of a shelf and let my arms go to the book I have chosen. They stretch out and I feel the whole body participating to this simple movement: while my hands grasp the book, legs flex, the pelvis rotates downwards, and the chest bends. Words have a weight.

LAURA—*I spend many hours in the university: four to five days a week, often more than nine hours daily, forty to forty-five hours each week. Sometimes I have a proper lunch (more likely, if I am alone, I swallow a sandwich in front of the computer). Sometimes I use the toilets (when it is* REALLY *urgent). Most of the time I stay in my recess, sitting at my desk, shoulders stiff, striking the keyboard in quite an unhealthy position. This scenario changes three months a year: when I teach (twelve hours a week) I have to walk (!) through the campus up to twenty minutes, to reach the classroom. During my courses, I* NEVER *sit. I walk up and down the aisle or central staircase, I often invite students to leave their desks, to spread out in the corridors, to form groups, especially when we practice aesthetic representations—drawing, performing, playing. Sometimes we reverse roles, and I enjoy sitting in the rows and listening to students' presentations.*

If I take the perspective of the body, I see a lot of bad habits, a steady and restless rhythm, disrespectful of physiological needs. And short breath. This is not new to me: I am fully aware of my contradictions and limits, thanks to personal reflection, dialogues with fellow colleagues, and the exploration of experience through æsthetic practices and languages. I feel disconnected, incoherent, and self-deceived when I think that outside academia I am able to cultivate beauty, harmony, mindfulness. I wonder: have I adapted too much to external pressure? And why?

IS THIS ALL ONLY ABOUT SUBJECTIVITY AND THE INDIVID-UAL? HOW IS OUR THEORISATION OF THE BODY A PART OF THE PROBLEM? WHAT IS THE ROLE OF THE UNIVERSITY, AND THE LARGER SOCIETY, IN SHAPING OUR BODIES?

> At the turn of the 21st century, the self seems above all a commodified self, the person is equated with their bodily form, and in control of their appearance via the body [...] The body in late modern societies is, then, one of the primary loci of personal and social standing.[12]

The 'discourse of the body', and the self as a body, based on processes of subjectification and objectification, is very strong in late modernity. Apparatuses[13] control bodies and the mobility of people through silent laws that define and limit the extension of individual action, by punishing every violation of established boundaries and rules. However, coercion is less visible in our times, and especially in academia, since a discourse of 'freedom' is dominant, and external pressures to conform are hidden and internalised. People—and their bodies—are expected to be productive and politically useful (usable) objects. The academic body appears as commodified as any other, hence reduced to a good, controlled by 'scrutiny', observation and assessment. The symbolic enactment of an epistemology of distance and technical knowledge, also related to the dominance of the positivistic epistemology and a functionalist view of research, hinders, then, 'empathetic perception' which is based on the reciprocal resonance of sensitive, expressive, emotional bodies. There is no space for breathing, in this disenchanted scenario.

In the reign of global visual culture, the body is not only silenced: it is constantly exposed, photographed, scrutinised, manipulated as an object. Issues of control, beauty and illness dominate a 'mass-mediated ethnographic exercise'[14] that imposes idealised and colonised images of the body and the self. Any sign of difference is banned. This culture also affects academic life, notwithstanding its claim to foster critical thinking and freedom of research.

What kind of theory can be developed, to re-enchant academy through awareness of the body? We see the body as a bridge, a material-symbolic link between subjectivity and reality, the individual

---

12   Justine Coupland and Richard Gwyn, *Discourse, the Body, and Identity* (New York: Palgrave Macmillan Books, 2003), 4.

13   Michel Foucault, *Psychiatric Power: Lectures at the College de France 1972–1973* (New York: Palgrave Macmillan Books, 1993), passim.

14   Coupland and Gwyn, *Discourse*, 3–4.

and society, and also between technique and meaning: both polarities are necessary aspects of human life, and the pattern which connects them could initiate a more ecological way of living in academia. Instead of bodies as (separated and static) objects, we try to address the trans-individual process of *bodying*, where the individual body is seen as a form that continuously shapes itself in relation to its environment. As in the work of dancer/philosopher Erin Manning, our 'individuation's dance'[15] is not necessarily on stage, neither does it require music; it performs anywhere, by its 'techniques', that are our concrete ways of interacting with the world. 'There are techniques for hoeing, for standing at a bus stop, for reading a philosophical text, for taking a seat in a restaurant, for being in line at a grocery store.'[16] Techniques shape the body, and each body in unique ways, while they shape the world. This resonates with the systemic notion of 'autopoiesis', or self-creation in structural coupling with the environment.

> More than its taking-form, 'body' is an ecology of processes (and practices, as Isabelle Stengers might say) always in co-constellation with the environmentality of which it is part. A body is a node of relational process, not a form per se. A body is a complex activated through phases in collision and collusion, phasings in and out of processes of individuation that are transformed—transduced—to create new iterations not of what a body is but of what a body can do.[17]

Bodies, subjects, institutions and cultures are different systemic levels, then, of the same 'bodying' process. To re-enchant the academy, a critical and complex theory is needed, able to sustain a healing process of recognition, voicing, and re-connection. Freedom and a more ecological, sustainable life in the academy require that we attend to the complexity of all these levels:

---

15   Erin Manning, *Always More Than One: Individuation's Dance* (Durham: Duke University Press, 2013), 33.

16   Ibid., 33.

17   Humberto Maturana and Francisco J. Varela, *The Tree of Knowledge: The Biological Roots of Human Understanding* (Boston: Shambhala, 1992), 19.

§ at a macro-level, academic bodying is subjected to dominant socio-cultural norms of desirability and commodification (e.g., youth, health, and standardised beauty), as well as productivity, that need to be addressed and challenged, to create space for creativity, uniqueness, and subjectivity;

§ at a meso-level, the academy is itself an institutionalised bodying of interacting subsystems and individuals; each subject/person/body is a node within a network of interdependent and coordinated actions. Hence, shared awareness of reciprocal influence and movement, in relation to body, space, time, and the material dimensions of organisational life, can foster new ways of interacting;

§ at a micro-level, subjectivity and the 'experience of acting as a body' are ways to foster the perception, attention, awareness, and deliberate action of the self and others, in contrast to automatic, anæsthetised responses.

Fourth cycle: learning

[INHALE]—We decided to explore more deeply our embodied experience and learning biography of breathing. The first step in our inquiry was autobiographical: we shared writings on our life history, and how we 'learned' to breathe. By writing, we re-presented an entangled process of bodying, where the material and the symbolic were woven together.

> HOW DO I BREATHE? HOW DID I LEARN IT? HOW DID I LEARN THIS WAY OF ANSWERING TO THESE KIND OF QUESTIONS? DO THESE QUESTIONS AND ANSWERS CONNECT TO MY IDENTITY AS A RESEARCHER?

[EXHALE]—*Autobiographical memories.*
   SILVIA—*...the radio is a component of my family...my mother was listening to the song Where one flies...'Let me breathe again, take me where one flies'...I found in my Amsterdam journal these words: 'Last night I slept very badly, I woke up many times with this song in my mind, "Blackbird singing in the dead of night, take these broken wings and learn to fly [...] you were only waiting for this moment to arise" Felt anxious, I cannot explain what's wrong, but I feel too many*

things inside, pushing to come out, but I am not able to let them out.

LAURA—*... my family motto was 'hang tough, and bite the bullet'...so my breathing is too short, I talk too much and I often hold my breath...and every time I connect to my body, I sigh heavily, shaken by these deep involuntary exhalations...when the body is engaged, it needs oxygen, but when my breath is short, fear and tension increase, and I snatch for air, feeding a vicious circle. Breathing through fear and tension is needed, to take care of yourself. How many things we should know, but nobody teaches us...I learnt this one at the childbirth course...breathing is a metaphor for birth itself, indeed, for what the body is able to do unconsciously...*

STEPS TOWARDS UNDERSTANDING: INSPIRATIONAL MASTERS AND OUR OWN PATHS

In order to re-enchant academy, we felt the need to re-embody our own experience of academic life, as a starting point of our research. In exploring breathing, we referred to our (different) practices and theories of embodiment. Silvia's inspiration came from Moshe Feldenkrais' work:

> Our breathing system is complicated. We breathe in different ways when we are asleep, running, singing, or swimming. The only thing all forms of breathing have in common is that when we inhale air enters the lungs and when we exhale it is expelled, because the entire system is so constructed as to increase the volume of the lungs for breathing in, and to reduce it for breathing out. This increase in volume can be produced by movement of the chest in front, behind, or at the sides, or by an up and down movement of the diaphragm. In general, only a part of this system is used, and that not to its fullest extent. All the possible forms of breathing are used simultaneously when breathing must be speeded up, as after rapid and prolonged running.[18]

---

18   Moshe Feldenkrais, *Awareness Through Movement: Easy-to-Do Health Exercises to Improve Your Posture, Vision, Imagination and Personal Awareness* (New York: HarperCollins, 1972), 164.

Moshe Feldenkrais celebrated, in his very physical and practical work, the (circular) connections between breathing and posture. He proposes a simple exercise to enable people to explore for themselves this deep relationship:

> Air must penetrate through the nose and mouth into the windpipe, bronchi and lungs—and be expelled again—properly, in order to supply sufficient oxygen at all times and under all conditions throughout a person's life. If breathing is internally disrupted we cannot survive more than a few seconds, though we can hold our breath for a few minutes. Most of the muscles of the respiratory system are connected to the cervical and lumbar vertebræ and breathing therefore affects the stability and posture of the spine, while conversely the position of the spine will affect the quality and speed of breathing. Good breathing therefore also means good posture, just as a good posture means good breathing.
>
> Lie on your back. Draw up your knees so that your feet can stand on the floor, close your eyes and try to remember the movement of the lung and diaphragm as they were just described. Breathe slowly, in small, short steps, making many movements of the chest and abdomen for every time to inhale or exhale. Observe your chest in your imagination, and see in your mind's eye how it pulls your right shoulder, between collarbone and shoulder blade, every time air is drawn into this section. Observe this spot only as you breathe and skip in your imagination the expelling half cycle. Air reaches this point from the middle of your body, about halfway between the breastbone and the floor, where the bronchi are, three on the right and two on the left. The chest sucks the lung in various directions at once: to the right shoulder, between the collarbone and the shoulder blade (in the direction of the ear), to below the armpit, to the shoulder blade resting on the floor, and the front of the chest.[19]

---

19   Ibid., 166.

In Feldenkrais' theory and practice, thinking and moving are interconnected. The four components of action are: moving, sensing, feeling, and thinking:

> in order to think, for instance, a person must be awake, and know that he is awake and not dreaming; that is, he must sense and discern his physical position relative to the field of gravity. It follows that movement, sensing and feeling are also involved in thinking.[20]

Our self-image, way of thinking, and level of awareness change through and by moving, and vice versa. As long as education is based on facts external to the individual, there will always be incomplete development. Breathing is a healing experience of movement that re-connects body and mind, outside and inside the physical and the symbolic, as in these words by Germana Giannini, who was inspirational in Laura's experience:

> The moment when air flows into the body is a fundamental symbol of receptive openness to the world: air should not be grasped for but received as the gift of inspiration. It is important not to originate the breathing gesture in the nose and mouth area, since the centre of breathing is in the centre of our body.[21]

The first movement in breathing, then, is imagined by Giannini as a gesture of opening, acceptance, and inspiration (by gods themselves, in traditional cultures). The following movement, complementary to this, is a creative, generative, and active gesture.

> The moment of exhalation, instead, is focused on the diaphragm's tonic movement...During the gesture of breathing and vocal emission (be it spoken words or singing), Germana invites people to adhere to themselves, by suggesting coincidence of the gesture with an inner disposition.[22]

---

20   Ibid., 11.

21   Germana Giannini and Andrea Marabini, *Il canto dell'Altro* (Sevilla: Padilla Lobros, 2014), 77. Our translation.

22   Ibid., 78. Our translation.

This creative coincidence of gesture and meaning, in true dialogue with the world, with nature, and/or with the gods, is the essence of 'authenticity'. However, what 'evidence' do we have of this process? The gap between authentic experience and the scarcity of words that we have to tell it, needs to be minded. We use narratives, and art, not only to celebrate it, but to investigate it. The dialogic investigation of our learning biographies was a revelation of how we both achieved some awareness, although via different paths, and learnt how to take responsibility for our breathing, moving, and living. Silvia practises—among other traditions—the Feldenkrais method, aimed at improving posture, vision, imagination, and personal awareness. Laura's practice of singing is inspired by Giannini's research on the 'geography of voice' within the human body, and its amazing resonance with many spiritual traditions.

Body practices (entailing rituals, disciplines, meditation, martial arts, sports, and so on) are a large (and somehow underestimated) part of human co-evolution through the centuries. In fact, they are rooted in history, co-created in time by millions of single subjectivities, taught by individuals to other individuals, and communities, who re-embodied in each generation the original practice, transforming and renewing it. Embodied learning connects us to our biological and cultural roots in space and time. Theories also transform, in space and time. We need to update our theories and practices in each generation, to adapt them to the present. Literature on breathing is amazing: it ranges from philosophy to spiritual practices, from mindfulness to childbirth, from sports practices to the training of actors and artists, far beyond medical and biological studies. In order to build an integrated theory, and to transform our practices in more liveable and sustainable ways, we refer to embodied and enacted knowing,[23] phenomenology, body pedagogy,[24] and spiritual traditions like Buddhist meditation. These theories compose a constellation of ideas that celebrates the pattern which connects the levels of life, of material and symbolic aspects, of personal and collective movements.

---

23   Francisco J. Varela, Evan Thompson, and Eleanor Rosch, *The Embodied Mind. Cognitive Science and the Human Experience* (Cambridge, MA: MIT Press, 1991), passim; Daniel Hutto and E. Myin, *Radicalizing Enactivism: Basic Minds without Content* (Cambridge, MA: MIT Press, 2013), passim.

24   Ivano Gamelli. *Pedagogia del corpo* (Milano: Raffaello Cortina, 2011), passim.

So what?

The first outcome of our research is an imperative: 'If you want to learn, take a breath'. Conscious breathing connects mind and body by bringing attention to something that we do not need to control, as in this simple exercise by Buddhist monk Thich Nhat Hanh:

> Present moment, wonderful moment. In our busy society, it is a great fortune to breathe consciously from time to time. We can practice conscious breathing not only while sitting in a meditation room, but also while working at office or at work, while driving our car or sitting on a bus, wherever we are, at any time, throughout the day. There are so many exercises we can do to help us breathe consciously. Besides the simple 'In-Out' exercise, we can recite these four lines silently, as we breathe in and out:
>
> Breathing in, I calm my body.
> Breathing out, I smile.
> Dwelling in the present moment,
> I know this is a wonderful moment![25]

Why does, in this historical moment, such a deep desire manifest itself, to re-enchant everyday life through such paths as meditation, martial arts, yoga, or any other form of body practices? Our research focuses on the process of learning and meaning entailed and enhanced by these practices, and on its effects on our lives. We are also aware that these activities can easily be narrowed down to fashionable and commodified 'well-being' practices. Paradoxically, they can reinforce objectification, when the body is used on purpose, for the sake of personal improvement or performance. But we also know, from direct experience, that sometimes these practices do open possibilities, in terms of awareness, presence, reflexivity, and deliberate action. They reveal the contradictions and disorienting dilemmas in our lives. They create new desire for meaning in life. When this happens, body practices are transformative.

---

25   Thich Nhat Hanh, *Peace is Every Step: The Path of Mindfulness in Everyday Life* (New York: Bantam Books, 1991), 9–10.

Looking back at the whole path of this research, we see that sharing our experience fostered a dialogue between us. It allowed us to go beyond established roles and ideas, to find some space for freedom. By juxtaposing our stories, in the process of duoethnography, we did not aim to grasp an ultimate truth, but to gain awareness of our own presuppositions and hidden curricula, which constitute those processes, contexts, and learning experiences which implicitly socialised us into academic life.[26] The experience of co-writing on breathing brought us to enact a process of bodying where we felt more alive in a more liveable context. We practised together, too—Feldenkrais, singing, yoga, meditation—on some occasions. The result of this is a more authentic subjective and inter-subjective understanding of academia as a world which we no longer perceive as a given space 'outside there', to which we may adapt or not, but as a co-constructed space, where we can bring a difference that makes a difference.[27] We have a choice, and all of us can experience more freedom, if we take the responsibility to listen to our own and others' bodies. Our diversity and commonalities, if recognised, can re-connect us with our sense of humanity and with the circularity of eco-systemic life.[28] This is what we mean, now, by re-enchanting the academy: a very concrete change of the bodying process, at a micro, meso, and macro level.

How could this allow for a different, more embodied and embedded, more aware experience of life within the university? To be honest, we will need much more time, and shared practice, to answer this question.

SELECT BIBLIOGRAPHY

BATESON, Gregory. *Mind and Nature: A Necessary Unity.* New York: Bantam Books, 1979.

_____. *Steps to an Ecology of Mind.* New York: Ballantine Books, 1972.

COUPLAND, Justine, and Richard GWYN. *Discourse, the Body, and Identity.* New York: Palgrave Macmillan Books, 2003.

26　Sawyer and Norris, *Duoethnography*, 45–46.

27　Bateson, *Mind and Nature*, 76–77.

28　Bateson, *Steps to an Ecology of Mind*, passim.

FELDENKRAIS, Moshe. *Awareness Through Movement: Easy-to-Do Health Exercises to Improve Your Posture, Vision, Imagination and Personal Awareness.* New York: HarperCollins, 1972.

FOUCAULT, Michel. *Psychiatric Power: Lectures at the College de France 1972–1973.* New York: Palgrave Macmillan Books, 1993.

GAMELLI, Ivano. *Pedagogia del corpo.* Milano: Raffaello Cortina, 2011.

GIANNINI, Germana, and Andrea MARABINI. *Il canto dell'Altro.* Sevilla: Padilla Lobros, 2014.

LAING, Ronald D. *The Politics of Experience.* New York: Pantheon Books, 1967.

MANNING, Erin. *Always More Than One: Individuation's Dance.* Durham: Duke University Press, 2013.

MATURANA, Humberto, and Francisco J. VARELA. *The Tree of Knowledge.* Boston: Shambhala, 1992.

MEZIROW, Jack. *Transformative Dimensions of Adult Learning.* New York: John Wiley and Sons, 1991.

SAWYER, Richard D., and Joe NORRIS. *Duoethnography.* New York: Oxford University Press, 2013.

_____., and Joe NORRIS. 'Duoethnography. A Retrospective 10 Years After'. *International Review of Qualitative Research* 8 (2015): 1–4.

THICH NHAT HANH. *Peace is Every Step: The Path of Mindfulness in Everyday Life.* New York: Bantam Books, 1991.

TISDELL, Elizabeth J. *Exploring Spirituality and Culture in Adult and Higher Education.* San Francisco: Jossey-Bass, 2003.

VARELA, Francisco J., Evan THOMPSON, and Eleanor ROSCH. *The Embodied Mind: Cognitive Science and the Human Experience.* Cambridge, MA: MIT Press, 1991.

Women with Wings

Right-brain Consciousness and the Learning Process
in Balkan Dance

LAURA SHANNON

INTRODUCTION

Before the emergence of modern science, information was encoded and transmitted through largely nonverbal means, in the realm of right-brain consciousness which precedes, surrounds, and runs parallel to the left-brain thinking dominant in academic institutions and the scientific worldview. An example of the right-brain learning process, using symbol, myth, and other forms of condensed wisdom, can be found in the artistic traditions of Eastern European village women, often semiliterate, who transmit information through a sophisticated system of interrelated customs, including songs, dances, and textiles. These interwoven artistic media activate both the right and left sides of the brain, and form a system of preserving and passing on information which has existed outside of, and parallel to, the academy, for many centuries.

I chose to immerse myself in the culture of Eastern European dance after earning degrees in Intercultural Studies and Dance Movement Therapy in the 1980s. This paper will briefly describe the methodology developed in the course of my lifelong research and teaching, and will examine one key motif, the woman with wings. The winged woman appears in myth, song, textiles, archaeological artefacts, and dance, frequently in association with life transitions such as puberty and marriage. Within the context of traditional Greek and Balkan dance customs, the woman with wings also symbolises joy and the journey towards fulfilment of creative potential, two important ingredients of a learning process based in right-brain consciousness. A closer look at this parallel, non-academic education system may inspire us to invite into our own learning process those things which have been missing from the academy: nature and the body, intuition, creativity, celebration and play, and a sense of meaning in the part we play in preserving knowledge and wisdom for future generations.

LEARNING FROM THOSE ON THE OUTSIDE

In our quest to restore enchantment to the academy, what might we learn from those whom the academy has excluded?

In the peace process in Northern Ireland, when they were making new policy, Inez McCormack, the trade unionist, came to the negotiations with three cleaning ladies from Belfast. She said, 'To make fair government, you have to look at who's been missing from the table'. So can we ask the question: Who or what is missing from the academic table?

I think most of us working in an academic context would agree that enchantment is missing. I suggest we look at who else is missing, people or qualities or aspects of being, and invite them back to the table in the ivory tower.

That's already an enchanting image: inside the tower, there's a table. Now let's imagine that it is set with a feast. There is a dance song from the mountains of Northern Greece—a wild landscape, with many towers—which begins, 'A thousand welcomes, dear friends, to this table set with silver and with gold'.[1] Gold and silver, in the language of fairy tales, are sun and moon, night and day, dark and light, sorrow and joy, and all the other pairs of opposite or complementary forces embodied in the nature of the universe and in the right and left sides of the brain. The fairy tale feast, where everyone is invited and everyone is present, is an image of wholeness on every level: mental, physical, emotional, spiritual, and community wholeness. So this image can guide us to welcome everybody, and all parts of ourselves, to the feast at the table in the ivory tower.

We know that esoteric and mystical knowledge used to be part of the academic and scientific learning process but have since been excluded. Also among the missing are women, nature and the body, joy, celebration and play, colour, creativity, beauty, a sense of the sa-

---

1   Kostantis Kourmadias and Laura Shannon, *Taxidi: Traditional Dance Music from Greece and Asia Minor* (Athens: Lavra Music, 2011), CD.

cred, communion with the divine, laughter and love of life.

It sounds good, doesn't it? It sounds like a party—like a place I would want to spend my life. That is partly why I left the academic realm for a life of independent scholarship, where I thought I might have a better chance of finding those missing things. I did not want to pursue knowledge without wisdom, or theory without experience; I wanted to work, learn, and teach using the right and left sides of my brain.

THE RIGHT-BRAIN LEARNING PROCESS OUTSIDE THE ACADEMY

How do people outside the academy teach and learn?

Non-literate and semiliterate peoples are no less intelligent, and have better memories, than those immersed in print culture, and oral cultures had complex ways of conveying information without the technology of writing. As Ian McGilchrist[2] has helped to clarify, the right-brain learning process is cyclical, artistic, and intuitive, condensing knowledge into symbol, metaphor, and myth. The reduction of information to its essence conveys nonrational nonlinear information while allowing scope for imagination, intuition, and individual understanding. This is the realm of right-brain consciousness, which runs parallel to the left-brain thinking now dominant in the academic world, and which Walter Ong identifies as primary to predominantly oral cultures. This mode of thinking is 'holistic', situational, and experiential rather than abstract, enabling people to learn 'from observation and practice with only minimal verbalized explanation' and 'produce amazingly complex and intelligent and beautiful organizations of thought and experience' without relying on overly analytical thought processes. Oral memory also has a high somatic component.[3]

The right-brain learning process may be missing from the academy, but it is alive and well in Eastern Europe, where for the last thirty years I have been researching dances, particularly village dances, and most particularly women's dances. Most people would agree

---

2   Ian McGilchrist, *The Master and His Emissary* (New Haven, CT: Yale University Press, 2009).

3   Walter Ong, *Orality and Literacy* (London: Methuen, 1982), 73, 43, 57, 66.

that Eastern European village women, who can often barely read and write, are good examples of those who have been excluded from the academy. And yet these women communicate through a sophisticated range of media including myths and rituals, songs and dances, folk dress and textile patterns. These various art forms facilitate education and expression. They activate the right and left sides of the brain. They are beautiful, joyful, and meaningful. Quite simply, they enchant. They comprise a very effective and very old system of preserving and passing on information. I contend that this system functions as a women's mystery school, where, beyond the scope of the academy, ancient wisdom, knowledge, and skills are taught not hierarchically, but in a circle: a dance circle.

ANCIENT ROOTS

Yosef Garfinkel confirms that 'scenes of dancing are among the oldest and most persistent themes in Near Eastern prehistoric art', reaching as far back as the 9th millennium BCE, and affirms that the history of dance can be shown to have started 'as early as the first appearance of modern humans in Europe, nearly 40,000 years ago'.[4] Garfinkel further states that before the emergence of literacy, 'community rituals, symbolized by dance, were the basic mechanisms for conveying education and knowledge to the adult members of the community and from one generation to the next'.[5] Elizabeth Wayland Barber describes a belief system which originated with the beginnings of agriculture in Europe in the Neolithic era and 'continued for millennia among people who knew little or nothing of literacy. What knowledge they thought important they passed down through visual apprenticeship and oral tradition', through myth, ritual, story, song, handicrafts, and dance. Essentially, this belief system 'sought to influence the flow of life by means of dance',[6] and it is still alive and well in the chain and circle dances of the Balkans.[7]

---

4   Yosef Garfinkel, 'Dance in Prehistoric Europe', *Documenta Præhistorica* XXXVII (2010), 305.

5   Yosef Garfinkel, *Dancing at the Dawn of Agriculture* (Austin: University of Texas Press, 2003), 3.

6   Elizabeth Wayland Barber, *The Dancing Goddesses* (New York: W.W. Norton, 2013), 2.

7   Mercia MacDermott, *Bulgarian Folk Customs* (London: Jessica Kingsley, 1998).

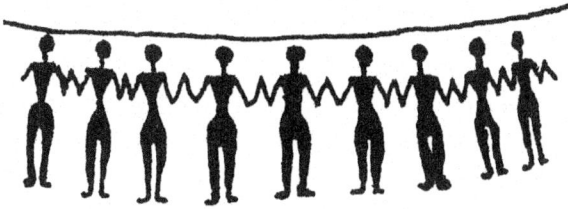

FIGURE 1:

Dancers on Neolithic pottery from Khazineh, Iran,
6ᵗʰ millennium BCE (University of Texas Press).

The many depictions of circles of women dancing with joined hands (in rock art, pottery shards, vases and frescoes, going back thousands of years) show that ritual dance was a primary means of women's worship (see FIGURE 1). Traditionally, women in Greece and the Balkans have tended to be in charge of dance and ceremonial matters, including birth, marriage, death, and fertility rituals; men have their own dance rituals,[8] and there are many mixed-gender customs. Existing dance traditions in this geographical area still serve as a primary means of celebration,[9] enabling dancers to pass on knowledge and navigate life passages within the supportive company of others. It is highly likely that many of these dance traditions and related customs are the direct descendants of ancient practices.[10]

Ronald Hutton[11] has argued against the possibility of pre-Chris-

---

8   For an example of men's seasonal dance rituals, see Laura Shannon, 'Theophania in Northern Greece: Men's Dance Rituals of Blessing and Protection', *Kef Times* (Fall 2014).

9   Yvonne Hunt, *Traditional Dance in Greek Culture* (Athens: Centre for Asia Minor Studies, Music Folklore Archive, 1996).

10   Correlations between ancient and modern dance practices have been explored by Dora Stratou, *The Greek Dances, Our Living Link with Antiquity* (Athens: Dora Stratou Dance Theatre, 1966), as well as by Barber, *The Dancing Goddesses*, and Garfinkel, *Dancing at the Dawn Of Agriculture*, who show that Balkan chain and circle dance structures and handholds originated with the beginning of agriculture in the Neolithic period.

11   Ronald Hutton, *The Triumph of the Moon: A History of Modern Pagan Witchcraft* (Oxford: Oxford University Press, 1999), 122-31.

tian rituals surviving into the present day in Britain. However, Hutton's stance, though influential with regard to contemporary pagan practice in the British Isles (which is the focus of his study), is not applicable to the traditional culture of Eastern Europe, where an enormous number of extant folk rituals have discernible roots in practices dating from antiquity.[12] These include ceremonial, culinary, sartorial, agricultural, marriage and funeral customs, agrarian offerings and animal sacrifice, and many rites marking life transitions and seasonal cycles with music and dance.[13] Academic specialists in Eastern European folk tradition have identified countless remnants of pre-Christian belief systems which survive today within the external framework of Christianity. Rachko Popov, for example, writing on the Bulgarian customs of Gherman and Peperouda—another winged woman figure in folk custom—states that they represent 'survivals of ancient conceptions and beliefs, of cult practices and rituals connected with the pagan pantheon of deities of the peoples belonging to the Balkan historical and ethnographic region.'[14]

Eastern and Western regions of Europe differ widely in this re-

---

12   See J.C. Lawson, *Modern Greek Folklore and Ancient Greek Religion* (Cambridge: Cambridge University Press, 1910), MacDermott, *Bulgarian Folk Customs*, and Barber, *The Dancing Goddesses*.

13   On the subject of animal sacrifice, see John Griffiths Pedley, *Sanctuaries and the Sacred in the Ancient Greek World* (Cambridge: Cambridge University Press, 2006), 80–82, and Loring Danforth, *Firewalking and Religious Healing* (Princeton: Princeton University Press, 1989), 16–17. On textile motifs, see Mary B. Kelly, *Goddess Embroideries of Eastern Europe* (McLean, New York: StudioBooks, 1989) and Sheila Paine, *Embroidered Textiles* (London: Thames & Hudson, 2008). On funeral laments, see Margaret Alexiou, *The Ritual Lament in Greek Tradition* (London: Cambridge University Press, 1974), Loring Danforth, *The Death Rituals of Rural Greece* (Princeton: Princeton University Press, 1982), and C. Nadia Seremetakis, *The Last Word: Women, Death and Divination in Inner Mani* (Chicago: University of Chicago Press, 1991).

14   Rachko Popov, *Butterfly and Gherman: Bulgarian Folk Customs and Rituals* (Sofia: Septemvri State Publishing House, 1989), 82. See also Georg Luck, *Arcana Mundi: Magic and the Occult in the Greek and Roman Worlds* (Baltimore: Johns Hopkins University Press, 1985), 35. Hutton himself acknowledges that '[t]he trappings of late antique and mediæval Christianities were taken over wholesale from paganism: the form of sacred buildings themselves and the use of clerical costume, altars, incense,

spect: those areas of western and northern Europe that were Christianised from Rome have predominantly couple dances, while areas to the east and south that were Christianised from Constantinople still feature almost exclusively line/chain dances, which were never banned by the Orthodox church.[15] The period of Ottoman rule, which lasted for nearly half a millennium in Bulgaria and Greece, also enabled the survival of pre-Christian folk customs in Eastern Europe. Firstly, the Ottoman conquest displaced or destroyed the aristocratic and urban educated classes which would otherwise have initiated the adoption of Western lifestyles and modes of thought; secondly, the Ottoman Balkan territories remained virtually untouched by the progressive influences of Renaissance, the Enlightenment, and the Industrial Revolution, and therefore maintained ancient customs for longer.[16]

MYSTERY SCHOOLS

The body of dances in a typical Balkan village represent an educational process, akin to a school in that the dances do compose an organised system, but it is a non-hierarchical, self-organising one. The dances are taught without teaching, and learnt without learning. People learn by participating, they learn with pleasure because dancing is fun, and yet they take it seriously because dance mediates every life event with both solemnity and joy. The 'school' of the dance aims to support each individual to successfully pass through all of life's challenges and to fulfil their potential, within an ethical framework that prioritises the overall good of the whole.[17] The steps, songs, and structures of dance and accompanying rites comprise a 'curriculum' of practical and ritual information which is passed down, seemingly without effort, from generation to generation.

Perhaps this is why Plato asserted that 'choral dance and song are

music, veils and cloths, decorative foliage, and several seasonal festivals'. In Ronald Hutton, 'Afterword', in *Ten Years of Triumph of the Moon*, ed. Dave Evans & Dave Green (Laverne, TN: Hidden Publishing, 2009), 217, quoted in Ben Whitmore, *Trials of the Moon: Reopening the Case for Historical Witchcraft* (Auckland: Briar Books, 2010), 58.

15   Barber, *The Dancing Goddesses*, 355.

16   MacDermott, *Bulgarian Folk Customs*, 106.

17   Ibid., 35–38.

identical with education as a whole'.[18]

The process of learning through doing corresponds to Burkert's definition of ancient mysteries as rituals that sought to bring about 'a change of mind through experience of the sacred'.[19] The fact that dances such as these are never formally taught, but are transmitted by doing them, reflects Aristotle's statement that 'at the final stage of mysteries there should be no more "learning" (mathein) but "experiencing" (pathein), and a change in the state of mind (diatethenai)'.[20] Mystery schools of antiquity also sought to facilitate processes of transformation, initiation, and changes of state or status. As Burkert describes, 'The change from childhood through puberty to maturity and marriage is the natural, archetypal model for change of status, and elements of this sequence may well be preserved in mysteries'.[21] In the Balkan worldview, '[h]umans are most vulnerable to supernatural forces in the course of the normal but critical events of birth, puberty, marriage, and death. Thus, special rites enable them to pass safely from one position to another'.[22] In Balkan countries, such rites of transformation and change are most often mediated through dance.[23] Transformation, of course, is another definition of enchantment.

METHODOLOGY

The methodology I have developed in the course of my research weaves together several different threads.[24] Along with the tradi-

---

18   Plato, Laws 672E, in *Complete Works* (Indianapolis: Hackett, 1997).

19   Walter Burkert, *Ancient Mystery Cults* (Cambridge, MA: Harvard University Press, 1987), 11.

20   Burkert, *Ancient Mystery Cults*, 89, citing Aristotle fr. 15, in Synesius, *Dion* 8.48A.

21   Burkert, *Ancient Mystery Cults*, 105.

22   Patricia Williams, 'Shawl and Cap in Czech and Slovak Rites of Passage', in *Folk Dress in Europe and Anatolia*, ed. Linda Welters (Oxford: Berg, 1999), 136.

23   'In traditional Bulgarian society, music and dancing were not luxuries, optional extras or even merely entertainment. They were an essential part of everyday life.' MacDermott, *Bulgarian Folk Customs*, 53.

24   Laura Shannon, 'Women's Ritual Dances: An Ancient Source of Healing

tional dances, which are my main interest, we look at folk songs, and we find that certain themes recur not only in songs and dances but in myths and legends, woven and embroidered designs,[25] and in archaeological discoveries going back more than 8,000 years.[26]

This continuity of motif through time and space, in my view, cannot be accidental or coincidental: it must be intentional. It has kept key images and symbols alive and active via multiple layers of expression which are mostly nonverbal (as even myth, song, and story, which use words, are 'verbal' in a right-brain way, a poetic way). Depth psychologist Jean Shinoda Bolen[27] states that 'poetry is compressed information', and like poetry, I see these women's songs and stories, dances and crafts as repositories of compressed information, systematically and purposefully transmitted within the sphere of right-brain consciousness.

Again and again in Balkan cultures, we see the same themes, images and symbols reiterated in myth, costume, textiles, dance steps, and song words. A neo-euhemeristic approach to this material looks at myth, legend and lore as sources of information about what was actually happening in the ancient world.[28] We cannot know the exact meaning these symbols may have had for the women who kept them alive, but we can be certain that they did have meaning. That is the view of archæologist Marija Gimbutas, who maintains that symbols on and in cultural artefacts can be 'read' as part of what she calls the 'language of the Goddess'.[29] Mary Kelly,[30] Sheila Paine[31] and other textile researchers have shown that embroidery is a language; what I see with the women in the Balkans is that textiles are their

---

in Our Time', in *Dancing on the Earth: Women's Stories of Healing Through Dance*, ed. J. Leseho and S. McMaster (Forres: Findhorn Press, 2011), 143.

25   Kelly, *Goddess Embroideries of Eastern Europe*.

26   Garfinkel, *Dancing at the Dawn of Agriculture*.

27   Jean Shinoda Bolen, *The Millionth Circle* (Berkeley, CA: Conari Press, 2003), 7.

28   For a definition of neo-euhemerism, see Marguerite Rigoglioso, *Virgin Mother Goddesses of Antiquity* (New York: Palgrave Macmillan, 2010), 9.

29   Marija Gimbutas, *The Language of the Goddess* (San Francisco: Harper & Row, 1989), xv.

30   Kelly, *Goddess Embroideries of Eastern Europe*.

31   Paine, *Embroidered Textiles*.

texts.[32] Anna Ilieva and Anna Shturbanova describe archæological and mythological symbols in ritual dance as the means by which living dances continue to transmit messages embedded in them since antiquity.[33] These symbols, which in so many cases have discernible roots in the Neolithic era, can be understood in the same sense with which Hazrat Inayat Khan speaks of symbols as living manuscripts which serve to keep ancient wisdom intact, transmitting ideas in unwritten form long beyond the lifetime of the teacher.[34] This is another way in which the 'mystery school' of Balkan dances, and the information encoded within them, are self-organising and self-perpetuating.

WOMEN WITH WINGS

Let us take a closer look at one of the motifs which turns up again and again, from thousands of years ago right up until the present day: the woman with wings.

Who are the women with wings? In archaeological artefacts, women with wings are goddesses or priestesses, shown with wings, with birds, as birds, as butterflies, with birdlike heads, with birdlike clothing, with sleeves like wings, with arms like wings, arms extended like wings, arms holding sacred objects, arms to the sky in gestures of invocation. These images are found all over the ancient world.[35]

We know that priestesses of antiquity were adepts of trance states and divination, and, according to Felicitas Goodman, probably used the actual stances depicted in folk art and archaeological finds.[36]

---

32   Shannon, 'Women's Ritual Dances: An Ancient Source of Healing in Our Time', 143.

33   Anna Ilieva and Anna Shturbanova, 'Some Zoomorphic Images in Bulgarian Women's Ritual Dances in the Context of Old European Symbolism', in *From the Realm of the Ancestors*, ed. Joan Marler (Manchester: Knowledge, Ideas & Trends, Inc., 1997), 309–21.

34   Hazrat Inayat Khan, *The Sufi Message: The Unity of Religious Ideals* (New Delhi: Mortilal Banarsidass, 2003), 213–21.

35   Laura Shannon, 'Der Tanz gibt uns Flügel', *Balance: Zeitschrift des Fachverbandes Meditation des Tanzes* (2014: 2): 16.

36   Felicitas Goodman, *Where the Spirits Ride the Wind* (Bloomington:

Greek and Balkan mythology is rich in depictions of nymphs and muses, semi-divine women with the power to fly. They were also considered to be bearers of fertility to crops, animals and people.[37] Marguerite Rigoglioso asserts that legends of winged women in some cases reference actual priestesses of pre-Christian times and their shamanistic ability to fly between the worlds;[38] we know that the priestesses of antiquity were real, historical women, whose spiritual, clairvoyant and visionary power was recognised by their society.[39]

FIGURE 2:

'Flying' priestesses with wing-like sleeves on a vessel in the shape of an astragalos (knucklebone), Aegina, Greece, 5th century BCE
(Copyright: The Trustees of the British Museum).

In the Christian era, the destruction of the earlier temples meant that these women of power had to go underground. After that, the motif of the woman with wings continued to be reiterated in versions

---

Indiana University Press, 1990).

37   Barber, The Dancing Goddesses.

38   Marguerite Rigoglioso, The Cult of Divine Birth in Ancient Greece (New York: Palgrave Macmillan, 2009), 88–94.

39   Joan Breton Connelly, Portrait of a Priestess (Princeton: Princeton University Press) 2007.

more abstract, more discreet, yet still recognisable to those with eyes to see. There are many examples of disguised or encoded versions of this pattern, the woman with upraised arms or wings. Important motifs are centrally located to underscore their significance, often on the bodice, the apron or the sleeves.[40] These embroideries are not merely decoration, but proclamations of power. Remember, for these women, textiles are text.

FIGURE 3:

Example of embroidery motif of woman with upraised arms or wings, author's collection.

After the imperial decrees of the late 4th century ordered the destruction of the pagan sanctuaries, women's knowledge of initiatory techniques, previously open, had to be disguised or encoded in order to survive. Of course much was lost, or greatly changed; however, I suggest that a central essence visibly remains, in the ways that Balkan women of today continue to use the arts at their disposal to preserve and pass on elements of ancient culture. They dance and sing, enact ritual, keep tradition, practise sacred arts and are often skilled in clairvoyance, divination and healing, even to-day. And like dancers in every part of the world, and in every era, they use physical, mental and spiritual techniques to consciously enter another frame of mind while they dance.[41] This is an initiatory process which can ultimately transform one's state of mind, just as Aristotle described.

---

40   Kelly, *Goddess Embroideries of Eastern Europe.*

41   Barber, *The Dancing Goddesses*, 337–51; see also Barbara Ehrenreich, *Dancing in the Streets* (New York: Metropolitan Books, 2007).

Burkert and others have claimed that the mystery schools of antiquity all died out and no living links remain,[42] but every Greek village I have visited for my research has been full of living remnants of
encoded ancient wisdom. The women's knowledge did not stop and
start again, to be resurrected later from written texts, because they
had no written texts; these women kept their body of knowledge
alive and handed it down orally in person for many generations, up
until the present, since dance cannot be transmitted any other way.[43]

The costumes themselves often feature wing-like aspects such as
extra-long or vestigial sleeves, long panels of fabric, or fringes which
move and sway with the dancers' arms. In some parts of Bulgaria,
these vestigial wings take the form of strips of fabric hanging from
the shoulders of the overdress,[44] and these may even be ornament-
ed with images of winged female figures. Elizabeth Wayland Barber has found in the ultra-long sleeve a link between dance rituals,
bird motifs, and priestesses of antiquity, providing further corrob-
oration for Marguerite Rigoglioso's theories connecting legends of
winged women with priestesses of pre-Christian times.[45] The dancers themselves also often use arm movements which seem to fly, and
of course if you are a dancer, you already know that that is exactly
what dancing feels like.

RITES OF PASSAGE

Wings are an obvious metaphor for transition and transformation,
and the image of the winged woman frequently appears in connec-

---

42 Burkert, *Ancient Mystery Cults*, 53. Burkert states that '[m]ysteries could
    not go underground because they lacked any lasting organization' but
    I would argue that dance traditions were and are self-organising and
    self-sustaining, and unlike official schools, institutions, or religion, they
    did not and do not require much in the way of external organisation.
    Women danced then and dance now simply because they have always
    done so.

43 Barber, *The Dancing Goddesses*; Hunt, *Traditional Dance in Greek Culture*;
    MacDermott, *Bulgarian Folk Customs*; Shannon, 'Women's Ritual Danc-
    es: An Ancient Source of Healing in Our Time'.

44 MacDermott, *Bulgarian Folk Customs*, 45.

45 Barber, *The Dancing Goddesses*, 183–200; Rigoglioso, *The Cult of Divine
    Birth*, 88–94.

tion with rites of passage such as puberty, engagement, and marriage. As bringers of fertility—also in the symbolic realm—the
women with wings are seen as guides who can help everyone fulfil
their creative potential, be it physical, artistic, intellectual, or spiritual. Birds also represent the ability to move between the worlds, including from puberty to marriage.[46] In many wedding songs, brides
are identified with birds, such as the dove and partridge, which in
pre-Christian times were sacred to Aphrodite, goddess of love. One
of these wedding songs, from the Greek island of Thassos, is called
'Ola ta poulakia', 'All the birds', and I would like to take a closer look
at that dance here. 'Ola ta poulakia' was sung and danced during
the wedding preparations, before the bride leaves her family home
forever for the house of her new husband.[47] This is a significant and
solemn moment in a woman's life,[48] and the ritual dance helps her
through the initiatory stages of separation and transition in her rite
of passage.[49] These folk rites took place outside the framework of
the Church, but 'were often regarded by the participants as religious
acts. Rites possessed special authority and in all probability represented remnants of pre-Christian beliefs'.[50] The change in social
status at the heart of the ritual dance mirrors the change in state of
mind at the conclusion of ancient mysteries.

---

46   Barber has noted the emphasis on bird images, women, or priestess-
      es dressed like birds or dancing like birds, in relation to the fertility of
      crops and females: she believes the ubiquitous bird-faced, bird-winged or
      winged-sleeved figures, sculpted in clay or depicted on Minoan seal rings,
      'refer to real women dressed as bird girls and to the selfsame bird-inhab-
      iting spirit maidens who bring moisture and fertility and whose history
      [can be] traced from modern times back to the threshold of the Bronze
      Age'. Barber, The Dancing Goddesses, 300.

47   Yiannis Prantsidis, Ο χορόσ στην ελληνική παράδοση και η διδασκαλία
      του (Athens: Ekdotiki Aiginiou, 2004), 330.

48   In Greece and the Balkans, marriage was a solemn rite of passage, in
      which 'a bride leaves her home and family of origin at marriage in or-
      der to live with her new husband in his father's home. For this reason, a
      woman's wedding, like her funeral, is for her parents and her other close
      relatives a sad occasion at which her departure evokes the expression of
      grief'. Danforth, The Death Rituals of Rural Greece, 75.

49   Arnold Van Gennep, The Rites of Passage (Chicago: University of Chicago
      Press, 1960), 10.

50   Williams, 'Shawl and Cap in Czech and Slovak Rites of Passage', 136.

The women would have danced this dance around the dow-ry—the *príka*—the weavings, bedcovers, clothing, embroideries, household goods and other skilfully crafted, exquisitely decorated items made by the bride throughout her girlhood years.[51] Many of these textiles feature the motif of the winged woman. As in most of the ancient world, a bride's dowry remained her property, so, then and now, it served as a form of insurance and a guarantee of economic independence for the married woman. I think it likely that the embroidered image of the winged woman served to help remind the bride of her essential independence and freedom, nei-ther lost nor forgotten despite being somewhat curtailed by her new circumstances.

In Balkan rural areas, life transitions were typically medi-ated by dance and by cloth; in this case, not only do the women dance around the dowry (composed of mainly textiles), the fes-tive costume they wear is also of significance. A very large silk shawl, the *diplárika*, is a key part of the women's folk costume of Thassos (FIGURE 4)

It is secured atop a coiled scarf arranged like a crown on the wom-an's head, and drapes down the length of her body at the back and sides to create a capelike effect resembling wings. The festive costume also features 'tongues' of fabric, trimmed with gold braid, added to the sleeve ends of the waistcoat, 'in such a way as to make it appear to have two sets of sleeves' which hang down over the hands.[52] The women dancers, thus adorned with the 'wings' of their large shawls as well as ultra-long sleeves, sing a song which portrays the bride as a bird,[53] while the bride herself metaphorically takes flight into her new life.

---

51   The fact that the women dance around the precious textiles which com-prise the dowry is also significant. Since ancient times, the act of dancing around a sacred object has been considered to have an apotropaic func-tion as well as a consecrating effect, both upon the dancers and the items encircled. W.O.E. Oesterley, *Sacred Dance in the Ancient World* (Mineola: Dover Publications, 2002), 37, 105, 183.

52   Christos Broufas, *40 Greek Costumes from the Dora Stratou Theatre Col-lection* (Athens: Dora Stratou Theatre, 2010), 64. As we have seen, wing-like elements in costumes go back at least to the 8th century BCE: Barber, *The Dancing Goddesses*, 285–87.

53   See Appendix to this chapter.

FIGURE 4: *Women's folk costume from the island of Thassos, Greece, 20th century (Christos Broufas, 40 GREEK COSTUMES FROM THE DORA STRATOU THEATRE COLLECTION, Athens: Dora Stratou Theatre, 2010).*

An initial movement analysis of this dance, which I learned on the island of Thassos during numerous visits over several years,[54] is rewarding here. The dance structure corresponds to the main ba-

---

54   In 2010, 2011, 2012, 2014, and 2015.

sic pattern found throughout the Balkans and Near East, with two steps progressing forward followed by two step-lifts symmetrically mirrored to both sides; the simplicity of this pattern, its ubiquity in a huge geographical area, and the infinite variety of variations, all indicate great antiquity.[55] The dance steps may not seem very vigorous at first glance, but a relatively large movement is required for the foot to lift across in front, emphasised further by the upper body leaning slightly towards the opposite diagonal. This creates a dynamic tension through each dancer's physical core, kindling a sensation of internal movement and a feeling of extending through a greater distance. In addition, the dance includes vigorous arm movements like flying wings, which reflect the key image of the text, that of the bride as bird. Like many Balkan dance songs, the song is sung in alternating phrases, first by a leader and then by a chorus. This antiphonal style originated in the earliest forms of Greek drama, where choral dancers also acted out the words being sung,[56] just as they do today on Thassos.

RITUAL CLEANING

I would like to suggest that we return, just for a moment, to the cleaners, with whom we began our discussion. Typically, these women are also excluded from the academy, and I mean *really* excluded. Our idea of someone in the academy is someone who is not a cleaner; our idea of someone who is a cleaner is someone who is not in the academy. And yet—who cleaned the rooms in which we gather for our conferences and classes, the corridors through which we walk? The cleaners. They *are* inside the academy, literally inside; present yet invisible, invisible yet present.

The Greek and Balkan women who enact rituals and dances like those described here are, in my view, initiates and adepts of a secret mystery school. They are also cleaners. In these places, the women who dance are the women who clean. Every ritual in every village begins with an orgy of cooking and cleaning. The women clean their homes, they clean the church, they clean the dancing ground, they clean themselves, their families, and their special festive clothing.

---

55   Hunt, *Traditional Dance in Greek Culture.*
56   Barber, *The Dancing Goddesses,* 273.

They light incense, just like the priestesses of antiquity,[57] and prepare the space, on every level, before they undertake the sacred work.

This practical and ritual cleaning affirms the home as a sacred space, and the woman of the house as its priestess, consciously tending its flame. As Joan Breton Connelly[58] and Kaltsas and Shapiro[59] have helped us to understand, women in the ancient world were largely in charge of spiritual affairs, which scholars of today often do not take into account. Just as women used to tend the flame on their home altar to Hestia or Vesta in ancient Greece and Rome, Orthodox women nowadays still keep an oil lamp burning in front of the icon in their home. The Greek term equivalent to 'housewife', *noikokyra*, literally means 'the lady of the house', clearly indicating a prestigious, even noble role of power and responsibility. These women were, and are, both priestess and potscrubber; Martha and Mary; sacred and secular; silver and gold.

ECSTASY AND SELF-CONTROL

I would like to describe one more example of right-brain consciousness in the learning process. Every year on 8th September, the feast day of Panayia Yiatrissa (Our Lady the Healer), a church festival takes place in a tiny mountain village in the Peloponnese region of southern Greece. The women of this little settlement spend days, unpaid, cleaning the church and preparing food for over a hundred people. When the church service is over and everyone has enjoyed an enormous feast of local, seasonal, home-made food and wine, another kind of work begins, which is the ritual dance. This dance creates a circle of joyful connection, just as important as the actual liturgy; both are believed to bestow a blessing on everyone present. The priest begins the dance, leads the dance, and invites people in one at a time, starting with those who contributed the most work to the celebration, to honour them: the cooks and the cleaners.

The custom of communal dancing in front of the church on holy

---

57   Connelly, *Portrait of a Priestess.*

58   Ibid.

59   Nikolaos Kaltsas and H.A. Shapiro, eds., *Worshipping Women: Ritual and Reality in Classical Athens* (New York: Alexander S. Onassis Public Benefit Foundation, 2008).

days, accompanied by a communal feast, can still be witnessed in rural villages all over Greece. At this particular festival, which I have attended on several occasions[60], many interesting things take place which could offer inspiration in our quest for the re-enchantment of the academy. We see everyone dancing together, men and women, rich and poor, young and old. People are remembering and reaffirming favourite steps and songs, and apparently without effort teaching the young ones this part of their common heritage and identity. The children quite naturally take their place at the end of the open circle and often dance with dexterity at a very young age.

All the adult women are expected to dance, even just for a few seconds. People know the right moment to join the line; they know how to assume leadership and also how and when to pass it on. People dance differently when they take the lead. The leader of the dance has greater freedom to move, to 'fly'; her movements both up and down show the path of the journey between heaven and earth, while her more vigorous arm movements express the expanded sense of self and vital energy which belong both to the sacred day and to the leadership role.

Nothing is ever taught, yet everyone in the community naturally learns, by immersion in the joy which both transports and transforms. Connection with others is a source of enchantment, and joyful, ecstatic feelings are another means by which we can 'fly'. In this case, because circle dancing requires concentration and self-control, euphoria is experienced without abandoning consciousness, in a state of mind which balances ecstasy and awareness, thus activating both hemispheres of the brain. In this state, learning and teaching—of dance, song, and leadership skills—take place almost without effort.

Each time I have attended this festival, I have seen the priest take in his hands a sacred object, to call people to the dance. This ritual tool signifies leadership and gives the first dancer, whoever it is, temporary authority to act as a priest or priestess, receiving and channelling the benevolent powers of the holy place and the holy day, as a blessing for the community. This hallowed item is, quite simply, an ordinary dishtowel. Once again, we are back with the cleaners.

---

60   In 2014, 2015, and 2016.

CONCLUSION

The customs described here present alternative methods of learning and teaching which enable both transformation and celebration. The woman with wings, as a symbol in traditional Balkan dance, mediates rites of passage and enables a state of euphoria without loss of concentration. The dances provide a fertile context for learning which emphasises a collective social structure rather than a hierarchical one, and fosters an ethic of using one's talents to contribute to the community. This holistic way of embodied, experiential learning closely resembles what McLean calls 'magical or hermetic thinking': 'the ability to see ideas as part of a whole—to see the interconnections, the correspondences, between seemingly diverse events, things, and ideas'.[61]

Could these traditions help us re-imagine the educational process as a journey towards personal transformation, creativity, and joy—while cultivating an ethic of compassion, connection, and social justice? Surely that would be a more enchanting, and enchanted, approach, to education, and might provide an antidote to academic systems which, in the past, have all too often served to suppress and stultify instead of nurture.[62] Perhaps the woman with wings can inspire us to embark on our own rite of passage, into a new understanding of what it means to learn and to teach—and to look in new ways at what we do with our learning.

In answer to the question: How do we re-enchant the academy? I suggest we invite the women—not just as cleaners, but as scholars, sources of wisdom, and teachers, from the past and the present—and welcome them into the academy. Invite the body. Invite the belly: your own gut instinct, your intuition, your enteric nervous system. Invite poetry, creativity, celebration, and play. Invite music and dance and the wish for everyone to fulfil their creative and in-

---

61   Adam McLean, *The Magical Calendar: A Synthesis of Magical Symbolism from the Seventeenth Century Renaissance of Medieval Occultism* (Grand Rapids, MI: Phanes Press, 1994), quoted in Whitmore, *Trials of the Moon*, 43.

62   In Patrick Leigh Fermor's memorable description, education based on indoctrination 'turns children—all of them, till then, near-geniuses trailing clouds of glory—into frightened, insufferable little conformist prigs'. Patrick Leigh Fermor, *The Broken Road* (London: John Murray, 2013), 221.

tellectual potential. It is not too late to reclaim these lost treasures, and to reweave intellect and intuition, the warp and the weft of the ancient fabric of our minds.

We can learn from those in the human family whose contribution has been overlooked. They can help us bring right-brain consciousness back into our learning process, fostering egalitarian community and connection with the natural world, a sense of past and future and a sense of purpose in the part we play preserving knowledge and wisdom for future generations.

As we seek to strengthen both wings of the mind, and to think with both hemispheres of the brain, we too can learn to fly between the worlds, out of the ivory tower and over the garden wall. And wherever that feast of gold and silver happens to be, in the tower, in the garden, or beyond, let us also invite, and honour, the hands that cooked, served and cleaned up after the meal. They are the hands that join us in the dance.

APPENDIX: *OLA TA POULAKIA*—ALL THE BIRDS

Wedding dance song from the island of Thassos, Greece.[63]

> Όλα τα πουλάκια ζυγά-ζυγά,
> το 'ρημου τ'αηδόνι το μοναχό.
> Το 'ρημου τ'αηδόνι το μοναχό,
> περπατεί στους κάμπους με τον αϊτό.
>
> Περπατεί και λέει και τραγουδεί
> άντρα μου πουλήτη πρηματευτή.
> Άντρα μου πουλήτη πρηματευτή,
> κι Μεσολογγύτη ξενητευτή.
>
> Που την ηδιαλέξες αυτή την νιά,
> την ξανθομαλλούσα την παρθενιά;
> Από ταξιδιώτης κατήβηνα,
> στου περιβουλάκι την ήβρηκα.

---

63   Learnt by the author through the oral tradition.

Τα βασιλικά της επότιζε
  και τις ματζουράνες εδρόσιζε.
Εκοψε κλωνάρι και μου 'δωσε,
  μου 'πε κι ένα λόγο και μ' άρεσε.

Βρε παλικαράκι κι αν μ>αγαπάς,
  τί συχνοδιαβαίνεις και δεν μιλάς;
Στείλε προυξινήτη στην μάνα μου,
  κι προυξινητάδες στον μπάρμπα μου.

ALL THE BIRDS HAVE PAIRED OFF
Except the lonely nightingale
The lonely nightingale
Walks in the fields with the eagle

She walks and talks and sings
My man, the travelling merchant
Travelling in Misolonghi

Where did you find this young woman,
This golden-haired virgin?
I came back from a voyage
And found her in her garden

She was watering her basil
And her marjoram plants
She cut a sprig and gave it to me,
And spoke words which pleased me

Young man, if you love me,
Why do you always come around here,
but you don't say anything?
Send a matchmaker to my mother

SELECT BIBLIOGRAPHY

BARBER, Elizabeth Wayland. *The Dancing Goddesses*. New York: W.W. Norton, 2013.

BURKERT, Walter. *Ancient Mystery Cults*. Cambridge, MA: Harvard University Press, 1987.

DANFORTH, Loring. *The Death Rituals of Rural Greece*. Princeton: Princeton University Press, 1982.

GARFINKEL, Yosef. *Dancing at the Dawn of Agriculture*. Austin: University of Texas Press, 2003.

GIMBUTAS, Marija. *The Language of the Goddess*. San Francisco: Harper & Row, 1989.

HUNT, Yvonne. *Traditional Dance in Greek Culture*. Athens: Centre for Asia Minor Studies, 1996.

HUTTON, Ronald. *The Triumph of the Moon: A History of Modern Pagan Witchcraft*. Oxford: Oxford University Press, 1999.

_____. 'Afterword'. In *Ten Years of Triumph of the Moon*, edited by Dave Evans and Dave Green. Laverne, TN: Hidden Publishing, 2009.

KALTSAS, Nikolaos, and H. A. Shapiro, eds. *Worshipping Women: Ritual and Reality in Classical Athens*. New York: Alexander S. Onassis Public Benefit Foundation, 2008.

KELLY, Mary B. *Goddess Embroideries of Eastern Europe*. McLean, New York: StudioBooks, 1989.

MacDERMOTT, Mercia. *Bulgarian Folk Customs*. London: Jessica Kingsley, 1998.

McGILCHRIST, Iain. *The Master and His Emissary*. New Haven, CT: Yale University Press, 2009.

ONG, Walter. *Orality and Literacy*. London: Methuen, 1982.

PAINE, Sheila. *Embroidered Textiles*. London: Thames & Hudson, 2008.

RIGOGLIOSO, Marguerite. *The Cult of Divine Birth in Ancient Greece*. New York: Palgrave Macmillan, 2009.

SHANNON, Laura. 'Women's Ritual Dances: An Ancient Source of Healing in Our Time'. In *Dancing on the Earth: Women's Stories of Healing Through Dance*, edited by Johanna Leseho and Sandra McMaster, 138–57. Forres: Findhorn Press, 2011.

_____. 'Der Tanz gibt uns Flügel', *Balance: Zeitschrift des Fachver-bandes Meditation des Tanzes*. 2014.

WHITMORE, Ben. *Trials of the Moon: Reopening the Case for Histor-ical Witchcraft*. Auckland: Briar Books, 2010.

The Walking Dead

Or Why Psychogeography Matters

SONIA OVERALL

Do you walk on autopilot? Do you find yourself moving through place without noticing where you are or how you got there? Does the world take on the soupy soft-focus of middle-distance or flit past in a bombardment of signs, notices, and advertising hoardings? Are you in danger of becoming one of the walking dead?

In the rush of movement, in our race to get from one meeting to the next, to catch a bus, park the car, fit in the school run, get the shopping, meet a friend—we rarely stop, breathe, and reconnect with the atmosphere, stories, details, history, or spirit of the place we are in. How can we redress the balance? One way which works for me, and which I have used with students to re-engage them with their surroundings, is to adopt a little psychogeographical attitude.

What is psychogeography?

The term 'psychogeography'[1] is rooted in the radical experiments of the Situationist International and their precursors, including the Lettrist movement in Paris. Guy Debord—popularly cited as the grandfather of psychogeography—explained it as a practice 'not inconsistent with the materialist perspective that sees life and thought as conditioned by objective nature', which 'sets for itself the study of the specific effects of the geographical environment (whether

---

1   The use of the term 'psychogeography' and its history, from the Letterist group and Situationist International to the early 21st century, is outlined in Merlin Coverley, *Psychogeography* (Harpenden: Pocket Essentials, 2010).

consciously organized or not) on the emotions and behaviour of individuals'.[2] Key to the practice of psychogeography is the drift or *dérive*, 'a technique of rapid passage through varied ambiences'.[3]

As a label, psychogeography has been through a repeated cycle of acceptance, rejection, and popularisation over the last sixty or so years. In her introduction to *Walking Inside Out*,[4] an anthology of writings on Contemporary British Psychogeography, Tina Richardson suggests that rather than using the term psychogeogra*phy*, we should think of psychogeogra*phies*. Richardson states that the 'bricolage nature of psychogeography means that its influence for a specific group or individual will be vastly different from that of another',[5] something which is evident when one looks at the resulting practices. Psychogeography has a role in the work of artists, writers, protest groups, performers, and just about anyone who uses walking 'with attitude' as part of their practice. It has been broken down, reworked, and renamed continually, spawning subgroups of practitioners wishing to differentiate themselves: Richardson cites 'psychogeophysics' and 'cryptoforestry' as examples of this, as well as her own take on map use, 'schizocartography'.[6]

Regardless of fine differences, the umbrella of psychogeography is broad enough to keep its many followers dry as they tramp through labyrinthine streets and across open fields. I would like to see the redemption of the term, and I am sticking to it. Helpfully, Richardson proposes that we consider the historic influences of the psychogeography movement as 'a kind of toolbox for contemporary practitioners'.[7] This is certainly what I do in my own work and teaching.

---

2   Guy Debord, 'Introduction to a Critique of Urban Geography' [1955], in *Situationist International Anthology*, ed. and trans. Ken Knabb (Berkeley: Bureau of Public Secrets, 2006), 8.

3   Guy Debord, 'Theory of the Dérive' [1959], in *Situationist International Anthology*, ed. and trans. Ken Knabb (Berkeley: Bureau of Public Secrets, 2006), 62.

4   Tina Richardson, 'Introduction: A Wander through the Scene of British Urban Walking', in *Walking Inside Out*, ed. Tina Richardson (London: Rowman & Littlefield International, 2015), 1–27.

5   Ibid., 3.

6   Ibid., 18.

7   Ibid., 3.

SO MUCH FOR THE DEFINITIONS:
WHAT IS IT IN PRACTICE?

In its broadest sense, psychogeography is a way of looking at place and our relationship with it. It is a two-way thing: we are influenced by our surroundings, but rather than blindly following whatever directions we are given, and simply 'zoning out', a psychogeographer will question, refuse, and occasionally disobey. Psychogeography is driven by curiosity and a desire to experience place more fully, on many levels. A *dérive*, then, is attentive walking. It is more than a stroll, and less than a march. It is not about getting from A to B, but about taking a route that suggests itself as the walk progresses. It encourages the walker to experience place, taking time to explore routes away from the everyday. It is, at its most radical, a means of pedestrian protest that disobeys the rules of urban planning, and attempts to shatter the 'spectacle' of commercialised and municipal spaces that the Situationists rejected so strongly. It is primarily an urban pursuit but can be practised anywhere. It reads and maps spaces across time, takes in the palimpsest of city streets and ancient byways. It is a process of defamiliarisation and re-enchantment, and I cannot recommend it highly enough.

We all know that exercise is good for us, and walking is a form of exercise that requires, at most, a stout pair of shoes. Aside from the health benefits, and the sense of well-being that a stroll in the fresh air can give us, a recent scientific study has demonstrated that walking in the outdoors also increases our ability to think novel, creative thoughts. The study was carried out by Marily Oppezzo and Daniel Schwartz of Stanford University.[8] In a report published last year in the *Journal of Experimental Psychology*, they summarised their findings:

> Four studies demonstrate that walking increases creative ideation. The effect is not simply due to the increased perceptual stimulation of moving through an environment, but rather it is due to walking [...] Walking outside produced the most novel and highest qual-

---

8   Marily Oppezzo and Daniel Schwartz, 'Give Your Ideas Some Legs: The Positive Effect of Walking on Creative Thinking', *Journal of Experimental Psychology: Learning, Memory and Cognition* 40.4 (2014): 1142–52.

ity analogies. The effects of outdoor stimulation and walking were separable. Walking opens up the free flow of ideas, and it is a simple and robust solution to the goals of increasing creativity and increasing physical activity [...] Walking also exhibited a residual effect on creativity. After people had walked, their subsequent seated creativity was much higher than those who had not walked. [9]

So, walking outdoors helps us to think creatively. Psychogeography helps us to see the everyday afresh. The benefits of the wider practice are clear. There are also two strands of contemporary psychogeographical practice that I feel are particularly pertinent to the notion of re-enchantment: Mythogeography and Deep Topography.

MYTHOGEOGRAPHY

In 1997, a group of four performance artists—Stephen Hodge, Simon Persighetti, Phil Smith and Cathy Turner—established the company 'Wrights & Sites'. Originally interested in site-specific performance, their projects gradually morphed into explorations of human responses to cities, landscape, and walking. Their practice of 'disrupted walking' has a playful Dadaist approach to collaborative experience, intervention and what they refer to as 'spatial meaning-making'.[10]

Wrights & Sites increasingly used *dérives* in their work, moving away from performance and spectacle and adopting what member Phil Smith (also known as 'Crab Man' for his sideways approach to walking) termed 'mythogeography'. Originally a misremembered version of the word psychogeography, mythogeography gradually took on its own mantle of meanings. By 2004, what the term had come to signify is highly suggestive of an attempt to 're-enchant' place:

> We have been exploring the potential of an approach to place through the lens of mytho-geography that places the fictional, fanciful, mistaken and personal on

9   Oppezzo and Schwartz, 'Give Your Ideas Some Legs', 1142–45.

10   Wrights & Sites, MisGuides (www.mis-guide.com).

equal terms with factual, municipal history. It suggests performance through the participation of active
spectators as researchers of the city, allowing authors
and walkers to become equal partners in ascribing
significance to place.[11]

As well as the *dérive*, or drift, Wrights & Sites employed 'catapults'
to disrupt a walk. Smith refers to his use of a taxi at the beginning
of a long walk as what 'might charitably be interpreted as a catapult;
a Lettriste device, an artificial stimulant a walker can use to disrupt
themselves. Leap onto a bus or train without knowing the vehicle's
destination, walk against the wind, follow the first animal you see'.[12]
The catapult is a useful item in the psychogeographer's toolbox.

In his own practice, and particularly in his recent publications,
Smith has re-emphasised the role of solitary walking: the psychogeographer as a lone figure traversing the urban landscape, seeking out evocative liminal spaces. In his books *Mythogeography*[13] and
On Walking ... And Stalking Sebald,[14] Smith revisits and revises past
walks and interventions, most notably W.G. Sebald's Suffolk walks
from *The Rings of Saturn*.[15] In his article 'Psychogeography and
Mythogeography: Currents in Radical Walking', Smith describes
mythogeography as 'a theorization of multiplicity and nobility that
hangs on the texture, grit, sweat, and emotion of individual journeys'.[16] While these journeys can be collective, the uniqueness of the
experience is what counts. By revisiting past walks, Smith is effectively exploring similarities and differences between these events.
He is seeking out, and creating, palimpsest.

---

11   Stephen Hodge, et al., 'Mis-guiding the City Walker' (paper presented by
      Wrights & Sights at Cities for People at The Fifth International Confer-
      ence on Walking in the 21st Century, Copenhagen, 9th–11th June 2004), 1.

12   Phil Smith, *Mythogeography: A Guide to Walking Sideways* (Axeminster:
      Triarchy Press, 2010), 44.

13   Ibid.

14   Phil Smith, *On Walking...And Stalking Sebald* (Axeminster: Triarchy
      Press, 2014).

15   W.G. Sebald, *The Rings of Saturn* (1998; repr. London: Vintage, 2002).

16   Phil Smith, 'Psychogeography and Mythogeography: Currents in Radical
      Walking', in *Walking Inside Out*, ed. Tina Richardson (London: Rowman
      & Littlefield International, 2015), 165.

Wrights & Sites' adventures in walking led them to reject what they saw as 'the municipal interpretations of the city', an echo of the Situationists' rejection of prescriptive urban planning.[17] Wishing to extend their mythogeographic reading of the city across time as well as space, they pursued—and continue to do so—a counter-touristic approach to walking. They described 'the burgeoning Heritage Industry' as 'dutifully concerned with historical accuracy and authentic reconstruction', but also accused it of employing 'the disingenuous and romantic sloganeering of the travel agent'.[18] In response, they produced a series of 'Mis-Guides', a 'disruption of city tour guides' that encouraged walkers to drift, 'seeking cities within cities', offering 'a forged passport to an "other" city and a hyper-sensitised way of travelling the familiar one'.[19] Maps were also 'misused':

> An overlay of maps seems to challenge our notions of time and space in a landscape or cityscape of sky, water and earth, merging contours, fluctuating and colliding in the flow or contra-flow of daily life [...] Hence, the strange journeys we make, walking in a place we think we know but allowing in a sense of don't know.[20]

This desire to see beyond the familiar and to reinterpret space; the overlay of maps and seeking the city 'within' the city: these are key psychogeographical concerns. Guy Debord refers to 'transposing maps of two different regions' in his 'Introduction to a Critique of Urban Geography', citing the example of using a map of London to negotiate a region of Germany.[21] Using and misusing maps is a valuable and practical way of defamiliarising and re-enchanting place—and one I will return to later.[22]

Smith took the Mis-Guide further with his quirky publication *Counter-Tourism: The Handbook* and its pocketbook edition.[23] These

---

17   Hodge et al., 'Mis-guiding the City Walker', 1.

18   Ibid.

19   Ibid.

20   Ibid.

21   Debord, 'Introduction to a Critique of Urban Geography', 11.

22   See exercises below.

23   Phil Smith, *Counter-Tourism: The Handbook and Counter-Tourism: A Pocketbook* (Axeminster: Triarchy Press, 2012).

books urge the heritage-lover to interact playfully and imaginatively with place: to give weight to the possible as well as the evidenced; to give story and history equal footing. Smith recently cited the growing influence of mythogeography as a term, pointing out that it is becoming common currency in books, student projects, community events, lectures, blogs—and now this paper. It is a sign of a persistent interest in psychogeography and walking studies, of the practice of walking artists and the long-standing relationship between walking and writing. Smith says:

> The variety of these practices, in tune with the mytho-geographical principle of multiplicity, is consistent with a growing variegation of dérive-influenced activities, both in Britain and beyond, in the last decade. Just as mythogeography has escaped its organization, so these practices resist centralization.[24]

Mythogeography is not a top-down movement, but it is taking up more room under the umbrella.

As a way of seeing and exploring the world, mythogeography's combination of pedestrian resistance and magical thinking has wide appeal. In a city like Canterbury, home of my current institute, rich in historical importance, sacred spaces and heritage sites, mythogeography's counter-touristic approach is hugely refreshing. 'Move along', say the signs and the roped-off areas; 'look over here, walk this way, keep out. These are the dates and facts'. But equally compelling are the possibilities, the overlooked or forgotten stories, the ghosts, folktales and urban legends that tell us so much about a place, its visitors and inhabitants.

DEEP TOPOGRAPHY

'Deep Topography' is a term employed by walker, collector and writer Nick Papadimitriou to describe his own practice. Papadimitriou has fostered an intense relationship with the landscape where he grew up, a place that continues to shape him and his interests. His recent book Scarp[25] explores the 'lost county' of Middlesex and

---

24   Smith, 'Psychogeography and Mythogeography', 170.
25   Nick Papadimitriou, Scarp (London: Sceptre, 2012).

its borders, in particular the looming presence of an escarpment
that gives the book its name. Papadimitriou has walked the area
for twenty years, and his immediate impressions, ruminations on
self and place, and fictional flights are combined with a deep study
of local history, flora and fauna, and the buildings and objects he
encounters. The book, along with a documentary film *The London
Perambulator*,[26] has caused a minor tectonic shift in the world of
contemporary psychogeography and made Papadimitriou something of a cult figure.

What is so refreshing about Papadimitriou's brand of psychogeography is its equal embracing of the real and imagined, the removal
of veils between the seen and unseen. This is not to be confused with
the so-called 'occultism' of certain London psychogeographers—
Iain Sinclair and Peter Ackroyd in particular. Nor is it about earth
mysteries and ley lines, although Papadimitriou would probably
embrace these too—Deep Topography is a broad church. What Papadimitriou sees in the landscape is the collective memory of place;
a vault of experiences and memories that can be accessed by attentive walking. Interviewed on a walk in the documentary, he says:

> When I walk I seem to access all sorts of levels. Pro-
> cesses taking place under hedges, or the memories of
> people I've never known. They're memories that aren't
> mine, and yet they seem so tangible.[27]

Deep Topography enables Papadimitriou to constantly reassess his
relationship with marginal and liminal spaces. He sees parallels between ancient temples and suburban water towers, and refers to bol-
lards in a residential area as 'deep storage vats for regional memory'.[28]
It is a re-mystification of the habitual and man-made: an embracing
of what is, has been and could be—a constant defamilarising. In this
sense, Deep Topography draws on the 'mytho' of mythogeography,
accepting the individual experience, the imagined and fictitious
along with the cherished historic and the contemporary overlooked.

---

26   *The London Perambulator*, dir. John Rogers, 45 min (Vanity Projects,
      2009), film.

27   Ibid.

28   Ibid.

Embracing the zombie within

Deep Topography, and Mythogeography, celebrate liminal spaces and explore the narrative possibilities of place. Following these ways of walking allows the practitioner to 'read' a place, however familiar or potentially unlovely, and interpret from or actively create a narrative around it.

'Unlovely' places are important here. It is one thing to seek out natural beauty, to take appreciative walks in stunning landscapes, soak up forests, follow coastal trails, or stroll across moors. Rewilding and re-enchantment are obvious companions: parks and seaside footpaths offer something similar to urban environments. I would advocate this kind of walking whenever possible, but I am also drawn to the flawed, decaying and ruined, much as I am drawn to flawed characters in film and fiction. Unlovely places have great narrative potential. They cause us to interrogate what we encounter. What happened here? Why is this building boarded up? Who lives in this semi-derelict site, and why?

If we can re-enchant, and be re-enchanted by, wastelands, edgelands, built and decaying environments, then we are well on the way to enhancing everyday experience. Celebrating the unlovely requires a certain amount of distance, and the ruined even more so, ruins being representative of loss. As Geoff Nicholson states in *Walking in Ruins*, 'one has a duty to respond decently to that loss, not to belittle it'.[29] One way of responding that is open to us is to become part of the narrative.

Having woken from the deathly autopilot of everyday pedestrianism, and embraced the practice of observing and attending, creating or recording, the challenge is to become a part of that story, an active protagonist. If we can walk attentively, seeking narrative, then why not extend the practice beyond ourselves? Why not walk *as* someone, or something, else?

In *The Footbook of Zombie Walking*,[30] Phil Smith advocates a form of mythogeography informed by zombie narratives. Contemporary society has, Smith suggests, resonant parallels with the

---

29   Geoff Nicholson, *Walking in Ruins* (Chelmsford: Harbour Books, 2013), 32.

30   Phil Smith, *The Footbook of Zombie Walking* (Axeminster: Triarchy Press, 2015).

zombie apocalypse.[31] Walking familiar streets as a lone survivor or infected agent is analogous with the Situationists' *dérives* in Paris: zombie walking becomes a political act, an attack on the Spectacle.

> Walking plays a distinctive and controversial part in this [the zombie] myth. They are not the walking dead for nothing; disrupting the banality-inducing acceleration of images, the algorithms of the contemporary media spectacle and our headlong rush with our terrain to mutual annihilation.[32]

In essence, Smith advocates using the zombie narrative as a framework for psychogeographical approaches, opening up levels of awareness. 'Adopting the fictional apocalypse as a way of seeing, things that have been invisible or concealed will make themselves known.'[33] This practice involves various degrees of walking in character, of inhabiting a role: not the outward slope and shuffle of the zombie parade, but a more subtle set of tactics, applying the senses, finding contrasting settings and exploring notions of threat. Rather than staggering like zombies, subject to our own passivity, we can be ambulant revenants reawakened to our surroundings. We can embrace the zombie within, or be freshly alert to the movement of the horde. Whichever role we choose, we will experience place in new ways. Here is how Smith suggests we begin:

> Make your first zombie walk in territory you know well. Touch, sniff, watch these familiar spaces as if they were the setting for an apocalypse. Then try less familiar places. Walk as quietly as possible [...] Feel for the sonic qualities of what is underfoot. If you step on a snail shell today it will sound like a gunshot (yesterday, you wouldn't have noticed). Stop. Listen [...] Sensitise yourself [...] Turn through the full 360 degrees, take in the horizon. Walk on very slightly tensed; ready to run, but not running.[34]

---

31   Ibid., 5–7.
32   Ibid., 5.
33   Ibid., 16.
34   Ibid., 15.

As well as readings of zombie films and social and political com-
mentaries, Smith's book includes several such walking exercises,
offering practical suggestions for how to reconnect with one's environment. These exercises aim to facilitate individual and group
walks shaped by the attitudes and expectations of a familiar fictional
genre. They are instructions for psychogeographical zombie walks.

When the walker takes on a role, an identity other than the attentive self, place is seen and understood through this lens. If we can do
this with a genre, as Smith does with zombies, then we can do it with
specific stories, and by extension, individual characters. Experience
can be filtered and interpreted according to the narrative framework
or character one assumes. This attitudinal walking is particularly
useful to creative writers. A writer can choose to walk as a particular
character in their fiction, a form of embodiment that works much
as an actor adopting elements of Lee Strasberg's infamous Method.[35]
Method walking, producing method writing. I am not suggesting
that writers should adopt a limp or wear a false beard, or affect any
other outward manifestations of a character—although this might
have its place—but to inhabit that character's internal concerns and
attitudes. By walking *as* a character, a writer may achieve a level of
insight that sitting at a desk may not bring. The result would be enhanced authenticity in their fiction (aspects of voice, point of view
or motive, for example). The writer walking *through setting as character* would be the ideal combination, providing the opportunity to
experience the field of a fiction through the eyes of its agent. This
is something I have tried when working on novels: an initial walk
through setting with map and notebook, identifying topographical
landmarks and considering the logistics of moving through the setting, then walking the same route *as* the protagonist. The horizon
shifts, and the details differ.

While it is difficult to write convincingly of a setting without a
certain level of familiarity, any place can be experienced 'in character', allowing the writer to dip into the process whenever it is needed. (If I have forgotten how to think as my protagonist, I can go
out walking *as* them.) Likewise, the walker can take on any number of identities: a creator of crime fiction may choose to walk in

35   See Lee Strasberg, *A Dream of Passion: The Development of the Method*
      (Boston: Little Brown, 1987).

turn as victim, perpetrator, or detective. A novelist struggling with the motivations of a suicide taking their final river-bound walk may seek despair with stones in their pockets. Dystopian writers would be alert to the possibilities of abandoned warehouses, CCTV cameras, and so on.

Is this process only useful to writers? The application to writing is obvious to me, because that is what I do. But walking 'in character' has potential for a variety of disciplines: creative, sociological, historical, literary. If we walk as a character in a piece of fiction, we may understand that character in new ways. (It is a process somewhat akin to the hunter moving like their prey, the better to understand, track, and catch them.) This works for the reader as well as the writer. The same could potentially apply, with varying degrees of imagination, to historical characters, contemporary individuals, or social groups.

Texts that are strong on setting lend themselves to literary pilgrimages: literature that features walking characters can inspire its readers to walk. Such texts lend themselves readily to walking 'in character'. Book-related walking tours are a familiar activity, especially within cultural festivals: witness the Bloomsday[36] events that follow in the footsteps of characters in Joyce's *Ulysses*.[37] What if we, as readers, took this further, walking *as* Leopold Bloom, empty-bellied before breakfast, passing through our own spaces of sensory overload during the course of a day? Would we not come to understand him more intimately? And does this not open up possibilities for teaching, using walking as a way of accessing literary texts with students?

Bram Stoker's *Dracula*,[38] with its numerous atmospheric settings, is a useful example, and one which fits neatly with notions of the ruined and undead. Combining urban and rural, contemporary buildings and ancient piles, it offers a variety of possible walks. A reader of *Dracula* wishing to walk 'in character' could choose to explore busy city streets, a decaying mansion, or just the local cemetery to get an 'authentic' feel. Dracula himself does plenty of walking. 'Some

---

36   See the extensive programme of walking events listed for the 2016 Bloomsday festival on the James Joyce Centre website (www. jamesjoyce. ie/bloomsday).

37   James Joyce, *Ulysses* (1922; repr. London: Penguin, 1992).

38   Bram Stoker, *Dracula* (1897; repr. London: Simon & Schuster, 2014).

claims are made for Dracula as a psychogeographer, walking around the metropolis eyeing victims, and certainly the novel *Dracula* is packed with walking: in London, Transylvania, and Whitby.[39] The claim Nicholson refers to here is made by Iain Sinclair in his book *London Orbital*[40] in which Sinclair details his walks around the M25. Throughout his perambulations of the London settings in *Dracula* ('Carfax' and Purfleet, the shadow of the city that is Thurrock), Sinclair detects vampirism: scenes of decay, criminal activity, economic crisis. 'Dracula is the original psychogeographer' Sinclair states, 'map fetishist, timetable freak.'[41]

I would argue that Dracula's search for victims suggests a predatory quest—more stalking than drifting—and his initial experience of London is tangential and indirect, accessed only through maps and guidebooks (and later, anecdote). More interesting is Sinclair's ability to read place through the lens of Stoker's book and its titular character. Sinclair is not overtly walking *as* Dracula, but he is seeing the city through gothic goggles. 'Dracula's Garden. Plants have had the juices sucked out of them.'[42] 'The smoking mass of the Procter & Gamble factory is Carfax Abbey.'[43] Walking in this way changes the experience of place to the point that Sinclair envisions London, not just as the vampire's hunting grounds, but as Dracula's metaphoric victim itself:

> The body of London solicits his bite. He knows just where skin is tender, where the stitches will part: the alleys and waste lots and riverside chasms where ancient crimes are unappeased.[44]

Walk as Dracula. Walk as Stoker. Walk as Sinclair. By applying this walking process, our experience of a fictional world becomes more embodied, less vicarious. Bringing together psychogeographical practices and fictional frameworks offers us, as reader-walkers, a way of re-enchanting literature. As Nicholson admits, when re-

---

39   Nicholson, *Walking in Ruins*, 204.

40   Iain Sinclair, *London Orbital* (London: Penguin, 2003).

41   Ibid., 488.

42   Ibid., 483.

43   Ibid., 489.

44   Ibid., 488.

flecting on *Dracula*, 'I've certainly walked along Piccadilly plenty of times [...] and I've looked at all the people walking around me [...] and wondered which ones might be geniuses of deep crime, which ones it might be fun to follow, and which ones are vampires'.[45]

PSYCHOGEOGRAPHY, LEARNING, AND TEACHING

It is clear that psychogeographical practices can enhance our experience of place, and walking will sharpen up our creative responses to it. It is a small step to adapt these into our teaching. Morag Rose, a co-founder of the Manchester-based Loiterers Resistance Movement, uses psychogeography as activism, but also believes in its pedagogic value. In her article 'Confessions of an Anarcho-Flâneuse', she remarks on 'the multi-sensual relationship between self, space, and left-behind traces: the reason [...] walking has terrific power as a kinaesthetic and learning tool'.[46] Taking teaching out of the seminar room, and recording, observing, and exploring beyond the prescribed or habitual, can help to free thought, inspire creativity and enhance problem-solving: useful skills in any academic discipline. To illustrate this point: an anecdote, and a brief return to W.G. Sebald.

A few years ago I taught a group of undergraduate students who were required to study an extract of Sebald's *The Rings of Saturn*. In the text, Sebald's protagonist walks from Dunwich Heath and, under a dark sky, hemmed-in by dense heather, he becomes lost in an apparent maze of snaking paths. The ensuing panic he experiences is related in painfully convoluted, winding prose: the walker-writer is trapped, claustrophobic and yet exposed, an experience so powerful that it repeats itself in a dream several months later. Dream and reality merge. At one point, the narrator describes climbing to a vantage point and looking out across the maze: from this spot he can view the terrain clearly.

> [...] I saw the labyrinth, the light sandy ground, the

---

45   Nicholson, *Walking in Ruins*, 204.

46   Morag Rose, 'Confessions of an Anarcho-Flâneuse, or Psychogeography the Mancunian Way', in *Walking Inside Out*, ed. Tina Richardson (London: Rowman & Littlefield International, 2015), 147.

sharply delineated contours of hedges [...] a pattern simple in comparison with the torturous trail I
had behind me, but one which I knew in my dream,
with absolute certainty, represented a cross-section
of my brain.[47]

My students struggled with this text, becoming equally lost in the
prose. To help them grasp the rhythm and complexity of Sebald's
writing, I asked them to pack away their books and took them on
a meandering walk around campus, leading them down corridors,
around tall-sided buildings and eventually, to the open grassy space
overlooking the city. Built into a slope is a labyrinth.[48] Having been
led a dizzying and disorientating dance around the site, walking the
labyrinth gave the students clarity. As they walked, I asked them to
imagine themselves walking *as Sebald's prose*: approaching the subject (the centre of the labyrinth), digressing (being led away again
by the circuits) and, by subtle gradients, reaching the desired goal.
The students' frustrations with the text quickly unravelled. The labyrinth's central point is, like Sebald's prose, always present, but at certain points in the walk the view is oblique. The pleasure of reading
Sebald's writing is in the path, in the knowledge that there is clarity
in digression and association, and that, like a labyrinth (and unlike
a maze) it contains no empty cul-de-sacs. Through walking, the students learned to trust the text and its author.

EXERCISES FROM THE
PSYCHOGEOGRAPHER'S TOOLBOX

Here are some items from my toolbox that I have used with writing

---

47   Sebald, *The Rings of Saturn*, 175.
48   The labyrinth at The University of Kent, Canterbury. For more on my use
      of the labyrinth with students, see Sonia Overall, 'Writing and Walking
      the Labyrinth' in *Learning with the Labyrinth: Creating Reflective Space in
      Higher Education*, eds. Jan Sellers and Bernard Moss (London: Palgrave
      Macmillan, 2016), 119–23, and other articles in this title on the pedagogi-
      cal use of labyrinths.

students and interdisciplinary groups.[49] Although they are necessarily geared towards a creative outcome, they can be readily adapted to other disciplines and situations. They should go some way towards shaking off the torpor of the deathly everyday, enabling you to step out, more re-enchanted than revenant.

A dérive—with instructions

Suitable for individuals, pairs or groups of three:

- ⸿ Take time to observe.
- ⸿ Stand still and listen.
- ⸿ Walk at different speeds.
- ⸿ Interact with spaces, or other people.
- ⸿ Write down what is seen, heard, and overheard.
- ⸿ Note the affect of different places on self and others.
- ⸿ Take notes while in motion as well as pausing.
- ⸿ Walk 'against the current'. If a crowd is surging in one direction, walk the opposite way.
- ⸿ Ignore directional signage—look instead for any alternative text or images to follow.
- ⸿ Be led by anything that interests.
- ⸿ Walk in any way that is not prescribed by crowds, street furniture, or habit.
- ⸿ Look up above street level, and down at feet.
- ⸿ Be prepared to look behind and under street furniture if necessary.
- ⸿ Treat all buildings and obstacles equally, rather than be led by landmarks.

If appropriate, add exercises, prompts, or seed words to encourage participants to respond in specific ways (I use writing prompts with creative writing students).

---

49   For more exercises and further discussion of them, see Sonia Overall, 'Walking Against the Current: Generating Creative Responses to Place', *Journal of Writing in Creative Practice* 8.1, Place-based Arts (2016): 11–28.

A group dérive—searching for synchronicity

Suitable for groups of three to six:

- ¶ *Dérive* as a group. Look for a thread running between places you visit, scenes, people, or objects. Record anything that strikes you as interesting or unusual.
- ¶ As you walk, discuss your findings and observations. What themes emerge?
- ¶ Create a 'narrative' for your *dérive* to recount later. Shape this narrative so that it can be told by the group, or agree on a written account.

Add constraints or catapults

- ¶ Give *dérive* participants randomly-generated directions to get them started in different directions.
- ¶ Flip a coin to decide on directions at junctions.
- ¶ Use the 'wrong' map. Negotiate one town using the map of another.
- ¶ At the end of a *dérive*, look at a London tube map. Using your current location as Victoria, navigate the streets in search of Liverpool Street Station.
- ¶ Treat your *dérive* like a scavenger hunt. While walking, focus on finding a particular element: a shade of blue, conversations in graffiti, overlooked objects, or markings underfoot. Don't collect—just absorb and record.

SELECT BIBLIOGRAPHY

COVERLEY, Merlin. *Psychogeography*. Harpenden: Pocket Essentials, 2010.

DEBORD, Guy. 'Introduction to a Critique of Urban Geography' [1955]. In *Situationist International Anthology*, edited and translated by Ken Knabb, 8–12. Berkeley: Bureau of Public Secrets, 2006.

_____. 'Theory of the Dérive' [1959]. In *Situationist International Anthology*, edited and translated by Ken Knabb, 62–66. Berkeley: Bureau of Public Secrets, 2006.

HODGE, Stephen, Simon PERSIGHETTI, Phil SMITH, and Cathy TURNER. 'Mis-guiding the City Walker'. Paper presented by Wrights & Sites at Cities for People: The Fifth International Conference on Walking in the 21st Century, Copenhagen, 9th–11th June 2004 (http://mis-guide.com/ws/documents/citywalker.html).

The London Perambulator. Directed by John ROGERS. 45 min. UK: Vanity Projects, 2009. Film.

NICHOLSON, Geoff. Walking in Ruins. Chelmsford: Harbour Books, 2013.

OVERALL, Sonia. 'Walking Against the Current: Generating Creative Responses to Place'. Journal of Writing in Creative Practice 8.1, Place-based Arts (2016): 11–28.

_____. 'Writing and Walking the Labyrinth'. In Learning with the Labyrinth: Creating Reflective Space in Higher Education, edited by Jan Sellers and Bernard Moss, 119–23. London: Palgrave Macmillan, 2016.

PAPADIMITRIOU, Nick. Scarp. London: Sceptre, 2012.

ROSE, Morag. 'Confessions of an Anarcho-Flaneuse, or Psychogeography the Mancunian Way'. In Walking Inside Out, edited by Tina Richardson, 147–62. London: Rowman & Littlefield International, 2015.

RICHARDSON, Tina. 'Introduction: A Wander through the Scene of British Urban Walking'. In Walking Inside Out, edited by Tina Richardson, 1–27. London: Rowman & Littlefield International, 2015.

SINCLAIR, Iain. London Orbital. London: Penguin, 2003.

SMITH, Phil. Counter-Tourism: The Handbook. Axeminster: Triarchy Press, 2012.

_____. The Footbook of Zombie Walking. Axeminster: Triarchy Press, 2015.

_____. Mythogeography: A Guide to Walking Sideways. Axeminster: Triarchy Press, 2010.

_____. On Walking…And Stalking Sebald. Axeminster: Triarchy Press, 2014.

Lightning Source UK Ltd.
Milton Keynes UK
UKOW04f1120010817
306439UK00002B/550/P

9 781943 710133